THE LETTERS OF LADY ANNE BACON

THE LETTERS OF LADY ANNE BACON

edited by
GEMMA ALLEN

CAMDEN FIFTH SERIES
Volume 44

CAMBRIDGE
UNIVERSITY PRESS

FOR THE ROYAL HISTORICAL SOCIETY
University College London, Gower Street, London WC1 6BT
2014

Published by the Press Syndicate of the University of Cambridge
The Edinburgh Building, Cambridge CB2 8RU, United Kingdom
32 Avenue of the Americas, New York, NY 10013-2473, USA
477 Williamstown Road, Port Melbourne, VIC 3207, Australia
C/Orense, 4, Planta 13, 28020 Madrid, Spain
Lower Ground Floor, Nautica Building, The Water Club,
Beach Road, Granger Bay, 8005 Cape Town, South Africa

First published 2014

A catalogue record for this book is available from the British Library

ISBN 9781107056541 hardback

SUBSCRIPTIONS. The serial publications of the Royal Historical Society, *Royal Historical Society Transactions* (ISSN 0080-4401) and Camden Fifth Series (ISSN 0960-1163) volumes, may be purchased together on annual subscription. The 2013 subscription price, which includes print and electronic access (but not VAT), is £142 (US $237 in the USA, Canada, and Mexico) and includes Camden Fifth Series, volumes 43 and 44 and Transactions Sixth Series, volume 23 (published in December). Japanese prices are available from Kinokuniya Company Ltd, P.O. Box 55, Chitose, Tokyo 156, Japan. EU subscribers (outside the UK) who are not registered for VAT should add VAT at their country's rate. VAT registered subscribers should provide their VAT registration number. Prices include delivery by air.

Subscription orders, which must be accompanied by payment, may be sent to a bookseller, subscription agent, or direct to the publisher: Cambridge University Press, The Edinburgh Building, Shaftesbury Road, Cambridge CB2 8RU, UK; or in the USA, Canada, and Mexico: Cambridge University Press, Journals Fulfillment Department, 100 Brook Hill Drive, West Nyack, New York, 10994-2133, USA.

SINGLE VOLUMES AND BACK VOLUMES. A list of Royal Historical Society volumes available from Cambridge University Press may be obtained from the Humanities Marketing Department at the address above.

Printed and bound by CPI Group (UK) Ltd, Croydon, CR0 4YY

CONTENTS

LIST OF FIGURES   vi

ACKNOWLEDGEMENTS   vii

LIST OF ABBREVIATIONS   x

INTRODUCTION   I

EDITORIAL CONVENTIONS   47

THE LETTERS OF LADY ANNE BACON   51

INDEX   289

FIGURES

1. *Nicholas and Anne Bacon to William Cecil*, 18 August 1557 (**4**), CP152/19, fo. 27r. Reproduced by permission of the Marquess of Salisbury.

2. *Anne Bacon to Robert Cecil*, 13 July 1594 (**109**), CP 27/33, fo. 59r. Reproduced by permission of the Marquess of Salisbury.

3. *Anne Bacon to Robert Devereux, earl of Essex*, 23 December [1595] (**146**), CP 128/68. Reproduced by permission of the Marquess of Salisbury.

4. Detail from *Anne Bacon to Anthony Bacon*, 1 April 1595 (**123**), LPL 651, fo. 108r. Reproduced by permission of Lambeth Palace Library.

ACKNOWLEDGEMENTS

This edition has been many years in the making and has left me with numerous debts. I first began working with Anne Bacon's letters during my doctoral research. After my initial despair over the indecipherable nature of Anne's handwriting, the correspondence formed an important part of my thesis and subsequent monograph. I owe a huge debt of gratitude to Felicity Heal, who supervised my doctoral studies and who has been kind enough to guide and encourage my labours ever since. The suggestion that I should compile an edition first came from James Daybell, over a cup of tea in Blackwell's coffee shop in Oxford. I am very much indebted to James for his support of the project ever since and for generously sharing his expertise in early modern epistolary culture. Lynne Magnusson and Alan Stewart both read the edition in its entirety at a particularly busy point in the academic year. I am hugely grateful for their herculean efforts; their erudition and detailed knowledge of the Bacon archive has saved me from countless errors. As literary director for the Camden series, Ian Archer has shown unstinting patience as more letters were discovered and deadlines were revised; I am grateful too for his perceptive comments on various letters. Many other scholars were generous with advice and references, including Timothy Barnes, Susan Brigden, Susan Doran, Clive Holmes, Diarmaid MacCulloch, Michael McVaugh, Alison Wall, and Alison Wiggins. My colleagues at both Pembroke College and, more recently, the Open University have encouraged my labours with the letters; I am most grateful to them all and in particular to Eleanor Betts, Amanda Goodrich, Helen King, Anne Laurence, Donna Loftus, Rosemary O'Day, and Gabriella Zuccolin. I must also acknowledge the patience shown by my students, for indulging my enthusiasm when Anne Bacon letters made appearances in tutorials.

This edition includes translations of Latin, Greek, Hebrew, and French, and I have to thank many colleagues for their help in the very difficult task of deciphering and translating the foreign languages used in the letters. Carolinne White and David Butterfield assisted with the Latin and Greek translations; they were hugely generous with both their expertise and their time. Joshua Teplitsky and Aaron Graham translated the Hebrew for me, while Dunlaith Bird and Thibault

Miguet provided guidance regarding the French translations. I am most grateful to them all for assistance. Without the great intellectual generosity shown to me by academic colleagues across the world, this would have been a much poorer edition. The errors that remain are, of course, my own.

Various institutions have provided financial support for the numerous archive trips involved in producing this edition, particularly Jesus College, Oxford, and the Open University. I am also indebted to the repositories that hold Anne Bacon's letters for allowing me to reproduce transcriptions in this edition. In particular I must acknowledge the kindness of Heather Wolfe at the Folger Shakespeare Library; Gill Cannell at the Parker Library; Mary Robertson at the Huntington Library; Cornelia Hopf at the Forschungsbibliothek Gotha; Daniel Meyer and Christine Colburn at the University of Chicago Special Collections; Michael Frost and Margaret Clay at the Inner Temple Library; and Robin Harcourt Williams and Vicki Perry at Hatfield House. I am also grateful to the staff at the British Library, the Bodleian Library, Cambridge University Library, and the Hertfordshire Archives and Local Studies Centre. My greatest thanks must be reserved for the staff at Lambeth Palace Library. They have provided invaluable assistance on my countless visits over the last few years, never tiring of repeatedly fetching the heavy Bacon volumes for me. It really is a special archive and I feel very lucky to have been able to spend so much time working there. Joaneath Spicer was kind enough to allow me to see the Anne Bacon miniature held by the Walters Art Museum when I visited Baltimore in 2008. The image now forms the cover of this edition and I am grateful to Ruth Bowler for making special arrangements for new colour photography. My sincere thanks also go to Daniel Pearce and the staff at Cambridge University Press for all their support of this volume, as well as to Hester Higton for her meticulous copy-editing.

Finally, I must thank my friends and family for their encouragement and patience during the completion of the edition. My mother and sister, Vanessa and Francesca Allen, chivvied me along the long road to completion; my mother's frequent refrain that 'it's just like a detective story' at times of particular bewilderment over Anne's handwriting or over the dating of letters was always a comforting spur to action. My greatest debt is to my husband, Edward Arnold. He has heard every development in the progress of the edition, has put up with me spending evenings and weekends at the computer, and has kept me going when it seemed an impossible task to complete. That it is eventually finished is all down to Edward. It will be strange for us both to live without Lady B. in our midst. While at times editing her letters has proved exasperating, they have never been dull; I'll miss having Anne around.

Gemma Allen,
Oxford, July 2013

ABBREVIATIONS

Bacon Letters and Life	J. Spedding (ed.), *The Letters and the Life of Francis Bacon, Including All His Occasional Works*, 7 vols (London, 1861–1874).
BL	British Library.
'Catalogue of field names'	C. Moor, 'Catalogue of field names occurring on the Hertfordshire estates of the earl of Verulam', *Transactions of the St. Albans and Hertfordshire Architectural and Archaeological Society* (1927), pp. 1–118.
Chicago	Sir Nicholas Bacon Collection, University of Chicago Special Collections, Chicago, Illinois, USA.
Cooke Sisters	G. Allen, *The Cooke Sisters: education, piety and politics in early modern England* (Manchester, 2013).
Corporation Records	A.E. Gibbs, *The Corporation Records of St Albans, with Lists of Mayors, High Stewards, Members of Parliament &c.* (St Albans, 1890).
CP	Cecil Papers, Hatfield House, Hertfordshire.
Folger	Folger Shakespeare Library, Washington, DC, USA.
Gotha	Gotha Forschungsbibliothek, Thuringia, Germany.
HALS	Hertfordshire Archives and Local Studies, Hertford.
History of Parliament	P.W. Hasler (ed.), *The History of Parliament: the House of Commons, 1558–1603*, 3 vols (London, 1981).
Huntington Library	Huntington Library, San Marino, California, USA.
Inner Temple	Inner Temple Library, Inner Temple, London.
LPL	Lambeth Palace Library, London.
'Money-lenders'	C. L'Estrange Ewen, 'Francis Bacon and the money-lenders', *Baconiana*, 3rd series, 21 (1934), pp. 238–253.
OED	*Oxford English Dictionary*.
ODNB	A.R. Matthew (ed.), *The Oxford Dictionary of National Biography* (Oxford, 2004).

Parker Library	Parker Library, Corpus Christi College, Cambridge.
SP	State Papers, The National Archives, London.
Stiffkey	A. Hassell Smith, G. Baker, and R. Kenny (eds), *The Papers of Nathaniel Bacon of Stiffkey*, 4 vols, Norfolk Record Society, 46, 49, 53, 64 (Norwich, 1979–2000).
Troubled Life	L. Jardine and A. Stewart, *Hostage to Fortune: the troubled life of Francis Bacon* (London, 1998).
VCH	*Victoria County History*.
Wealth of the Gentry	A. Simpson, *The Wealth of the Gentry, 1540–1660: East Anglian studies* (Chicago, 1961).

INTRODUCTION

Lady Anne Bacon (*c*.1528–1610) was a woman who inspired strong emotion in her own lifetime. As a girl, she was praised as a 'verteouse meyden' for her religious translations, while a rejected suitor condemned her as faithless as an ancient Greek temptress.[1] The Spanish ambassador reported home that, as a married woman, she was a tiresomely learned lady, whereas her husband celebrated the time they spent reading classical literature together.[2] During her widowhood, she was 'beloved' of the godly preachers surrounding her in Hertfordshire; Godfrey Goodman, later bishop of Gloucester, instead argued that she was 'little better than frantic in her age'.[3] Anne's own letters allow a more balanced exploration of her life. An unusually large number are still extant; she is one of the select group of Elizabethan women whose surviving correspondence includes over fifty of the letters they wrote themselves, a group that incorporates her sister, Lady Elizabeth Russell, and the noblewoman Bess of Hardwick, the countess of Shrewsbury.[4]

---

[1] G.B., 'To the Christen Reader', in B. Ochino, *Fouretene sermons of Barnadine Ochyne, concernyng the predestinacion and eleccion of god*, trans. A[nne] C[ooke] (London, 1551), sig. A2r. For Walter Haddon's comparison of Anne to Cressida, a character from ancient Greek mythology, see BL, Lansdowne MS 98, fo. 252r.

[2] M.A.S. Hume (ed.), *Calendar of Letters and State Papers Relating to English Affairs Preserved Principally in the Archives of Simancas, 1558–1603*, 4 vols (1892–1899), I, p. 20; N. Bacon, *The Recreations of His Age* (Oxford, 1919), p. 27.

[3] T.W. [Thomas Wilcox], *A short, yet sound commentarie; written on that woorthie worke called; the Proverbes of Salomon* (London, 1589), sig. A3r; G. Goodman, *The Court of King James the First*, ed. J.S. Brewer, 2 vols (London, 1839), I, p. 285. Goodman was writing many years after Anne's death. For more on Goodman's characterization of Anne, see *Cooke Sisters*, pp. 219–220.

[4] Both these women have recently had new editions compiled of their correspondence. See P. Phillippy (ed.), *The Writings of an English Sappho (Elizabeth Cooke Hoby Russell, 1540–1609)* (Toronto, 2012), and the online edition of the letters of Bess of Hardwick, http://www.bessofhardwick.org/. There are over seventy extant letters written by Elizabeth Bourne in the 1570s and 1580s, as well as a rich body of surviving letters of Joan and Maria Thynne. See J. Daybell, 'Elizabeth Bourne (fl. 1570s–1580s): a new Elizabethan woman poet', *Notes and Queries*, 52 (2005), pp. 176–178; A. Wall (ed.), *Two Elizabethan Women: correspondence of Joan and Maria Thynne, 1575–1611*, Wiltshire Record Society 38 (Devizes, 1983). There are over a hundred surviving letters written by Arbella Stuart, although many of these are Jacobean: see S.J. Steen (ed.), *The Letters of Lady Arbella Stuart* (Oxford, 1994).

Anne's letters have never been entirely forgotten. Thomas Birch's 1754 *Memoirs of the Reign of Queen Elizabeth* included some extracts from her correspondence and in 1861 James Spedding included whole transcriptions of a small number of Anne's letters in the first volume of his work on her son, as did William Hepworth Dixon in his biography of Francis Bacon.[5] While these were valuable resources, they only made accessible a very small proportion of Anne Bacon's surviving correspondence. However, in manuscript form Anne's letters have continued to receive attention from scholars working on her sons and their wider circle and, in recent years, they have started to be studied for what they reveal about Anne herself.[6] A primary obstacle which surely prevents more scholars from using the letters is Anne's handwriting. It has been despairingly described as 'hardly legible' and 'indecipherable'; without long and painful acquaintance, it is decidedly impenetrable.[7]

This edition brings together for the first time nearly two hundred of the letters which Anne sent and received, scattered in repositories throughout the world. It allows fresh light to be shed on Anne's life and

[5] T. Birch, *Memoirs of the Reign of Queen Elizabeth*, 2 vols (London, 1754); *Bacon Letters and Life*, I; W.H. Dixon, *The Personal History of Lord Bacon: from unpublished papers* (London, 1861). Gustav Ungerer included two letters in his work on the correspondence of Antonio Pérez: G. Ungerer, *The Correspondence of Antonio Pérez's Exile*, 2 vols (London, 1974–1976), I, pp. 219–221.

[6] For the use of Anne's manuscript letters by those working on her sons, see especially *Troubled Life*. Paul Hammer also made use of her correspondence in his work on the earl of Essex: see 'Patronage at court: faction and the earl of Essex', in J. Guy (ed.), *The Reign of Elizabeth I: court and culture in the last decade* (Cambridge, 1995), pp. 65–86; *idem*, *The Polarisation of Elizabethan Politics: the political career of Robert Devereux, second earl of Essex, 1585–1597* (Cambridge, 1999). For work on Anne Bacon herself, see M.E. Lamb, 'The Cooke sisters: attitudes toward learned women in the Renaissance', in M.P. Hannay (ed.), *Silent but for the Word* (Kent, OH, 1985), pp. 107–25; A. Stewart, 'The voices of Anne Cooke, Lady Anne and Lady Bacon', in D. Clarke and E. Clarke (eds), *This Double Voice: gendered writing in early modern England* (Basingstoke, 2000), pp. 88–102; L. Magnusson, 'Widowhood and linguistic capital: the rhetoric and reception of Anne Bacon's epistolary advice', *English Literary Renaissance*, 31 (2001), pp. 3–33; J. Daybell, *Women Letter-writers in Tudor England* (Oxford, 2006); K. Mair, 'Anne, Lady Bacon: a life in letters' (unpublished PhD thesis, Queen Mary, University of London, 2009); G. Allen, '"A briefe and plaine declaration": Lady Anne Bacon's 1564 translation of the *Apologia Ecclesiae Anglicanae*', in P. Hardman and A. Lawrence-Mathers (eds), *Women and Writing, c.1340–c.1650: the domestication of print culture* (Woodbridge, 2010), pp. 62–76; G. Allen, 'Education, piety and politics: the Cooke sisters and women's agency, *c.* 1526–1610' (unpublished DPhil thesis, University of Oxford, 2010); L. Magnusson, 'Imagining a national church: election and education in the works of Anne Cooke Bacon', in J. Harris and E. Scott-Baumann (eds), *The Intellectual Culture of Puritan Women, 1558–1680* (Basingstoke, 2010), pp. 42–56; J. Daybell, 'Women, news and intelligence networks in Elizabethan England', in R.J. Adams and R. Cox (eds), *Diplomacy and Early Modern Culture* (Basingstoke, 2010), pp. 101–119; K. Mair, 'Material lies: parental anxiety and epistolary practice in the correspondence of Anne, Lady Bacon and Anthony Bacon', *Lives and Letters*, 4 (2012), pp. 58–74; G. Allen, *The Cooke Sisters: education, piety and politics in early modern England* (Manchester, 2013).

[7] Ungerer, *Antonio Pérez's Exile*, I, p. 220; Daybell, *Women Letter-writers*, p. 96.

on her wider circle, including her children, her sisters, and her privy councillor relatives, as well as controversial figures such as the earl of Essex. Freed from the difficulties of Anne's handwriting, this edition makes accessible the more productive challenges which her letters pose to our knowledge of early modern women. Her correspondence allows us to question, for example, the practical utility of a humanist education for sixteenth-century women, as well as the extent of their political knowledge, from their involvement in parliamentary and local politics to their understanding of political news and intelligence. Furthermore, Anne's letters provide insights into her understanding of diverse issues, including estate management, patronage networks, finance, and medicine, as well as allowing an exploration of her religious views and her experience of motherhood and widowhood.

Although the edition that follows includes letters from all but the first decade of Anne's life, the coverage is uneven. Most of the letters date from after the death of her husband, Nicholas Bacon, in 1579; more particularly, the main body of her surviving letters are those exchanged between Anne and her son Anthony after his return to England in 1592. The types of letters included in this edition also vary: the published, dedicatory letters, which are concentrated in the earlier decades of Anne's life, have a very different function and audience in mind than the quotidian correspondence exchanged between Anne and Anthony during her widowhood, often written in haste. The introduction that follows seeks to outline Anne's biography and the thematic content of the letters, before considering the nature of the archive in more detail and the material issues which influence the reading of her correspondence.

Early life

Anne Bacon was born around 1528 at Gidea Hall in Essex. She was the second of five daughters and four sons born to Sir Anthony Cooke and his wife; her sister Mildred had been born in 1526, and Anne's birth was followed by those of three other sisters, Margaret, Elizabeth, and Katherine. Of her four brothers, Anthony and Edward died while still young, but Richard and William both lived to serve as MPs.[8]

[8] Anne noted her brother Anthony's death of the sweating sickness in her Greek copy of Moschopulus's *De ratione examinandae orationis libellus* (Paris, 1545): see p. 5, n. 16. Edward Cooke died in France, shortly after accompanying his sister Elizabeth and her ambassador husband, Thomas Hoby, to Paris. For more details on these brothers, see M.K. McIntosh, 'Sir Anthony Cooke: Tudor humanist, educator, and religious reformer', *Proceedings of the American Philosophical Society*, 119 (1975), p. 239. For Richard and William Cooke, see S.T.

Anne was named after her mother, who was the daughter of Sir William Fitzwilliam, a merchant tailor and sheriff of London, and later Northampton.[9] Her father, Anthony Cooke, was also politically well connected. After the death of his father, John Cooke, in 1516, he had been raised by his uncle Richard Cooke, a diplomatic courier for Henry VIII, and his stepmother, Margaret Pennington, lady-in-waiting to Katherine of Aragon.[10] Anthony Cooke was renowned for his humanist education and he acted as a tutor to Edward VI, most probably as a reader after the retirement of Richard Cox in 1550.[11] It seems that his contemporaries regarded Cooke as largely self-taught and there is no evidence that he attended university.[12]

Education

Sir Anthony Cooke's greatest claim to posthumous reputation is that he provided both his sons and his daughters with a thorough humanist education, in both classical and modern languages.[13] The Cooke sisters were lauded in their youth for their remarkable learning. Anne was singled out for particular praise in 1551, when John Coke wrote that 'we have dyvers gentylwomen in Englande, which be not onely well estudied in holy Scrypture, but also in Greek and Latyn tonges as maystres More, mastryes Anne Coke, maystres Clement, and others'.[14] Walter Haddon described a visit he made to the Cooke household: 'While I stayed there,' he wrote, 'I seemed to be living among the Tusculans, except that the studies of women were flourishing in this Tuscany'.[15] The Cooke household was therefore acclaimed as a little academy, in which the girls were educated alongside their brothers, reading the same texts. In a copy, in the original Greek,

Bindoff (ed.), *The History of Parliament: the House of Commons, 1509–1558*, 3 vols (London, 1982), I, p. 691; *History of Parliament*, I, pp. 646–647.

[9] M. Davies, 'Sir William Fitzwilliam', *ODNB*.

[10] M.K. McIntosh, 'The Cooke family of Gidea Hall, Essex, 1460–1661' (unpublished PhD thesis, Harvard University, 1967), p. 12.

[11] McIntosh, 'Sir Anthony Cooke', p. 241.

[12] *Ibid.*, p. 237.

[13] Marjorie McIntosh suggests that Cooke started serious study in the 1530s and may have pursued his education at much the same time as his children. See *ibid.*, pp. 235, 237, 240.

[14] The 'maystres More' and 'maystres Clement' to whom Coke referred were Thomas More's daughter and his adopted daughter, respectively Margaret More, later Roper, and Margaret Giggs Clement. See J. Coke, *The debate betwene the Heraldes of Englande and Fraunce* (London, 1550), sig. K1r.

[15] '*Equidem ibi versans, in Tusculanis mihi videbar viuere, nisi quod foeminarum etiam in hoc Tusculano vigebat industria.*' W. Haddon, *G. Haddoni Legum Doctoris ... lucubrationes* (London, 1567), sig. R2r.

of Moschopulus' *De ratione examinandae orationis libellus* (Paris, 1545), Anne wrote the following inscription: 'My father delyvered this booke to me and my brother Anthony, who was myne elder brother and scoolefellow with me, to follow for wrytyng of Greke'.[16]

Alongside Greek, Anne's childhood education included schooling in Latin and Hebrew, as well as Italian, which she used to translate the sermons of the Italian evangelical Bernardino Ochino. In the prefatory letter which she appended to the first volume of her translated sermons, the twenty-year-old Anne described herself as a 'begynner' in Italian, although that may have been an expression of modesty rather than the literal truth (**1**). Together with her sisters, Anne's schooling also covered the five-part *studia humanitatis*, extolled by sixteenth-century educationalists, which consisted of grammar, poetry, rhetoric, moral philosophy, and history. Furthermore, her sisters Mildred and Elizabeth were interested in logic and dialectic, so it is possible that Anne also read works on those subjects.[17]

One result of this education was that it enabled Anne to become a translator. Bernardino Ochino had been invited to England in 1548 by Thomas Cranmer, archbishop of Canterbury, to assist with the reform of the English church. In the same year, Anne translated five of his sermons, the text being published anonymously.[18] By 1551, she had translated another fourteen of his sermons, which were published in two editions that year. One was an anonymous amalgamation of all of Anne's translations, plus a reprint of six of Ochino's sermons rendered into English by Richard Argentine in 1548.[19] The other 1551 edition contained only Anne's fourteen new sermons, this time printed under her own name.[20] Thus, by 1551, Anne was known as a published translator in her own right. These publications were Anne's contribution to the evangelical cause. In the prefatory letter to her second set of Ochino translations, she describes her mother's previous dislike of her Italian studies, 'syns God thereby is no whytte magnifyed'

[16] This quotation is included in an anonymous cutting held by Essex Record Office: Sage 773. I have located its original context as a note by a 'J.H. Mn' on 'Lord Bacon's mother' included in *Notes and Queries*, 95 (1857), 327. However, I have not been able to locate Anne's volume of Moschopulus.

[17] For a reconstruction of Anne's education and that of her sisters through their reading material, see *Cooke Sisters*, pp. 18–55.

[18] B. Ochino, *Sermons of Barnardine Ochine of Sena godlye, frutefull, and very necessarye for all true Christians*, trans. anon (London, 1548).

[19] B. Ochino, *Certayne Sermons of the ryghte famous and excellente Clerk Master Barnadine Ochine*, trans. anon (London, 1551). These twenty-five sermons were also reprinted in 1570, but then they were published as Anne's work: B. Ochino, *Sermons of Barnadine Ochyne (to the number of 25) concerning the predestinacion and eleccion of god*, trans. A[nne] C[ooke] (London, 1570).

[20] B. Ochino, *Fouretene sermons of Barnadine Ochyne, concernyng the predestinacion and eleccion of god*, trans. A[nne] C[ooke] (London, 1551).

(**2**). In dedicating this work to her mother, Anne emphasizes that the activity fulfilled her mother's insistence on godly labour and the letter makes clear her developing Calvinist beliefs in God's determination 'wythout begynnynge, al thynges [. . .] to hys immutable wyll'.

Anne's scholarly pursuits continued after her marriage to Nicholas Bacon in 1553, shown by her 1564 translation into English of John Jewel's *Apologia Ecclesiae Anglicanae*. The production of Jewel's original Latin tract was closely associated with her husband's political circle, particularly William Cecil, her brother-in-law.[21] One of the major challenges facing the nascent Church of England during the early Elizabethan period was ensuring the preaching of the word to the laity. Close analysis of Anne's text reveals her intention to use her translation to engage with these issues, offering a creed for the Church of England, written for a wide readership in plain English.[22] However, the prefatory letter to the first published edition of the translation, written to Anne by Matthew Parker, the archbishop of Canterbury, chooses to present her text very differently. Parker suggests that Anne conceived the translation as a private, domestic act. He writes that he instigated its publication without her knowledge, stating that such action was necessary 'to prevent suche excuses as your modestie woulde have made in staye of publishinge it' (**6**). The presentation of Anne's translation in the prefatory letter is a deliberate framing device, designed to obscure any suggestion that this translation fulfilled official needs, yet Catholic observers astutely saw through such a ruse. Richard Verstegan later acknowledged Anne's role as translator, perceiving it as part of William Cecil and Nicholas Bacon's 'plot and fortification of this newe erected synagog', accurately identifying the usefulness of Anne's work to the early Elizabethan Church of England.[23]

Beyond her activities as a translator, Anne's letters reveal the impact of her humanist training more widely. Five of her letters are written entirely in Latin. She sent two Latin letters to the theologian, Théodore de Bèze; she also received three letters written completely in Latin, including one from her sister Mildred.[24] The majority of

[21] J.E. Booty, *John Jewel as Apologist of the Church of England* (London, 1963), pp. 42–45; Hume, *Calendar of State Papers, Spain*, I, p. 201.

[22] For analysis of Anne's intentions with her translation of the *Apologia*, see Allen, 'Lady Anne Bacon's 1564 translation'. For a later analysis, see P. Demers, '"Neither bitterly nor brablingly": Lady Anne Cooke Bacon's translation of Bishop Jewel's *Apologia Ecclesiae Anglicanae*', in M. White (ed.), *English Women, Religion, and Textual Production, 1500–1625* (Aldershot, 2011), pp. 205–218.

[23] R. Verstegan, *A Declaration of the True Causes of the Great Troubles* (Antwerp, 1592), p. 12.

[24] For the letters to Bèze, see **16**, **17**. For the Latin letters written to Anne, see **3**, **20**, **III**. **35** is also primarily written by Anne in Latin. However, she also included an English postscript.

Anne's own letters are written in English, but even in these letters she frequently included odd lines in Latin, Greek, and, more rarely, Hebrew. She turned to classical languages when trying to conceal the contents of her letters, as will be discussed later, or particularly when seeking to persuade her correspondents. Such a motivation was behind her regular adoption of a sententious writing style in her letters. Through classical *sententiae*, pithy moral quotations, Anne was able to access the persuasive power of the cited authors in her correspondence. For example, she used Seneca's wisdom in his *Moral Epistles* to bolster her unwelcome advice to her son Anthony regarding his ungodly choice of friends.[25] Along with Seneca, Anne cited Publilius Syrus, Terence, Horace, and Pindar, as well as drawing on her reading of *The Life of Severus Alexander*.[26] Biblical quotations abound in her letters, unsurprisingly given that Anne described scripture as the 'infallible towchstone' of all believers (**19**). Although she used acknowledged and unacknowledged citations from both the Old and New Testaments in her letters, the greatest proportion of biblical quotations in her correspondence is drawn from the New Testament epistles, fittingly given the genre in which she was writing.[27] In acknowledgement of her learning, Anne's correspondents also frequently adopted a sententious style in their letters to her. Matthew Parker consciously employed such a style when seeking to persuade Anne to intervene with her husband on his behalf in 1568, quoting in Latin from scripture, particularly the Psalms, as well as from Sallust and Horace.[28] Anne's humanist learning is therefore a constant presence in letters from throughout her life.

Marriage

In February 1553 Anne Cooke married Nicholas Bacon, as his second wife; Nicholas Bacon was a close friend of William Cecil, who had married Anne's sister Mildred in 1545. However, Anne had earlier been courted by Walter Haddon, shortly before he was appointed Master of Magdalen College, Oxford.[29] Haddon sought the assistance of both William and Mildred Cecil in his suit and when Mildred wrote to her sister to advise that she accept Haddon's hand, she

[25] See **113**.
[26] See **96**, **100**, **109**, **120**, **142**, **148**, **186**.
[27] For detailed engagement with Anne's use of scriptural citation, see *Cooke Sisters*, pp. 109–111.
[28] See **7**. Nathaniel Bacon, Anne's stepson, also quoted one of Erasmus' *Colloquies* to his stepmother in a petitionary letter (**8**).
[29] For more on Haddon's appointment, see p. 55, n. 20, below.

chose to correspond in Latin (3).[30] Their shared knowledge of the classical language was appropriate for a letter so concerned with the importance of humanist education in sixteenth-century society, but, in spite of her sister's counsel, Anne eventually chose Nicholas Bacon instead of Haddon.[31]

The death of Edward VI ushered in an anxious period for the couple, as they were both well known for their Protestant convictions; not only was Anne the translator of the evangelical Bernardino Ochino, but Nicholas had been closely involved with many of those advancing religious reform during Edward's reign.[32] On the accession of Mary I, Anne had ridden to join her at Kenninghall in Norfolk and had pledged her support to the new queen. She was thus instrumental in securing Mary's goodwill towards her husband and her brother-in-law, William Cecil, who had been a reluctant witness to the king's instrument to alter the succession. Kenninghall was Robert Wingfield's house and he recorded that Anne was 'their chief aid in beseeching pardon for them'.[33] In many ways, Anne's actions in 1553 were fortuitous and contingent on circumstance, for Kenninghall was but a few miles from where the Bacons were then living at Redgrave in Suffolk, but they also reveal her understanding of the unfolding political events.[34]

The Bacons outwardly conformed during Mary's reign, but the years were ones of seclusion. The couple were comforted by their learning. Nicholas Bacon wrote a poem celebrating their shared intellectual interests, which concluded with the following verse:

> Thinkeinge alsoe with howe good will
> The idle tymes whiche yrkesome be
> You have made shorte throwe your good skill
> In readeinge pleasante thinges to me.
> Whereof profitte we bothe did se,
> As wittenes can if they could speake
> Bothe your Tullye and my Senecke.[35]

---

[30] For Haddon's letter to William Cecil regarding the match, see BL, Lansdowne MS 3, fo. 19r.

[31] For possible reasons for Anne's rejection of Haddon, see 3.

[32] R. Tittler, *Nicholas Bacon: the making of a Tudor statesman* (London, 1976), pp. 19–20, 52.

[33] D. MacCulloch, 'The *Vita Mariae Angliae Reginae* of Robert Wingfield of Brantham', *Camden Miscellany* 28, Camden Society, 4th series, 29 (London, 1984), p. 270.

[34] See Tittler, *Nicholas Bacon*, p. 53. For Anne's political awareness in seeking pardon for her husband and brother-in-law, see *Cooke Sisters*, p. 124.

[35] N. Bacon, *The Recreations of His Age* (Oxford, 1919), p. 27. By 'your Tullye and my Senecke', Nicholas Bacon was referring to Cicero and Seneca.

However, these years were not simply filled with intellectual pleasures. Later letters provide evidence of Anne's domestic skills. Her correspondence reveals that she taught other women how to brew and that she had some culinary knowledge: 'Trowts must be boyled as soone as possible because they say a faynt harted fysh' (**143**).[36] A verse written about Anne by the clergyman Andrew Willett confirms her expertise in 'huswifery'.[37]

The Bacons' fortunes rose with the accession of Elizabeth I in 1558, as Nicholas Bacon was shortly after made a privy councillor and lord keeper of the great seal. His position was a source of great pride for Anne, who long into her widowhood recalled her status as a 'cheeff cownsellour's wyffe' and widow of the lord keeper (**131**).[38] Nicholas bought Gorhambury manor in Hertfordshire in 1560; construction of a new house there was complete by 1568 and thereafter much of the couple's time was split between Hertfordshire and residence at York House in London. The marriage seems to have been a happy one. Anne's frequent postscripts to Nicholas' letters reveal her intimacy with the contents of his personal correspondence (see figure 1).[39] She was perceived by others to hold considerable power over her husband: Matthew Parker described her in his letter from February 1568 as Nicholas Bacon's '*alter ipse*', his other self (**7**). Parker was loath to write to Nicholas directly, fearing the reception to his overture, but he was convinced that Anne would persuade her husband to help him ensure godly preaching for the people of Norwich.

While wife of the lord keeper, Anne contributed a Latin verse to an Italian manuscript treatise entitled the *Giardino cosmografico*; the work was compiled by Bartholo Sylva, a physician from Turin and Protestant convert seeking favour from the earl of Leicester.[40] Her sister Katherine and Anne Locke, another contemporary female translator, also wrote dedicatory verses for the treatise in 1571.[41] A little over a year later, the volume became a vehicle to regain courtly favour for Anne Locke's husband, the ostracized godly clergyman Edward Dering, at which point Anne's sisters Mildred and Elizabeth contributed Greek dedicatory poems.[42] Nicholas Bacon became the primary examiner of Edward Dering when he was called before the Star Chamber in 1573,

---

[36] For Anne's tuition in brewing, see **127**.

[37] A. Willet, *Sacrorum emblematum centuria una* (Cambridge, 1592), sig. F1v.

[38] For subscriptions referencing Anne as widow of the Lord Keeper, see **16**, **17**, and **193**.

[39] See **4**, **10**. Her sister Mildred was likewise widely thought to read her husband's correspondence. See *Cooke Sisters*, p. 135.

[40] For her verse, see Cambridge University Library, Ii.v.37, fo. 8r.

[41] *Ibid.*

[42] For their poems, see *ibid.*, fo. 5v. For more detail on the Cooke sisters' involvement with this volume, see *Cooke Sisters*, pp. 169–172.

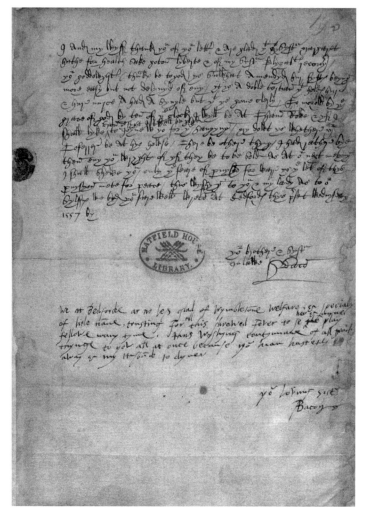

Figure 1. *Nicholas and Anne Bacon to William Cecil*, 18 August 1557 (**4**).

and so Anne's name was partially erased from the manuscript, with only her initials remaining and the spaces for the name which would once have read '*Anna Baconia*'.[43]

---

[43]Cambridge University Library, Ii.v.37, fo. 8r.

Motherhood

The marriage brought multiple pregnancies, but only two of Anne's children survived into adulthood, Anthony and Francis Bacon. John Walsall, the Bacons' household chaplain, later praised the couple's care in 'demeaning your selves in the education of your children' (**14**). Anne's memories of her sons' boyhoods occasionally come to the fore in her later letters: when she sent pigeons to the adult Anthony and Francis, she sent more birds to her younger son, explaining to Anthony that Francis 'was wont to love them better then yow from a boy' (**126**).

Anne was also close to at least some of her stepchildren during her husband's lifetime. In a letter from 1579, she referred to the long 'continuance of more then common amytee' shared with her stepson Nicholas, and a similarly close relationship is testified to by the extant correspondence between Anne and Nathaniel Bacon, prior to her husband's death (**15**). Nathaniel arranged for his stepmother to be involved in the education of his wife shortly after their marriage.[44] Anne Gresham Bacon was the acknowledged illegitimate daughter of Sir Thomas Gresham and a household servant. In order that she acquire the gloss of a gentlewoman, Nathaniel arranged 'to have her placed' with his stepmother (**8**). Anne Gresham Bacon wrote to her stepmother-in-law after her return from Gorhambury, stating herself to be 'greatly bounden to yow for the great care that yow alwaies had of my well doinge duringe my beinge with yow' (**9**). Relations were still close in 1573, when Anne Bacon was asked by Nathaniel and his wife to act as godmother to their new daughter; Anne asked her stepdaughter Elizabeth to deputize for her at the christening.[45]

Nicholas Bacon died on 20 February 1579. His will made thorough provision for Anne and it also detailed bequests to the children of both his marriages.[46] However, the magnitude of the late lord keeper's debts led both branches of the family to dispute their inheritance and William Cecil, by then Lord Burghley, was sought to intervene. The matter was eventually settled by 1580, although Anne's relationship with her stepsons Nicholas and Nathaniel thereafter seems to have been strained.[47] Although Anne mentioned Nicholas in a later letter,

---

[44] See **8**.

[45] See **12** and **13**.

[46] Anne received a life interest in Gorhambury manor in Hertfordshire and in the lease and copyhold lands surrounding the estate, the remnant of the lease of York House in London, and sheep stocks from her stepson Nicholas from Ingham and Tymworth in Suffolk, properties related to her jointure. She also received plate, jewels, horses, coaches, litters, and the household stuff from York House, as well as half the household contents at Gorhambury. See *Stiffkey*, II, pp. 25–29.

[47] For more details on this dispute, see **15**.

his message was relayed via another family member.[48] Two years later, Anne did not know in advance that her stepdaughter Elizabeth would marry Sir William Peryam, lord chief baron of the exchequer.[49] However, Anne's last known letter is to Nicholas, reminding him to pay her annuity on time; there she describes herself as 'Your Lordship's mother, in the Lord, very frend' (**197**).

On the death of Nicholas Bacon I, Anne's elder son, Anthony Bacon, decided to use his inheritance to travel, first to Paris, with the aim of sending intelligence back to his uncle, Lord Burghley, and to Francis Walsingham. In 1581, he moved on to Geneva and stayed with the theologian Théodore de Bèze. Anne felt that the theologian would provide particularly trustworthy paternal guidance, as shown by her letters to Bèze from that year (**16** and **17**). Anthony's travels then took him to various French cities, with his continued absence from England authorized by the queen.[50] Walsingham's secretary, Nicholas Faunt, kept Anne apprised of her son's movements on the Continent; in April 1582, he reported back to Anthony that he had met Lady Bacon in Burghley's garden and had answered her questions 'in all such demand[s] as you may imagin shee did make, touching your estate of health, being, moction of employing your tyme, charges of lyving in those partes, and purpose of further travayle'.[51]

By October 1584, Anthony was resident in the Huguenot town of Montauban, collecting information from Henry of Navarre's court to report back to England.[52] Increasingly, his continued stay in France caused consternation, never more so than with his mother. In April 1585, Anne petitioned the queen 'with importune show' to insist on her son's return; by the end of 1586, she was refusing to send funds to Anthony.[53] She particularly feared his friendships with the English Catholic figures Thomas Lawson, a servant, and Anthony Standen, a double agent now working for his home country. Lawson felt the effects of Lady Bacon's wrath when sent as a messenger to England in 1588. He was imprisoned for ten months by Burghley, the result of what Anthony later described as 'my mother's passionate importunitie, grounded uppon false suggestions and surmyses'.[54] Another messenger, Captain Francis Allen, reported Anne's state of mind in August 1589 regarding her son's continued Continental sojourn: 'she let not to say

[48] See **102**.
[49] See **138** and also **140**.
[50] *Troubled Life*, pp. 87, 94.
[51] LPL 647, fo. 125r.
[52] *Troubled Life*, p. 102.
[53] LPL 647, fos 189r and 219r. J.T. Freedman, 'Anthony Bacon and his world, 1558–1601' (unpublished PhD thesis, Temple University, 1979), p. 80.
[54] LPL 659, fo. 25r.

you ar a traitre to God and your contry. You have undone her, you sieke her death, and when you hav that you sieke for you shall have but on [*sic*] hundered pounds mor then you hav now'.[55] By 1591, Anne was even more resolute to procure Anthony's return; the godly preacher Thomas Cartwright found that he could not persuade her to soften her stance towards her son in this regard, nor induce her to a better opinion of his companion, Thomas Lawson.[56]

There is no evidence, however, that Anne knew of Anthony's prosecution on charges of sodomy in France in 1586.[57] She received a letter during this period from Michel Berault, the minister in Montauban, explaining her son's continued absence in France and alluding to the fact that she might hear 'some more serious opinion' of him; in that case, Berault argued, Anne must 'immediately set aside the matter' (**20**). It is possible that Berault wrote this during the summer of 1586 in response to Anthony's arrest; it could also refer to the hostility that Philippe du Plessis-Mornay and his wife held towards Anthony at this time.[58] However, Anne's later letters make fleeting allusions to both her sons' almost entirely masculine lifestyles.[59] She lamented their lack of wives and her consequent lack of grandchildren, in terms that recalled Anthony's Continental exile: 'I shulde have ben happy to have seene chylder's chylder, but Frannce spoyled me and myne' (**188**).

Anthony's return: a mother's political counsel

Anthony's return to England in February 1592 marks the start of a voluminous correspondence between mother and son; Anne initially welcomed her son back to the country by letter.[60] A major concern

---

[55] LPL 647, fo. 245r.

[56] A. Pearson, *Thomas Cartwright and Elizabethan Puritanism, 1535–1603* (Cambridge, 1925), pp. 464–465.

[57] For Anthony's prosecution, see *Troubled Life*, pp. 108–111.

[58] Alan Haynes has suggested that Anthony's prosecution was connected to his dispute with Madame du Plessis-Mornay. For more details, see p. 93, n. 178, and A. Haynes, *Invisible Power: the Elizabethan secret services, 1570–1603* (Stroud, 1994), pp. 105–106.

[59] For her condemnation of 'that bloody Peerce', as Anthony's 'coch companion and bed companion', see **44** and **45**.

[60] See **22**. For discussion of other early modern women's maternal letters of advice, see L. Mitchell, 'Entertainment and instruction: women's roles in the English epistolary tradition', *Huntington Library Quarterly*, 66 (2003), pp. 331–347; R. Anselment, 'Katherine Paston and Brilliana Harley: maternal letters and the genre of mother's advice', *Studies in Philology*, 101 (2004), pp. 431–453; Daybell, *Women Letter-writers*, pp. 179–182.

of this letter, and subsequent correspondence, was how her newly returned son should advance himself in England. The secretary Nicholas Faunt was suggested as a suitable companion, described by Anne as 'one that feareth God in dede, and wyse with all having experience of our state' (**22**). She was concerned that without a detailed knowledge of past political affairs, Anthony would be a poor judge of his new acquaintances. 'Beleve not every one that speakes fayre to yow at your fyrst comming', she told him; 'It is to serve their turn' (**25**). His understanding of state matters was a particular cause of anxiety: 'Yow have ben long absent and by your sickliness cannot be your own agent and so wanting right judgment of our state may be much deceaved' (**32**).

For Anne, the combination of her educational background and her hard-earned political experience was a potent one: 'I think for my long attending in coorte and a cheeff cownsellour's wyffe few *preclarae feminae meae sortis* are able or be alyve to speak and judg of such proceedings and worldly doings of men' (**131**).[61] Her warning to Anthony about the duplicitous nature of the countess of Warwick, a gentlewoman of the Privy Chamber and one of the queen's closest intimates during this period, was therefore based on past experience.[62] Her sense of political intelligence was not simply self-aggrandisement. Her political understanding was acknowledged by Matthew Parker: in comparing Nicholas Bacon to three former lord chancellors, Thomas More, Thomas Audley, and Thomas Goodrich, Parker assumed Anne's knowledge of these late politicians. The freedom with which Parker discussed his affairs with Anne contrasts with his statement that he had not spoken of any such matters with his own wife, Margaret Harleston Parker, a woman whom he admitted as being not without 'reason and godlynes' (**7**).[63]

After the death of their father in 1579, the assistance of their uncle, William Cecil, Lord Burghley, was crucial to Anthony's and Francis' career advancement. Francis, for example, sought help in September 1580 from the lord treasurer and his aunt Mildred in obtaining an honorary legal post from the queen.[64] On his return from Europe in 1592, Anthony Bacon and his mother expected that Burghley would aid his career. Anne approached Burghley in August 1593 but, while his subsequent letter declared his goodwill towards his nephews, it lacked

---

[61] For translations of the foreign languages included in the Introduction, see the relevant letter.
[62] See **140**.
[63] For more on Margaret Harleston Parker, see p. 62, n. 57.
[64] See *Troubled Life*, p. 80; *Cooke Sisters*, pp. 145–146.

any practical assurance to further Anthony and Francis.[65] Anne also approached Robert Cecil in January 1595 regarding Francis' bid for the post of solicitor-general; after the latter's assurances that his father was seeking to advance his nephew with the queen, Anne concluded that Robert Cecil's 'spech was all kindly owtward and dyd desyre to have me think so of him' (**116**).

Despite such protestations, there is an increasing sense of unease regarding Anne's perception of her Cecil kin. Anne told Anthony in March 1594 that he should be careful in his 'use' of his relatives, particularly Burghley (**98**). Such suspicions were only increased upon the appointment in July 1596 of Robert Cecil to the post of principal secretary, after which Anne told her son, 'He now hath great avantage [*sic*] and strength to intercept, prevent and to toy where he hath ben or is, sonne, be it emulation or suspicion, yow know what termes he standeth in toward your self [. . .] The father and sonne are affectionate, joyned in power and policy' (**158**). Anthony kept his mother informed of changes in his relationship with his cousin; he told her in December 1596 that Robert Cecil had declared any past ill will as forgotten, with 'earnest protestation [. . .] he would be gladd and redye to doe me any kinde office' (**183**). Such information would have been welcome to Anne; despite her concern regarding Robert Cecil's goodwill towards her sons, he and his father had long been recipients of her more general requests for patronage.[66]

The failure of Burghley to act as a patron meant that Anthony and Francis Bacon sought the advancement of another well-connected figure, Robert Devereux, the second earl of Essex. Francis' friendship with Essex had begun in the late 1580s and he introduced his brother to the earl on his return in 1592. When the position of master of the rolls became vacant in early 1593, it was widely assumed that it would be filled by the current attorney-general, Thomas Egerton. Essex thus tried to secure the post of attorney-general for Francis Bacon; Anthony relayed his efforts with the queen to Anne.[67] Anthony declared to his mother in September 1593 that the earl was 'more like a father then a frende' towards Francis Bacon, arguing that, if only Lord Burghley would join with Essex, then Francis would succeed in his attempts at preferment (**69**). However, the Cecils sought to place Edward Coke as attorney-general; Francis, they suggested, would do better to try for Coke's post as solicitor-general. Anthony informed his mother, in minute detail, of the earl's efforts on Francis' behalf, reporting that Essex told their cousin Robert Cecil, 'Digest me noe digestinge, for the

---

[65] See **67**.
[66] See **19**, **109**, **132**, **193**.
[67] See letters **52**, **60**, and **85**.

Attourniship is that I must have for Francis Bacon' (**85**). When Edward
Coke was made attorney-general on 10 April 1594, Francis' attentions
shifted to securing Coke's old position. His mother, however, feared
that his continued struggle for preferment was affecting his well-being,
writing that her younger son 'hindreth his health' with 'inwarde secret
greeff' (**140**).

Despite Anne's appreciation of Essex's efforts to advance her sons,
his relationship with them caused her great anxiety. Anthony was
soon organizing a secretariat for Essex, which gathered information
from across Europe.[68] To be closer to this operation, Anthony moved
from Gray's Inn into a house in Bishopsgate Street in April 1594.
His mother was horrified at the relocation, given the lack of 'edifieng
instruction' and the close proximity to the 'corrupt and lewde' Bull
Inn (**101**). After a short residence in Chelsea during the spring and
summer of 1595, Anthony had decided to move again, into the earl of
Essex's residence on the Strand in August. His mother was opposed
to the move from its inception, telling her son 'yow shall fynde many
inconveniences not lyght' (**141**).[69] It would also bring Anthony closer to
those whom she worried might infect him with Catholic sympathies.
The influence of Anthony Standen and Thomas Lawson had long
been a concern, but Anne now feared Anthony's closer association
with members of Essex's circle, such as Antonio Pérez, the former
secretary of Philip II of Spain, and particularly Lord Henry Howard,
later the earl of Northampton. She described Howard as a 'dangerous
intelligencyng man', adding 'No dowt a subtill papist inwardely and
lyeth in wayte' (**123**).[70]

The political circles of Elizabethan London were not the only arena
in which Anne sought to guide her son; she was concerned too with his
political standing in Hertfordshire. She was a keen observer of local
politics close to the Gorhambury estate and she informed Anthony
of his failure to be elected as MP for nearby St Albans in 1593; her
opinion was that the town had always been set on re-electing the
same two principal burgesses and that the offer of support was a
superficial one.[71] Anthony was instead elected MP for Wallingford in
Oxfordshire that year.[72] When he was asked to serve as a justice of
the peace, his mother's advice was clear: 'Take it not yet sonne, *si
sapis*' (**98**). Recent work on sixteenth-century women and politics has

---

[68] P. Hammer, 'The uses of scholarship: the secretariat of Robert Devereux, second earl
of Essex, *c*. 1585–1601', *English Historical Review*, 109 (1994), pp. 26–51.

[69] See also **142**.

[70] For more references to Howard, see **123**, **125**, **131**, **137**, **145**, **186**, **194**.

[71] See **35**.

[72] See *History of Parliament*, I, p. 372.

sought to reconceptualize their activities away from the traditional arenas of politics.[73] Anne's involvement in local politics, and, as we shall see, parliamentary politics, instead reveals that women in this period understood and participated in these 'conventional' political processes.

The counsel of a godly widow

Anne did not only seek to counsel her sons regarding secular politics. Religion is a central issue in her surviving letters, in contrast to the correspondence of many of her female contemporaries.[74] One reason why Anne wrote so frequently concerning religion in her correspondence is that she felt the need to provide spiritual counsel to her son Anthony. She wanted Anthony to demonstrate his godly credentials clearly on his return to England, especially as he had 'ben where Reformation is' (**22**). She advised him to ensure that his household was ordered upon godly lines, telling him to 'exercyse godlynes with prayours and psalmes reverently, morning and evening' (**64**). Moreover, she urged him to place his trust in those of the 'syncerer sort' of religion; she had a particular regard for the Calvinist worship of the French Stranger Church in London (**22**).[75]

Anne frequently reflects on the spiritual progress of England in her letters from the 1590s. At times she refers to the need for further reform, suggesting that the country was 'styll wayting for our conversion' (**148**). Overall, however, there is a perception of religious decline in her correspondence. The queen was criticized, albeit somewhat obliquely, for her deficiency in stemming such a decline: 'God preserve her from all evell and rule her hart to the zeallus setting forth of his glory,' Anne wrote of Elizabeth I in October 1595, adding 'want of this zeale in all degrees is the very grownde of our home trobles. We have

[73] The literature in this area is extensive. Barbara Harris' work is seminal; see particularly B. Harris, 'Women and politics in early Tudor England', *Historical Journal*, 33 (1990), pp. 259–281. Another important volume is J. Daybell (ed.), *Women and Politics in Early Modern England, 1450–1700* (Aldershot, 2004).

[74] James Daybell has suggested that one reason why there are so few surviving sixteenth-century women's letters discussing religion is that letter-writing was 'largely a secular domain'. See J. Daybell, 'Women's letters, literature and conscience in sixteenth-century England', *Renaissance Studies*, 23 (2009), p. 519. For religion in the letters of other early modern women, see *ibid.*; S. Doran, 'Elizabeth's religion: clues from her letters', *Journal of Ecclesiastical History*, 51 (2000), pp. 699–720; J. Eales, 'Patriarchy, puritanism and politics: the letters of Lady Brilliana Harley (1598–1643)', in J. Daybell (ed.), *Early Modern Women's Letter Writing, 1450–1700* (Basingstoke, 2001), pp. 143–158; M. Morrissey and G. Wright, 'Piety and sociability in early modern women's letters', *Women's Writing*, 13 (2006), pp. 38–50.

[75] For the French Stranger Church, see also **138** and **142**.

all dalied with the Lorde, who wyll not ever suffer him selff [to] be mocked' (**145**). The lack of godly preaching at court was particularly condemned, as infecting not only the queen's counsellors but also beyond through their 'lamentable example': 'For by expownding well the law and commandments of God, sinne is layde open and disclosed to the hearers and worketh in them by God his spirit more hatred of evell and checketh our pronness naturall, to all synn' (**146**).

Sections of Anne's letters almost encroach on the masculine domain of the jeremiad sermon, bewailing the misfortunes of late sixteenth-century England as just punishment for society's impiousness.[76] In April 1595, she wrote that 'evell dayes [were] imminent to be feared' (**123**). She went further in a letter to the ecclesiastical judge Edward Stanhope, condemning his role in England's spiritual decline, through his persecution of godly preachers:

> By report, the enemies of God, of her Majestie and of our cuntrie are mighty and with cruell and fiery hartes preparing the readie to the pray and spoile of us all. We had need with most humble submission intreat the Lord of hostes … to torne away his wrath so greatlie provoked daily by the fearfull contempt of his holie gospell. (**189**)

Anne's letters reveal her attempts to inspire personal moral reformation. One particular recipient of her godly counsel was the earl of Essex, who received letters from Anne urging him to cease swearing and his adulterous acts.[77] She not only attempted to reform Essex's ways directly but also raised her concerns with her son Anthony and with other members of the Essex circle.[78] Anne's religious counsel was connected to her status as a widow. For her, widowhood was an opportunity to concentrate on spiritual matters.[79] She told Burghley in a letter from 1585 that she understood she must attend public preaching as 'a cheff duty commanded by God to weedoes' (**19**). Widowhood, however, had a further resonance for Anne, revealed through her correspondence. She chose to sign herself as 'ABacon $X\eta\rho\alpha$' in ten of her letters, '$X\eta\rho\alpha$' being the Greek for widow.[80] Two of the letters were directed to the earl of Essex, one went to Lord

---

[76] For jeremiad sermons, see M. Morrissey, 'Elect nations and prophetic preaching: types and examples in the Paul's Cross jeremiad', in L.A. Ferrell and P. McCullough (eds), *The English Sermon Revised* (Manchester, 2000), pp. 43–58.

[77] See **146** and **174**. For Essex's response, see **176**; Anne's subsequent reply is **177**.

[78] For her letters to Anthony, see **140** and **166**. For Anthony's response, see **168**. See also **148** to Francis Goad, an army captain, regarding the morality of Essex's soldiers.

[79] In this, she contrasts with her sister Elizabeth Cooke Hoby Russell, who continued to be actively involved in political circles in her widowhood. See *Cooke Sisters*, pp. 146–157.

[80] See **29**, **62**, **114**, **115**, **118**, **132**, **133**, **174**, **190**, **197**. See also **146** for Anne's description of herself as 'husbandless' in Greek.

Burghley, six were sent to her son Anthony, and one was written to her stepson Nicholas Bacon II. It seems likely that Anne's use of the Greek term for widow in these letters derives from the role of godly widows expounded in the Pauline epistles, in his first letter to Timothy.[81] The biblical passage discusses how poor widows will be maintained and advises that a special group of widows receive assistance from the Church; the passage suggests that in return these godly widows will 'continueth in supplications and prayers night and day'.[82] The ten letters that Anne signed 'ABacon $X\eta\rho\alpha$' are united by the fact that they all include some form of intercessory prayer on behalf of the recipient; the letters to Anthony and Nicholas are familial correspondence, covering diverse matters, but all include at least a short intercession. Anne frequently incorporates written prayers in other letters, without the Greek subscription, even explicitly concluding three of these epistolary prayers with an English 'Amen' and four with the same word in Hebrew.[83] In some ways, the use of written prayers is a strategy for offering advice: the value of intercessory prayer for Anne, as a female counsellor, was that she could offer bold and authoritative godly advice through what was a religiously sanctioned act.[84]

'but quod my Lorde': reporting speech

When offering both political and religious counsel, Anne relied heavily on incorporating reported speech into her epistolary advice. Linguists have drawn attention to the use of reported speech in other forms of early modern writing, particularly in news serials, and it is striking that Anne's correspondence contains so much reported speech.[85] She has a particular awareness of the gap between the spoken word and

---

[81] For wider discussion of this point, see Magnusson, 'Widowhood', pp. 28–32; and *Cooke Sisters*, pp. 112–113.

[82] See 1 Timothy 5:5. For another New Testament discussion of the role of the godly widow, see Luke 2:36–37.

[83] For the use of Amen in English, see **120**, **123**, **148**. For the use in Hebrew, see **22**, **142**, **177**, **188**.

[84] For more on Anne's use of written prayers, see *Cooke Sisters*, p. 113.

[85] For reported speech in other types of early modern writing, see in particular A. Zucker, '"but 'tis believed that . . . ": speech and thought presentation in early English newspapers', in N. Brownlees (ed.), *News Discourse in Early Modern Britain* (Bern, 2006), pp. 105–126; N. Brownlees, 'Spoken discourse in early English newspapers', in J. Raymond (ed.), *News Networks in Seventeenth Century Britain and Europe* (Abingdon, 2006), pp. 67–84. For the use of reported speech in diplomatic correspondence, see N. Brownlees, 'Reporting the news in English and Italian diplomatic correspondence', in M. Dossena and G. Camiciotti (eds), *Letter Writing in Late Modern Europe* (Amsterdam, 2012), pp. 121–138.

action. She tells Anthony of a conversation between Lord Burghley and a quack physician,

> a soden startupp glorious stranger, that wolde nedes cure him of the gowt by boast, but quod my Lorde, 'Have yow cured eny; let me know and se them'. 'Nay', sayde the fellow, 'but I am sure I can'. 'Well', concluded my Lorde and sayde 'Go, go and cure fyrst and then come again or elce not'. (**113**)

Her entire conversation with Robert Cecil in January 1595 is reported back to Anthony, and she also records her sister Elizabeth's speech to her in April of that year.[86] When Anne counsels the earl of Essex against swearing, she reports how she learnt of his behaviour in discussion with a court friend after a sermon and she includes much of the dialogue that ensued, which in turn involves the retelling of an even earlier conversation.[87]

There is the sense that Anne quotes so many speech-acts because they provide evidence for her advice-giving. This, in many ways, is similar to her use of *sententiae* to bolster her counsel, yet here the usage of reported speech functions as a form of rhetorical proof. Classical and renaissance rhetoricians emphasized that inartificial proofs were particularly persuasive, such as the judgments of earlier courts or the testimony of witnesses.[88] Anne's reportage of speech-acts, the testimony of her witnesses, is another technique designed to persuade her reader that her epistolary advice was based on strong, incontrovertible evidence.

'For occurents'

Another basis for Anne's counselling activities was her access to intelligence. There has been much recent scholarly interest in early modern women's involvement with news.[89] Anne Bacon's letters provide an opportunity to expand our understanding of sixteenth-century women's acquisition of and interest in news. Her correspondence reveals her diverse intelligence networks. She was well served for local news; for example, she knew that Anthony had been

---

[86] See **116** and **125**. For an acquaintance's description of Bishopsgate Street, reported in his own words, see **101**.

[87] See **146**.

[88] See particularly Aristotle, *Rhetoric*, 1.2.2; and Quintilian, *Institutio oratoria*, 5.1.1.

[89] See particularly J. Daybell, 'Suche newes as on Quenes hye wayes we have mett': the news and intelligence networks of Elizabeth Talbot, Countess of Shrewsbury (*c.* 1527–1608)', in Daybell, *Women and Politics*, pp. 114–131. See also Daybell, *Women Letter-writers*, pp. 152–157; *idem*, 'Women, news and intelligence networks'; N. Mears, *Queenship and Political Discourse in the Elizabethan Realms* (Cambridge, 2005), pp. 54–55, 110–113.

approached about becoming a JP before he confirmed the fact to her by letter.[90] She also maintained extensive contacts at court, including Ursula Walsingham and her daughter Frances Devereux, Lady Mary Scudamore, and Lady Dorothy Stafford.[91] Sometimes Anne heard news first-hand through conversation with these courtly figures, but on other occasions she received intelligence in letters from the women: 'My Lady Stafford sent me word that her Majesti marveled yow come not to see her' (**144**). Anne even had European contacts who supplied her with news. Captain Francis Goad wrote to her from Dieppe in June 1593 with details of Henry IV's struggles to claim the crown of France, prior to his abjuration of Protestantism the following month.[92]

The greatest source of Anne's intelligence, however, was her son Anthony. His letters supplied her with the latest news from London. Often this was closely concerned with her sons' personal advancement. Anthony wrote on 5 February 1594 to his mother regarding his brother, Francis; he told her that what followed came to him via the earl of Essex, adding 'I alter not one worde, thinkinge it best to set it downe as it hath bene delivered from my Lord' (**85**). Similarly, a week later, Anthony again wrote to his mother, enclosing a letter written to him by Henry Gosnold, a young lawyer at Gray's Inn, concerning Francis' reputation.[93]

The news provided for Anne in her letters went beyond information concerning family members. In two different letters, Anthony told his mother of the progress of the investigation of Roderigo Lopez, former physician to Elizabeth I; Lopez was arrested at the end of January 1594 for conspiring to poison the queen and was executed on 7 June.[94] Anthony also provided information about household appointments at court and about City figures, telling his mother of the death of two London aldermen, one the lord mayor, in December 1596.[95] Anne was also interested in parliamentary activity. In the aftermath of the April 1593 parliament, Anthony answered each of his mother's queries directly, providing information on the fate of her nephew Sir Edward Hoby after he had quarrelled with a parliamentary committee member, and the consequences of Peter Wentworth's activities to reintroduce the issue of succession into parliament.[96]

[90] See **40**.
[91] See **114**, **123**, **132**, **144**, **145**, **174**, **196**.
[92] See **51**, and especially p. 132, n. 384, which discusses Goad's correspondence with Anthony Bacon.
[93] See **89**.
[94] For Lopez, see **83** and **85**.
[95] See **169** and **183**.
[96] See **43**.

European news was also relayed to Anne via Anthony. This was wide-ranging in its coverage; Anthony's letter of 13 July 1596 discussed the Thirteen Years' War and the Franco-Spanish War, as well as developments in the Nine Years' War in Ireland.[97] Much of this information was derived from Anthony's own political contacts with the earl of Essex and his circle. He provided his mother with detailed information regarding the duc de Bouillon's diplomatic activities to forge the Triple Alliance against the Spanish in 1596, much of which seemingly came directly from the Frenchman himself.[98] Anthony also heard French news through members of the French Stranger Church, which he relayed to his mother.[99] He was swift to inform his mother of the freshness of the news he provided: details regarding the Thirteen Years' War and the Franco-Spanish War were provided as 'newes arrived at the Court yesterday' (**154**).[100]

The news from London was sometimes clearly offered in exchange for goods from the Gorhambury estate. A letter from February 1594, reporting the reception of Francis Bacon's first cases in the King's Bench, was concluded, rather prosaically, with an appeal for another quarter of wheat.[101] Similarly, Francis Bacon concluded a letter lamenting his mother's ill-health with a postscript asking that she send him a bed from Gorhambury.[102] In each case, the request was seemingly purposefully left until the very end of the letter, as if an afterthought. Anthony's sustained dissemination of news to his mother, however, meant that he continued to facilitate her advice-giving activities, even if he did not always welcome the constant stream of epistolary counsel in return.

Receiving advice

Anne certainly often worried that her advice was mocked and, worse, ignored by her sons, writing, for example, 'But my sonns hast not to harken to their mother's goode cownsell in time to prevent' (**27**).[103] Her exasperation even caused her to utilize the additional persuasive power of Latin: '*haud inane est quod dico*' (**133**). There is little direct evidence of Francis' reactions to his mother's counsel. When she tried

<hr/>

[97] See **159**.
[98] See letters **147**, **157**, **165**, **168**.
[99] See **83**, **178**.
[100] For more European news, see **63**, **164**.
[101] See **86**.
[102] See **105**.
[103] For more discussion of the reception of Anne's advice, see Magnusson, 'Widowhood'; Mair, 'Material lies'; and *Cooke Sisters*, pp. 114–116.

to advise him on how to order his finances in April 1593, he accused
her of treating him like a ward, which Anne retorted was 'a remote
phrase to my playn motherly meaning' (**45**). Anthony's responses to
his mother's advice were varied. Sometimes he resorted to silence,
something which enraged his mother and necessitated him providing
a further justification:

> so in matter of advice and admonition from a parent to a childe, I knowe
> not fitter nor better answerre then signification of a dutyfull acceptance and
> thankes, unlesse there were juste cause of replie, which howe reasonable soever
> it be, manie times is more offencive then a respective silence. (**65**)

Such cool anger was also frequently his response to what he termed
her 'misconceite[s], misimputatione[s] or causeles humorous threates'
(**150**). The sheer quantity of correspondence between mother and son,
however, suggests that Anthony did value the relationship, if at times
only to ensure a supply of goods and money from Gorhambury.[104]
There is also evidence that he read his mother's letters closely. In
answer to her comment regarding the stormy weather in June 1596,
he responded with a sentiment designed to appeal to his godly mother:

> the changes whereof as they were used for threatnings by the prophettes in an-
> tient time, so ~~no dout but~~ ^God graunt^ they ^may^ worke more ~~in all good~~
> ~~Christians minde amongst~~ ^in^ us as due and timelie apprehension of God's
> hevie judgements, imminent over us, for the deep prophane securitie that
> rayneth to much amongs us. (**154**)

The many corrections made to this draft suggest that Anthony was
trying to please his mother with his response to her advice. Moreover,
when he received word of the queen's kind comments about him
in October 1593, he was swift to tell his mother, writing that his
motivation was not 'vaine glory', but that she would be 'partaker of
my comforts, as advertised of my crosses' (**73**).

Patronage power

The political roles held by early modern women within their patronage
society has been the subject of much scholarly research.[105] Anne's
letters provide evidence as to her role as an intermediary to influential
patrons. She would write on behalf of kin: for example, she appealed
to Matthew Parker in 1561 for a distant cousin.[106] After a letter of
request by her son Anthony, Anne also wrote to Burghley concerning

---

[104]Magnusson, 'Widowhood', pp. 12–13.
[105]See above, p. 17, n. 73.
[106]See **5**.

a wardship dispute involving Robert Bacon, her nephew.[107] She told her
brother-in-law that this was the first patronage request that Robert had
ever made of her, and that kinship compelled her to write on his behalf.
In this instance, she was more persuaded by their close kinship than
was her sister Elizabeth, whom Robert also approached for assistance
with the wardship.[108] Anne also intervened on behalf of servants. When
Anthony's servant 'little' Peter sought new employment at the Doctors'
Commons, she wrote to Julius Caesar, the master of requests, and to
her relative Thomas Stanhope on his behalf, although she was explicit
that this was her first and last intervention for Peter.[109] She would also
intervene on behalf of neighbours in Hertfordshire, if they shared her
godly beliefs.[110]

During her widowhood, Anne's energies as an intermediary
were particularly focused on intense support of godly preachers, in
response to John Whitgift's attempts to enforce religious conformity
as archbishop of Canterbury from 1583. Nicholas Faunt described
Anne's activities at court on behalf of the suspended preachers, writing
to her son Anthony 'that I have bene a wittenes of her earnest care
and travaile for the restoring of some of them to their places, by
resorting often unto this place to sollicite those causes'.[111] Her letter to
her brother-in-law, Lord Burghley, from February 1585, demonstrates
not only the nature of her religious beliefs but also her willingness
to use her family connections to further the godly cause. Anne was
'extraordinaryly admitted' through Burghley's favour into the House
of Commons, when Whitgift gave his response to a petition against
his 'Three Articles', which had led to the suspension of many godly
preachers.[112] Following this particularly heated session, Anne asked
that her brother-in-law, perhaps with other privy counsellors, grant
some of the godly preachers a private audience:

> And yf they can not strongly prove before yow owt of the worde of God that
> Reformation which they so long have called and cryed for to be according to
> Christ his own ordinance, then to lett them be rejected with shame owt of the
> church for ever. (**19**)

[107] Anne described Robert Bacon as her husband's 'elldest brother's onelie sonne' (**193**).
[108] For Elizabeth's involvement with Robert Bacon, see *Cooke Sisters*, pp. 143–144.
[109] See **163**.
[110] See **109** and **179**. The godly Sir Henry Cocke, the deputy lieutenant of Hertfordshire,
also sought Anne as an intermediary in his repeated petitions to Burghley. See *Cooke Sisters*,
p. 142.
[111] LPL 647, fo. 145r.
[112] The longer history of women listening to parliamentary debates is discussed in E.
Chalus, *Elite Women in English Political Life, c. 1754–1790* (Oxford, 2005), pp. 47–52. For an
alternative view, see Magnusson, 'Imagining a national church', pp. 42–56.

Despite Anne's energetic petition, there is no evidence as to any positive outcome from her appeal to Burghley.

Anne also acted as a religious patron in her own right. In his letter of 1581, Théodore de Bèze suggested that his dedication to Anne of his meditations on the penitential psalms was inspired purely by her humanist learning.[113] However, the dedication was a calculated move. In 1583 and 1590, Anne donated funds to the Genevan church.[114] In 1593, she was once again prevailed upon to contribute to the European cause and was presented with a recent edition of Bèze's meditations.[115] However, Anthony's letters reveal that no contribution was forthcoming from her, so he himself sent a gift to Bèze. The draft of his letter to his mother, explaining the gift which he had sent, is revealing through its multiple corrections and additions, as Anthony struggled to find the right words to write to his mother.[116] It would appear that by 1593 Anne was less predisposed to donate to the European cause, perhaps because her primary concern was with local provision of godly preaching.

Anne's letters thus reveal her considerable support of puritan preachers at Gorhambury in the 1590s. In May 1592, she made reference to the 'comfortable company' of Percival Wyborn and Humphrey Wilblood, both of whom had been deprived of their benefices. Her condemnation of those who persecuted the godly was clear: 'Thei may greatly be afraide of God his displeasure which worke the woefull disapointing of God his worke in his vineyarde by putting such to silence in these bowlde sinning dayes' (**26**). Wyborn and Wilblood stayed at Gorhambury at various points throughout the early 1590s, providing 'fatherly and holsome heavenly instructions' to the household and local community (**185**).[117] Anne frequently tried to send them to her sons in London; she urged that Anthony should interpret the visits of these 'learned men [. . .] as tokens of [God's] favour' (**58**).

During her widowhood, Anne presented the clerical livings to two benefices in Hertfordshire: St Michael's in St Albans and the nearby Redbourn parish. Her clerical presentations were all godly preachers, who were subjected to close scrutiny by the ecclesiastical authorities.[118] The archdeaconry of St Albans was under the diocese of London at that time and John Aylmer, bishop of London from 1577 to 1594,

[113]See **18**.
[114]See Stewart, 'Voices of Anne Cooke', p. 96; *Cooke Sisters*, p. 186.
[115]See **52**.
[116]See **53** and *Cooke Sisters*, p. 186.
[117]See also **48**, **62**, **64**, **92**, **100**, **103**, **120**, **139**, **182**, **185**.
[118]For these presentations, see *Cooke Sisters*, pp. 177–183.

was described by Anne as a 'godles Bishop', committing even worse persecution in her eyes than the Marian bishop Edmund Bonner (**103**). Those serving the archdeaconry of St Albans were described as 'byting vipers, the hole pack of them [. . .] hindrerers of goode men' (**102**).[119]

Anne's correspondence reveals in detail the dealings of one of her clerical choices, Rudolph Bradley, with the ecclesiastical authorities. Appointed vicar of Redbourn parish in 1592, Bradley was required to send a certificate of orders in February 1597 to Edward Stanhope, chancellor to the London diocese, and, on the latter's failure to receive them, Bradley was declared excommunicate.[120] Anne's response was to send a vehement letter of reproach to Stanhope, arguing that his role should instead be to 'incouradge the faithfull and painefull preachers of Jesu Christ' (**189**). After further intervention from Anthony Bacon, Bradley was reinstated and continued at Redbourn until 1602, although Anne refused to see herself as beholden to Stanhope, whom she had earlier condemned as a 'fylthy adulterer, yf not fornicator too' (**163**).[121] Anne's correspondence concerning Bradley reveals her belief that if the parishioners were not guided by a preacher, they would fall away from godly living; she wrote to Anthony that she feared that, in the absence of scriptural instruction from the pulpit, 'Now belyke Robin Hoode and Mayde Marian are to supply with their prophan partes, for leave is geven' (**33**).

Anne's letters demonstrate that even after clergymen ceased to live under her direct patronage she continued to perceive them as being under her care; in 1597, she used her connections with the earl of Essex to help William Dike, who had previously been an assistant curate at St Michael's, even prevailing upon her son to add his influence to her suit.[122] Edward Spencer, one of Anthony's servants, wrote to his master in August 1594 from Gorhambury, informing him of Anne's financial support of godly preachers: 'Mr Willcockes had a paper withe agrete delle of gould in it, Willblod had 2 quartares of whete, Dicke had somthinge the other day, what I know not'.[123] Anne's local religious patronage as a widow even went beyond her own clerical candidates. In 1589, Thomas Wilcox, one of the authors of the 1572 Presbyterian manifesto, *An Admonition to the Parliament*, wrote of the 'sundrie favours' she had shown towards 'many worthie ministers' over the years (**21**).

[119] See also Anne's description of Thomas Rockett, the official and registrar to the archdeacon of St Albans, in **167**.
[120] For Bradley's appointment, see HALS, ASA 7/15, fo. 8v.
[121] For Anthony's intervention, see LPL 655, fo. 1r, and *Cooke Sisters*, p. 182.
[122] See **190** and **191**. For Dike borrowing Anne's coach in 1596, see **161**.
[123] LPL 650, fo. 253r. 'Mr Willcockes' was Thomas Wilcox, 'Willblod' was Percival Wilblood, and 'Dicke' was William Dike.

Anne has also long been associated with the puritan apologia, *A Parte of a Register*, published in 1593. John Field was responsible for collecting this mass of documents recording the struggle of the godly; the aim was to form a puritan register which would imitate Foxe's *Acts and Monuments*. William Urwick, the Victorian historian of nonconformity, suggested that *A Parte of a Register* was 'probably issued with the sanction and at the expense of Lady Bacon' and this suggestion has been echoed by later scholars.[124] A letter written by Anne in July 1593 to Anthony makes a cryptic reference, perhaps to the documents that formed the *Register*: 'I wolde have the two kallenders very saffly returned hether' (**58**).[125]

Sisterhood

Despite the fact that Anne's historical reputation is partly based on her status as one of the learned Cooke sisters, little mention is made of her sisters in her letters. Nicholas Bacon's letter to William Cecil, husband to Anne's sister Mildred, refers to Elizabeth and Margaret Cooke as living with the Cecils during the Marian period, although Anne's postscript to the letter makes no further direct mention of her sisters.[126] There is greater evidence of Anne's relationship with Elizabeth during their widowhoods. She referred to receiving a letter from Elizabeth Cooke Hoby Russell, but stated that she had replied, advising her not to visit in person while she was unwell.[127] She borrowed her sister's coach on occasion and visited her Blackfriars house after attending Stephen Egerton's sermons at the nearby St Anne's church.[128] There Elizabeth tearfully revealed their nephew Robert Cecil's rejection of her advice. Anne's response was to write to Robert on her sister's behalf, but Elizabeth was resolutely opposed to such a course: '"No, no", *inquit*, "It is to late, he hath marred all and that against my cownsells lyking at all"' (**125**).

Anne counselled her sons not to take notice of their aunt's actions, or become embroiled in such courtly intrigue. Elizabeth, Anne believed, could be a fickle ally; she told Anthony that Henry Howard would

---

[124]W. Urwick, *Nonconformity in Herts. Being Lectures upon the Non-conforming Worthies of St Albans and Memorials of Puritanism and Nonconformity in All the Parishes of the County of Hertford* (London, 1884), p. 82.

[125]See Magnusson, 'Widowhood', p. 30; Magnusson, 'Imagining a national church', p. 49. For further discussion of Anne's role in *A Parte of a Register*, see *Cooke Sisters*, pp. 189–192.

[126]See **4**.

[127]See **70**.

[128]See **151** and **125**.

surely betray him to his aunt Elizabeth.[129] There is evidence in Anne's letters that her sister certainly did try to become involved in Anthony's affairs. In October 1593, he told his mother that he had heard from his aunt that the queen had openly lamented his ill-health and three years later Elizabeth Russell tried to heal the mistrust which had developed between the two sides of the family, the Bacons and the Cecils, since Robert Cecil's elevation to the secretaryship in July 1596.[130] To assuage this bad feeling, Elizabeth went to and fro between her brother-in-law, Burghley, and her nephew Anthony, on 8 September 1596.[131] That Anthony was suspicious of his aunt's intentions was confirmed by a later letter to his mother. He told her that he was pleased that his aunt had solicited a profession of goodwill from Burghley, stating that her mediation 'hath dried upp the torrent of my Lord Tresurer's mightie indignation, at the least by show and his owne profession and so autenticall a testemony as my Lady Russell's' (**172**). In the reference to Elizabeth's 'autenticall' testimony, there is surely the suggestion that, like his mother, Anthony felt that his aunt would publicize her actions.

Inheritance and finances

Anne's letters provide important evidence regarding the financial dealings of a sixteenth-century woman, which complements recent research on eighteenth-century women and their money.[132] It seems that Anne kept relatively detailed accounts; in June 1596, for example, she broke down the £220 of payments made by her that year.[133] Her sons proved a great and unpredictable drain on her finances. A frequent refrain in her letters is that she had spent all her wealth on

---

[129] See **123**.
[130] See **73** for Elizabeth relaying a message from the queen.
[131] For a reconstruction of the saga, see *Cooke Sisters*, pp. 149–157.
[132] For eighteenth-century women, see A. Laurence, 'Lady Betty Hastings, her half-sisters and the South Sea Bubble: family fortunes and strategies', *Women's History Review*, 15 (2006), pp. 533–540; R. O'Day, *Cassandra Brydges (1670–1735), First Duchess of Chandos: life and letters* (Woodbridge, 2007), pp. 14–26; A. Laurence, 'Women investors, "that nasty South Sea affair" and the rage to speculate in early eighteenth-century England', *Accounting, Business and Financial History*, 16 (2007), pp. 245–264; eadem, 'The emergence of a private clientèle for banks in the early eighteenth century: Hoare's Bank and some women customers', *Economic History Review*, 61 (2008), pp. 565–586; A. Laurence, J. Maltby, and J. Rutherford (eds), *Women and Their Money 1700–1950: essays on women and finance* (London, 2009); R. O'Day, 'Matchmaking and moneymaking in a patronage society: the first duke and duchess of Chandos, c. 1712–35', *Economic History Review*, 66 (2013), pp. 273–296.
[133] See **156**.

them: 'Goodes shall I leave none as mony or plate [...] I have ben too ready for yow both till nothing is left' (**44**).[134]

Many of Anne's letters discuss the financial ramifications of her husband's will. Francis Bacon's financial difficulties stemmed from the fact that he had been less well served by his inheritance, gaining some marsh lands in Kent and in Essex.[135] Due to her 'natural love and affection' for her younger son, Anne granted him the manor of Marks and associated land near Romford, Essex, in January 1584; however, her grant had the proviso that, upon payment of ten shillings, Anne could void the agreement.[136] Anne and Francis jointly leased the manor to George Harvey in October 1584.[137] In April 1592, Francis, ignoring the conditional nature of the grant from his mother, mortgaged Marks to Harvey, the lessee.[138] In order to repay £1,300 on 30 April 1593, Francis proposed selling Marks to Harvey, although he needed his mother's agreement. Anthony reminded her of her 'motherlie offer' to bestow the whole interest in Marks upon his brother (**42**), but Anne initially angrily protested that Francis had told her he would not part with the property, but would instead borrow money from other creditors; she then softened her stance, but demanded that Francis produce a written note of all his debts and that she handle the financial settlement with Harvey.[139] Francis responded with outrage, to which Anne protested that her 'playn purpose was and is to do him good' (**45**). Francis rejected his mother's offer on such terms and instead arranged a second mortgage with Harvey on 26 May 1593, which he repaid in full in May 1594.[140] Marks was again mortgaged to Harvey in May 1595, but Anne seems to have released all her interest in the property, for Francis alone conveyed the property to Harvey in May 1596, when unable to find the funds to reclaim the manor.[141]

Anthony had been better served by his father. He had inherited the three Hertfordshire manors of Minchenbury, Abbotsbury, and Hores in Barley, although the estate was entailed and his half-brother Nicholas had an interest as 'remainderman', which meant that he would have inherited the estate on the death of Anthony.[142] Nicholas

---

[134] For other letters in which Anne is adamant that all her finances are spent, see **99** and **140**.

[135] 'Money-lenders', p. 239.

[136] See Essex Record Office, D/DMs/T12/4.

[137] 'Money-lenders', p. 239.

[138] *Ibid.*, p. 240. On 24 February 1593, Harvey wrote to Anthony, demanding his brother's six-month interest on the money. See LPL 648, fos 153r–154v.

[139] See **44**.

[140] Anne referenced the Marks lease in July 1593 (**58**). For Francis' new mortgage with Harvey, see 'Money-lenders', p. 240.

[141] *Ibid.*, pp. 242–243.

[142] *Bacon Letters and Life*, I, p. 246.

Bacon II therefore had to approve any sale of the land. Several of the letters discuss Anthony's attempts to sell Barley in 1593.[143] Difficulties arose because Nicholas was loath to agree to the sale.[144] The potential buyer of the estate, Alderman John Spencer, also drove a very hard bargain.[145] An indenture dated 4 September 1593 records the sale of Barley estate to John Spencer, although the agreement of Nicholas was still uncertain.[146] Anne also gave her life interest in the manors of Windridge, Burston, and Napsbury in Hertfordshire to Anthony on 10 November 1593, along with lands around Gorhambury and Redbourn rectory, with the proviso that she could reclaim them for the payment of 20 shillings.[147]

In spite of waiving her interest in these properties, Anne repeatedly argued that the sale of land for reasons of expediency caused her sons' financial ruin. 'Have yow no hope of posterite?', she asked Anthony. 'Only my chyldern cownted in the worlde unworthy their father's care and provyding for them' (**188**). The last evidence of Anne's activities before her death concerns these inherited properties: on 1 March 1606 she gained licence to alienate Gorhambury manor and on 14 June 1608 she received a pardon for improperly alienating her interest in the manors which she signed over to Anthony in November 1593.[148]

Anne's letters also reveal that she paid many of her sons' bills.[149] She questioned the huge bill that Anthony had run up for coal in the summer of 1596; likewise, the bill of £16 for coal in March 1597 was declared by Anne to be 'monstrous' (**194**).[150] She also questioned Anthony's grocery bills. She asked the grocer himself to inform her of her son's balance, without Anthony's consent; Robert Moorer told her that Anthony owed him £15 or £16 and that his bill had not been settled since the previous autumn.[151] Anne advised that this was a common ploy and one she had known used by the apothecary Hugh

---

[143]See **41**, **48**, **58**, **62**, **63**, **64**, **65**, **66**, **68**, **69**. For an overview of the sale of the Barley estate, see *Bacon Letters and Life*, I, pp. 246–250; and Freedman, 'Anthony Bacon and his world', pp. 184–185.

[144]See **66**, **68**, **69**. For Francis Bacon's draft of a letter to be sent by Anthony Bacon to Nicholas Bacon II to convince him of the sale, see *Bacon Letters and Life*, I, p. 247. For Anthony's attempts to persuade his half-brother, see LPL 649, fo. 305r–v.

[145]See **63**, **65**, **66**, **68**. Both Francis Bacon and the barrister Nicholas Trott attempted to help Anthony with the sale; see **66** and *Bacon Letters and Life*, I, pp. 248–250. For John Spencer's reputation for truculence, see I.W. Archer, 'John Spencer', *ODNB*.

[146]See **68**, **69**; 'Money-lenders', p. 241; *Wealth of the Gentry*, p. 102.

[147]'Money-lenders', pp. 241–242.

[148]*Ibid.*, pp. 240–241, 253. **36** discusses Nicholas Bacon I's posthumous fine for alienation of the Barley and Napsbury estates.

[149]This included settling payment on a tailor's bill due to her stepson Nathaniel. See **11**.

[150]See **170** and **171**.

[151]See **151** and **156**.

Morgan, who had treated Nicholas Bacon; Morgan had wanted to wait until prices rose to submit his bills, rather than submit them quarterly, although Anne sought to counteract this scheme.[152] Anne stated that she would pay the grocer's bill for Anthony only if he would sign an itemized version, for fear he was being overcharged.[153]

It was not only money that Anthony and Francis required of their mother; goods and services from Gorhambury were sought by the brothers to save further expenditure. Anthony thus made frequent requests for goods from Hertfordshire, particularly for beer.[154] Anne's letters often detail plans for the transportation of beer to London, along with other produce from the estate, including game birds, fish, and strawberries.[155] Francis also asked his mother for household implements, for he had discovered, he reported, 'howe costlie the buyinge of it newe is' (**91**). Anne complained that her sons stripped the Gorhambury manor of all its finery; in response to Anthony's request for a long carpet and the pictures of the 'ancient learned philosophers', she lamented 'yow have now bared this howse of all the best' (**133**). The exchange only very occasionally went the other way. Anthony sent Spanish dainties and wine to Anne from London; the latter was not for herself, Anne protested, but to offer to the clergymen who regularly visited her at Gorhambury.[156]

At home in Hertfordshire: Gorhambury manor

Barbara Harris has shown that aristocratic widows in the late fifteenth and early sixteenth centuries were energetic estate managers.[157] Anne's letters provide later evidence of such activity, revealing in close detail her management of the Gorhambury estate during her widowhood. Anne had considerable involvement in the leaseholds held by some of the Gorhambury tenants. These were fixed-term

---

[152] See **156**. For an earlier mention of Morgan, see also **151**.
[153] See **151** and **156**.
[154] For Anthony's requests for beer, see **54** and **151**.
[155] See **29**, **31**, **32**, **112**, **126**, **142**, **143**, **144**, **145**, **166**, **170**.
[156] See **100**, **121**, **122**, **140**, **142**, **164**, **185**.
[157] B. Harris, *English Aristocratic Women, 1450–1550* (Oxford, 2002), p. 145. There is also evidence of late sixteenth- and early seventeenth-century wives running estates in their husbands' absence. See A. Wall, 'Elizabethan precept and feminine practice: the Thynne family of Longleat', *History*, 75 (1990), pp. 23–38; Eales, 'Patriarchy, puritanism and politics'. For an example of an unmarried early modern woman's involvement in estate management, see R.G. Griffiths, 'Joyce Jeffries of Ham Castle: a seventeenth-century business gentlewoman', *Transactions of the Worcestershire Archaeological Society*, 10 (1933), pp. 1–32; 11 (1934), pp. 1–13; 12 (1935), pp. 1–17.

agreements, bounded either by a number of years or by life span.[158] She often interceded on behalf of tenants with her son and she also had the authority to grant new leases.[159] The lease held by Hugh Mantell, Anthony's steward, was described by Anne as 'subtile and combersome' and she sought further advice on how to proceed (**61**).

She was also forthcoming in passing judgement on tenants, again advising caution from Anthony at his return from Europe: 'they wyll all seek to abuse your want of experience by so long absence' (**27**). Furthermore, the letters reveal Anne's concern with the Gorhambury manorial court. Every manorial lord had the right to hold such a court and they enforced the manorial customs, copyhold land transfers, and local community matters, including the administration of local justice for minor crimes.[160] Although it had some powers of social control, the court leet, held once or twice a year, had greater powers concerning local order, such as regulating misbehaviour, including drunkenness and assault.[161] These courts were usually presided over by a steward, often a senior estate official, appointed by the lord of the manor.[162] Anne was adamant that William Downing, a London notary, should act as steward for the Gorhambury courts, ideally with the assistance of the lawyer Thomas Crewe.[163] She also revealed a particular interest in holding regular sessions of the court leet, which may suggest that she valued its ability to enforce social regulation.[164] She certainly noted tenants who had particular business with the court; William Dell's 'nawghty dealing' meant that her court steward 'hath had much a doo with him' (**82**). Anthony's letters reveal that he was happy to leave the organization of the court to his mother: 'For the time of keeping the Court, as it hath ben, so shall it be allwaies of your Ladyship's pleasure and appointment' (**119**).[165]

In line with Anne's interest in the moral regulation provided by the court leet, her letters reveal her concern with behaviour on the estate and in the local parish. Her fear was that ungodly behaviour would spread: 'I wrong my men lyving well and christianly in their honest

---

[158] R.W. Hoyle, 'Tenure on Elizabethan estates', in R.W. Hoyle (ed.), *The Estates of the English Crown, 1558–1640* (Cambridge, 1992), p. 164.

[159] See **79**, **114**, **118**, **119**, **126**.

[160] C. Harrison, 'Manor courts and the governance of Tudor England', in C. Brooks and M. Lobban (eds), *Communities and Courts in Britain, 1150–1900* (London, 1997), p. 49–50.

[161] J. Hamilton-Baker, *Oxford History of the Laws of England: 1483–1553* (Oxford, 2003), p. 317; Harrison, 'Manor courts', p. 44.

[162] M. Bailey, *The English Manor c. 1200–c. 1500* (Manchester, 2002), p. 170; Hamilton-Baker, *History of the Laws of England*, p. 315.

[163] See **117** and **167**.

[164] Anne wrote in August 1596 that the 'next coorte is lete also, which wolde not be neglected' (**167**).

[165] For Anthony's correspondence on the manorial court, see also **135**.

vocation to suffer them to be ill entreated and my selff contemned'
(**125**). Yet Anne encountered difficulties in exerting her authority over
Anthony's multiple inherited manors. Many of Anthony's tenants
clearly recognized Anne's jurisdiction over her son's properties. She
interceded for a tenant from the Barley estate, who had heard that
his farm was to be sold by Anthony; Anne protested that the same
family had dwelt in the farm for a hundred and twenty years and so
should continue there.[166] Yet nearby properties held by Anthony also
represented a threat to Anne's authority at Gorhambury. She argued
that her position was contested by Anthony's men from his Redbourn
estate, stating that 'Idle Redborn men have hunt here allmost dayly; yf
I were not syckly and weak I wolde owt my selff with all kind of doggs
against them and kyll theirs' (**93**). She told Anthony that she must
be held in authority over her own servants and over Gorhambury
manor: 'Elce I geve over my authorite to my inferiours, which I think
is a discreadit to eny of accompt that knows rightly their place from
God' (**194**).

Anne's interactions with Edward Spencer, another of Anthony's
servants, provide further evidence of the difficulties that she had
in establishing her authority. During the summer of 1594, Spencer
relayed to his master in a series of letters from Gorhambury how
'unquiet my Lady is with all her household', suggesting that Anne
was in dispute not only with her household servants but also with
Anthony's friends and servants at Redbourn manor:

> She have fallen out with Crossby and bid him get him out of her sight. – Now
> for your Doctor at Redbourn, she saith he is a Papist or some sorcerer or
> conjurer or some vild name or other. – She is as far out with Mr. Lawson as
> ever she was, and call him villain and whoremaster with other vild words.[167]

Previous scholarship has placed emphasis on Spencer's accounts as
evidence of Anne's mental instability, together with the later testimony
of Godfrey Goodman, bishop of Gloucester, who wrote that Anne was
'little better than frantic in her age'.[168] Yet Anne's collected letters reveal
that she and Spencer were regularly in dispute, and that undue weight
should not be placed on his testimony from the summer of 1594; Anne
described him in May 1593 as 'an irefull pevish fellow yf he be looked
into and checked for his loose demeanour' (**48**).[169]

---

[166] See **57**.

[167] This modernized version of Spencer's letter is from *Bacon Letters and Life*, I, p. 312 (though note that Spedding retains 'vild' for 'vile'). For the original, in Spencer's idiosyncratic spelling, see LPL 651, fo. 254r.

[168] Goodman, *Court of King James*, p. 285.

[169] For other disputes with Spencer, see **46**, **47**, **50**, **111**, **114**, **127**. For further discussion of these disputes, see *Cooke Sisters*, pp. 219–223.

Anne's authority was partially contested by her status as the life-tenant at Gorhambury; many of her servants thus looked towards Anthony as their master instead of her. Anne acknowledged the difficulty of her position: 'I have it as I myght not, greving liberly to their hurt and my discredit, because I wold yow shulde every way be well and comfortably here' (**127**). Anthony promised not to interfere with his mother's business and, on occasion, actively sought to defend her from attacks on her authority. In January 1594, Winter had acted towards Anne with 'undewteyfull demeanour and speeches', according to Anthony Bacon, who came to hear of his mother's treatment (**81**). He urged his mother that Winter should 'be called to account' for his words and actions; as he was at Redbourn, Anthony proposed sending Richard Lockey, a principal burgher of St Albans, to intervene on his behalf. Anne's response was to reject his offer, entreating her son not to call upon Lockey: 'He is an open mowthed man with owt all discretion, full of foolysh babling. He wolde make all the town ryng of his foolyshnes. I pray yow defend not me this way; I nether lyke it ner nede.' Anne argued that she was accustomed to such treatment and so she did 'rather contemn then regarde' (**80**). Yet the combination of her decreasing status and her decreasing funds was a source of much grief to her: 'I am halff impotent now my selff,' she wrote in July 1596, 'and every thing decaies with me' (**161**).

Medicine

Early modern women's interest in medicine has been well established, particularly through analysis of the textual evidence of women's expertise in healing.[170] Anne's letters contain frequent discussion of afflictions and their treatment. She regularly described her own health to Anthony and asked for details about his state in return. When suffering from kidney stones, Anthony told his mother that he was in much less pain after having passed three stones, 'the leaste as bigge as a barlie corne' (**65**). Anne was concerned that her sons' loose living caused their ill health; she lamented that Francis' weak stomach was exacerbated by 'untimely late going to bed and then musing *nescio quid* when he shuld slepe and then in conseqwent by late rising and long lyeing in bed' (**27**). Her great fear in terms of health was extreme behaviour of any kind: 'Extremitees be hurtfull to whole, more to the

---

[170] See, for example, L. Pollock, *With Faith and Physic: the life of a Tudor gentlewoman, Lady Grace Mildmay, 1552–1620* (London, 1993); J. Moody (ed.), *The Private Life of an Elizabethan Lady: the diary of Lady Margaret Hoby 1599–1605* (Stroud, 1998); P. Bayer, 'Lady Margaret Clifford's alchemical recipe book and the John Dee circle', *Ambix*, 52 (2005), pp. 271–284.

syckly' (**28**). Keeping to his bed would only prolong Anthony's gout, in her opinion: 'The gowt is named *pulvinarius morbus* because it lyketh softness and ease' (**62**). She feared that taking the warm water on a trip to Bath would only increase Anthony's 'hote' gout (**50**). Too strong beer was also mistrusted as it would 'bestur' the gout (**133**). Purging was questioned as too extreme, for Anne told her son 'me thinkes it shuld make nature nether to work digestion ner strength being so long still pulled' (**196**).

Anne feared the actions of certain doctors, particularly those whose prescriptions were too extreme. Much of her knowledge of kidney stones and gout was drawn from her experience of her husband's affliction with the same complaints.[171] For example, when Anthony was suffering from kidney stones, she told him that his father had found relief by anointing his genitals with oils, drinking almond milk, and taking a bath strewn with herbs; describing the bath, she told her son, 'Yf yow wyll lett me, I wyllingly wyll come and make it for yow' (**84**). It may be that Anne also first learnt the effectiveness of distilling strawberries for their medicinal properties when treating her husband (**29**). Other positive first-hand recommendations of treatments were also trusted. After receiving encouraging reports from her stepson Nicholas, Anne suggested that leeches might bring comfort from the gout.[172] Ultimately, she considered that illness was providentially ordained, a sign of 'fatherly correction' (**133**).[173] The only sure cure was prayer, through which God would work in the 'syck body to the reviving of his sowle' (**120**).

Composition

The content of the letters, discussed in detail above, needs to be considered in relation to their composition. Most, but not all, of Anne's letters are written in her own hand. While this means that her message was unmediated by a scribe, it poses its own difficulties, both for the contemporary reader and, presumably, for her sixteenth-century readers. Anne's hand, a loose form of italic, is infamously difficult to decipher.[174] It has been noted that it was acceptable for high-ranking men and women to have illegible handwriting, labelled

---

[171] See **84** and **114**.

[172] See **102**.

[173] For a restatement of this view, see **186**.

[174] Anne's hand is closer to her sister Mildred's handwriting than it is to the much clearer italic handwriting of her younger sister Elizabeth. For Mildred's hand, see Bodleian Library, Carte MS LVI, fo. 475r. For Elizabeth's hand, see, for example, SP 12/255, fo. 37r.

by Graham Williams as 'uglyography'; Anthony Bacon described the
earl of Essex's hand to his mother as being as hard to read as any
cipher, 'to those that are not thoroughlie acquainted therewith' (**73**).[175]
Anne's handwriting may reflect her sense of high status, but it certainly
worsened as she aged (see figures 1 and 2). The fact that her letters
are almost all in her own hand did not preclude the involvement of
others in their composition; for example, she sent drafts of important
letters to her son for his advance approval before sending.[176]

Almost all of Anthony's letters, and those of most of Anne's other
correspondents, are not holograph. Most of Anthony's extant letters
to his mother are drafts. It is likely that he worked closely with his
secretaries over their composition, but it is impossible to reconstruct
the particular authorship roles held in this process.[177] As has been
discussed, the various changes made to these drafts reveal the effort
placed upon their composition and the message that Anthony sought
to convey to his mother. There are complex issues regarding the
composition of other letters in the edition, too. Anne Gresham Bacon's
letters to her stepmother-in-law are actually in her husband's hand,
revealing his role in their composition.[178] There are also questions
regarding the composition of the letter from Mildred to Anne in 1552.
The letter, seeking to persuade Anne to accept the proposal of Walter
Haddon, is actually written in Haddon's own hand, so may possibly
have been composed by him; more probably, however, Haddon was
shown and then made a copy of Mildred's letter of advice.[179]

Furthermore, epistolary conventions dictated the form of some of
the letters in the edition. Anne's sister Mildred owned a copy of
Erasmus' letter-writing manual, *De conscribendis epistolis*, and Anne's
own letters reveal her familiarity with contemporary epistolary
practices.[180] The majority of Anne's correspondence is familial.
Erasmus had designated that such letters should be defined as a
separate category of correspondence, differentiated from the classical
rhetorical categories of judicial, demonstrative, and deliberative
correspondence. In terms of internal structure, then, most of Anne's

---

[175] J. Daybell, *The Material Letter in Early Modern England: manuscript letters and the culture
and practice of letter-writing, 1512–1635* (Basingstoke, 2012), p. 89; G. Williams, 'Theorizing
uglyography: the socio-cultural implications of George Talbot's gouty hand' (unpublished
paper given at the Cultures of Correspondence Conference, University of Plymouth, 2011).
[176] See **90**.
[177] For an example where the process can be reconstructed, see A. Stewart and H. Wolfe,
Letterwriting in Renaissance England (Washington DC, 2004), p. 55.
[178] See **9** and **13**.
[179] See **3**.
[180] Mildred's copy of Eramus' work is held at Hatfield House, with her signature mark on
the title-page. Hatfield House, D. Erasmus, *Opus de conscribendis epistolis* (Antwerp, 1564).

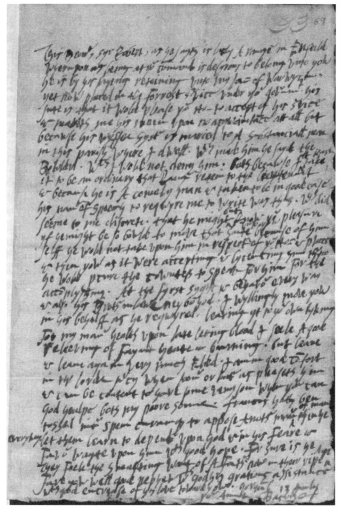

Figure 2. *Anne Bacon to Robert Cecil,* 13 July 1594 (**109**).

letters are freely formed, although her letters to Essex, unlike the majority of her correspondence, occasionally adopt the formal rhetorical structure of early modern letters.[181]

---

[181] For more formally structured letters, see **146** and **174**. The formal rhetorical structure of early modern letters consisted of an *exordium* (introduction), *propositio* (declaration of the

Epistolary conventions also had an impact on specific areas of Anne's letters. Letter-writing manuals were explicit that the wording of the subscription should be reflective of the social status of the writer and the recipient. In *The Enimie of Idlenesse* (1568), William Fulwood made the point that sixteenth-century correspondents writing to their superiors must close by stating 'By your most humble and obedient sonne, or servaunt, &c. Or, yours to commaund, &c.'; inferiors only necessitated a sign-off of 'By yours, &c.'.[182] Such social considerations govern Anne's writing of subscriptions. To potential patrons, such as Théodore de Bèze or Edward Stanhope, Anne's subscription noted that she was the 'late Lord Keper's widow' (**189**).[183] As has been discussed, she used the Greek for widow, '$X\eta\rho\alpha$', in ten of her letters. To her sons, her subscriptions varied; generally she closed with 'Your mother' in either English or Latin, but she also used the subscription to amplify the emotional persuasion of the letter. In December 1594, she felt that she needed to emphasize her status as a godly widow and affectionate mother, signing off as 'your loving and careful mother for yow. ABacon $X\eta\rho\alpha$' (**114**). On other occasions, too, the personal descriptions used in subscription reveal Anne's emotional state. After informing Anthony of the death of John Finch in 1593, she signed the letter 'Your sad mother, ABacon' (**72**). In this, she followed the practice of her sister Elizabeth, who likewise utilized the subscription of her letters to bolster their emotional resonance.[184]

The addresses or superscriptions, providing the name of the recipient and their location, included on the outside of the letters, are also illuminating. Details are provided as to the necessity for swift carriage: a letter to Anthony in May 1595 was addressed with the note that it was to be carried 'with some spede' (**129**). Sometimes notes were even written on the outside of letters, perhaps because news had reached Anne after the rest of the epistle had been sealed. 'Part not with your London howse *temere ne forte peniteat tei*', she wrote on the outside of a letter to Anthony in June 1595 (**135**).

---

substance of the letter), *confirmatio* (amplification), *confutatio* (countering of objections), and *peroratio* (conclusion). For more on this structure, see J. Gibson, 'Letters', in M. Hattaway (ed.), *A Companion to English Renaissance Literature and Culture* (Oxford, 2000), pp. 615–619; Daybell, *Women Letter-writers*, pp. 240–243.

[182] W. Fulwood, *The Enimie of Idlenesse* (London, 1568), sig. B2v.

[183] Her letters to Theodore de Bèze used the Latin version of this subscription: '*vidua Domini Custodis*'. See **16** and **17**.

[184] See, for example, her subscription to SP 12/255, fo. 37r: 'By your aunt that hath not above 600 l *de claro* in the world to live on left, Elizabeth Russell, that liveth in scorn of disdain, malice and rancor, fearing, serving and depending only upon God and my sovereign, Dowager'.

The material nature of Anne's letters also has much to tell us about how the letters would have been read. The use of space on the page was significant in early modern letters; the space between the salutation and the main body of the letter, and between that and the subscription, reflected deference towards the recipient, in an age when paper was an expensive resource.[185] It has been remarked that, in practice, such conventions governing the use of space were often loosely followed and Anne Bacon's letters reflect a general application of this principle. Letters to Théodore de Bèze and to the earl of Essex all have a marked space between the salutation and the body of the letter (see figure 3).[186] On occasion, there is some space left between the body of the letter and the subscription; the greatest space left in any of her surviving letters between the main letter and her sign-off is in her second letter to Théodore de Bèze, but even then Anne did not place her subscription at the bottom of the page, indicating that, while she wanted to show Bèze deference, she was aware of her own status as the 'widow of the Lord Keeper' (**17**).[187]

While Anne was familiar with contemporary epistolary practice, her letters reveal the additional constraints placed on their composition. Time pressures limited the ability to write. She told her brother-in-law, William Cecil, that she was cutting her message short 'because your man hasteth away and my husbande to dyner' (**4**); another letter was written '*raptim*', in haste (**35**).[188] As she aged, Anne's eyesight also hindered long periods of letter-writing.[189] Often letters were written in stages and postscripts are a common feature in her correspondence. During her marriage, Anne frequently wrote postscripts to her husband's letters, amplifying her husband's message, rather than providing new information to the reader.[190] Here it appears that a holograph postscript itself conveyed an important message to the recipient, by its presence highlighting Anne's own interest in the matter in hand.[191] During her widowhood, she more often used postscripts

---

[185]See, for example, A.R. Braunmuller, 'Accounting for absence: the transcription of space', in W. Speed Hill (ed.), *New Ways of Looking at Old Texts* (Binghamton, NY, 1993), pp. 47–56; J. Gibson, 'Significant space in manuscript letters', *Seventeenth Century*, 12 (1997), pp. 1–9; A. Stewart, *Shakespeare's Letters* (Oxford, 2008), pp. 39–74; Daybell, *Material Letter*, pp. 90–95.

[186]See **16** and **146**.

[187]There is also a relatively large space left between the body of the letter and the subscription in Anne's May 1595 letter to Lord Burghley (**132**).

[188]See also the letter written by her sister Mildred, which stated to Anne that she would like to write more, but travelling made it impossible (**3**).

[189]See **19** and **179**.

[190]See **4** and **10**.

[191]Anne only signed and wrote the postscript to **12** in her own hand. For the message conveyed by holograph writing, see Daybell, *Material Letter*, p. 86.

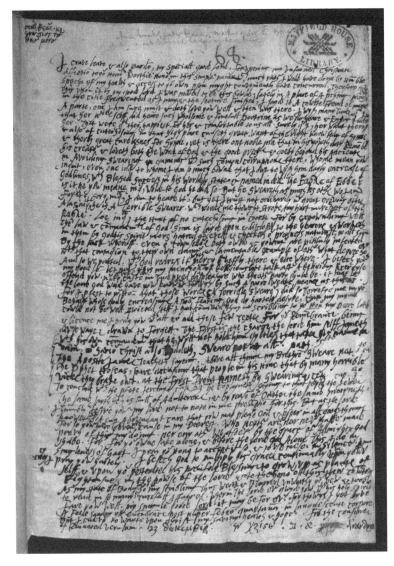

Figure 3. *Anne Bacon to Robert Devereux, earl of Essex*, 23 December [1595] (**146**).

to provide afterthoughts concerning letters written in stages or for additional emphasis, often about the destruction of the letters.

Delivery

As private correspondence, most of Anne's letters were carried by bearers. Information concerning the letter carrier is frequently included on the page and Anthony's secretaries also often noted who delivered Anne's letters.[192] Neighbours and servants were regularly trusted to carry letters for Anne to London; when utilizing a new bearer unknown to Anthony, Anne provided a justification in her letter.[193] In line with Anne's concern over the quality of her mail carriers, it is clear that not all letters written by her were actually delivered to their intended recipient.[194]

Anne and Anthony's correspondence networks were interlinked, to the point where the same letter could be inscribed by both parties: Anne returned one of his letters to Anthony, adding a postscript detailing another letter she was enclosing.[195] Anthony likewise recorded sending other letters to St Albans with the bearer of the letter to his mother.[196] Anne's correspondents sometimes sent their letters to Anthony for him to forward to her. Captain Francis Goad, for example, sent his letter from Dieppe to Anne via Anthony Bacon at Gray's Inn, as can be seen from the superscription; the seal, however, is still extant, so presumably his message to Anne was secure until it reached her.[197] Anne sent letters to Essex via Anthony and they were returned to her by the same process. However, this did not mean that Anthony was initially privy to all correspondence between his mother and the earl; Anthony asked to see a sealed letter sent to his mother by Essex and to see a copy of his mother's reply, which she wrote out again in her own handwriting.[198] It seems that Anthony did not see at least one other of his mother's letters to Essex. Her letter condemning the earl's swearing is held in the Cecil Papers at Hatfield House, rather than at Lambeth Palace Library in Anthony's papers. She was explicit in the letter that she would not show her message to her sons: 'my

---

[192] For example, Anthony's servant, 'little' Peter, was often recorded as delivering letters. See **83** and **86**.

[193] For neighbours as bearers, see **41**, **43**, **44**, **45**, and **143**. For the warning about a new bearer, see **124**.

[194] For the failed delivery of one of Anne's letters, see **136**.

[195] See **135**.

[196] See **169**.

[197] See **51**.

[198] See **175** and **177**.

deerest, who neyther are, nor never shalbe made prevy of this my doing' (**146**). Its eventual inclusion in the Hatfield archive suggests that it was part of the cache of Essex papers that was acquired by Sir Robert Cecil after his rival's downfall.

Anne's correspondence also highlights how much communication occurred off the page. She told her stepson Nathaniel that she understood the finer details appertaining to his daughter's christening from his 'man' (**12**). This reliance on bearers to impart additional information was connected to the fear of epistolary insecurity, something that frequently worried Anne.[199] She feared that Thomas Lawson, 'that foxe', was 'acqwainted' with all her letters, telling Anthony that Lawson 'commonly opened undermyningly all lettres sent to yow from cowncell or frends' (**22**).

One response for Anne as a learned women was to turn to her knowledge of classical languages. Sometimes she used her knowledge of the Greek alphabet purely to conceal information in her letters. The technique of transliteration, using characters from the Greek alphabet instead of Roman letters, was an established method of seeking epistolary privacy for Anne's contemporaries.[200] Although not a fool-proof system, only providing protection from the prying eyes of bearers, a letter from Anne in March 1595 reveals the utility of this method, for she transliterated the names of Henry Howard, Anthony Standen, Antonio Pérez, the earl of Arundel, and her sister Elizabeth Cooke Hoby Russell into Greek characters (see figure 4). Latin was a far less secure means of concealing information, but sometimes it would suffice for letters written in haste. When informing Anthony that he had failed to be elected as MP for St Albans in 1593, Latin at least meant that the message was hidden from the bearer of the letter.[201] Anne also attempted to ensure additional epistolary privacy through the folding of her letters; she folded her letters with the 'tuck and seal' method, which meant that there was generally an additional folio of paper covering her writing.[202] She also then sealed her letters

---

[199] For the response of other early modern letter-writers to concerns about epistolary privacy, see Daybell, *Material Letter*, pp. 148–174.

[200] For the use of Greek transliteration by the Edwardian diplomat Richard Morison, see, for example, SP 68/6, fo. 213r. For the use by Anne's brother-in-law, William Cecil, see BL, Lansdowne MS 118, fo. 83v.

[201] See **35**. See also Anne's Latin comments regarding the countess of Warwick in **140**.

[202] For the 'tuck and seal' method, see C. Burlinson and A. Zurcher, '"Secretary to the Lord Grey Lord Deputie here": Edmund Spenser's Irish papers', *The Library*, 6 (2005), pp. 59–60; Daybell, *Material Letter*, p. 49. For the more varied use of folding by Bess of Hardwick, see A. Wiggins, *Bess of Hardwick: reading and writing Renaissance letters* (Aldershot, forthcoming).

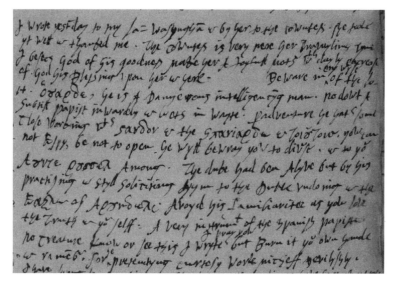

Figure 4. Detail from *Anne Bacon to Anthony Bacon*, 1 April 1595 (**123**).

with wax; she mentions her seal ring to Anthony and evidence of her seal can still be seen on her letters.[203]

After reading, Anne felt that the only way her correspondence could be kept confidential was for it to be returned, burnt, or torn.[204] Otherwise, she was certain that her letters were not secure from Anthony's servants: 'Your men and your brother's prye in every matter and lysten. I pray send back or burn this [letter] to be sure' (**114**). The secretarial endorsements on the letters both received and sent by Anthony Bacon, noting the sender and the date in French, reveal that Anne's fears were not ungrounded. However, it must be remembered that Anne did not necessarily want all her letters to remain secure. Her condemnation of Edward Stanhope has been noted to read almost like a jeremiad sermon. It is plausible to think that Anne may have wondered whether her letter would have been circulated beyond its intended recipient, in which case it offered her an opportunity to

[203] For Anne's seal ring, see **194**. For complete seals on her letters, see **61**, **123**, **124**, **145**, **163**.
[204] For Anne's messages to Anthony on this subject, see **35**, **46**, **58**, **97**, **102**, **123**, **125**, **126**, **134**, **145**, **158**.

provide religious admonition to those whom she perceived as the
enemies of the godly.[205]

Afterlives: the making of the Bacon archive

The locations of Anne Bacon's letters are revealing as to their
afterlife.[206] The vast majority are contained within the papers of her
elder son, Anthony Bacon. The boundaries of the Bacon archive
at Lambeth Palace Library therefore dictate much of the breadth
of Anne's surviving correspondence. None of Anthony's letters after
1598 survive; it seems likely that he destroyed his correspondence after
that date when he left Essex House in March 1600.[207] After his death,
Anthony's papers were first in the possession of his brother, Francis,
and they were then passed to Francis' chaplain, William Rawley. After
the latter's death in 1667, the papers came to Thomas Tenison, a close
friend of Rawley's only son, also called William. Anthony's papers
arrived at Lambeth Palace Library when Thomas Tenison was made
archbishop of Canterbury in 1695.[208]

The Bacon papers are now in fourteen volumes at Lambeth
Palace Library. Another volume of Anthony Bacon's papers is held
at the British Library, although that contains no correspondence
with his mother.[209] Correspondence with other family members
lies primarily within their respective papers: letters from Anne's
stepchildren are held within the collections of their papers at the
Folger Shakespeare Library and at the University of Chicago Library,
while correspondence with her sister Mildred and her brother-in-law,
William Cecil, is found within their papers at Hatfield House and the
British Library.

There is a hinterland of additional correspondence behind that
included in the current edition. Much of Anne's correspondence has
been lost. There are very few letters extant sent between Anne and
Francis Bacon; those that do survive are copies made for Anthony.[210]

---

[205] See **189**.

[206] For work on the afterlives of correspondence, see Stewart and Wolfe, *Letterwriting in
Renaissance England*, pp. 181–205; Daybell, *Material Letter*, pp. 217–228.

[207] It is also possible that the correspondence was confiscated, but, if so, it must have been
subsequently destroyed.

[208] See Birch, *Memoirs of the Reign of Queen Elizabeth*, I, p. 2; T. Birch (ed.), *Letters, Speeches,
Charges, Advices, &c. of Francis Bacon* (London, 1763), sig. A5v; Ungerer, *Antonio Pérez's Exile*, I,
p. xiv.

[209] See BL, Additional MS 4125. This volume was compiled by Thomas Birch, around the
time when he was writing his 1754 *Memoirs of the Reign of Queen Elizabeth*; some of the papers
were probably originally held at Lambeth.

[210] See **23**, **78**, **91**, **105**, **112**. Anne sent letter **100** to both Anthony and Francis jointly.

These were often copied because the letter discussed particularly important matters, rather than more prosaic concerns.[211] Bar the published dedicatory letter written by Thomas Wilcox to Anne in 1589, none of their other correspondence survives; a manuscript volume of Wilcox's letters has been lost, although Anne is listed as a correspondent in a surviving note made on the preacher's letters.[212] This edition has attempted to bring together all the extant letters written by and to Anne Bacon. That decision has therefore precluded the many other letters that were not written directly by or to Anne, but that she would have seen and read. Her correspondence certainly reveals the presence of further epistolary communication, as other letters were frequently noted as included with correspondence directed to Anne. Matthew Parker sent her a copy of his letter to her husband, contained within his letter to her in 1568.[213] Anthony also forwarded letters he had received to his mother. Thus he sent her a letter written to him by Henry Gosnold, concerning his brother Francis, in February 1594; he also forwarded a letter from Robert Cecil in July 1596.[214] Anne likewise provided covering letters which enclosed patronage requests from clients.[215] These letters were all part of the wider world of Anne Bacon's correspondence, but beyond the scope of this volume.

Every attempt has been made to locate and bring together all of Anne's direct, extant correspondence for this edition. It is possible, however, that more of her letters still survive, awaiting discovery by future scholars of the formidable Lady Bacon.

---

[211] For example, a copy was made of Francis Bacon's letter to his mother in February 1594 because it '*touchant le fait de Mr Kempe*', according to the endorsement by Anthony's secretary. See **91**.

[212] See **21** and P. Collinson, 'The role of women in the English Reformation illustrated by the life and friendships of Anne Locke', in P. Collinson (ed.), *Godly People: essays on English Protestantism and puritanism* (London, 1983), p. 275.

[213] See **7**.

[214] See **89** and **162**.

[215] See **190**.

EDITORIAL CONVENTIONS

Letters have been ordered by chronology. Dates are given in Old Style, with the year taken to begin on 1 January; when the letter was originally dated in New Style, the equivalent Old Style date has been provided in the heading for consistency. Primarily the letters were given Old Style dates, either by the writer or by Anthony Bacon's secretaries, who endorsed most of his letters. Very occasionally, however, Anthony's secretaries are inconsistent as to whether they take the year to begin on 25 March or 1 January; unless there is evidence to the contrary, it has been assumed that endorsements follow the standard practice of the year beginning on 25 March, which in this edition is then altered to reflect the year beginning on 1 January.[1] The endorsement and the date given by the letter-writer are often the same; Anne's letters reveal evidence that she expected the bearer to deliver her letter to London and return to Hertfordshire on the same day.[2] On other occasions, the date given in the letter and the endorsement can be days apart.[3] When there is no dating given by the letter-writer, however, then the date of endorsement has been taken as the date. Undated letters have been placed in chronological order, as far as the internal evidence allows, and the reasoning behind the decision is explained fully in the footnotes. In some cases, this has presented particular difficulties, when the internal evidence is very inexact.

The location of the letter is given in terms of repository of origin and volume; folio numbers are given whenever possible, but when there are no folios numbers then the document number is provided. The Lambeth letters have an earlier 'article' number for each letter as well as more recent folio numbers, but only folio numbers have been given in this edition. The majority of Anne's letters are bifolium: she folded her sheets of paper in half to create four writing sides, although, like her contemporaries, she aimed only to write on the front side of

[1] For example, **34** and **35** are dated by Anne as written in January 1592, but endorsed as January 1593.
[2] Katy Mair has suggested that the journey from Gorhambury to London could be completed in four hours. See K. Mair, 'Material lies: parental anxiety and epistolary practice in the correspondence of Anne, Lady Bacon and Anthony Bacon', *Lives and Letters*, 4 (2012), p. 69.
[3] See, for example, **158**.

the first folio.[4] Anthony's drafts are generally only written on one folio, although sometimes utilizing both sides. In each instance, the folio numbers for the entire letter are given in the heading, although, unless otherwise indicated, the body of the letter is written on the recto side of the first folio. If the text of the manuscript letter continues on further folios, then that is noted in italic square brackets and the text broken up to reflect the material nature of the original letter. It is indicated whether or not the letter is 'holograph'.[5] Endorsements are given whenever present; any later markings on the letters are not given. The superscription on the letter is also given, where present, under 'Addressed'.

Original spelling has been retained throughout. The use of 'u'/'v' and 'i'/'j' has been regularized according to modern usage, and the 'con'/'cion' suffix has been amended to the modern 'tion' form; 'ff' is rendered as 'f' or 'F', depending on context. Additional punctuation has been provided; Anne, for example, often used the edge of the paper to infer the ends of sentences, so it was felt that adding more punctuation would aid the reader. Capitalization has been modernized, excluding titles, discussed further below. The original paragraph structure has largely been kept, although letters have been broken into additional paragraphs on occasion, in order to help the reader. Lineation has not been kept, because the majority of the letter-writers included in this edition 'justified' their own writing (see figure 3), so it was felt that preserving lineation did not always preserve the way that the letter looked on the page.

Abbreviations have generally been silently expanded; unnecessary abbreviation marks have been ignored. Exceptions are 'Mtr' or 'Mr', 'Mrs', and 'Dr', which are left abbreviated in line with modern usage. Other titles (such as 'Matie', 'Lo', 'La', 'S^r') have all been silently expanded but left capitalized. Abbreviations of 'lettre' ('lttr', 'lre') within the body of letters have been expanded, but left in the original French; as it was a widely used abbreviation, 'lettre' has not been italicized to indicate a foreign word. Anne used 'dd', as did many of

---

[4] For more on bifolium manuscript letters, see J. Daybell, *The Material Letter in Early Modern England: manuscript letters and the culture and practice of letter-writing, 1512–1635* (Basingstoke, 2012), pp. 2, 6.

[5] 'Holograph' (meaning the letter is entirely in the handwriting of the person under whose names it appears) is used in this edition rather than 'autograph' (denoting that the letter is written and signed in the author's hand); although most of Anne's letters are written in her own hand, she does not sign all of them, perhaps relying on her distinctive handwriting to act in place of a signature. For the deficiencies with the terms 'holograph' and 'autograph', see J. Daybell, 'Women, politics and domesticity: the scribal publication of Lady Rich's letter to Elizabeth I', in P. Hardman and A. Lawrence-Mathers (eds), *Women and Writing, c.1340–c.1650: the domestication of print culture* (Woodbridge, 2010), p. 133.

her contemporaries, to stand for 'delivered', so that has been silently expanded; her use of 're' to stand for 'receive/d' has likewise been expanded.[6] Thorns have been rendered as 'th' and ampersands as 'and'; et cetera ('&c') has been left abbreviated. Numerals have been transcribed as written, a mixture of Roman and Arabic. Abbreviations concerning money have also been left as they were written; pounds, shillings, and pence were written as 'l' for *librae*, 's' for *solidi*, and 'd' for *denarii*. Names, both forenames and surnames, have been transcribed as they were originally written, although abbreviated names have been expanded in unambiguous cases. Place-names have likewise been transcribed as written and silently expanded, if there is no confusion over the location.

Additions or corrections have been noted by the use of ˆ at the beginning and end of the insertion; the use of ˆˆ denotes the start and finish of corrections within an addition. Some of the letters are damaged and in those cases attempts have been made to supply obscured words in square brackets. When sections of the letter are completely obscured, then the missing sections are indicated '[. . .]'. Deleted words are given in the body of the text, but crossed through, so that the reader can see the drafting process clearly. Repetition of words by the writer has been noted in the footnotes.

Anne's handwriting has caused particular difficulties. Her use of the so-called 'swash e' is very variable. Sometimes she uses it to stand for a terminal 'es', while at other times it merely indicates a terminal 's'.[7] For consistency, unless modern usage demands the additional 'e', then Anne's use of the 'swash e' has simply been transcribed as a terminal 's'. For her correspondents' letters, the swash 'e' has been transcribed as an 'es'.

The use of foreign languages within letters is italicized. Accents and breathing signs have been noted where they occur in the original manuscript. In the transcription of Greek, sigmas have been preserved as they were written, for example retaining medial sigmas when used in place of terminal sigmas. Greek ligatures have been expanded. In most cases, an English translation is given in the footnotes, with an indication as to the language of the original phrase. One exception to this rule regards the endorsements. Anthony's secretaries endorsed his letters in French; the standard endorsement was '*lettre de Madame*' ('letter from the mistress') or '*lettre a Madame mere de Monsieur*' ('letter to

---

[6] For the abbreviation 'dd', see M. Markus, 'Abbreviations in early English correspondence', in M. Dossena and S. Fitzmaurice (eds), *Business and Official Correspondence: historical investigations* (Bern, 2006), p. 115.

[7] For both uses of the 'swash e', see A.G. Petti, *English Literary Hands from Chaucer to Dryden* (London, 1977), p. 23.

the mistress, mother of the master'). For these standard endorsements, or endorsements where the only additional information is the date or additional writer/recipient, then no translation is given. Where the endorsement provides additional information regarding delivery, then an English translation is provided in the footnotes. Another exception to the rule regarding translations relates to Anne's provision of dating details in the letters, as she often gives the day and the month in Latin. As the date is also provided in the letter heading, the majority of these details are not translated in the footnotes. Where the entire letter is in a foreign language, then the language of the letter is noted in the heading and the translation follows the original. In those cases, references have been provided to the complete English translation, for the reader's convenience.

Unless otherwise stated, quotations from scripture are from the Geneva Bible (1560).[8] Anne must have owned a copy of this version, as she followed its division into chapter and verse in her letter to the earl of Essex; Anthony also followed the exact translation of the Geneva Bible in one of his letters.[9]

For individuals occurring regularly in the letters, biographical details are supplied at their first appearance. Many of the letters concern tenants and servants and, in those cases, any information known about the individual is likewise provided at their first mention.

---

[8] See *The Geneva Bible: a facsimile of the 1560 edition* (Madison, WI, 1969).
[9] See **104**.

THE LETTERS OF LADY ANNE BACON

1. *[Anne Cooke] to her 'good reader'*, 1548

Published, prefatory letter. B. Ochino, *Sermons of Barnadine Ochine of Sena godlye, frutefull, and very necessarye for all true Christians*, trans. anon[1] (London, 1548), sigs A2r–A4r.
Addressed (sig. A2r): The interpretour to the gentle reader, healthe in Christe Jesu.

Death (good reader), as scripture declareth, and our dayly experience practeseth, to all mankynde is a thing most certeine and sure. For who is he that shall lyve and not se nor tast of deathe's cuppe; the longest lyvers at length dyed, neyther kyng ne[2] keysar[3] can avoyde the duyte of death, but of necessitie, as al are of earth and asshes, so shall they returne into the same.

Notwythstandynge thys that sure we be to dye, yet when it shall come, the Lord hath lefte secret to hys owne wysdom, chefelye bycause we shulde ever kepe watche, and warde, and be styll in aredines[4] wyth our lampes burnyng to wayte upon the bridegrom, whych commeth we can not tell when, whether at mydnyght, or at the cocke's crowynge, wherfore our mayster Christ gave us warnyng that we shulde be alwayes wakyng, and loke vigilantly for he cometh closlye lyke a thefe, wythoute warnynge us, at what houre he wyll come.[5]

Then as he findeth every man, so wyll he judge hym, and where the tree falleth, whether it be towarde the south or north, there it lyeth;[6] there is then no respite to be had, but streyght waye due execution of Godde's justice shal come upon all fleshe. Happy is he therfore,

---

[1]**anon** Anne's translations of five of Bernardino Ochino's sermons were published anonymously in 1548, only appearing under her own name in the 1551 edition. For the 1551 edition, see **2** below.
[2]**ne** nor.
[3]**keysar** Caesar.
[4]**in aredines** in readiness.
[5]**chefelye ... come** Anne was here alluding to the parable of the ten virgins in Matthew 25:1–13, and to the warnings to be vigilant in Mark 13:35 and Luke 12:39.
[6]**where ... lyeth** See Ecclesiastes 11:3.

whome hys maister at hys returnynge fyndeth wakynge, for hym shall he put in auctoritie over all hys treasure.[7]

And for so moche as then the [ma]tter shall hange al together in clearenes of conscience, whyche at that tyme shall accuse a man, or defende hym, acordynge as he hath kepte it cleane with vertues, or stayned wyth vices (for in the booke of menne's concience are all theyr dedes layed uppe, to be opened at the audit day of our death) me thynk nothyng can be a greatter staye to the concience[8] of man, then to know how he ought to go owt of thys present lyfe, and what to cary wyth hym to hys account, or leve behynd hym in the world.

In consyderation wherof I have translated into my natyve spech out of Italien a sermon of maister Barnardine Ochin,[9] teaching how a true Chrysten ought to make hys last wyll, and for so moche as the divell is at that instant of deth very bragging busyly wyth man, and diversly troblith hym, and the justice of God on the other side fearith hym, I have, to staye and strengthen the consience on thes behalfes, turned into English two sermons enstructyng us how to aunswer the divel when he tempteth us at what tym, and by what meanes to quiet our myndes, as touching God's justice. Other two have I also translated, whych enforme us of the true workes that God requireth of us, and the way to go to heaven, and that our saviour, Christ Jesus, hath by hys most precious death purchased for us paradise with out our deservynges.

Wich fyve sermons taken out of the first part of Maister Barnardine sermons,[10] as they be wrytten and publyshed of good zeale to the wealth of many, so it is thy curtisye (gentle reder) to accept them in good parte, and pardon my grosse tearmes as of a begynner, and beare wyth my translation, as of a learner. Obteynynge thys of the good reader, I shalbe redye and wyllynge hereafter when God geveth better knowlege (accordyng as my talent wyll extende) to turne mo[11] godly sermons of the sayd Mayster Barnardine into Englishe for the enformacion of all that desyre to know the truth. For they truely conteyne moch to the defacyng of al papistrie, and hipocrysie, and to

[7]**maister . . . wakynge** This is an allusion to Luke 12:35–40 and an inversion of Mark 13:34–36. The description 'in auctoritie over all hys treasure' may recall Acts 8:27.

[8]**concience** conscience.

[9]**Barnardine Ochin** Bernardino Ochino, the Italian evangelical. See the Introduction, p. 5.

[10]**five . . . sermons** Anne's five 1548 sermons were translated from the first book of Ochino's published Italian sermons, his *Prediche de Bernardini Ochini da Siena: novellamente ristampate & con grande diligentia rivedute & corrette*, 5 parts (Geneva, ?1543–1562). There is some confusion over the publication dates of the first two parts of the *Prediche*; a letter at the end of the second part is dated 7 April 1543, which gives some indication as to dating.

[11]**mo** more.

the advancement of the glorye of God, and of the benefytes of Christ Jesus.[12] To whom wyth the holye ghost be all honoure and glorye for ever and ever. So be it.

God save the kyng and graunt us the truthe of hys worde.

2. *Anne Cooke to Lady F,*[13] 1551

Published, prefatory letter. B. Ochino, *Fouretene sermons of Barnardine Ochyne, concernyng the predestinacion and eleccion of god* (London, 1551), sigs A3r–A4v.

Addressed (sig. A3r): To the right worshypful and worthyly beloved mother, the Lady. F., hyr humble daughter wysheth encrease of spirituall knowledge, with ful fruition of the fruites thereof.

Since the orygynal of what so ever is, or may be converted to ani good use in me, hath frelye proceded (thoughe as the minister of God) of youre Ladyshype's mere carefull, and motherly goodnes, as well in procurynge all thynges thereunto belongeynge, as in youre many, and most godly exhortacyons, wherein amonge the rest it hath pleased you, often to reprove my vaine studye in the Italyan tonge, accompting the sede thereof, to have bene sowen in barayne, unfruitful grounde (syns God thereby is no whytte magnifyed), I have at the last, perceived it my duty to prove howe muche the understandynge of youre wyll could worcke in me towardes the accomplyshynge of the same. And for that I have wel knowen your chyfe delight to rest in the destroynge of man hys glorye, and exaltynge wholy the glory of God, whych may not be unles we acknowledge that he doth fore se and determyne from wythout begynnynge al thynges, and cannot alter or rewarde after our deserved worckes, but remayne stedefaste, accordynge to

---

[12] **For ... Jesus** These five sermons are far less Calvinist than the second set of Ochino's sermons translated by Anne and published in 1551, containing only a few references to election and reprobation. See *Cooke Sisters*, p. 59.

[13] ***Lady F*** There has been debate over the precise identification of Lady F, referred to as 'beloved mother' in the letter. Beginning with John Gough Nichols, some historians have identified 'Lady F' as Anne's maternal grandmother, Lady Jane Fitzwilliam, third wife of Sir William Fitzwilliam. However, this Lady Fitzwilliam made her will in January 1541 and it was proved on 25 October 1542, so it seems unlikely that Anne was addressing her long deceased grandmother in this letter. It is surely more likely that she is here addressing her actual mother, Lady Anne Fitzwilliam. For J.G. Nichols, see his *Narratives of the Days of the Reformation*, Camden Society, old series, 57 (London, 1859), p. 313. For Jane Fitzwilliam's will, see J.W. Clay (ed.), *North Country Wills: abstracts of wills held at Somerset House and Lambeth Palace, 1383–1558*, Surtees Society 116 (Durham, 1908), p. 136.

hys immutable wyll,[14] I have taken in hande to dedicate unto youre
Ladyship this smale number of sermons (for the excelent fruit sake
in them conteined) proceding from the happy spirit of the santified[15]
Barnardyne, which treat of the election and predestination of God,
wyth the rest (although not of the selfe title) a perteynig[16] to the same
effect to the end it might appere, that your so many worthy sentences
touching the same, have not utterly ben without some note in my
weake memory, and al be it, they be not done in such perfection,
as the dignitie of the matter doth requyre, yet I trust and know, ye
wil accept the humble wil of the presenter, not weghing[17] so much
the excelnecy[18] of the translation, al thoughe of ryghte it oughte to
be such as should not by the grosnes therof deprive the aucthor of
his worthynes. But not meanynge to take upon me the reache to his
hygh style of thealogie, and fearyng also, least in enterprisynge to
sette forth the bryghtnes of hys eloquence, I shuld manyfest my selfe
unapte to attaine unto the lowest degre therof, I descend therefore to
the understanding of myne own debilitye. Only requiring that it may
please youre Ladyshippe to vouchsafe that thys my smal labor may
be alowed at your handes under whose protection only it is commited
wyth humble reverence, as yeldyng some parte of the fruite of your
motherly admonitions, in this my wyllinge servyce.

Your Ladyshyppe's daughter most boundenly obedient.
A.C.

---

[14]**whych … wyll** The pastoral ramifications of Calvinist doctrine were at the heart
of this set of translations, which Anne drew from the later sermons in the second book of
Ochino's *Prediche* (see above, p. 52, n. 10).

[15]**santified** sanctified.

[16]**a perteynig** appertaining.

[17]**weghing** weighing.

[18]**excelnecy** excellency.

3. *Mildred Cooke Cecil to Anne Cooke*,[19] [after 9 July 1552][20]

Draft/copy in Walter Haddon's hand.[21] Latin. BL, Lansdowne MS 104, fos 156r–157v. 2pp.

Addressed (fo. 156v): ανvή κοκή αδελφή γλυκύτατη[22]

Mea soror, Cantabrigis fui. Tuum vidi Haddonum, quem amabis, si sapis, et plane tuum esse statues. Nihil illi praeter fortunam deest, nec haec quidem diu abesse potest in tanto reliquorum concursu vel ornamentorum, vel oportunitatum. Interim erit brevi, mediocris conditio, quae tuam potest honestam et ingenuam quietem sustentare. Neque minimum cogitare velis quid ortu tuo, quid communi tuoram expectatione, quid summa spe patris dignum sit; aut cum haec cogitas (ut certe debes) simul illud pondera, nullam fere rem in ipso principio se universaliter solere effundere, sed quaedam esse temporum intervalla, et certos quasi gradus vitae, quibus ad perfectionem ascendi solet. A[d] me specta, que licet nunc affluente sum et ubere fortuna, tamen principio spem non rem sequuta sum. Idem in Checo repititum est, et iterum in Smitho, qui in eisdem eruditionis et ingenii fotibus ad huiusmodi famam profluxerint. Cur non iis in Haddono sit tuo consequiturum. Sed patris voluntas tibi resistit; difficilis sane locus et lubricus; tamen, aut iis quod ille vult Deus efficiet, aut illum ita praemolliet, ut in hac tum incerta vita, non omnia velit certa postalare. Sed tamen ante omnia tibi in illius authoritate acquiescendum esse arbitror, quam si Deus ad hanc causam accommodaverit, licet fundi nonnihil haereant, nec quicquam, sit preter Oxoniensem conditionem et Regium vectigal infusum, optabilior est cum his parvis facultatibus Haddonus quam sexcenti sunt ex hoc aulico strepitu quorum, quasi pecudum solas externas videre licet corporum exuvias mentem vero tanquam porcis iures illis pro sale datam esse. Scis quanti te semper fecerim; tibi tam vehementer non suaderem nisi res valde inprobaretur sed tamen ad te refero, nam et in Haddono et in omnibus, hoc tibi semper positum et fixum sit alios ut audias, sed hac in causa tibi ipsa obtemperandum esse statuas.

---

[19] ***Mildred . . . Cooke*** See the Greek address below. The sister writing to Anne must be Mildred, owing to the internal references to her marriage. See p. 56, n. 25.

[20] **[after 9 July 1552]** William Cecil visited Cambridge on 9 July 1552, presumably with his wife, Mildred, given the contents of this letter. The letter refers to Walter Haddon's Oxford post; although he was not formally appointed to the mastership of Magdalen College, Oxford, until October 1552, the previous incumbent had been prevailed upon to resign before July that year and letters had been sent to the college from the king, recommending Haddon as his successor. For Cecil's visit to Cambridge, see C.S. Knighton, *Calendar of State Papers Domestic, Edward VI, 1547–1553* (London, 1992), p. 238. For Haddon and Magdalen College, see H.A. Wilson, *Magdalen College* (London, 1899), pp. 97–98.

[21] **Draft/copy . . . hand** See the discussion of the letter's composition in the Introduction, p. 36.

[22] *ανvή . . . γλυκύτατη* [Greek, transliteration and direct] 'To her dearest sister, Anne Coke'.

Tua enim res agitur et quidem totius vitae. Plurima vellem, sed in itinere sum itaque non licet. Post videbimus. Vale.

> *Tua soror tui amantissima.*

[Translation]

My sister, I have been in Cambridge.[23] I saw your Haddon, whom you will love, if you have sense, and will decide that he is completely yours.[24] He lacks nothing except good fortune and this indeed cannot long be wanting where there is such a combination of other distinctions and advantages. Meanwhile there will be for a short time a middling status which can sustain your honourable and free-born tranquillity. Please consider not the least what may be worthy of your birth, of the shared expectation of your family and of the very high hopes of your father; or when you consider these things (as you certainly should) at the same time you must reflect on this, that hardly anything tends in all cases to pour forth at the very beginning, but that there are certain periods and certain stages of life which usually have to be scaled in order to reach perfection. Look at me; although I now have an abundant and plentiful fortune, nevertheless at the beginning I followed hope and not actual things.[25] The same is true in the case of Cheke,[26] and again in the case of Smith,[27] who have progressed to a reputation of this kind in the same quickening of learning and talent. Why should there not be a similar outcome also in the case of your Haddon? But your father's will stands in your way. This is a difficult and slippery place, to be sure. And yet, either God will bring about what he wants, or he will soften him in such a way that in this life, which is at present uncertain,

[23]**Cambridge** Mildred Cooke Cecil had a close relationship with her husband's *alma mater*, St John's College. There is evidence of her personal patronage of the college in her later years: a copy of a letter she wrote to the college, accompanying her gift of a polyglot bible, is still extant. See *Cooke Sisters*, pp. 30, 36, 84, 188; BL, Lansdowne MS 104, fo. 158r.

[24]**Haddon ... yours** Walter Haddon, the civil lawyer, had been a Cambridge fellow from 1536, and was friends with Sir John Cheke and Roger Ascham. Haddon sought the assistance of Mildred Cecil with his suit for her sister Anne's hand, as seen in this letter, but he also drew on his friendship with William Cecil. For Haddon's later letter to William Cecil, see BL, Lansdowne MS 3, fo. 19r, 11 November 1552. Haddon recorded the eventual rejection of his suit in poetry. See *Cooke Sisters*, p. 205.

[25]**I now ... actual things** Mildred had become the second wife of William Cecil in December 1545, when he was only the chief clerk of the Court of Common Pleas. The accession of Edward VI marked the beginning of his advancement in governmental service. See S. Alford, *Burghley: William Cecil at the Court of Elizabeth I* (London, 2008), pp. 33–49.

[26]**Cheke** Sir John Cheke, father of William Cecil's first wife, had been appointed royal tutor to the future Edward VI in 1544. His standing rose after Edward's accession in 1547 and he was knighted in 1551.

[27]**Smith** Sir Thomas Smith was another figure whose career accelerated with the accession of Edward VI; he became secretary of state in 1548 and was knighted in 1549.

he will not wish to demand everything be certain. But above all I think you should give in to his authority, which if God accommodates to this case, although they refuse to pour forth anything, and there is nothing apart from his Oxford status and the payment of the royal honorarium, Haddon is more desirable with these small resources, than six hundred from this courtly din, of whom one can only see the external skins of their bodies, as of cattle, while you would swear that their mind has been given as it were to the pigs to serve as preserving salt.[28] You know how much I have always tried to do for you; I would not have urged you so forcefully if the matter were not greatly disapproved of, but nevertheless I return to you, for in the case of Haddon and all things, may this always be set and fixed for you that you should listen to others, but in this case you should decide to obey yourself. For it is your business which is at stake, and indeed the business of your whole life. I would like to write more, but I am on the road and thus it is not possible. Afterwards, we shall see. Farewell.

Your sister who loves you most dearly.

4. Nicholas and Anne Bacon to William Cecil, 18 August 1557

Holograph, in Nicholas Bacon's hand from 'I and my wyff', in Anne Bacon's hand from 'We at Bedfordes'. CP 152/19, fo. 27r–v. 1p. *Endorsed (fo. 27v):* 1557 18 August Mr Bacon

I and my wyff thank you of your letter and are glad that my syster Margaret hathe for health sake goton lyberte and of my sister Elizabeth's recovery.[29] Your goddowghter[30] (thanks be to God) ys somwhat amendyd, hir fytts beyng more easy but not delyvyd of

---

[28] **the external skins ... salt** Mildred has drawn this idea from Cicero, who in turn derived it from Chrysippus; the suggestion is that life is only given to a pig – whose primary function is to be eaten – to prevent it going bad, acting therefore like salt. See Cicero, *De finibus*, 5.13.38 and *De natura deorum*, 2.64.160. Erasmus also quoted Cicero in his *Adages*. See D. Erasmus, *Adages I i to I v 100*, ed. R.A.B. Mynors, *Collected Works of Erasmus*, XXXI (Toronto, 1982), p. 89.

[29] **my syster ... recovery** Anne's sister Margaret Cooke served Mary I at court, but she may also have stayed with the Cecils during this period. Another sister, Elizabeth Cooke, had lived with the Cecils in Wimbledon since her father's departure for Continental exile in 1554. For Elizabeth's stay with the Cecils, see E. Powell (ed.), *The Travels and Life of Sir Thomas Hoby, Kt of Bisham Abbey, Camden Miscellany* 10, Camden Society, 3rd series, 4 (London, 1902), pp. 126–127.

[30] **goddowghter** Presumably Susan Bacon, Nicholas and Anne's daughter, who died in infancy. An image of Susan is included in a tree of Jesse showing the offspring of Nicholas Bacon by both his wives. See *Cooke Sisters*, p. 208.

eny. Yt ys a doble tertian that holds hir and hir nurse a had a syngle but yt ys gone clerly.[31] To morow by the grace of God by tenn of the clock I wyll be at Chanon Rowe[32] and yf I shall lyke ^upon the syght I shall be glad^ to joyne with you for the hangyng. My dowt ys whether Mr Coferrer[33] be at hys howse. There be other thyngs I had rather bye than eny you wryght of; yf they be to be sold as at our next metyng I shall shewe you.[34] Only the feare of provysion for warr ys the let of thys provysion mete for peace. Thus wysshyng to you and my lady as to our sylffs, we byd you farewell. Wreton at Bedfords[35] thys present Wednysday 1557 by

> your brother and sister
> in lawe NBacon.

We at Bedfords ar no less glad of Wymbledonns[36] welfare, and specially of litle Nann's,[37] trusting for ^all^ this shrewed fever to se ^her and myne^ then play fellows many tymes. Thus wyshing *contynuans*[38] of all goode thyngs to yow all at once because your man hasteth away and my husbande to dyner.

> Your loving sister,
> ABacon.

5. *Anne Bacon to Matthew Parker, 27 June 1561*

Holograph. Parker Library, MS 114a, p. 124. 1p.

Please yt your grace, at the sute of one Fyzwyllyams which hath ben your grace's servaunt, I am so bowlde as to be a means to yow for your favour towardes hym, wherof he is an earnest craver whylest he

[31]**doble tertian ... clerly** A single tertian fever is characterized by an attack every alternate (i.e. third) day, whereas a double tertian is marked by two sets of paroxysms every other day.
[32]**Chanon Rowe** William Cecil began negotiations for a house in Cannon Row in Westminster in 1550 and kept the residence until Elizabeth's reign. See Alford, *Burghley*, p. 43.
[33]**Mr Coferrer** Sir Richard Freeston was cofferer of the household until 1558. See S.T. Bindoff (ed.), *History of Parliament: the House of Commons, 1509–1558*, 3 vols (London, 1982), II, pp. 571, 583.
[34]**There ... shewe you** This is presumably a reference to the sale of Anne of Cleves' effects in August 1557. William and Mildred Cecil bought several kirtles and gowns at the sale in Chelsea. See BL, Lansdowne MS 118, fo. 78v.
[35]**Bedfords** A manor close to Gidea Hall in Essex.
[36]**Wymbledonns** The Cecils had lived at the Old Rectory in Wimbledon since 1550.
[37]**litle Nann's** Anne Cecil, born in December 1556.
[38]*contynuans* [Latin] 'continuing'.

served your grace. I nether was acqwaynted with hymse[lf] ner yet understoode that he was my cosyn.[39] Yf I had, I wolde have ben his frende sooner. But ˆnowˆ that I know so much, I besech your grace to be his goode Lorde, that yt wyll please yow to remitt eny thyng past and to graunt hym your favour and also goode worde, yf occasyon so serve. I promiss your grace I do heare some honest report of hym or elce I wolde not thus troble yow. Yf my sute may stande hym in steade more then others as he hath heretofore labored herin he sayth, your own ˆhowseˆ can well wyttness. I shall take my selff much beholdyng to yow on his behalff. For thowgh I can do ether frend or kynn but small pleasure, yet I wolde gladly procure them my husbande's goode opinion of them and wellcome them to me, which I do not now so effectually tyll he have recovered your goode cowntenance and report agayn. Wherin he entendeth to wayt shortly on your grace hymselff and I also trust that he shall retorn with obteynyng of your favour. And thus I wysh your grace much godly success.

From my house this 27 of June 1561.

Your grace's well wyller,
ABacon.

6. *Matthew Parker to Anne Bacon,* 1564

Published, prefatory letter. J. Jewel, *An Apologie or Answere in Defence of the Churche of Englande,* trans. Anne Bacon (London, 1564), sigs 1st unpaginated leaf r–2nd unpaginated leaf v.
Addressed (1st unpaginated leaf r): To the right honorable learned and vertuous Ladie A. B.,[40] M.C.[41] wisheth from God grace, honoure, and felicitie.

Madame, according to your request I have perused your studious labour of translation profitably imploied in a right commendable work.[42] Whereof for that it liked you to make me a judge, and for that the thinge it selfe hath singularly pleased my judgement, and delighted my mind in reading it, I have right heartely to thanke your Ladiship, both for youre owne well thinking of me, and for the comforte that

---

[39]**my cosin** Anne was related to the Fitzwilliams on her mother's side. Her mother, also named Anne, was the daughter of Sir William Fitzwilliam (d. 1534) of Gaynes Park, Essex.
[40]**A.B.** Anne Bacon.
[41]**M.C.** *Matthaei Cantuariensis* [Latin] 'Matthew of Canterbury', i.e. Matthew Parker, the archbishop of Canterbury.
[42]**I have … work** Anne had translated John Jewel's *Apologia Ecclesiae Anglicanae* (London, 1562) from Latin into English. Jewel's text was written for a foreign, scholarly audience and it justified the secession from Catholicism using scriptural and patristic sources.

it hathe wrought me. But far above these private respectes, I am by greater causes enforced, not onely to shewe my rejoyse of this your doinge, but also to testify the same by this my writing prefixed before the work, to the commoditie of others, and good incouragement of your selfe. You have used your accustomed modestie in submittinge it to judgement, but therin is your prayse doubled, sith[43] it hath passed judgement without reproche. And whereas bothe the chiefe author of the Latine worke[44] and I, severallye perusinge and conferringe youre whole translation, have without alteration allowed of it, I must bothe desire youre Ladiship, and advertise the readers, to thinke that wee have not therein given any thinge to any dissemblinge affection towards you, as beinge contented to winke at faultes to please you, or to make you without cause to please your selfe; for there be sundry respectes to drawe us from so doinge, althoughe we were so evil minded, as there is no cause why we should be so thought of. Your own judgement in discerning flatterie, your modestie in mislikinge it, the layenge open of oure opinion to the world, the truth of our friendship towardes you, the unwillingnesse of us bothe (in respecte of our vocations) to have this publike worke not truely and wel translated,[45] are good causes to perswade that our allowance is of sincere truth and understanding. By which your travail, Madame, you have expressed an acceptable dutye to the glorye of God, deserved well of this Churche of Christe, honourablie defended the good fame and estimation of your owne native tongue, shewing it so able to contend with a worke originally written in the most praised speache,[46] and besides the honour ye have done to the kinde of women and to the degree of ladies, ye have done pleasure to the author of the Latine boke, in deliveringe him by your cleare translation from the perrils of ambiguous and doubtful constructions, and in makinge his good woorke more publikely beneficiall; wherby ye have raysed up great comforte to your friendes, and have furnished your owne conscience joyfully with the fruit of your labour, in so occupienge your time, whiche must needes redounde to the encoragemente of noble youth in their good education, and to spend their time and knowledge in godly exercise, havinge delivered them by you so singular

[43]**sith** since.
[44]**chiefe author . . . worke** John Jewel, the bishop of Salisbury.
[45]**this publike worke . . . translated** There had been another English translation of the *Apologia*, published in 1562. Parker's suggestion that this earlier English translation was flawed was designed to obscure governmental intentions with Anne's new translation. See *Cooke Sisters*, pp. 61–62, 65–71.
[46]**good fame . . . speache** There were reservations about the ability of the English language to match the richness of Latin at this time. Anne's translation, however, draws on colloquial English to engage with its readers. See *Cooke Sisters*, pp. 68–69.

a president. Whiche youre doinge, good Madame, as God (I am sure)
doth accept and will blesse with increase, so youre and ours moste
vertuous and learned soveraigne Ladie and Mastres shal see good
cause to commende, and all noble gentlewomen shall (I trust) hereby
be alured from vain delights to doinges of more perfect glory. And I
for my part (as occasion may serve) shal exhort other to take profit by
your worke, and followe your example, whose successe I beseche our
heavenly Father to blesse and prospere. And now to thende bothe to
acknowledge my good approbation, and to spread the benefit more
largely, where your Ladishippe hathe sent me your boke writen,[47] I
have with most hearty thankes returned it to you (as you see) printed,
knowing that I have therin done the beste, and in this poynte used a
reasonable pollicye, that is, to prevent suche excuses as your modestie
woulde have made in staye of publishinge it.[48] And thus at this time I
leave furder to trouble youre good Ladishippe.

M.C.[49]

7. *Matthew Parker to Anne Bacon*, 6 February 1568

Copy. Inner Temple, Petyt MS 538.47, fos 59r–62v. 4pp.
Endorsed (fo. 62v): Mathew Canterbury to my Lady Bacon of her
husband's binding a poore man to give v li a year to a kinsman
of his in Cambrige.

Madame, my hartie salutations to your Ladyship presupposed, *in
Christo servatore et judice.*[50] I understand that ye use otherwhiles to be a
good sollicitor to my Lord your husband in the causes of the pore for
justice, &c, and I doubt not that ye remember the Christian duetie ye
beare to him as well in respect of conscience to Almigtie God, as for
his honorable estimation and fame to the world. *Et hoc est esse, juxta
divinam ordinationem, vere adjutorium salutare coram Adam datum a Deo, tempore
vanitatis nostrae.*[51] Upon which grounde I thought good, nowe in thend
of the terme,[52] after my Lorde's angrie busynes nye defrayde, to write
a fewe wordes to you; to my Lorde I perceive I maye not write, except

---

[47]**writen** written.
[48]**you[r] Ladishippe ... publishinge it** Given that Anne had already seen her
translations of Ochino in print under her own name, this is simply a modesty trope. See
Ochino, *Fouretene sermons*, trans. A[nne] C[ooke].
[49]**M.C.** See p. 59, n. 41.
[50]*in ... judice* [Latin] 'in Christ the saviour and judge'.
[51]*Et hoc ... nostrae* [Latin] 'And this is to be, according to God's ordinance, truly an
aid to salvation, given by God in the presence of Adam in the time of our vanity'.
[52]**terme** The Hilary 'term' of the legal year.

they be *placentissima*[53] and therefore I shall staye my hande. My Lorde, as by his fewe lynes written to me in awnswere to my frindlye lettres, dothe saye he hathe conceyved that he thought not to have heard at my handes before I had spoken with himself, and not so contented, but sent me an harde awnswere in worde by my mann yet externe to us bothe, whome I wisshed not to have knowen any inckling of our private dealinges so privatelie, I saye, written of my partie, that I tell you the truthe, *coram Deo servatore meo*,[54] the talke not opened nor conferred within any signification to my yokefellowe,[55] thoughe yet, I trust not so great a daye bodye[56] and without God's feare, and can consyder bothe reason and godlynes.[57] Yet I have kept my greife within myself from her, not as to have you thinke that such a matter were to be much regarded, howsoever it be taken of such two as we maye be estemed, but that I have used frindship towarde my Lord in all poyntes, whatsoever he conceiveth. But I am sorye he can so sone conceive displeasantlie againste me not deserved, I saye, and to abyde thereby not deserved, for I ment not only prudently but christianlye, godlie and frindlie, howsoever yt be taken. The testimonye of my conscience shall make me take this his storme quietlie to Godwarde, rather offering him in my prayers to God, then carefull of any submission as having offended, which I entended not, as fawtie.[58] In his conceyving (as he writeth) for to have suspended my such writing till I had heard from him or spoken with him &c, ye shall understand that the partie whoe came up with the Duke's Grace's lettres resorted to me a little before dynner, and shewed me in his talke that he was appoynted to come againe that afternone to have receyved his lettres to the Duke's Grace in awnswere &c. Whereupon I thought the tyme present such as that before he should write to his Grace to put to his wisedome and consyderation so much as I did write, for after that tyme yt had bin to late

[fo. 59v] to speake with himself who at that after none had no leysure if I had come to him, and yet sending my lettres by that messenger nor making him prevye of the sending &c. But, concerning the matter yt self, forsothe I am sure I did so reasonablie write that if he had bin

---

[53]*placentissima* [Latin] 'most pleasing'.
[54]*coram . . . meo* [Latin] 'in the presence of God, my saviour'.
[55]**yokefellowe** Matthew Parker's wife, Margaret Harleston Parker.
[56]**daye bodye** Overly concerned with daily matters, as opposed to loftier thoughts.
[57]**yokefellowe . . . godlynes** Margaret's virtue was apparently well known to her contemporaries, as Nicholas Ridley praised 'the fame of her virtue in God' in 1551, although he had not met Margaret personally. See J. Bruce and T.T. Perowne (eds), *The Correspondence of Matthew Parker* (Cambridge, 1853), p. 46.
[58]**fawtie** faulty.

the prince of the realme, or I but his chapleyn, I might have written privately as I did. And where he findeth lacke in me that I did so write, peradventure I might finde some lack in him for not staying his displeasure till he had knowne what great cause ~~he ha~~ I had to write, yea much more then I did write both in conscience and in good love of frindship. Madame, be not offended with my plainenes as thoughe I would make comparison with him. I knowe his office, I knowe his giftes of God, and his place, and yet maye Matthewe Parker write privately to Nicolas Bacon in matter of good frindship without offence. In all humilitye of heart I will not stick to submytt my self to his page of his chamber and will be admonished by him in reason, thoughe he were myne enimye, and againe in doing myne office to God, and my duetie of frindship to them whome I will sincerely love and honor. I will not be abasshed to saye to my prince that I thinke in conscience in awnswering to my charging, as this other daye I was well chidden at my prince's hande, but with one eare I heard her harde words, and with thother and in my conscience and heart, I heard God. And yet her highnes being never so muche incensed to be offended with me, the next daye comyng by Lamhithe bridge into the feildes, and I according to duetie meting her on the bridge,[59] she gave me her verie good lokes and spake secretly in myne eare, that she must nedes countynance myne auchoritye before the people to the credit of my service, whereat diverse of my Arches[60] then being with me peradventure merveiled &c. Where peradventure some bodye would have loked over the shoulders and slily slipt awaye to have abashed me before the worlde &c. But to enter the matter of late. I sent my visitors into Norwiche, Dion's his countrye[61] and myne, to set order and to know the state of the countrye whereof I heard of credible and of worshipfull persons that Gitzi[62] and Judas had a wonderfull haunte in the countrye that *Quid vultis mihi dare?*[63] had so much prevailed there amonge the simonyans[64] that nowe to sell and to buy benefices, to flease parsonages and vicareages, that *omnia erant venalia.*[65] And I was

[59]**Lamhithe . . . bridge** The archbishop of Canterbury's seat was Lambeth Palace in London, surrounded by fields in Parker's time.

[60]**Arches** Formally the dean of the Court of the Arches. However, at this time the term also meant an archbishop's official. See G. Elton, *Studies in Tudor and Stuart Politics and Government* (Cambridge, 1974), p. 97.

[61]**Dion's his Countrye** By Dion, Parker presumably means Zeus and so is referring to the paganism of the county of Norfolk.

[62]**Gitzi** Gehazi was a covetous Old Testament figure. See 2 Kings 5:20–27.

[63]*Quid . . . dare?* [Latin] 'What will you give me?' See Matthew 26:15.

[64]**simonyans** Those who practise simony, namely the buying and selling of benefices.

[65]*omnia . . . venalia* [Latin] 'everything was for sale'. This is a reference to Sallust: see *Bellum Jugurthinum*, 8.1: '*Romae omnia venalia sunt*' ('In Rome, everything is for sale').

enformed the best of the countrye not under the degree of knightes, were infected with this sore[66]

[fo. 6or] so far that some one knight had fower or fyve, some other seven or eight benefices clouted together, fleasing them all, defrauding the Crown's subjectes of their duetie of prayers, some where setting boyes and there serving men toe beare the names of such lyvinges. Understanding this enormitye, howe the Gospell was thus ^universally^ pynched to the discoraging of all good laborers in God's harvest I ment to enquier of it, &c. In such inquisition was presented at Norwiche that my Lord had sett a serving man not ordered, a mere laye bodye, in the face of the whole citye to be a prebendarie of the churche there, and that he had an other at home at his house, an other prebendarie, and bearing them selves great under my Lorde's aucthoritye, despised myne to be at the churche's visitation &c. This matter hathe bin longe tossed amonge that people of theis two places thus used, which I knewe not of till my visitors came home againe, and enquiring of them first of the cathedrall churche &c I was enformed of theis two, of whome I tolde my Lord himself what was spoken, who not remembring their names, I ceased of talke, and yet he semed not well content that they should not doe their dueties. My commissionors unknowing to me when they were at the churche charged the Deane &c to paye them no rent of their prebendes till they had shewed good cause to me of their absence. After the visitation Smythe,[67] one of them, came thether and was denyed his monye, and after came one of them to me for a letter of release. When I perceived what he was, and perceiving that yet he had honest learning, I moved him to enter order to avoyde the speache of the worlde and not to lyve so contrarie to lawes, and so to honest that smale nombre of the churche, besides being but six prebendaries thoughe they were all at home where one could hardlie be spared, not so well as in churches where be xl or l prebendes. After many wordes he awnswered me that thoughe he had bin brought up in some prophane learning, yet in scripture he had no knowledge and thereupon would not enter into the ministerie. He there upon asked further my counsell. I tolde him that I thought yt best for him for the necessitye of life after his service

[fo. 6ov] spent with my Lorde reserving some pension to resigne yt to such an one as were able to doe good in that churche. He tolde me that certayne had offered him well, but he liked not their judgments.

---

[66] **this sore** Repeated on fo. 6or.

[67] **Smyth** Thomas Smyth, the cause of the dispute between Nicholas Bacon and Parker, was eventually deprived of his seat in 1570. For Smyth's connections with the Bacon family, see *Stiffkey*, I, p. 289.

In fyne he thought good to gratefie the whole citye and to resigne yt to Mr Walker,[68] who was desired for his gifte of preaching to continue there in the citye and so to be from the daunger of *non residens*[69] from a little benefice he hathe in the countrye, whether he must be fayne els to goe and leave the citye destitute, for ^such^ kindes of informations be nowe redily made and heard in the King's Benche, as I heard this other daye of a verie honest man keping at his greater benefice a verie good house, is charged with *non residens* by a promoter from his lesse benefice not yet far of[70] from his other, for every monethe's absence x li. This Smythe had my lettres of release to the Deane to receive his payment, after what tyme he resigned his prebend upon a penson[71] of v li assured by the churche, upon which vacation the Duke's Grace did write to my Lord in Mr Walker's favor, this partie travailed hether with his lettres, but he could not be admitted, the cause was awnswered that Smythe was bounde to my Lord to paye v li penson of his prebend to a sister's sonne of my Lorde's studying at Cambridge. The partie tolde me that my Lord made the awnswere himself, and that was the lett, when I heard yt, I was sory to heare yt of him, *qui foenum habet in cornu,*[72] as I thinke yt will be in the Grene Yarde[73] a common place shortly of the preachers there. I excused the matter as well as I could, who told me the usage of this kinde of doing in all the countrie, and merveiled that they which favour the gospell should so use yt with diverse wordes more whereby I gathered the sequell what was like to followe of his repulse. In this verie article of tyme, reteyning this Walker at dynner in my house of purpose, I in dynner time did write to my Lord my lettres, only to put the matter to his wisedome and consideration, without any of the harde circumstannce of the cause, howe yt was like to be taken, saving only of my Lord of Norfolke's plesuring &c, who I am suer would have taken yt thankfully to have sped, and so made yt knowne amongest his frindes in the citye, which should have, I doubte not, promoted the creditt of the gospell[74]

[fo. 61r] for his Grace to be the motyoner and bringer into the churche and into that citie such a preacher, whereby the people of the citie might have receyved joye and gladnes, and thenemyes of the gospell disapoynted of their triumphing on that preacher, if he had sped at the

---

[68]**Walker** John Walker, who was presented to a prebendal stall in the cathedral by the lord keeper on 25 January 1570. See J. Craig, 'John Walker', *ODNB*.

[69]***non residens*** [Latin] 'not resident'.

[70]**of** off.

[71]**penson** pension.

[72]***qui … cornu*** [Latin] 'who has hay on his horn'. See Horace, *Satires*, 1.4.34.

[73]**Grene Yarde** An open space used for preaching to the north of Norwich cathedral.

[74]**gospell** Repeated on fo. 61r.

Duke's requeste &c. But all this woulde not serve, for the messenger sayd this v li pencion was the stop and lett &c. Marye he tolde me that my Lord woulde awnswere the Duke's Grace that he should be sure of the nexte vacante romme when yt channced there. I pray God send my Lord many joyfull yeares to contynue both in life and in office till that daye and tyme, but I thinke this offer wold have bin taken in tyme, and I wishe I had borne this v li pencion of myne owne purse that the common slaunderouse speache might have bin stayed, where I feare yt will by this doing be further wondred at. But yt may be sayde, 'Let such as talke of yt, remedie yt if they can'. Oh, Madame, God is the rewarder of all good doinges, and reformer of all disorders. I see this countrie so much without remorse of conscience in this outrage that the stones will speak of yt, if it be not reformed. Yf my Lord be angrie with me for my plainenes, I feare not Almightie God. *Deus, ultionum Deus*[75] wilbe content, yea and he will aske accompte of me if I holde my peace, when bothe my Lord and I shall stande dreadfully before his Chauncerie, and therefore I will not so covett the favour of man to displease God. And suerlie, Madame, I coulde no lesse doe of tender heart to his estymation. And lothe would I be that his example should be alledged for diverse spoylers in that countrye of the ministerye, thoffice of manne's salvation, thoffice of Christe's crucifyed misteries, howesoever the carnall princes of the worlde do deride God *et omnia sacra, sed qui habitat in coelis irridebit eos.*[76] For God's love, Madame, helpe you *tanquam una caro cum viro tuo, sed ambo Christi membra charissima,*[77] to helpe to elyminate out of his house this offendicle, *ut ne ponat maculam in gloria senectutis suae. Labi et falli humanum, sed perseverare durum.*[78] I will not write that I heare reported, nor will creditt all tales. Fye on the world to carie God's good, elect and principall members of his kingdome,

[fo. 61v] so to be drowned in the dregges of this mortalitye, not to regard theis so cheife causes. What shalbe hoped for in frindship if the advertising of one an other in true faithfull frindship, and to God warde, shall stirre up emnitye and disliking? Let the blinde world saye, '*Suaviora sunt fraudulenta oscula odientis, quam vulnera diligentis*'.[79] Let

[75] *Deus* ... *Deus* [Latin] 'God, the God of vengeance'. See Psalm 94:1.

[76] *et* ... *eos* [Latin] 'and all things sacred. But he who dwells in the heavens shall laugh at them'. See Psalm 2:4.

[77] *tanquam* ... *charissima* [Latin] 'just as one flesh with your husband, but both most dear members of Christ'.

[78] *ut ne* ... *durum* [Latin] 'and so that it may not place a stain on the glory of his old age. To fall and to err is human, but to perservere is obstinate'.

[79] *Suaviora* ... *diligentis* [Latin] 'The deceitful kisses of the enemy are more sweet, than the wounds given by a friend'. Proverbs 27:6 reads '*meliora sunt vulnera diligentis quam fraudulenta odientis oscula*', 'The wounds of a friend are faithful, but the kisses of an enemy are deceitful'.

the wise man say contrarie, '*Quam meliora sunt vulnera diligentis, quam fraudulenta oscula odientis*'.[80] I am jealous over my Lord's conscience, and over his honorable name. Yt maye become my office to him warde, thoughe he be great in office, to heare the voyce of a pore pastor, for there is one which saithe *Qui vos audit, me audit; qui vos spernit, me spernit; qui vos tangit, tangit pupillam oculi mei*,[81] as contemptible so ever the vaine world estemeth us. I have alwaye joyed in my Lord, alwaye honorablye reported him. I have in good places, and before the moste honorable, compared him with More[82] and Audeley[83] for their eloquence, witt, and learning in lawe, with Bisshop Goderick[84] for his sinceritye towardes justice, althoughe they all had their faultes which God kepe from my Lord and me. The first embrued with papistrie, the seconde *omnino passim et ab omnibus*,[85] the third a dissembler in frindship who used to entertayne his evill willers verie courteousely, and his verie frinds verye imperiousely, thinking thereby to have the rule of bothe, whereby he loste bothe. For while his evill willers spred howe he would shake up his acquayntance, they gathered thereby the nature of his frindship towarde his olde frinds, and therefore joyed not much of his glorious interteyning, and his frinds in dede joyed lesse in him for such his discoragement that they felt at his handes. *Expertus loquor*[86] &c. Nowe what will be judged of many of the worlde, which peradventure love neither of us, if it maye be heard howe we two in that place that we be in by God's providence and the Quene's favour, bothe professing God's veritie as we doe, so longe conjoyned as we have bin nowe to fall at square, so nighe to fall into our earthlie pitt, he to contemne me, I to be dulled in my contentation towarde him? What will this worke in the common wealthe, and specially yf it[87]

[fo. 62v] should breake out upon what grounde this greife is conceyved and taken? I would be lothe to breake frindship with any meane bodye,

80 ***Quam . . . odientis*** [Latin] 'How much better are the wounds given by a friend, than the deceitful kisses of the enemy'.

81 ***Qui . . . mei*** [Latin] 'He who hears you, hears me; he that despises you, despises me; he that touches you, touches the apple of my eye'. This seems to be a mixture of biblical sources, both Old and New Testament. Luke 10:16 includes '*qui vos audit me audit et qui vos spernit me spernit*' ('He that heareth you heareth me; and he that despiseth you despiseth me'), while Zechariah 2:8 includes '*qui enim tetigerit vos, tangit pupillam oculi sui*' ('for he that toucheth you toucheth the apple of his eye').

82 **More** Thomas More, lord chancellor from 1529 to 1532.

83 **Audeley** Thomas Audley, lord chancellor from 1533 to 1544; he was named lord keeper before he became chancellor, in May 1532.

84 **Bisshop Goderick** Thomas Goodrich, lord chancellor from 1552 to 1553; he was appointed lord keeper in December 1551.

85 ***omnino . . . omnibus*** [Latin] 'altogether everywhere and by everyone'.

86 ***Expertus loquor*** [Latin] 'I speak from experience'.

87 **yf it** Repeated on fo. 62v.

much lesse with my Lord, and yet either King or Cesar, contrarie to my duetie to God, I will not, nor entend not, God being my good Lorde. It is not the solempnitye or commoditye of myne office that I so much esteme. I was sorie to be so accombered, but necessitie drave me, and what fate shall thrust me out, *susque deque fero.*[88] I am growne nowe into a better consideration by myne age, then to be aferde or dismayed with such vaine terriculaments of the worlde. I am not nowe to learne howe to fawne upon man, *cuius spiritus in naribus eius,*[89] or that I have to learne howe to repose my selfe quietlye under God's protectyon, against all displeasure of frinds and against all malignitye of thenimye. I have ofte sayd and expended that verse, *Cadent a latere tuo mille* &c.[90] In this mynde I truste to lyve and dye. Here I will not awnswere as a panyme[91] did to a panyme, *Cur habeam eum pro principe, qui me non habet pro senatore.*[92] But while I lyve I will praye to my Lord that all grace and good fortune maye assiste him in himself and in his posteritie, and shalbe as glad and redye to the duetie of godlie frindship to him, if it may be reasonablie taken, as any one whatsoever with whome he is best pleased and lest provoked with, as any one that fawneth most upon him for his office sake, or for his vertue, to my power.

And thus reposing my self *in bona et constante conscientia*[93] in this brittle time, I commytt your Ladyship to God as my self. Bycause ye be *alter ipse*[94] to him, *unus spiritus, una caro,*[95] I make you judge, and therefore I transmytt the verie copie of my lettre sent to him to expend the rather of my writinge. Whereby ye may take occasion to worke as God shall move you. And thus I leave. From my house at Lamhithe, this vi of Februarie. 1567.

Your frind unfeyned in Christe,
Matthaei Cantuariensis.[96]

---

[88] *susque . . . fero* [Latin] 'I take it, up or down'. See Aulus Gellius, *Noctes Atticae*, 16.9.1.
[89] *cuius . . . eius* [Latin] 'whose breath is in his nostrils'. See Isaiah 2:22.
[90] *Cadent . . . mille* [Latin] 'A thousand will fall at your side'. See Psalm 91:7.
[91] **panyme** pagan.
[92] *Cur . . . senatore* [Latin] 'Why should I have him as a leader, who does not have me as a senator?'
[93] *in bona . . . conscientia* [Latin] 'in a good and constant conscience'.
[94] *alter ipse* [Latin] 'another self'.
[95] *unus . . . caro* [Latin] 'one spirit, one flesh'.
[96] *Matthaei Cantuariensis* [Latin] 'Matthew of Canterbury', i.e. Matthew Parker, the archbishop of Canterbury..

8. *Nathaniel Bacon to Anne Bacon*, [late 1569–1572][97]

Draft in Nathaniel Bacon's hand. Folger Library, L.d.48. 1p.

Madame, I am sorie, that I am no more able than I am, to shewe that goodwill and dutie which I justly owe unto your Ladyship. A poore amendes I must confesse it is of a man endetted, only to confesse his det. A poores amendes do I nowe make, who am not a litle endetted to your Ladyship. Howe it cometh to passe that I especially am moved thus to writ, I dout not but I maie utter without havinge any ill thought therof. Your Ladyship knoweth how, beinge matched in mariage as I am, it stode me upon to have some care of the well bringinge up of my wife,[98] for these wordes of Erasmus are very trewe: *plus est bene instrui quam bene nasci*.[99] Yf she sholde have had the want of both, I had just cause to feare what might befall. Herupon, beinge not able to remedie the one, I did as mutch as in me lay to provide for the other, and therfore I sought by all the meanes I colde to have her placed with your Ladyship; and at length, though with mutch adoe ^first^ and those stickinge most who had lest cause to sticke at it,[100] ~~I~~ ^was^ brought the matter to passe.

This is it for which I thinke my self so greatly beholdinge to your Ladyship, in that yow were content to troble your self with havinge my wife ~~with yow~~, and not that alone, but duringe her beinge with yow to have sutch care over her and better to use her than I my self cold have wisshed. Yea, I often saied, and yet saie, a more strait maner of usage wolde have wrought a greater good. Yet sutch was your Ladyship's goodwill, which I will not live to be unmindfull of.[101] For the care had

---

[97] **[late 1569–1572]** The letter refers to events since Nathaniel Bacon's marriage, in the summer of 1569. Nathaniel Bacon, Nicholas Bacon I's son by his first wife and so Anne Bacon's stepson, had married Anne, the illegitimate daughter of Sir Thomas Gresham by one of his household servants. As his new wife needed schooling in the demands of her new position, he arranged for her to live with his stepmother at Gorhambury. Nathaniel wished his new wife to spend 'half a year or a quarter' with his stepmother, so this letter must, at least, date from late 1569. For the duration of stay proposed by Nathaniel, see *Stiffkey*, I, p. 11.

[98] **beinge . . . wife** See n. 97.

[99] ***plus . . . nasci*** [Latin] 'it is better to have been well educated than well born'. See D. Erasmus, *Colloquies*, in C.R. Thompson (ed.), *Collected Works of Erasmus*, XXXIX (Toronto, 1997), p. 264.

[100] **those stickinge . . . at it** Both Sir Thomas Gresham and his wife had protested against the arrangement, with the former questioning whether Lady Anne Bacon, Nathaniel's stepmother, would use 'over sharpness' towards his daughter. See *Stiffkey*, I, pp. 11–12.

[101] **not . . . unmindfull of** Nathaniel admitted in a letter to Lady Anne Gresham that while he had a 'great likinge' of his stepmother in some ways, 'in other things . . . it maie be I have as great mislikinge of her'. See *Stiffkey*, I, p. 12.

of her, I accompt it had of me; the good done to her, I accompt it done to me, for I perswade my self it was done in respect of me. ^But^ howsoever that be, ^at the lest^ this am I suer of, that I am he who am like to enyoye some benefit of the good which was than done ^upon^ her.

[verso] Your Ladyship seeth how redy I am in wordes to acknowledg this good torne. I shall desier yow, Madame, to thinke me as redy also in minde to requite the same, wherof I make faithfull promise, whensoever occasion shalbe geven. And thus I take my leave wisshinge your Ladyship long well to do.

9. *Anne Gresham Bacon to Anne Bacon* [late 1569–1572][102]

Draft in Nathaniel Bacon's hand. Folger Library, L.d.15. 1p.

My dutie most humbly remembred unto your good Ladyship. I am in good hope that your Ladyship conceiveth no ill of me, notwithstandinge that I have not sins my departure from Gorrhambury written any lettre to yow. The time hath not bene long sins my cominge from thence, and fewe convenient messengers have chaunced, at the lest none more convenient than my brother Windam,[103] who is the bearer herof. How well I am here placed in his house and how mutch to myne owne contentment, though perhappes your Ladyship hath alredy hard somwhat therof, yet none maie better certefie yow therof than my self, so mutch am I beholdinge to my brother and sister.[104] I have but litle besides to writ unto your Ladyship, except it be to acknowledg my self greatly bounden to yow for the great ^care^ that yow alwaies had of my well doinge during my beinge with ^yow^ which (wolde to God) it had bene soner and so might have bene longer. I am to crave that your Ladyship will take in good part this token of my goodwill untill I shalbe better able to shewe my self thankfull, and in the meane time I shall praie to God that your

[102] **[late 1569–1572]** See p. 69, n. 97.
[103] **my brother Windam** Two years earlier, Francis Wyndham had married Elizabeth Bacon, sister to Nathaniel Bacon and daughter to Nicholas Bacon I by his first wife, Jane Fernley.
[104] **placed ... sister** Nathaniel and his bride were living with Elizabeth and Francis Wyndham in Norwich. In another letter, Anne Gresham Bacon complained of the difficulty of this scenario. See *Stiffkey*, I, p. 26.

Ladyship maie live many a yeare in all happines. Yf I might be so bolde, I wolde sende commendations to my brother Anthonie and my good brother Franck.

Most bounden to your Ladyship,
Anne.

10. *Nicholas Bacon I and Anne Bacon to Nicholas Bacon II, Francis Boldero, and George Nunn,*[105] 16 November 1572

Holograph in Nicholas Bacon I's hand from 'N. Bacon C.S.'; in Anne Bacon's hand from 'I pray yow'. Chicago, 4123A. 2pp.
Addressed: To my sonne Nicholas Bacon and to my servauntes Frauncis Boldero and Georg Nunne geve theise

Complaynt is made unto me, by Buckes wief this bearer, that the will of her former husbond Howlot is broken by my servaunt Howlot. Theise ar therfor to will you to calle before you Howlot my servaunt and this bearer and her husbond Buck my servaunt also as you knowe, and after the matter fully examyned to take such order as the justice of the cause shall requyre. And yf you shall fynd eyther of the parties obstinate and not conformable to that that you shall thinke reasonable. Then to signifie unto me the state of the matter and in whom you shall fynd the default to thend I may deale therein as justice shall requyre. And so fare you well. From my howse besides Charing Crosse, this xvith of Novembre 1572.

N. Bacon C.S.

I pray ^yow^ sonne do that you may to healpe the owlde mother to lyve in qwiett and comfort with her own childerine in her owlde and few dayes by liklyodd, and spare not to enforme ~~the~~ my Lorde the truth. She sayth it greveth her ~~she sayth~~ to have her childern at variance, and she is very sori for her eldest sonne.

Your father is in the gowte at this present, but his payne now is tollerable, God be thanked.

Your mother,
ABacon.

---

[105] ***Francis Boldero and George Nunn*** Boldero and Nunn were servants of Nicholas Bacon I. See D. MacCulloch (ed.), *Letters from Redgrave Hall: the Bacon family, 1340–1744* (Woodbridge, 2007), p. xviii.

11. *Nathaniel Bacon to Anne Bacon* [early 1573][106]

Holograph draft. Folger Library, L.d.64. 1p.

Madame, I humbly thanke your Ladyship for the discharge of sutch mony as was due to the taylors for my wife. It was not my meaninge that your Ladyship sholde have bene charged with ~~all~~ it, for I had takinge[107] order with my brother Edwarde[108] for the paiment of it. I understande by a lettre of my brother's how my Lorde hath a likinge that Paternoster[109] sholde attende upon my brethren at ther goinge to Cambridge.[110] I told the felowe of this, and I will trewly writ your Ladyship worde what aunswere he mad me. He said he was loth to have my Lord's displeasure, but to take that paines which he had taken duringe his beinge at Cambridg before, he was no waies able.[111] For ever sins his lat siknes and the breakinge of his fote, both which happened to him at ons about two yeares past, he hath bene often trobled with paine in his bake, and likewise yf he ~~went~~ goeth any thinge mutch, with paine in his fote; and besides considering ^he was above L yeare old and^ he had served me and my brethren these ix or x yeares, that he were nowe loth to enter into an newe service, of whom he was not able any waie to deserve well, in as mutch as he was not able to take any paines. Herto I said that yf he went not, the let shold be judged in me, wherto he aunswered that he had before this said as mutch unto my brother Anthonie. But herof I shall talke further with your Ladyship upon my cominge to London.

---

[106] **[early 1573]** This letter refers to Anthony and Francis Bacon going up to Cambridge, which happened in April 1573, so the letter must have been written at least a few months earlier.

[107] **takinge** taken.

[108] **my brother Edwarde** Edward Bacon, the third son of Nicholas Bacon I.

[109] **Paternoster** Bernard Paternoster, a servant of Nathaniel Bacon's. See *Stiffkey*, I, p. 40.

[110] **my brethren ... Cambridge** Anthony and Francis Bacon went up to Trinity College, Cambridge, in April 1573.

[111] **paines ... able** Nicholas, Nathaniel, and Edward Bacon, Nicholas Bacon I's sons by his first marriage, had all matriculated at Trinity College, Cambridge, in 1561.

12. *Anne Bacon to Nathaniel Bacon*, 6 August 1573

Holograph from 'ABacon'. Huntington Library, FBL3. 2pp.
Addressed: To my sonne Nathaniell Bacon at Wraxham.

Sonne, as you wrote unto me, so am I very well content with my Lady Gressham[112] to be godmother to your dawghter.[113] And understanding by your man, who hath bene with my Lady Gressham, that she hath appoynted Mrs Read[114] to be for her, so for me, my desire is to have my dawghter Wyndham,[115] yf her health will so suffer it, which yf it showld not (as my hope is it will) then would I have my cosin Townesend,[116] to take the paynes for me. For the daye (because all thinges will not be convenyently redie as I thinke by Sonday), my Lord and I thinke it good that it be uppon Wednesdaye next, or soner or longer ~~by~~ as you shall thinke best. And so have I sent word to my Ladie Gresham as her desire was. I have sent by this bearer ii peces of gowld, ^one^ for the nurse and thother for the mydwife. But my gifte for the child[117] I cannot ~~se~~ (as I gladly would) send nowe by this bearer, because I cannot in so short tyme send to London for it, where it is, but assone as I shall go thether and have a fit mesenger, I will send it. The name for my part I put to the ~~discrecion~~ ^choyse^ of the mother ^for eny name she lyketh^, to whom with my harty comendacions I wishe ~~Go~~ spedie recovery with perfect healthe. From my hows at Gorhambury this vi of August 1573.

Your mother,
ABacon.

God be thanked for my dawghter's saff delyveraunce. Desyre her from ^me^ not to be to bowlde of her selff in childebed for all she is so yowng and strong.

---

[112]**Lady Gressham** Lady Anne Gresham was married to Sir Thomas Gresham, father to Nathaniel's wife, Anne Gresham Bacon.
[113]**godmother . . . dawghter** Anne Gresham Bacon had given birth to a daughter, also named Anne.
[114]**Mrs Read** Lady Anne Gresham's first husband was the mercer William Read; Sir Thomas Gresham was her second husband. Anne Gresham had two sons by her first marriage, so Mrs Read was presumably one of her daughters-in-law.
[115]**my dawghter Wyndham** Elizabeth Bacon Wyndham, Anne Bacon's stepdaughter.
[116]**my cosin Townesend** Jane Stanhope Townshend, wife of Sir Roger Townshend, was a distant relation of Anne Bacon's on her father's side.
[117]**my gifte . . . child** Letter **13** suggests that the gift was a cup.

13. *Anne Gresham Bacon to [Lady Anne Bacon]*[118] [*c.*October 1573][119]

Draft in Nathaniel Bacon's hand. Folger Library, L.d.476. 1p. Damaged.

Madame, I c[ra]v[e par]don yf any ill be thought of m[e becau]se I have not sins my delivery [before] nowe written to your Ladyship. I am su[re y]our Ladyship heareth how my husband ha[th] removed ^me^ from Waxam[120] to a house of his owne for the time to dwell upon, and I am very glad of it, and though the house be meane, yet I am very well content withall.[121] I humbly thanke your Ladyship for the cup which yow bestowed upon my dawghter at her christeninge. She is nursed at Styfkey[122] and is very well, and I dwell with in a quarter of a mile of her, so that I maie, as I will, loke unto her. Thus hartely wisshing your Ladyship a longe and happie life, I humbly [ta]ke my leave. From Cocthorpe.

14. *John Walsall*[123] *to Anne Bacon,* 1578

Published, dedicatory letter. J. Walsall, *A sermon preached at Pauls Crosse by John Walsal, one of the preachers of Christ his Church in Canterburie* (London, 1578), sigs A2r–A5v.
Addressed (sig. A2r): *To the right worshipfull, vertuous, and his verie good Ladie, the Ladie Anne Bacon, John Walsall hartily wisheth mercy and peace from God our Father, and from our Lord Jesus Christ.*

---

[118] *[Lady Anne Bacon]* It cannot be conclusively proven that Anne Bacon was the recipient of this letter. However, the reference to the christening gift suggests that it may have been written by Anne Gresham Bacon to one of her daughter's godmothers and letter **12** mentions Anne (Cooke) Bacon's plans to present a gift to the child.
[119] **[*c.*October 1573]** This letter must date from after Nathaniel and Anne had moved to Cockthorpe manor. See n. 121.
[120] **Waxham** Nathaniel and Anne had been living with Nathaniel's sister Anne and her husband, Henry Woodhouse, at Waxham in Norfolk.
[121] **my husband . . . withall** In the autumn of 1573, Nathaniel Bacon rented Cockthorpe manor in Norfolk.
[122] **Styfkey** Nicholas Bacon I had bought Stiffkey manor for his son in 1571, but it needed extensive rebuilding before the couple could move into the house. See H. Smith, 'Concept and compromise: Sir Nicholas Bacon and the building of Stiffkey Hall', in C. Harper-Bill, C. Rawcliffe, and R. Wilson (eds), *East Anglia's History: studies in honour of Norman Scarf* (Woodbridge, 2002), pp. 159–188.
[123] **John Walsall** John Walsall had been the household chaplain for the Bacons at Gorhambury after graduating from Oxford in 1566; he also acted as tutor to Anthony and Francis while in the Bacons' employment. He held this position until at least 1569, possibly until the brothers went up to Cambridge in 1573. See V.B. Heltzel, 'Young Francis Bacon's tutor', *Modern Language Notes*, 63 (1948), pp. 483–485.

This my present attempt and enterprise will, perhaps, minister unto the reader double cause of admiration, the one, by reason of the publishing, the other in the respect of the dedication of this simple and plaine discourse. Touching the first, albeit I may justly depose, and call God to witnesse that this sermon is thus imprinted and made common, not by any vaine desire of mine, or terrene[124] purpose in me, but at the importune suite of divers godly men both of the citie where it was preached, and of the countrie where I inhabite. Yet I am enforced openly to acknowledge that it is my bounden dutie of my selfe, without request, every way to seeke the glorie of my God, by exhorting privately, by preaching publikely, by writing generally, to the verie uttermoste of my power and abilitie. Howbeit, I am here constrayned humbly to bewraye[125] myne owne infirmities, with heartie prayer for greater strength. For mine own simplicitie and want of profounde knowledge, the aboundaunce of most learned volumes dayly set out, together with consideration of many curious heades and carping tongues, these so prevailed with my flesh, as neither I could, of my selfe, be moved, nor by the importunitie of others, for a good space, induced, to publishe this treatise. But at length my weakenesse was somewhat strengthened, and I persuaded, not onely by the reasons of men, whome I have good cause greatly to reverence, but also by the holy spirite of God, to collect this sermon out of my notes, and send it abroad, to the end, that, as by uttering thereof it pleased the Lord God mercifully to touch the heartes of some, so, by writing and imprinting thereof, it may like the same Lord as graciously to touch the heartes of many. So that my onely drift and purpose herein is to seeke the glorie of our good God, by attempting, as he hath inhabled mee, to reclaime the wicked, to confirme the godlie, to converte the deceived, to encourage the converted, that, as God hath created all, offered salvation to al, and nourished us all, so through his sonne our Saviour Christ, he may be glorified by us al.

   This glorie of our God ought to bee of so precious and deare accounte with us, that we shoulde directe whatsoever good thing wee have to the advauncement of his glorie. This is not the doctrine of carnall man, but of that moste excellent doctour Jesus Christ, and of his holy apostle S. Paule. Christe the maister saith, 'First seeke the kingdome of God and his righteousnesse, &c'.[126] And Paule the servant, speaking of the Lord God, telleth us, that, 'Of him, throughe him, and for him, are all thinges', and therefore addeth, 'to him be glorie for ever, Amen'.[127] These, and many the like scriptures, teach us that we are

[124]**terrene** worldly.
[125]**bewraye** expose or reveal.
[126]'**First . . . righteousnesse, &c'** Matthew 6:33.
[127]'**Of him . . . Amen'** Romans 11:36.

created, redeemed, sanctified, and preserved, yea, that all the Lorde's blessinges so without measure dayly powred upon us, tend to this end that his most glorious name maye bee continually extolled by us. Both Moses and Paul were so zealous for this glory, as they preferred the same to their own salvation. But alas, such is the miserable condition of the world, that few are founde willing to take anye little paine, or to susteine the short displeasure even of the vilest men, thereby to shewe their longing desire of God his glorie. Men, of all sortes, are made so drunken with their own vaine glorie, and in such manner bende them selves to maintaine that ignominious and shamefull glorie, as in the meane time, the glorie of God is cared for, accounted of, and longed for, but of verie fewe, and as it were, of an handfull, in respecte of the huge multitude of so innumerable people. From this most impure and deadly impoysoned fountaine of vaine glorie issueth the papistes' glorious opinion of their meritorious workes, their proude conceipt of man's righteousnesse, their bloudie argumentes against justification by faith, their obstinate defences of most grosse impieties, their daily coyning of newe counterfeit miracles for the underpropping of their nowe falling kingdome. From this filthie puddle of vaine glorie springeth the contemptuous disdayning of overmanie to submitte their stiffe necks to the sweet and easie yoke of Christe. Hence it is that the verie angelles of God his church, and true ministers of his worde are sternly frowned uppon, injuriously thrust to the walles, and handled unreverently, unles with popishe dirige,[128] they will sing, 'Placebo';[129] and as the Jewes willed Esay, speak 'Placentia';[130] and with the Terentian Gnato, 'ait, aio; negat, nego';[131] that is to say, unlesse they will with Judas betray their maister Christe, and frame them selves to feede the sinfull humours of carnall men, by wilfull neglecting the severe commaundementes of Almightie God. Hence it is, that, if contempte of true religion, lothing of Christ's holy gospel, counternauncing of the wicked, cormeranting of earthly thinges,[132] carnall talke, vaine delectations, horrible blasphemie, pride in apparell, epicurisme in diet, deceite in bargaining, unchristian conversation, if these, and the like enormities be reproved, and the terrible judgementes of God denounced againste them, vaine glorie will then be inflamed and set on fire with revenging

---

[128] **dirige** dirge.

[129] **popishe … Placebo** Placebo [Latin], 'I will please', was the first word of the first psalm (116:1) in the office (vespers) for the dead, according to the Vulgate.

[130] **the Jewes … Placentia** In Isaiah 30:10, the Jews are described as only wanting to hear 'placentia' [Latin], 'smooth/pleasing things'.

[131] **ait … nego** [Latin] 'If he assents, I assent. If he denies it, I deny it'. In Eunuchus, Terence has the parasitical Gnatho say these lines of his patron. See Terence, Eunuchus, 250–253.

[132] **cormeranting of earthly thinges** Cormorants are a traditional symbol of greed, so it seems that Walsall is alluding to the greedy gathering of worldly goods.

anger, and at daggers drawing with such preachers. Thus I might proceede to proove that vaine glorie doth every way so abound, as the advauncement of God his glory is lamentably neglected.

Oh, that man had regenerate eyes to looke throughly upon, and deepely into himself, he should then wel perceive that no glorie, but all shame is due to him; he shoulde then be compelled to confesse, that whatsoever good thing he hath of the bodie or minde, the Lorde God hath there with adorned him, that he the authour therof might be glorified with and for the same. Saint Paul to extinguish and quench out man's greedie thirst of vain glory demaundeth of man this question, 'What hast thou that thou hast not received?'.[133] To the same ende that universall speach of Saint James may be fitly applied: 'Every good giving and every perfect gift is from above &c'.[134] Wherein the holy ghost teacheth that all the good things we enjoy, either temporall, or spirituall, they have streamed from the everlasting founteine of God his unspeakable liberalitie, that for and with the same we shoulde magnifie and praise his most glorious name. The Lord therefore in mercie graunt, that every man, in his severall vocation, may so hartely bend all his affections, giftes, welth,[135] wisedome, worship, honour, or what soever the Lorde hath blessed him withal, to the magnifying of him our most gratious and loving Father, that every one of us may with a good conscience and truly say with holy David, 'Not unto us, o Lorde, not unto us, but unto thy name, give the glorie, &c'.[136] And with Saint Paul, 'God forbid that I should glory or rejoice, but in the crosse of our Lord Jesus Christ, whereby the world is crucified unto me, and I unto the worlde'.[137]

Thinke not (right Christian Ladie) that these words are uttered so much to instruct you, as to enforme the reader of this letter unto you. For by good experience I have comfortably found both in the right honorable my very good Lord, your wise and loving housbande, and in your good Ladiship, his godly and obedient espouse, such care of God's glorie in advauncing true religion, in demeaning your selves in the education of your children, in governing your family, in countenauncing of vertue and learning, in cherishing the poore and needie, as I might deservedly be deemed unwise, if I had not observed it; carelesse, if I did not remember it; unthankefull, if upon offred occasion, I would not testifie it.[138] But thanked be the king of eternal glorie, this your care of God his glory is so universally knowne to

---

[133] **What . . . received?** 1 Corinthians 4:7.
[134] **Every . . . above &c** James 1:17.
[135] **welth** wealth.
[136] **Not . . . glorie, &c** Psalm 115:1.
[137] **God . . . worlde** Galatians 6:14.
[138] **For . . . testifie it** See p. 74, n. 123.

the whole realme, and so joyfully acknowledge[139] of the godly therein, that I neede not produce my self for an experienced witnes of the same. Wherfore to conclude this branch, I will heartily offer uppe mine incessant prayers to the Lorde God, in the name of his sonne our saviour Christe, that both you, and all Christians, may daily and continually growe not onely into such contempt of vaine glory, and al vaine thinges, but also into such love and longing of his true glorie, and all heavenly things, as, in these evill dayes, ye may have the sure testimony of your owne consciences, that you have zealously sought God his glory, and in the end, through Christ, be made partakers of his eternall glorie.

As this care of God's glorie hath drawen others to desire, and me to publish this sermon, which I trust, will prevent the uncharitable suspicions of some, and stay the rash tongues of others, so me thinketh, I am to be blamed neither by you, nor of any other for dedicating the same to your Ladishippe. For, notwithstanding nothing to be therin taught, which you have not long ago learned, and nothing in such manner delivered by me, but hath ben and may be much bettered by others, yet your Ladiship, by perusing thinges alreadie learned, shall not be altogether unprofitably occupied, and at the least this my fact shall make some outwarde shewe of mine inwarde heartie thanksgiving for the benefits bestowed upon, and the trust reposed in me your humble and faithfull servaunt.

And when I considered, that by my Lorde and your Ladiship I was first called from the universitie to teach your two sonnes (and those such children, as for the true feare of God, zealous affection to his word, obedience to their parents, reverence to their superiours, humility to their inferiours, love to their instructour, I never knewe any excell them) and also that by the same meanes I was likewise first called from teaching of children, to enstruct men, verely I coulde not but dedicate the first fruites of these my so generall labours to some of that house, whence I was first sent out to be a poore labourer in the Lord's great harvest.[140] You shall here find no profounde learning, no exquisite art, no curious eloquence to delight your learned eares, but finde you shal the simple truth now imprinted as it was then uttered, to comfort your Christian hearte. And I am throughly perswaded that as I have the sure warrant of God's expresse worde for confirmation of the trueth herein conteined, so the holy spirite of God will in such wise affect you with a like and love thereof, that he will compel your heart to think, and your toung to say, Amen, yea, and to confesse that,

---

[139] **acknowledge** acknowledged.
[140] **poore . . . harvest** See Matthew 9:37–38 and Luke 10:2.

albeit a sinnefull man was the homely utterer, yet the holy Ghost is the undoubted authour of the same.

Nowe least the portall shoulde be as great as the house, and the preface as long as the treatise, I will conclude and cease from further troubling you. But, I trust, not to surcease from hearty praying the Lord God so to devor[141] the harts of your good Ladiship, of your children and whole family with the holy fire of his heavenly spirite, that ye may 'dwell in his court, and be satisfied with the pleasure of his house, even of his holy temple';[142] 'that the zeale of the Lorde's house may eate ye up';[143] that with good consciences and joyfull spirites, ye may truely say, 'o Lord, I have loved the habitation of thy house, and the place wher thine honour dwelleth'.[144] Finally, that ye may be of that bright heavenly wheate, whiche shall bee gathered into the celestiall garner by the Lorde Jesus, who, for ever, mightily protect, and mercifully preserve you.

At Easeling by Feversham in the countie of Kent.[145]

> Your Ladiship's heartie orator, and humble servant,
> John Walsall.

15. *Anne Bacon to Nicholas Bacon II*, [May–July 1579][146]

Holograph, excluding the address. Chicago, 4140. 2pp.
Addressed: To Sir Nicholas Bakon

Syr, as yow sent me worde by Osborn,[147] as soone as I understoode of my Lorde Treasurer's[148] coming from the coort ^this^ afternoone I lett him know what yow sayde of Nathanaell's lett of coming. That the lett shulde be trew which is named ^I am^ sorye, for it is a great pain, but to be playn, as I can not now change, when I fyrst harde his

---

[141]**devor** devour.

[142]**dwell ... temple** Psalm 65:4.

[143]**that ... ye up** Psalm 69:9.

[144]**o Lord ... dwelleth** Psalm 26:8.

[145]**At Easeling ... Kent** Walsall had been appointed rector of Eastling parish near Faversham in Kent in 1574. He had previously held other livings; the dispensation to hold them in plurality may have come through his service to the lord keeper. See Heltzel, 'Young Francis Bacon's tutor', pp. 484–485.

[146][**May–July 1579]** It was during this period that Anne and Anthony were in dispute with Nicholas Bacon I's sons from his first marriage over inheritance issues. See below, p. 80, n. 150.

[147]**Osborn** John Osborne, steward and secretary to Nicholas Bacon I. See *Stiffkey*, II, p. 51.

[148]**Lorde Treasurer's** William Cecil, Lord Burghley, had been appointed lord treasurer in 1572.

wyffe[149] was come and not he, I looked not for him. My Lord Tresurer hath appointed to morow at ii of the clock in the afternoone ˆto heare the matterˆ and so wylled to certefye yow.[150] I pray God worke in your hart as ˆreadyeˆ a dispotion[151] to ende ˆwellˆ, as I at the fyrst by his grace gave a very rare example to beginn well immediatly upon your father's death, of a most faythfull hart ever to him, and the lyke desyre to confyrm your goode will still. Yf eny yll cownsell, as the worlde is full of subtiltee, go abowt to alter your own nature, which hetherto I have taken to be well enclyned. I pray ˆyowˆ, goode Syr Nicolas Bacon, lett it do no hurt betwyxt us where there hath ben so long a continuance of more then common amytee. Yow being the sonne, and I the wyff, and now the weedoe of the same ˆgoodˆ father and husbande. So I byd yow hartely fare well and shalbe very glad when wee may mete together frendely. From Shudloes Howse[152] this Monday.

Your well wyller alweyes,
ABacon.

16. *Anne Bacon to Théodore de Bèze*, 18 May 1581

Holograph, excluding the address. Latin. Gotha, Cod. A 405, fos 282r–283v. 2pp.
Addressed (fo. 283v): Monsieur, Monsieur de Beze, à Geneve.[153]

Salutem in Christo Jesus.

Habes, vir eximie, jamdudum apud te, ut spero, filium meum, Antonium Bacon. Hic multumque cupiebam ut ˆhinc profectusˆ Genevam tuam, immo Dei potius, et faciem quoque tuam videret. Amisso patre, ingenti correptus ˆestˆ desiderio exteras salutandi regiones; quo morbo laborant plerique Angli hisce presertim temporibus. Faxit Deus ut in commodum Ecclesiae suae et huius regni succedat. Adjuva illum, te praecor, vir Dei, consilio tuo et in tuam tutelam suscipito eum. Egomet ignara sum quem nactus est itineris sui comitem, sed, ut conjicio, Blanchardum quendam Gallum, cui permagnam habet fidem, quemadmodum ex litteris suis mihi aliisque

---

[149]**his wyffe** Anne Gresham Bacon. See **8**, **9**, **12**, and **13**.

[150]**My Lord ... certefye yow** Nicholas and Nathaniel Bacon, two of Nicholas Bacon I's sons from his first marriage, were in dispute with Anne and Anthony Bacon over their inheritance. Burghley, one of Nicholas Bacon's executors, attempted to settle the disagreement. For Nicholas Bacon's will, see *Stiffkey*, I, pp. 25–29. For letters from Nicholas Bacon II and Nathaniel regarding the dispute and for Burghley's responses, see *Stiffkey*, I, pp. 77–79, 81–82, 93–95, 101–107. A resolution seems to have been reached by early 1580: see *Stiffkey*, I, pp. 119–120.

[151]**dispotion** disposition.

[152]**Shudloes Howse** Presumably Shardeloes manor, Amersham.

[153]*Monsieur ... à Geneve* [French] 'Master, Mr de Bèze, at Geneva'.

per Blanchardum ipsum traditis facile prospexi superiore mense Februario. Multo foelicior esset si vivente patre peregrinatus transmarinas vidisset terras, fultus auxilio et crebro consilio pii et vere prudentis patris; quod quidem fratri suo Edouardo benignitate Dei contigit. Verum cum secus visum est ^coelesti^ patri nostro, spes mea est, Deo hortante filium meum hoc iter ingressum esse et divini Spiritus ductu illum et proficisci et in bonarum rerum cognitione indies proficere.

Dominus maritus reliquit ex me, secunda sua uxore (et sane inter secundas res meas duco, precipue duco, quod me Deus voluit talis viri uxorem esse), ex me inquam, duos tantum reliquit filios, totam spem prolis meae in iis praeterea annis, qui potissimum meo judicio desiderant et indigent gubernaculo paternae autoritatis et cura sollicita chari parentis. Sed idem Deus qui abstulit patrem assumsit, ut confido, et me et filios meos in suam curam et patrocinium. Oro te, ut hanc meam quasi necessitate coactam audaciam ad te scribere velis excusatam habere et internum animi affectum viduae matris erga filium absentem respicere potius quam laceram et claudicantem latinitatem meam aut notare aut culpare. Valeat prestantia tua diu incolumis Ecclesiae Dei et reipublicae tuae.

Londini, 18 Maii 1581.

Tua in Christo ABacona,
vidua Domini Custodis.

[Translation]

Greetings in Christ Jesus.

You already for some time have with you, excellent sir, my son, Anthony Bacon, as I hope. I was greatly desirous that he should set out from here and see your Geneva – or rather, God's Geneva, as well as your face.

After the loss of his father he was seized by a great desire to visit foreign regions; this is a disease affecting many Englishmen, particularly in these times. May God grant that he succeeds to the benefit of his church and of this commonwealth. Assist him, I beseech you, as a man of God, with your counsel and take him into your protection.

I myself am unaware who he had as a companion on his journey but I presume it was Blanchard, a Frenchman,[154] in whom he has great faith, as I readily noticed from his letters delivered to me and to others by this same man Blanchard last February.[155] He would have been much

---

[154]**Blanchard, a Frenchman** Honoré Blanchard had been a student at Trinity College, Cambridge, with Anthony and had impressed the latter with his scholarship, particularly his 'grounded knowledge in Hebrew, Greek and Latin', and his past travels 'throughout Germany, the Lowe Countreis and the most part of England'. See SP 12/147, fo. 99r–v.

[155]**I readily . . . last February** Anthony had sent Blanchard to England in 1581 with a letter to his uncle, Lord Burghley. See *ibid*.

happier if he had travelled abroad and visited foreign lands while his
father was alive, supported by the help and frequent counsel of a godly
and truly prudent father, as indeed his brother Edward managed to
do through God's goodness.[156] But since our heavenly Father deemed
it otherwise, it is my hope that it was with God's encouragement that
my son undertook this journey and that it was under the guidance
of the Holy Spirit that he set off and makes daily progress in the
understanding of good things.

My lord husband has left me, his second wife (and certainly among
my blessings I especially count the fact that God wished me to be
the wife of such a man), has left me, I say, just two sons, the whole
hope of my offspring in these years moreover; in my judgement they
particularly miss and need the guidance of a father's authority and
the solicitous concern of a loving parent. But this same God who took
away their father has, as I firmly believe, taken up both me and my
sons in his care and protection. I beg you to excuse this boldness of
mine in writing to you as something forced by necessity, and to look
upon the deep affection of a widowed mother for her absent son,
rather than rebuking or censuring my mangled and halting Latinity.
May your excellence long remain safe and healthy for the church of
God and for your republic.

London, 18 May 1581.

Yours in Christ A. Bacon,
widow of the Lord Keeper.

17. *Anne Bacon to Théodore de Bèze*, 24 July 1581

Holograph. Latin. Gotha, Cod. A 405, fos 284r–285v. 2pp.
Addressed (fo. 285v): Domino reverendo D. Bezae.[157]

*Accepi tuas literas, vir eximie, quae mihi merito et sunt et debent esse gratissimae,
tum quod tu, vir omni eruditionis genere praestantissimus et hac nostra etate propter
zaelum Domus Dei maxime celebris, non dedignatus sis ad me scribere mulierem
viduam et imbecillem, tum vero quod per te certior facta sum de adventu filii mei ad
Genevam. De qua re non parum hactenus anxia fui, ac vehementer optatum hunc
audire nuncium diu desideravi. Ob id igitur, ex animo gratias ago Deo nostro qui
Anthonium meum salvum et incolumem ad te misit.*

---

[156]**brother Edward ... goodness** During his Continental travels, Edward Bacon,
Anthony's half-brother, had stayed with Théodore de Bèze in 1578. See H. Aubert, F.
Aubert, and H. Meylan (eds), *Correspondance de Théodore de Bèze*, 38 vols (Geneva, 1970),
XVIII, p. 145.

[157]***Domino ... Bezae*** [Latin] 'To the Reverend Lord D. Bèze'.

Biduo post acceptas tuas litteras, allatae sunt mihi literae quoque a filio inclusae in aliis ad quendam suum amicum exaratis, in quibus scribit se non modo tibi et vultu et verbis gratum venisse, verum etiam maxima cum humanitate et serio rogatu in hospitium tuum amicissime receptum fuisse. Hic vero, eloquar ne an sileam plane ignoro. Quantum ˆenimˆ tuae dignitati debeo propter hanc immensam ac spontaneam tuam benevolentiam erga filium, juvenem tibi penitus ignotum, nec loquendo nec scribendo satis exprimere possum. Quod si talem amicitiam erga eum tam mihi charum silentio preter mitterem, aut filium meum summae ingratitudinis, quod nollem, aut me, matrem suam tanti beneficii parum memorem, jure incusare posse videris. Deo idcirco propitio hoc omnino relinquo, cuius instinctu, ut spero, rem illi perutilem et mihi perjucundam fecisti, cuius etiam benignitas non desinit paternum suum amorem in me et meos cum maxime opus sit semper ostendere.

Dum Anthonius apud te manet, et quo diutius eo melius mihi placet, sis illi, obtestor te, loco patris et consilio tuo et auxilio, tum ad pietatem tum ad consultius et satis tuto tua prudentia reliquum iter peragendum, si modo sit illi in animo diutius adhuc foris manere, quo Dei Optimi Maximi misericordia, assiduaque tua familiaritate et sana doctrina, morumque integritate magis auctus et ditatus cum gaudio ad suos redeat.

Vale, pater celeberrime, in Christo; me meosque precibus ˆtuisˆ mando.

Ex edibus meis, Gorhamburiae, 24 Julii 1581.

> *In Christo Jesu*
> *semper tua, ABacona.*
> *Vidua Domini custodis.*

[Translation]

I received your letter, excellent sir, which rightly is and ought to be most pleasing to me, both because you, a man outstanding in every kind of learning and most celebrated in our day and age on account of your zeal for the house of God, were kind enough to write to me, a widow and a weak woman, and also because you informed me of my son's arrival in Geneva. I have up till now been not a little anxious about this and I have long wished to receive this news which is greatly desired. And so for this, I heartily thank our Lord who has sent my Anthony safe and sound to you.

Two days after I received your letter, a letter was delivered to me also from my son enclosed in another letter written to a friend of his,[158] in which he writes that he has not only arrived and been welcomed by you with a friendly countenance and words, but that he has also been received in a most friendly manner and with the greatest kindness and

---

[158] **a letter . . . of his** Anthony Bacon sent a raft of letters, including one to Mildred Cooke Cecil, his aunt, back to England in July 1581. See, for example, Edinburgh University Library, Laing MS iii. 193, fos 116a–116b.

a serious entreaty into your hospitable house. But here I am entirely unsure whether I should speak out or remain silent. For I cannot express in speech or in writing how much I owe your dignity for the immense and unasked-for kindness you have shown my son, a young man who is a complete stranger to you. But if I were to pass over in silence such friendship towards him who is so dear to me, you would seem to be able justifiably to accuse my son of extreme ingratitude, which I would not wish, or me, his mother, of failing to remember such a great kindness. And so with God's favour I completely leave this, at whose urging, so I hope, you did this thing which benefits him so much and gives me so much pleasure, whose goodness even now does not cease, ever to show his fatherly love towards me and my family when it is most necessary.

While Anthony remains with you – and the longer he stays, the happier I am – act as a parent to him, I beseech you, giving him your counsel and assistance, both for the sake of piety and so as to carry out the rest of his journey more advisedly and safely by means of your wisdom, if now he decides to remain abroad still longer, so that by the mercy of our Almighty God, and by your continued intimacy and wise teaching, his moral integrity may develop and grow richer and he may return to his family with joy.

Farewell, most distinguished father, in Christ; I commit myself and my family to your prayers.

From my house at Gorhambury, 24 July 1581.

Ever yours in Christ Jesus,
A. Bacon,
widow of the Lord Keeper.

18. *Théodore de Bèze to Anne Bacon*, 1 November 1581

Published, dedicatory letter. French. T. de Bèze, *Chrestienes meditations sur huict pseaumes du prophete David composees et nouvellement mises en lumiere par Theodore de Besze* (Geneva, 1581).[159]
Addressed: A Madame, Madame Anne Bacon, vefve de feu Monseigneur Nicolas Bacon, garde des seaux de royaume d'Angleterre.

Madame, estant le livre de Pseaumes de singuliere recommandation entre tous ceux de la saincte escriture, il y a quelque temps qu'après m'estre employé à la traduction et exposition d'iceux, je me suis mis aussi à esbaucher quelques

---

[159] **T. de Bèze ... (Geneva, 1581)** There are very few extant copies of the early editions of Bèze's meditations in French. For a discussion of the availability of these early editions, see Aubert, Aubert, and Meylan, *Correspondance de Théodore de Bèze*, XXII, p. 186.

meditations sur ce suject, ayant choisi comme pour un essay les sept Pseaumes pieçà nommez penitentiaux, pour estre lors specialement dediez à ceux lesquels, après avoir satisfait à la penitence publique et canonique, estoyent r'alliez au corps de l'Eglise, le tout pour mon instruction et consolation particuliere.

Et depuis encores ayant esté requis d'une grande et vertueuse Princesse de luy dresser quelque formulaire de prieres, je les ay reprins en main et polis aucunement, en esperance mesmes de les publier: ce que n'estant venu à effect par le soudain decez d'icelle Dame, je les ay gardez entre mes papiers comme chose de peu de prix: où ils fussent demeurez, n'estoit qu'à la venue de Monsieur Antoine Bacon vostre fils par deçà, voyant qu'il prenoit plaisir à ce petit ouvrage, et d'autre part ayant cognu par les lettres Latines desquelles il vous a pleu m'honorer, les grandes et singulieres, voire extraordinaires graces desquelles Dieu vous a douee, et desquelles je recognoy un vray pourtrait en vostre dict fils, je me suis persuadé que ne prendriez à desplaisir que ce petit livret, portant vostre nom sur le front, vous fust presenté pour tesmoignage de l'honneur et reverence que je porte à la vertu vostre et des vostres: esperant aussi qu'en cest estat de vefvage auquel il a pleu à Dieu que soyez reduite par le decez de ce tres vertueux et à bon droict tres-renommé Seigneur, Monseigneur Nicolas Bacon vostre mari, et tres digne garde de seaux d'Angleterre, vous y trouverez quelque consolation après la lecture de ces grands et saincts docteurs Grecs et Latins qui vous sont familiers, pour vous confermer de plus en plus en la meditation des choses spirituelles, et en ceste constance et patience Chrestienne de laquelle le Seigneur vous a tellement ornee, qu'en vous est vrayement recognue ce chrestiennement magnanime courage que j'ay veu par deçà reluire en feu de tres-heureuse memoire Monseigneur Antoine Koouk Chevalier, durant les grandes calamitez publiques du royaume, et particulieres à luy et à toute sa maison. Voilà le fondement de mon dessein, lequel s'il vous plaist avoir pour agreable, comme je vous en supplie tres-humblement, ce me sera peut estre une occasion de passer plus avant en ceste besongne, aydant nostre Seigneur, lequel je requiers, Madame, vous accroissant ses plus grandes graces, vous conserver avec toute vostre tres-noble famille tres-longuement en toute saincte et entiere prosperité. De Geneve, ce premier de novembre, 1581.

> *Votre bien humble et obeyssant serviteur,*
> *Theodore de Besze.*

[*Translation from T. de Bèze,* Christian meditations upon eight Psalmes of the prophet David, *trans. J.S. (London, 1582) sigs A4r–A5v*]
Addressed (sig. A4r): To my lady, the lady Anne Bacon, widowe of the deceased Syr Nicolas Bacon Knight, Lord Keeper of the great seale of England.

Madame, among other bookes of holy scripture, that of the Psalmes wel deserveth to bee singularly recommended to us. It is nowe some time, since having bestowed some payne in translating and expounding the same, I gave my selfe also to take some more libertie of dealing with them by way of meditating upon that subject, choosing (as it were for an assaye) the seven psalmes called some time Penitential, because they were appointed to such as after having satisfied open and canonical penaunce, were reunited to the body of the Church, wholy doing it for my particular instruction and consolation. After this, beeing required by a great and vertuous princesse, to frame for her some forme of prayers,[160] I tooke them afresh into my hands, polishing them over, and that with hope of publishing them, which being letted by the sodayne decease of that Lady, I reserved them among my papers as things of no great price, where they had lyen still, had not bene the comming of master Anthony Bacon your sonne, into these partes. Whom when I sawe to take pleasure in this litle piece of woorke, and againe knowing by the Latin letters wherewith it hath liked you to honour me,[161] the great and singular, yea extraodinarie graces wherwith God hath indewed you, and whereof I acknowledge a very paterne in your said sonne, I perswaded my selfe that it should not be displeasing to you, if this small volume carying your name upon the browe, were offered to you, in testimonie of the honour and reverence I beare to the vertue of you and yours. Hoping withall that this estate of widowehode whereunto it hath pleased God to call you by decease of that right vertuous and of right renowned Lord, my Lord Nicolas Bacon, your husband and most worthy Keeper of the seale of England, you might perhaps therein finde some consolation, after the reading of those great and holy doctors of Greeke and Latine so familiar to you, for your better confirming in the meditation of spiritual things, and in this constancie and Christian patience wherewith God hath so beautified you, that in you is verily acknowledged that Christianly high minded courage, which I sawe in these partes shining in the deceased, of very happy memorie, Syr Anthony Cooke Knight, during those great calamities publique to the realm, and particular to him and his whole familie.[162] See the ground of my purpose, which if it may please you to take in good part, which I very humbly crave, it may be perhaps an occasion of proceeding in this busines, our Lord ayding, whom I beseeche, Madame, that increasing in you his greatest graces, he will preserve you and your verie noble familie, long in all holy and perfect prosperitie.

From Geneva this first of November. Anno 1581.

Yours very humble and serviceable to commaunde,
Theodore Besze.

[160]**great ... prayers** Bèze may have been inspired by Jeanne d'Albret, whom he had met in 1571. See S. Barker, *Protestantism, Poetry and Protest: the vernacular writings of Antoine de Chandieu* (Aldershot, 2009), p. 250.
[161]**the Latin ... me** See **16** and **17**.
[162]**which I sawe ... familie** During the reign of Mary I, Anthony Cooke had embarked upon a self-imposed Continental exile.

19. *Anne Bacon to William Cecil, Lord Burghley,* 26 February 1585

Holograph. BL, Lansdowne MS 43, fos 119r–120v. 2pp.
Addressed (fo. 120v): To my very goode Lorde, the Lorde Tresurer of Englande
Endorsed (fo. 120v): 26 February 1584. The Lady Bacon for the preachers.[163]

I know well, myne especiall goode Lorde, it becometh me not to be troblesome unto your Honor at eni other tyme, but now cheefly in this season of your gretest[164] affayres and small or no leasure. But yet because yesterdaye's morning spech, as in that I was extraordinarly admitted yt was your Lordship's favour, so fearing to stay to long I cowlde not so playnly speak ner so well receave your answer therto as I wolde truly and gladly in that matter, I am bowlde by this writing to enlarge the same more playnly and to what ende I did mean.[165] Yf it may like your goode Lordship, the report of the late conference at Lambath hath ben so handled to the discrediting of those learned that labour for right reformation in the ministery of the gospell, that it is no small greff of mynde to the faythfull preachers, because the matter is thus by the othersyde caried away as thowgh the^ir^ cawse cowlde not ~~not~~ sufficiently be warranted by the worde of God.[166] For the which proffe they have long ben sadd sutors and wolde most humbly crave still both of God in heaven whose cause it is and of her Majestie, their moste excellent soverein here in earth, that they might obtein qwiett and convenient audience ether before her Majestie her selff, whose hart is in God his hande to towch and to turne, or before your honours of the cownsell, whose wysdome they greatly reverence. And yf they can not strongly prove before yow owt of the worde of God that Reformation which they so long have

---

[163]**26 ... preachers** This endorsement is in Burghley's own hand. An addition to the endorsement seems to be in a later hand: 'that they might bee allowed to shew their reasons before the Queen and her Counsel'.

[164]**gretest** greatest.

[165]**But ... did mean** Anne was admitted through her brother-in-law's, Burghley's, favour into the House of Commons when Whitgift gave his response to a petition against his 'Three Articles', which had led to the suspension of many godly clergymen. In a particularly heated session, Whitgift dismissed every point of the petition.

[166]**the report ... God** A two-day conference on Whitgift's articles had been hastily convened at the request of the earl of Leicester in December 1584. Owing to lack of time, discussion had been kept to limited issues; objections to the Prayer Book were not treated at all and Walter Travers evaded an attempt by Whitgift to discuss their more radical objections to the government of the Church. See P. Collinson, *The Elizabethan Puritan Movement* (London, 1967), p. 269.

called and cryed for to be according to Christ his own ordinance, then to lett them be rejected with shame owt of the church for ever. And that this may be better don to the glory of God and tru understanding of this great cause, they reqwyre fyrst leave to assemble and to consult together purposely, which they have forborn to do for avoyding suspetion of privat conventicles.[167] For hetherto thowgh in some writing they have declared the state of their, yea God his cause, yet were they never allowed to conferr together and so together be hard fully. But now some one and then some two called upon a soden unprepared, to fore prepared, to catch them rather then gravely and moderatly to be hard to defend their right and goode cause. And therfore for such weyghty conference they appeale to her Majesty and ^her^ honorable wyse cownsell, whom God hath placed in hyghest authority for thadvancement of his kingdom, and refuse the byshopps ^for judges^ who are parties partiall in their own defence, because the[168] seek more worldely ambition then the glory of Christ Jesus.[169]

For myn own part, my goode Lorde, I wyll not deny but as I may I heare them in their publyck exercyses, as a cheff duty commanded by God to weedoes,[170] and also I confess, as one that hath fownde mercy, that I have profyted more in the inwarde feeling knowledg of God his holy wyll, thowgh but in a small measure, by such syncere and sownde opening of the scrypture by ^an^ ordinary preaching, within these 7 or 8 yeres then I dyd by hearing ^odd^ sermons at Powles[171] well nigh 20 yeres together. I mention this unfaynedly the rather to excuse this my bowldness toward your Lordship, humbly beseching your Lordship to think upon their sute and, as God shall move your understanding hart, to further yt. And yf opportunite will not be had as they reqwire, yet I once again in humble wyse am a suter[172]

For thinnes of the paper I write in the other leaff. For my yll eyes.

[fo. 120r] unto your Lordeshipp that yow wolde be so goode as to chewse ii or iii of them which your Honour lykes best and lycence them before your own selff or other at your plesur to declare and to prove the truth of the cause, with qwiet and ^an^ attentyve eare. I have harde them say

---

[167]**which ... conventicles** The 1581 *An Act for Retaining the Queen's Subjects in their Due Obedience* decreed the various punishments due to those gathering in Conventicles, although it was primarily targeted at Catholics.

[168]**the** they.

[169]**the seek ... Jesus** For a similar conclusion on the role of bishops, see **22**.

[170]**a cheff ... weedoes** For scriptural commandments to widows, see in particular 1 Timothy 5:3–16.

[171]**Powles** Paul's Cross, an open-air pulpit in the churchyard of St Paul's cathedral.

[172]**a suter** Repeated on fo. 120r.

or[173] now they wyll not come to dispute or argew to brede contention, which is the maner of the byshopps' hearing, but to be suffred patyently to lay down before them that shall commande they[174] excepted, how well and certeinly they can warrant by the infallible towchstone of the worde the substantiall and mayn grownde of their cause. Surely my Lorde I am perswaded yow shulde do God acceptable service herin. And for the very entier affection I owe and do beare unto your honour, I wysh from the very hart that to your other rare gyfts sondrywyse yow were fully enstructed and satisfyed in this princypall matter, so contemned of the great rabyes to the dishonoring of the gospell so long amonst[175] us. I am so much bownde to your Lordship for your comfortable dealing towards me and myne as I do incessantly desyre that by your Lordship's meanes God his glory may more and more be promoted, the greved godly comforted and yow and yours abowndantly blessed. None is prevy to this and in dede thowgh I heare them, yet I see them very seldom.

I trust your Lordship wyll accept in best part my best meaning.

In the Lorde dutifully and most hartely,
ABacon.

20. *Michel Berault*[176] *to Anne Bacon*, 19 July [1585–1589][177]

Copy. Latin, with Greek words. BL, Harleian MS 871, fo. 75r–v. 1p.
Addressed (fo. 75r): Observandissimae dominae Annae Bacon Michael Beraldus verbi minister salutem in Christo Deo.

Fieri non potest, nobilissima religiosissimaque Domina, quin tibi quantacumque constantia ac firmitate animi praedita, Domini Antonii Bacon filii tui merito carissimi diuturna in his regionibus turbulentissimo praesertim tempore mora ac inde nata eius absentia atque desiderium, et solicitudinis et molesiae plurimum

---

[173] **or** before.
[174] **they** Repeated.
[175] **amonst** amongst.
[176] **Michel Berault** Michel Berault (Bérauld), a French Protestant theologian, was a minister in Montauban. In 1598, he published a *Brieve et Claire Défense de la Vocation des Ministres de l'Évangile* (*A Brief and Clear Defence of the Vocation of the Ministers of the Gospel*) in Montauban, in reply to the writings of the French Catholic convert Jacques du Perron.
[177] **19 July [1585–1589]** Berault dated the letter in New Style dating, but it is here given in the Old Style equivalent. Anthony Bacon was resident in Montauban by 24 October 1584 and he left in 1590; he was in Lisle-sur-Tam in July 1590, so it seems unlikely that the letter would have been sent that year, as it refers to his continued stay in Montauban. For Anthony's movements in France, see *Troubled Life*, pp. 102, 125, 544. It is most likely that this letter dates from either July 1586 or July 1587: see pp. 92–93, n. 178.

attulerit. Nam ut maternum animum omittam qui propensior fere in primogenitos esse solet ac proinde omnis mali metuentior, tum Dominus Deus pro sua in suos liberalitate eum tot tamquam raris cum animi tum corporis exornavit, ut eius discessus non popularibus modo, sed etiam alienigenis qui semel excellens eius ingenium, singularem comitatem placidosque mores noverint, non minus futurus sit gravis, quam aspectus quibus frui licet iucundus; tum hac tempestate tam graves tam repentini subinde intervenerint casus etiam iis, qui ubique terrarum, praecipue vero in hac infaelici Gallia tutissimo loco esse videntur ut nis sit mirum quod cum praetiosissimum pignus loco non solum a tuo conspectu, verum etiam a praesidio procul remoto habeas, omnia adversa atque infausta suspiceris et reformides, nec non ut te cura et metu filium periculo exolvas tum ad te denique revocare quam primum cogites, studeas, omni denique ope nitaris, horum equidem nihil a verae parentis officio alienum aut discrepans, ad quod malevoli quidam vel potius malesani homines conati sunt, ut audeo tibi longe meliora de filio iure expectanti persuadere. At si iam commemoratus filius vel captus loci amoenitate et civium nostrorum deliciis, obsequiis, blandimentis illectus, ultro Montalbani moras proderes necteret atque produceret, vel purae religionis, quam a teneris didiscerat, taedio a patriae conspectu in qua Deus per Christum unice colitur, a qua superstitio omnis eiulat singulari Dei beneficio abhorreret plane cum ipsa humanitate; nedum cum veritate pugnat. Certo autem certius est ei postquam sese huc paulo antequam coniurationis Guisiacae consilio in apertam vim erupisse, ut alteri pedi ex laxatione in comitatu regis Navarroe accepta, graviter affecta mederetur, nullam quamvis cupienti summaque cura reditum in patriam quaerenti, oblatam hinc exeunti, sine aperto salutis discrimine rationem fuisse; tantum abfuit ut Rupellae portum quot unde navigaret in Angliam, tuto pervenire posset. Enim vero, si qua forte militum manus satis firma et idonea perrumpendis quae passim struebantur insidiis in Xantones aut Pictavos profectura quod bis aut ad summum ter toto hoc quinquennio contigit diceretur hinc extrema εφοδιω inopia (ut interim nihil dicam de aeris alieni magnitudine, quod sui etiam frugalissime imo tenuissime victitans tanto tempore traxerat) illinc valetudo parum prospera, nec dicam adversa, ita sanctissimis eius consiliis obstiterunt et reflarunt. Ut non sine summo animi sui dolore, in hoc obscuro Galliae angulo carpendum ei adhuc fuerit, prout in clarissima luce orbis Christiani cuius dignus est versaretur. Quamquam neque urbis ignobilitas, neque iniquitas temporum ita virtutibus eius tenebras offundere potuerunt, quin permultis mihi vero in primis et exemplo et sermonum gravitate in his comunibus miseriis praeluxerit. Quocirca nunquam dubitabo palam affirmare cum quisquis ille fuerit, qui aliter vel dixerit vel scripserit, suam magis impudentiam, quam latissimi et ornatissimi iuvenis innocentiam prodiisse. Cum a me stet non dubia veritas, nequaquam vereor, ne ulla unquam ullius etiam disertissimi oratoris eloquentia aut vagorimi veteratoris, calliditas huic testimonio fidem derrogare aut me mendacii coarguere posse. Quamobrem ego matri aequi satisfaciendi, ac tuendae filii existimationis studiosus, te colendissima Domina oro atque obtestor et si fas est moneo atque hortor, ut si quam graviorem de filio opinionem quasi aliquid de veteri in Deum

vel in patriam, vel denique in te ipsum studio remiserit comprehendisti, eam me
sponso rem protinus deponas, tibique persuadeas multo plus animo eius accessisse
quam de pecuniis decessisse, hocque quinquennali usu et exercitationi provectiorem
filium pietate reliquisque virtutibus quam aetate factum, quod ipse brevi σαν θεω
praecipua cum animi voluptate cognosces et experieris. Vale. Datum Montalban.
Quarto Calendas Augusti novo calendo anno Domini.

[Translation]
Addressed: Michel Berault, minister of the word, sends greetings in
Christ God to the most honourable lady Anne Bacon.

It is impossible most noble and most pious lady, for you who are
endowed with such great constancy and firmness of mind, not to be
affected by a great deal of anxiety and concern because your son, Lord
Anthony Bacon, who is justifiably very dear to you, is staying a long
time in these parts at this particularly turbulent time. His absence must
cause you great longing. But I say nothing about the maternal mind
which tends to be almost more partial towards first-born children and
therefore more fearful of every evil; furthermore the Lord God, by his
generosity towards his own, has adorned him with so many rare gifts
of both mind and body that his departure will be no less serious than
the sight of him is pleasing to those who can enjoy them, not only to
his countrymen but also to foreign-born men who have come to know
his outstanding talent, his singular courtesy, and peaceable nature.
Moreover at this time such serious and sudden things have happened
repeatedly to those who seem to be in the safest place anywhere in the
world, but particularly in this wretched country of France, so that it
is not surprising since you have this most precious dear son not only
far from your sight but also from your protection, you suspect and
fear that everything is calamitious and unlucky and also that you may
free your son from danger by solicitude and anxiety, so you plan, try
and strive with all your efforts to bring him back to you as soon as
possible; of which is nothing foreign from or at odds with the true
role of a parent against whom some ill-willed or unsound men have
striven, as I dare to persuade you who are justifiably awaiting far better
things from your son. But since your already-mentioned son has been
captured by the pleasantness of the place and seduced by the delights,
services, and kindnesses of our citizens, so he voluntarily contrives to
prolong his stay at Montauban because he finds it useful, or through
its pure religion, which he had learned from his tender years, wearied
from the sight of his homeland in which God is solely worshipped
through Christ, bewailed by all superstition, utterly horrified by the
singular benevolence of God fighting with humanity itself, nay even
with truth. Certainly it is clearer to him that after he came here a little

before the Guise conspiracy deliberately erupted into open violence, so that by means of a period of rest received in the retinue of the king of Navarre, he might be healed in the other foot which had been seriously affected, there was no reason for him to leave here without an obvious and sudden improvement in his health, despite his desire to do so and even though he sought a return to his own country as a matter of the greatest concern. So far was he from being able to reach La Rochelle safely, from where he should sail to England, having realized that to go forth hence without clear health to be reckoning with danger. For indeed, if by chance a troop of soldiers sufficiently strong and suitable for breaking the ambushes (which were being set up everywhere) was to set out against the people of Saintes and Poitiers, which has happened twice or at most three times in this whole period of five years, there would be said to be, as a result, an extreme shortage of travelling supplies (to say nothing of the size of the debt which he had drawn out for such a long time by living very frugally, indeed very meagrely), or on the other side hardly prosperous, not to say bad, health would have hindered his most sacred plans and blown them in the opposite direction. So that not without the greatest mental anguish, he had to live in this dark corner of France until now, in so far as he should live in the brightest light of the Christian world of which he is worthy. Although neither the dishonourable nature of the city nor the wickedness of the times could extend the darkness over his virtues and prevent him shining forth to many and to me, especially by his example and the gravity of his conversation in these shared miserable conditions. For this reason I will never hesitate to affirm publicly that whoever it was who said or wrote differently, has revealed his own shamelessness rather than betraying the innocence of the most generous and distinguished young man. Since undoubted truth stands by me, I in no way fear that any eloquence of even the most learned orator or the cunning of a roaming crafty fellow could ever revile the fidelity from this testimony or prove me a liar. For this reason I am eager to satisfy the mother and to protect the son's reputation and I beg and beseech you, most worshipful lady, and, if it is proper, I warn and urge you that if you apprehend some more serious opinion about your son, such as if he has fallen away at all from his former devotion towards his homeland, towards God, or lastly towards you yourself, you should immediately set aside the matter,[178] with me as your pledge, and you should persuade yourself

---

[178] **I warn … the matter** It is unclear as to what Berault is referring to. Anthony had earned the wrath of Charlotte d'Arbaleste du Plessis-Mornay, owing to his failure to marry her daughter, to her reluctance for Anthony to be repaid a debt by her husband, and for his siding with Michel Berault, who was intent on enforcing the sumptuary rules against the ornate headwear which she favoured. Anthony later revealed that he believed 'false

that he has gained much more spiritually than he has lost financially, and that he has increased in piety and other virtues more than in years during the practice and efforts of these past five years, as you will find and experience yourself shortly, God willing, with particular pleasure of mind. Farewell. Written at Montauban on 29 July in the new calendar year of the Lord.

21. *Thomas Wilcox*[179] *to Anne Bacon*, 25 September 1589

Published, dedicatory letter. T.W. [Thomas Wilcox], *A short, yet sound Commentarie; written on that woorthie worke called; The Proverbes of Salomon* (London, 1589), sigs A2r–A4v.
Addressed (fo. A2r): To the honorable and his very good Ladie, the Ladie Bacon, T.W. wisheth abundance of all felicitie outward and inward in this life, and afterwards eternal blessednes through Christ in that life which lasteth for ever.

Amongst the great, unmeasurable and infinite benefites, that God most rich in mercie and faithfull in performance, hath given unto men of all estates and degrees, in this last (though worst) age of the world, as evident and infallible testimonies of his singular love and bountie towards them, and as notable instruments to drawe and allure them soundly to knowe, unfeignedlie to love, and reverently to feare him alone that is the only giver thereof, this in my poore judgement (good Madame) seemeth unto me (and I hope that others inlightned from God are of the same minde with me) not the least nor to be reckoned in the last place, namely, the excellent and most wonderfull light, not of manifold tongues onely, as Hebrew, Greeke, Caldee, Siriake, Latin, &c, neither yet of sundrie arts alone, as grammar, rhetoricke, logicke, musicke, arithmetick, geometrie, &c, but of the holy scriptures and Christian religion speciallie; all which doubtles

suggestions and surmyses' from du Plessis and his wife to have reached his mother, and his uncle, Lord Burghley, confirmed that 'Plessy complayned here of yow'. See LPL 659, fos 25r, 104v, 106r. For more on Madame du Plessis-Mornay's dispute with Michel Berault, see *A Huguenot Family in the XVI Century: the memoirs of Philippe de Mornay Sieur du Plessis Marly written by his wife*, trans. L. Crump (London, 1926), pp. 71, 198–217. It could also be that Berault is referring to Anthony's prosecution for sodomy. Informal testimony against Bacon was taken in August 1586; there was a second, formal hearing in November 1587. The outcome of these hearings seems to be that Anthony was sentenced for the crime, but that Henri de Navarre appealed on his behalf and had him released. Alan Haynes has suggested that the bad feeling held towards Anthony by du Plessis and his wife may have been connected to his prosecution. For Anthony's arrest, see *Troubled Life*, pp. 108–111; and A. Haynes, *Invisible Power: the Elizabethan secret services, 1570–1603* (Stroud, 1994), pp. 105–106.
[179] **Thomas Wilcox** For Anne Bacon's support of the godly clergyman Thomas Wilcox, see the Introduction, p. 26.

being heretofore through Sathan's malice and man's ignorance, not cast aside amongst wormes and moathes, by little and little to wast and consume them, but sumptuouslie laied in grave, and deepely buried, and that almost without hope of quickning, God (that alwaies had and hath the fulnes of power in his hand) hath been pleased now at the last, for the overthrowe of superstition, idolatrie, and wicked life, and for the advauncement of his glorie, and furtherance of men's salvation, to recall as it were even from the grave it selfe, and revive from the dead. Wherin howsoever the Lord have graciouslie vouchsafed to declare his incomprehensible power, accomplishing so miraculous a worke, and to manifest his unspeakable love not onely in the multitude and varietie, but in the evidencie thereof, so that even bleare eyed men and barbers (as is in the common byword) may cleerely perceive the same, yet the strength of sinne hath so not onely obscured, but as it were defaced, though not the sight, yet the power and efficacie of God's favour, with the fruites and effects which should followe thereupon, that some through naturall blindness and dimnes of their eyes cannot behold them; other some againe through dumnes of mouth, and having their tongues tied, will not acknowledge them; other some againe through want of good judgement, do with polluted hands irreverently receive them; and almost all through prophanenesse of hart, and cursed corruption unsanctifiedlie (if not irreligiouslie) use them. So fewe are there found in the world now adaies that profite by them to faith unfeigned, and humble thankfulnes before him that plentifully hath provided the same for their good, if they could tell how to accept and use the same. The contemplation and memorie wherof (I willingly and unfeignedly confesse it) leaveth behind it no small skarre, but a great wound rather in mine heart, and that not only so much for mine owne iniquitie in that behalfe (though I knowe the same to bee high and hainous) as for the common abomination, that every where as a mightie streame that will not be stopped, and forcible floud that cannot be withstood, overfloweth all, and for the fearefull desolation that in all probabilitie and likelihood of man's judgement will ensue thereupon, because howsoever God be of long suffering and great goodnes, yet he cannot, nor will not (for we are sure he is zealous over his owne glorie) continuallie suffer the vile and abominable of the world to trample and tread under their beastlie feete his exceeding blessings and singular favours. And yet I cannot hide this within my selfe, but must of necessitie breake foorth into the declaration thereof, that I am againe somewhat recomforted, in that whether soever I cast mine eyes whether at home or abroad, I certainlie beholde, and that without deceit of sight, some amongst all estates and degrees of men, high, lowe, rich, poore, young, olde, noble, unnoble, magistrates, ministers, and people, and sundrie of them of my Christian acquaintance, on whose behalfe I daylie offer up unto God through Christ the duetie of thanks giving, perswading my self further, that there is upon the face of the earth a mightie number besides (though not known to me) whom God hath pleased in the multitude of his mercies doubtles, and for much good towards them and others in them, not onely to single and cull out as it were from the huge heape and wicked fellowship of the polluted and prophane, but richlie to replenish and adorne them (as it were with most precious pearles) with the singular graces of sound knowledge, stedfast faith, comfortable feeling, unfeigned obedience, and sundrie such like holie and heavenlie gifts. Amongst whom, your sexe rightly considered, and the place you have been in wisely respected, and your present estate well weighed, I know fewe matchable with you (good Madame, flatterie is farre from my words, I humbly thanke God for it, and I hope pride removed farre from your selfe in hearing your owne praise, as I with envie may bee from others as in regard of your due commendation) and not many to go beyond you. For though to be borne not onlie of worshipful parents, but of a sanctified stock, be some thing both before God and man; and though learned and holie education bee a good helpe towards the reformation of our corruption, and as it were the instilling of another nature into us; and though to be richlie joyned in holy matrimonie be a token doubtles of God's great favour and love; and though to have in the undefiled mariage bed, a blessed seed and lawfull issue, be special blessing and mercie from God; and though to leade and live a vertuous and unreproveable life in the sight of men (who are wont neglecting themselves, with evill and curious eyes to looke upon others) bee a happie thing (with all which favours you have by the divine providence, been even laden as it were in your birth, bringing up, youth, old age, virginitie, mariage, widowhood and posteritie); yet because many bee degenerate and start aside from their ancestors' godlines; and some through carelesnes cause to perish the cost that hath been bestowed upon them in good bringing up; and others make themselves both in single and maried life lothsome to the Lord, and infamous before men, because either they have not begun well, or have not held on unto the end; and other some by evill example, have done the children of their wombe more hurt in the world, than they have done them good in bringing them foorth to behold the light of the sunne; and other some have added to the weakenes of their sexe, not watchfulnes against sinne, as their duetie required, but laied the raines of their severall iniquities and manifold inticements to evill in their owne neckes; and many have misused their places of honor and credit to all licentiousnes of the flesh, and carelesnes of God, and of the waies of his worship, and so consequently of eternal salvation; (from all which inconveniences and mischiefes the

Lord hath mercifullie kept you in everie condition of life wherein he hath been pleased to place you) me thinketh you have wherein to rejoyce, and that not onlie so much in the things themselves, freelie and plentifullie bestowed upon you, as in the happie continuance and mightie encrease of these his goodnesses in you, you also having received grace from God to beautifie them with an unblameable and holy conversation. By meanes whereof it is come to passe, that as you are much beloved at home in the midst of God's sainets and faithfull servants here, and these not onlie common professors, but many worthie ministers (for kindnes towards whom, and particularlie towards my selfe, I doo humblie here in all our names thanke God, and you as his gracious instrument), so you are made truely famous abroad in forraine Churches and countries, and highly reverenced of many worthie men there, indued doubtles with singular graces for God's glory, and the building up of the bodie of the fellowship of sainets. But what meane I to enter into this broad field of Christian commendation, where breath would rather faile me, and time I am sure, with abilitie to wade into it as I should, than matter any manner of way bee wanting. Give me leave therefore (good Madame), I beseech you, to desist from your praise (which I knowe you doo not willingly heare, though it be deserved as on your part, and though perhaps it might bee as a quicke spurre in the dull sides of others to provoke them to good things) and to turne my speach to exhortation rather and comfort. The course that you are entered into, and the race that now you have a long time runne in, is holie and honorable. Hold on therfore in the same chearefullie, notwithstanding the manifold hinderances that within and without bee cast in your way to turne you aside, if it might be; and bee not wearie of well doing at any hand, for as you knowe that your profession requireth it, so God hath promised that the time will come wherein you shall reape (as the sainets of God have done before you), if you faint not. Let the assured faithfulnes and infinite power of him, that hath in his word made you large promises, be a pricke unto you herein. And forasmuch as he hath given you grace to begin well, and to hold on hetherto, doubt not, but he hath both the will and the deed in his owne hands to bestowe them where and as it pleaseth him, will make perfect in you every good worke, even till the day of Jesus Christ. Is it possible, that that incorruptible crowne of eternall glorie, which in his onely beloved he hath prepared for you, should fade away? Upon these things, I beseech you (having cast away worldly cares), fixe continuallie the eye of your faith, that you may end your old yeeres in the Lord's peace, and be indeed gathered unto your fathers comfortablie, saying, as that holie apostle old Paule saied, 'I have fought a good fight, I have finished my course, I have kept the faith; from hence forth there is laied up for me

the crowne of righteousnes, which the Lord the righteous judge shall
give me at that day; and not to me onely, but unto all them also that
love his appearing'.[180] Your learned father, your honorable husband,
your loving brother, your deare sisters some of them, and (if I bee
not deceived) some also of your owne holie seede (all of them having
yeelded up their spirites in the faith and feare of God) are I doubt not
gone thether before you;[181] and why should you your selfe, or any other
thinke that you should be sundred from them? As for the lengthning
of your life, above many before reckoned, surely God hath done it
for his owne glorie, and the good of his Church, into which also you
being religiouslie gathered as a sound member thereof, you have even
in that an assured testimonie given unto you, that warfaring here with
his saincts as you doo, against sinne, the world and the divell, you
shall in good time, through him that hath loved you and washed you
in his bloud, become more than a conqueror, and eternallie truimph
together with them and the rest in heaven. Till which time, as I rest
resolved, that God the author and perfecter of every good thing in
all his, will not withdrawe his gracious hand from you in any grace,
speciallie spirituall and heavenlie. So I am certainlie perswaded that
manie such as are led by his spirit, and know you in Christ Jesus, and
love you in the trueth, will not (God ayding them) neglect any duetie
either outward or inward, that possiblie they can performe to further
that worke. Amongst whom I, though the least and most unworthie,
as in respect of my selfe, yet tied thereto by the duetie of my profession
from God, and bound to it by sundrie favours received from you,
will in my poore measure strive to do, though not so much as others,
neither yet so much as I owe (which I freelie acknowledge as being
privie to mine owne disabilitie and insufficiencie that way, and not
utterlie unacquainted with other men's fulnes and unheaped store)
yet what God hath or shal be pleased to enable me to accomplish.
Which that your good Ladiship may be the better assured of, I am
bold now to present unto you, and to publish under your name some
short notes and meditations of mine (long since written for the dearest
friend I had in the world) uppon that worthie booke of Salomon's
Proverbes. What it is, I leave to you, and the Church of God to judge of;
and yet this much I hope I may without pride protest, that though it

---

[180]**I have ... appearing** 2 Timothy 4:7–8.
[181]**holie seede ... before you** Two of Anne's daughters, Mary and Susan, had died
in infancy. See *Cooke Sisters*, p. 208.

bee not exquisite like unto the worthie workes of manie Bezaleels[182] in our age, yet it is sound; and though it bee not finelie polished, either in fitnes of wordes, or great store of arte, yet the trueth it is I hope, and never a whit the more to be misliked, because it is naked and plaine, but the rather to be imbraced of God's people; who I hope will shewe me this favour, that as they wil not reject any good thing in it for any evil that may be found or suspected to be therin, neither yet admit any evil for the good's sake, but in a discerning spirit refuse the one and receive the other; so they will assist me with their praiers to God for the increase of any good thing that is within me, to God's glorie, and the benefite of his people; and in much love, according to the spirit of love wherwith they are replenished, either Christianly cover that which is amisse, or curteouslie cure it. And as for you (good Madame) though I rest perswaded that it shall bee well accepted of you, yet can I not but againe and againe beseech you to receive it, not only as from the hand, but as from the heart of him, who, if either his poore praiers in absence, or speach in presence, or any thing els either within him or without him, could any many manner of way, either further you, or answere some part of that Christian kindnes which he hath received from you, would not bee wanting in any duetie toward you or yours that God shal inable him to performe. Now the very God of peace sanctifie you throughout and grant that your whole spirit, soule and bodie may be kept blameles unto the comming of our Lord Jesus Christ. London, the xxv. of this September 1589.

> Your good Ladiship's, as very much bounden,
> so in al things very readie in Christ to his poore power,
> T.W., the Lord's unworthie servant.

---

[182]**Bezaleels** See Exodus 31:1–5.

22. *Anne Bacon to Anthony Bacon*, 3 February 1592

Holograph. LPL 653, fos 343r–344v. 2pp.
Endorsed (fo. 344v): lettre de Madame
Addressed (fo. 344v): To my sonne Antonie Bacon geve theis

The grace of God be dayly multiplied in yow, with mercy in Christ our Lorde.

That yow are retorned now at length, I am right glad.[183] God bless it to us both. But when I harde with all that Lawson, who I foresuspected stale hence unto yow, and so belyk hath wrought upon yow again to your hurt to serve his own turn as heretoofore, how welcome that cowld be to your long greeved mother, judg yow.[184] I can hardly say whether your gowt or his company was the worse tidings. I have entreated this gentleman Mr Faunt[185] to do somuch kindnes for me as to jorny to yow, because your brother is preparing your loging at Grayes Inn very car[e]fully for yow. I thanke God that Mr Faunt was willing so to do and was very glad because he is not only an honest gentleman in civill behavour, but one that feareth God in dede and wyse with all having experience of our state and is able to advyse yow both veri wysely and frendly. For he loveth yourselff and needeth ˆnotˆ yours as others have and yet dissemble with yow. He doth me pleasure in this, for I cowlde not have fownde another so very mete for yow and me in all the best and most necessary respects. Use him therafter, goode sonne, and make much of such and of their godly and sownde ˆfrendlyˆ cownsell. This one cheffest cownsell your christian and naturall mother doth geve yow, even before the Lorde, that above all worldely respects yow carie yourself even at your first coming as one that doth unfeinedly profess the tru religion of Christ and hath the love of the truth now by long continuance fast settled in your hart and that with judgment, wysedome and discretion, and are not ether afrayd or ashamed to testify[186] the same by hearing and delighting in those religious exercises of the syncerer sort, be they French or

---

[183]**That ... glad** After bad weather delayed his crossing, Anthony Bacon landed at Dover on 4 February 1592.

[184]**But ... judg yow** Anne had long mistrusted Thomas Lawson, an English Catholic, and Anthony later alleged that his mother was the reason for Lawson's ten-month imprisonment in 1588. For more details, see the Introduction, p. 12.

[185]**Mr Faunt** Nicholas Faunt, secretary to Francis Walsingham and then William Cecil, Lord Burghley, had met Anthony Bacon in Paris in 1580 and they had remained friends and long-term correspondents.

[186]**ashamed to testify** 2 Timothy 1:8: 'Be not thou therefore ashamed of the testimony of our Lord'.

Englysh.[187] *In hoc noli adhibe^re^ fratrem tuum ad consilium aut exemplum, sed plus dehinc.*[188] Yf yow wylbe wavering (which God forbid, God forbyd) yow shall have examples and ill encoragers to many in these dayes and that αρch βισhοπ[189] since he was βουλευτὴσ ἐστὶ ἀπολεία τῆσ εκκλησιασ μεθ ἡμῶν, φιλεῖ γαρ την ἑαυτοῦ δοξαν πλεον τησ δοξησ τοῦ χρίστου.[190] Beware therfore and be constant in godly profession withowt faynting and that from your hart. For formalitee wanteth none with us but to ^to^ common. Be not readi of speche nor talk sodenly but where discretion reqwireth and that soberly then. For the propertie of our world is to sownde one at first comming and after to contemn. Curtesy is necessary, but common, too common familiaritee in talkyng and words is veri unprofitable and not withowt hurttaking *ut nunc sunt tempora.*[191] Remember yow have no father and yow have litle inowgh, yf not too litle regarded your kinde and no symple mother's holsome advyse from time to time. And as I do impute all most humbly to the grace of God whatsoever he hath bestowed upon me, so dare I affirme it had ben goode for yow everi way yf yow had followed it long er this. But God is the same who is able to heale both mynd and bodie, whome in Christ I besech to be your mercyfull Father and to take care of yow, gwyding yow with ~~holy~~ his holy and most comfortable spirit, now and ever. אמן.[192]

Let not Lawson, that foxe, be acqwainted with my lettres. I disdayn both it ^and^ him. He commonly opened undermyningly all lettres sent to yow from cowncell or frends. I know it and yow may to much yf God open your eyes, as I trust he wyll. Send it back to be sure by Mr Faunt sealed. But he wyll prye and prattle. So fare yow well and the Lorde bless yow and kepe yow from evell.

3 February.

Your mother,
ABacon.

[187]**be they French or Englysh** Anne's support of the French Stranger Church in London is extolled in other letters. See also **138** and **142**.

[188]*In ... plus dehinc* [Latin] 'In this, do not follow your brother's counsel or example. But more hereafter'.

[189]α**ρch β**ισ**h**οπ [partial Greek transliteration] 'Arch bishop'. John Whitgift had been the Archbishop of Canterbury since 1583.

[190]β**ουλευτὴσ** ... χ**ρίστου** [Greek] 'councillor, he is the destruction of the Church among us, for he loves his own glory more than the glory of Christ'.

[191]*ut ... tempora* [Latin] 'as the times are now'.

[192]אמן [Hebrew] 'Amen'.

I trust yow with your servants use prayour twyse in a day having ben where Reformation is. Omitt it not for eny. It wilbe your best credit to serve the Lorde duly and reverently and yow wylbe observed at first now. Your brother is to negligent herin. But do yow well and zealously. It wilbe lookt for of the best ^learned^ sorte and that is best.

23. *Francis Bacon to Anne Bacon*, 18 February 1592

Copy. LPL 648, fos 8r–9v. 2pp.
Endorsed (fo. 9v): Mr Francis Bacon to my Lady Bacon 1591

Madame, Alderman Haywood[193] is deseassed this nyght; his eldest sonne is fallen ward. My Lord Treasorer doth not for the most part hastely dispose of wardes.[194] It were woorth the obtayning if it were but in respect of the widow, who is a gentlewoman much commended. Your Ladyship hath never had any ward of my Lordship. It was to early for my brother to begynne with a sute to my Lord before he had seen his Lordship. And for me, I dar[195] at this tyme reserve my Lord to be my frend with the Queen. It may please your Ladyship to move my Lord and to promise to be thankful to any other my Lord oweth pleasure unto. Thear would be no tyme lost hearin. And so I most humbly take my leave.

From my lodging this xviii of February 1591.

Your Ladyship's most obedient sonne,
Francis Bacon.

[193]**Alderman Haywood** It would seem that Francis is referring to Sir Rowland Hayward, as he was the only Hayward/Haywood to serve as a London alderman in the sixteenth century. However, Hayward died on 5 December 1593, so Francis may have been given incorrect information. For sixteenth-century London aldermen, see A.B. Beaven, *The Aldermen of the City of London* (London, 1908), pp. 17–224.
[194]**My Lord ... wardes** Lord Burghley was master of the Court of Wards from 1561 to 1598.
[195]**dar** dare.

24. *Anne Bacon to Anthony Bacon*, 28 February 1592

Holograph. LPL 648, fos 6r–7v. 2pp.
Endorsed (fo. 7v.): lettre de Madame 1591
Addressed (fo. 7v): To my sonne Antony Bacon at Grayes Inne

Gratiam et salutem in Christo.[196]

I am looking for Redborn writings.[197] Yow will not think how loth most part of the neybours be yow shulde sell it away. Some cownsell rather to lease it is much better. They cownsell to sell Colney Chappell[198] and Meriden lease[199] or some such smaller thing. Thowgh less did ryse, yet one might borow some. God sende yow above all his true feare in your hart and goode health to do your long discontinued duty to her Majestie and cowntry. I pray yow be carefull and kepe goode diet and order. It is here marvelous colde and sharpe, too sharpe yet for yow, I think. On Thursday or ~~Wensday~~ Fryday I mean to be at London, yf the Lorde wyll be so. Many syck hereabowte and one of my howsholde since I came. Yf I come not shortly, I wyll send your boy, who is trobled with colde and wylling to be with yow. I wolde gladly yow had well seene her Majestie but be in some goode state of health fyrst and regard it carefully for eny, with God his blessing. The Lorde kepe yow both from evell and gwyde your wayes to please him and encrease your health. Looke well to your servaunts and ^to^ your own things.

Gorhambury *ultimo Februarii*[200] 1591.

Your mother,
ABacon.

---

[196]*gratiam . . . Christo* [Latin] 'Grace and salutations in Christ'.
[197]**I am . . . writings** Redbourn rectory was purchased by Nicholas Bacon I in 1560. See *Wealth of the Gentry*, p. 48. Anthony's inheritance of the lease had caused much dispute with his half-brothers, Nicholas and Nathaniel Bacon. See **15**.
[198]**Colney Chappell** Colney Chapel in Hertfordshire was held in fee by Anthony Bacon. See *VCH, A History of the County of Hertford*, 2 vols (London, 1908), II, p. 269; *Wealth of the Gentry*, p. 102.
[199]**Meriden lease** Nicholas Bacon had leased meads in Meriden (also known as 'Meryden' and 'Laggershott') in Warwickshire. See *Stiffkey*, II, p. 39. The lease was bringing in £8 a year in 1579, when the meads first came into Anthony's possession. See LPL 647, fo. 97r.
[200]*ultimo Februarii* [Latin] 'the last day of February'.

25. *Anne Bacon to Anthony Bacon*, 2 **March 1592**

Holograph. LPL 648, fos 12r–13v. 2pp.
Endorsed (fo. 13v): lettre de Madame, ma mere datee du 2 de mars 1591
Addressed (fo. 13v): To my sonne Anthony Bacon

Gratia in Christo.[201]

The goodeman Finch[202] amongst others is desirous to se yow and commeth purposely. Yt may be yow remember him. When yow are better acqwainted with him and can rightly judg yow shall have cause to lyke well of him. He is carefull for my business, honest and trusty; I thank God for him. I cannot yet go hence as I thowght. Lawrence[203] partly can tell. I wolde gladly here how all things go with yow; I wrote lately to yow. Beleve not everyone that speakes fayre to yow at your fyrst comming. It is to serve their turn. When your health and leisure serveth to be here, yow shall know diversites of frend by dealing in your absence and yet 'My yowng master' in their mowths. I commende yow both to the grace of God in Christ Jesu, who bless yow and kepe yow from evell.

Gorhambury 2 *Martii* 1591. Regard your health and serve the Lorde in truth.

Your mother,
ABacon.

26. *Anne Bacon to Anthony Bacon*, 17 **May 1592**

Holograph. LPL 648, fos 167r–168v. 2pp.
Endorsed (fo. 168v): Lettre de Madame ma mere de Gorambery receue ce 18eme may 1592
Addressed (fo. 168v): To my sonne Anthonie Bacon

God bless yow dayly more and more both in sowle and bodie. I send to know how yow do. For my selff I am but *languescens*[204] but in goode

<hr/>

[201] *Gratia in Christo* [Latin] 'Grace in Christ'.
[202] **goodeman Finch** John Finch (d. 1593) of Nicholls and Butler's Farm, Redbourn.
[203] **Lawrence** Lawrence was later described by Francis Bacon as a 'servant' of his mother's (**91**). The Lawrences were a large family in St Albans and were closely involved with town affairs; John Lawrence had served as mayor in 1575. For the Lawrence family, see *Corporation Records*, pp. 19, 21, 29, 32, 42–43, 48.
[204] *languescens* [Latin] 'Languishing' was a term associated with illness at this time. See *OED*.

chere and comfort, I thank God. The goodeman Rolff,[205] my tenant at Burston[206] but lately recovered, is desyrous to see yow. He is an honest man and a kinde tenant and of discretion and dealing. I sent my man Bury to direct him and to see yow and your brother, how it is with yow both. I humbly thank God for the comfortable company of Mr Wyborn and Wylblud.[207] Thei may greatly be afraide of God his displeasure which worke the woefull disapointing of God his worke in his vineyarde[208] by putting such to silence in these bowlde sinning dayes. *Haud impune ferent*,[209] come when it shall. God encrease in yow true knowledg and stablish[210] your hart in the love of his eternall truth. ^*Cura ut valeas*^.[211] Gorhamburi 17 *Maii* 1592.

Your mother, ABacon.

Think on your lettre wysely. Be not overruled still ~~with~~ by subtile and hurtfull hangers on.

---

[205] **goodeman Rolff** The Rolfe family was spread throughout the surrounding area. William Rolfe, a mercer, was mayor of St Albans in 1573 and 1586; his son, Rafe, was also a member of the Mercers' Company. Given that Anne describes goodman Rolfe as 'honest' and 'kind', it is unlikely that he is James Rolfe, official to the archdeaconry of St Albans. Rolfe is not recorded as a tenant in the 1569 survey of Burston. See *Corporation Records*, pp. 16, 16, 21, 32, 39, 43, 55, 292; H. Chauncey, *The Historical Antiquities of Hertfordshire* (London, 1826), p. 394; HALS XI/2.

[206] **Burston** Nicholas Bacon was granted Burston manor in 1545, along with Thomas Skipwith. Bacon received licence to alienate the manor in 1566. See *VCH, A History of the County of Hertford*, 2 vols (London, 1908), II, p. 425.

[207] **Mr Wyborn and Wylblud** Percival Wyborn and Humphrey Wilblood (sometimes known as Wildblood) were both godly preachers who had been deprived of their livings for their nonconformity. Wyborn had been appointed as a household chaplain by Nicholas Bacon in 1560 and Gorhambury continued to offer him a refuge during Anne's widowhood. Wyborn stayed at Gorhambury at various points throughout the early 1590s, assisting the household in its spiritual edification. Anne Bacon appointed Wilblood to the living of Redbourn on 25 November 1589, but he was deprived in 1592, although remaining in Hertfordshire under Anne's household patronage. He was licensed again in 1594 to officiate and teach in the archdeaconry, but was forbidden from preaching or acting as a schoolmaster. Through Anne's intercession, he was eventually instituted to the living of Pinner vicarage in 1601. See *Cooke Sisters*, pp. 176–177, 180–181.

[208] **his worke in his vineyarde** The parable of the wicked husbandmen is told in Matthew 21:33–46, Mark 12:1–12, and Luke 20:9–19.

[209] *Haud impune ferent* [Latin] 'they will not escape unpunished'.

[210] **stablish** establish.

[211] *Cura ut valeas* [Latin] 'Take care of your health'.

27. *Anne Bacon to Anthony Bacon,* 24 May 1592

Holograph. LPL 648, fo. 172r–v. 1p.
Endorsed (fo. 172v): lettre de Madame ma mere, de Goramberi, ce 27eme may 1592
Addressed (fo. 172v): To my sonne Antony Bacon at Grayes Inn

Gratia et salus.[212]
    That yow encrease in amending I am glad, God continue it every way. When yow cease of your prescribed diet, yow had nede I think to be very warie both of your soden chang of qwantite and of season of your feading, specially suppers late or full. Procure rest in convenient time. It helpeth much to digestion. I verely think your brother's weake stomack to digest hath ben much ~~begun~~ caused and confirmed by untimely ^late^ going to bed and then musing *nescio quid*[213] when he shuld slepe and then in conseqwent by late rising and long lyeing in bed. Wherby his men are made slewthfull and himselff continuall syckly. But my sonns hast not to harken to their mother's goode cownsell in time to prevent. The Lord ^our heavenly Father^ heale and bless yow both as his sonns in Christ Jesu.
    I promyss yow towching your coch, yf it be so to your contentation, it was not wysdome to have ^it^ seene and known at the coorte.[214] Yow shulbe so much preased to lende and your man for gayn so ready to agree that the discomodite theroff wylbe as much ^as^ the comoditie. I wolde your health had ben such as yow neded not to have provided a coche but for a wyffe, but the wyll of God be don. Yow were best to excuse yow by me that I have desired the use of it, because as I fele it to true. My going is allmost spent and must be fain to be bowlde with yow.
    It is lyke Robert Baylye and his sonne have ben to seeke some commoditee of yow. The father hath ben but an ill tenant to the wodd and a wayward payer and hath forfayted his bonde, which I entende not to lett slipp. His sonne a dissolute yowng man and both crafty. Lykewyse yowng Carpenter[215] may sue to be your man. Be not hasty. Yow shall finde such yowng men prowd and bowlde and of no servyce but charg and discredit. Be advised. Overshoote not your selff undiscretely. I tell yow, plain folk in apperence wyll qwickly comber one here and they wyll all seek to abuse your want of experience by so

[212] ***Gratia et salus*** [Latin] 'Grace and health'.
[213] ***nescio quid*** [Latin] 'I know not what'.
[214] **towching … the coorte** For Anne's advice regarding the use of the coach, see also **28**.
[215] **yowng Carpenter** Presumably either Thomas or Anthony Carpenter; their father, Edward, died in 1597. The 1609 survey reveals that Thomas held considerable lands in Redbourn. His brother, Anthony, surrendered three acres of meadows to the trustees of Francis Bacon in 1620. See HALS X/C/7/A and 'Catalogue of field names', p. 30.

long absence. Be not hasty but understand well first your own state.
There was never less kindeness in tenants commonly then now.

Vale in Christo,[216]
24 *Maii* 1592.
Your mother, ABacon.

Let not your men see my lettres. I write to yow and not to them.

Yf yow nede eny writings from hence, let me know in time. I stay
till next weke because of a coort, yf the steward can.[217] *Cura ut valeas.*[218]

28. *Anne Bacon to Anthony Bacon*, 29 May 1592

Holograph. LPL 648, fo. 178r–v. 1p.
*Endorsed (fo. 178v): Lettre de Madame ma mere le 29eme may 1592 l[e] Willam
Hoult.*[219]
Addressed (fo. 178v): To my sonne Antony

I am glad and thank God of your amendement. But my man sayde
he harde yow rose at 3 of the clock. I thowght that was not well so
sodenly from bedding much to rise so early, newly owt of your diett.
Extremitees be hurtfull to whole, more to the syckly. Yf yow be not wyse
and discrete for your diett and seasoning of your doings, yow wylbe
weakish, I feare, a goode while. Be wyse and godly too and discern
what is goode and what not for your health. Avoyde extremitees. What
a great fawt[220] were it in yow to take colde to hinder your amendment
being not compelled but upon voluntary indiscretion. Seing the cost
^of phisick^ is much, your payn long, your amendement slow and your
duty not yet done, geve none occasion by negligence. Yow go *ut vulgo
dicitur*[221] of your own errand. I lyke not your lending your coch yet to
eny Lorde or Ladie. Yf yow once begin yow shall hardely end; but
that in hope yow shall shortly use it, I wolde it were here to shun all
offending. It was not well it was so soone ^sene^ at coort to make talk
and at last be mocked or mislyked. Tell your brother I cowncell yow

---

[216] *Vale in Christo* [Latin] 'Farewell in Christ'.
[217] **I stay . . . steward can** The lord of the manor appointed the steward as the presiding officer in English manor courts. For more details, see the Introduction, p. 32.
[218] *Cura ut valeas* [Latin] 'Take care of your health'.
[219] *Lettre . . . Hoult* [French] 'Letter from the mistress, my mother, the 29 May 1592, [delivered] by William Hoult'. There is an additional endorsement in the same hand on this folio, repeating '*lettre de Madame, 1592*'.
[220] **fawt** fault.
[221] *ut vulgo dicitur* [Latin] 'as it is commonly said'.

to send it no more. What had my Lady Shrewssbury[222] to borow your coche; your man for mony and sombody elce for their ^vain^ credit wyll work yow but displeasure and loss and they have thanks. *Disce sapere huius modii rebusque et ne quid temere.*[223] In hast, late this Sabbath.

Vale et cura ut valeas et Deo placens.[224]

AB.

29. *Anne Bacon to Anthony Bacon*, 29 June 1592

Holograph. LPL 648, fo. 177r–v. 1p.
Endorsed (fo. 177v): lettre de Madame 1592

Grace and health. I am very glad yow draw to a goode ende. Er yow deale with Mr Elsdon I pray yow regarde my due which is a C li at Michall tyde.[225] L marks due last Annunciation,[226] the C marks for the next now at harde frutes.[227] I have had great comber and evell payment and wyll not folyshly at thend loose by craft. Yf yow deale with Elsdon, be very well advised. For he is heat and peradventure stepp over and geve yow the lurch at a pinch. Be wyse and circumspect; these days are full of fraude.

My man sayde yow ~~wolde~~ ^wyshed to^ have strawberies ^to still^.[228] I have sent, I thinke, all there be ^and^ this day gathred. I had ~~had~~ ment to ^have^ stilled for my selff, but they be as well thus. I sende them by the boy of my kitchen, a shrewd witted boy and pretely caterchised, but yet an ~~unhappy~~ untowarde ^crafty^ boy. He wyll mark, I warrant, yow throwghly. I looke for him again at night. I pray yow stay him not. I have so charged him. He is able inowgh to do it, God wylling. Do not pitie; it wyll make him worse. Yf yow geve him vi d of your own selff, it is too much. Let me know towching yow and towching me as yow

---

[222]**Lady Shrewssbury** Presumably Mary Talbot, the countess of Shrewsbury, rather than Elizabeth Talbot (Bess of Hardwick), the dowager countess.

[223]***Disce ... temere*** [Latin] 'Learn to be wise in matters of this kind and to do nothing rashly'.

[224]***Vale ... placens*** [Latin] 'Farewell, take care of your health, and please God'.

[225]**Michall tyde** 29 September, the feast of St Michael the Archangel, was one of the quarter days, the days on which payments were traditionally due.

[226]**Annunciation** 25 March, Lady Day, was the feast of the Annunciation of the Virgin Mary, another quarter day.

[227]**harde frutes** Lammastide, 1 August, was the feast of the First Fruits and one of the cross-quarter days, which fell between the quarter days of the year.

[228]**strawberies to still** Distillations of strawberries were thought to have numerous medicinal properties, including treating inflammation of the bladder and of the feet and hands. Anthony Bacon may therefore have used such distillations to treat his gout and kidney stones. See N. Culpeper, *The English Physitian Enlarged* (London, 1653), p. 347.

have cause. It is here very hote in dede. Let not your men drink wyne this hote wether, nor your brother's nether; tell him. Diverse syck of hote agews.[229] God kepe us sownd in the fayth and send us health and a care to please God above all.

All ^the^ strawberyes were gatherd in the oke woodd. None or as none in garden and orchard. It is ever hote and dry here. I thank your brother for Mr Wylblud. Much goode may he do for such and take no hurt by the others, I pray God. Impart this because I mean to both my lettre. God ever bless yow both in Christ our Lord. Gorhambury 29 *Junii* 92.

Your mother,
ABacon.
Χηρα.[230]

Let none other see this.
Do yow think on your stock with Burbage.[231] I heare he challengeth liberally your father.

30. *Anne Bacon to Anthony Bacon*, 6 July 1592

Holograph. LPL 648, fo. 200r–v. 1p.
Endorsed (fo. 200v): lettre de Madame 1592

I pray God yow have don well and wysely. I feare yow have yealded to th[a]t which was first shott at, I meane Barly.[232] Mr Maynarde's[233] frendshipp is then less to be accompted of in that ~~point~~ ^dealing^, yf he alse[234] were sowght in thother to drive to that. I am sory for it and must nedes be worse for yow as I yet can think.

---

[229]**hote agews** fevers.
[230]*Χηρα* [Greek] 'widow'.
[231]**Burbage** William or, more likely, his son, Edward Burbage. William was the troublesome tenant of Pinner park and farm, a property left to Anthony by his father. See D. du Maurier, *Golden Lads: a study of Anthony Bacon, Francis and their friends* (London, 1975), pp. 45, 48, 51. Anthony took Edward Burbage into his service, although he admitted that he suffered much 'unthankfulness' from the younger Burbage. *Ibid.*, p. 102.
[232]**Barly** Barley in Hertfordshire, comprising the manors of Abbotsbury, Minchenbury, and Hores, which Anthony Bacon inherited from his father. The negotiations to sell Barley were not concluded until late 1593. See *Wealth of the Gentry*, p. 102; 'Money-lenders', p. 241.
[233]**Mr Maynarde's** Henry Maynard, who served as a secretary first to Nicholas Bacon I and, after his death, to his brother-in-law, Lord Burghley. See R.C. Barnett, *Place, Profit, and Power: a study of the servants of William Cecil, Elizabethan statesman* (Chapel Hill, NC, 1969), pp. 94–103.
[234]**alse** likewise.

Baithforde sayd yow desyred some moe[235] straburies ^sende^.[236]
Almost the last throwgh stealers. The weather here is veri hote and
dry and seasonable rayn wyshed, if it please God, by whose wyll and
favour I mean to be at London on Saturday next upon some cause.

The uppermost ^straburis[237]^ are goode to be eaten and were more
choycely gatherd for that purpose for yow or your brother. The Lorde
direct yow both with his holy spirit and bless yow.

6 July 1592 Gorhambury.

Your mother,
ABacon
and
late Lordkeper's wydow.

31. *Anne Bacon to Anthony Bacon*, 14 July [1592][238]

Holograph. LPL 653, fos 326r–327v. 2pp.
Endorsed (fo. 327v): lettre de Madame

Grace and health.

I sende ^to^ yow, sonne, by this boy bearer to know your
determynation, with God his mercy and favour. When, what and how
in dede I mistooke it when yow spake of one your page, as yow called,
but after I remembred he is tall and not one of your litle boyes. Write
what yow wolde I send, and when and whether yow have eny stuff
sent upon Monday that I may send for it upon Tewsday to the town.
Make it readie yf yow do send, upon ~~to morow~~ Saturday because of
the Sabbath. Knight[239] knowes the order. I sende yow pescodds.[240] I
think ~~not veri goode~~ better for your frende then your selff. Byd they
be tenderly soden[241] because they be great. I wolde be loth to encrease
your payn eny way but yf yow tast, let it be at diner and not at night
and soden in goode care.

A few strawburies, pease of the first and those of the last almos[t
ha]d. God bless yow both and kepe yow from synn and evell. Wryte

---

[235]**moe** more.
[236]**sende** sent.
[237]**straburis** strawberries.
[238]**14 July [1592]** The internal references in this undated letter to Knight and to Peter
are inexact. The letter has been placed here owing to Anthony's request on the 29 June
1592 for strawberries (**29**), although it could equally date from another year.
[239]**Knight** Thomas and Robert Knight both initially served Nicholas and Anne Bacon
as 'grooms ordinary'. See *Stiffkey*, II, p. 55. By the 1590s, it seems that Thomas still served
Anne at Gorhambury, while Robert Knight served her son Anthony. Thomas Knight acted
as a juror for the Gorhambury manorial court in 1596. See HALS X/B/3/A.
[240]**pescodds** peas (in the pod).
[241]**soden** boiled.

your mynde and forbyd the boy of speche. Peter[242] and the other must nedes go on foote. Yow wyl[l] go but softly. Let me know perfectly as yow may. I look for the boy at night; dispatch him, I pray yow. Many wycked stalkers abroad. 14 July Gorhambury.

Your mother,
AB.

32. *Anne Bacon to Anthony Bacon*, 24 July 1592

Holograph. LPL 648, fos 196r–197v. 2pp.
Endorsed (fo. 197v): lettre de Madame 1592
Addressed (fo. 197v): To my sonne Antony Bacon at Grayes Inne

I thank yow for your lettre but I understand not that one cheffe point, nor do not desyre yet. But yow had nede be veri circumspect and wyse. Beware in such matters how yow venture before yow be called by God and your prince. I assure yow I aske not, nor know not where Lawson ^is^. But this I cownsell. Be very ware that his veri subtile and working head work not to your comber. Yow have ben long absent and by your sickliness cannot be your own agent and so wanting right judgment of our state may be much deceaved. That which yow did for the merchannts was scantly well taken and fell not owt as yow looked;[243] and I remember once yow dealt ^with Matinian[244]^, I wot ^not^ now, wherfore it is a goode whyle since, but both envy and also dislyke did appere. Some dowting your sowndeness in religion, yow were so great with some ^such^ great papists then. Have a sure warrant and grownd, least yow may purchase encombrance withowt goode success contrary to your expectation. Be not to bowlde with $\kappa\upsilon\rho\iota\omega\ \theta\eta\sigma\alpha\upsilon\rho\alpha\rho\iota\omega$.[245] Loose not his $\varphi\iota\lambda\iota\alpha\nu$,[246] yow know what I mean. God geve yow understanding in the best things and direct your

---

[242] **Peter** Presumably Peter the cook, mentioned in **32**, and not 'petit Pierre', a servant of Anthony Bacon's.

[243] **That . . . yow looked** Anthony Bacon had attempted to help the English merchants in the French town of Blaye in obtaining passage up the river Garonne to Bourdeaux. However, some of the merchants repudiated his efforts, with one of them apparently stating that Anthony Bacon had no authority to meddle in the matter, either from the Privy Council or from the merchants themselves. See R. Wernham (ed.), *List and Analysis of State Papers: foreign series III: June 1591–April 1592* (London, 1980), p. 358.

[244] **Matinian** Presumably a reference to Jacques de Goyon, comte de Matignon, the lieutenant-general of Henri III, who protected Anthony in Bordeaux against accusations that he was the 'receptacle of all rebellious Huguenots, [his] pen their intelligencer and director of their commotions'. See *Troubled Life*, pp. 92–93. This word is, however, much obscured by the binding.

[245] $\kappa\upsilon\rho\iota\omega\ \theta\eta\sigma\alpha\upsilon\rho\alpha\rho\iota\omega$ [Greek] 'lord treasurer', William Cecil, Lord Burghley.

[246] $\varphi\iota\lambda\iota\alpha\nu$ [Greek] 'friendship'.

mynde to walk wysely and religiously. Be not overcredulous nor to open. *Sub omni lapide latet anguis.*[247] Get health to serve God and your cowntry as he shall enable and call yow. And so the Lorde multiply his grace in yow with goode health to please him in all things. I thowght goode to write thus much unto yow. *Cogita tu ipsi.*[248] Cast it not abowt to be seene. When yow can welcome in the Lorde, send me worde. *Vale et bene vale.*[249] Gorhambury 24 *Julii* 1592.

Your moother,
ABacon.

I malice not thowgh to justly must mislyke Lawson, but take yow great heede he still play not upon yow to serve more him selff then your goode. No ill warning this. Be not yet too forward in state matters. Wyse have withdrawn *hisce diebus.*[250] On Monday last week Grimell and Ayre came hether as yow appoinnted thei sayde and this Monday one browght hether for yow from Mr Gray dosen ½ pigeons, whereof I send yow the doson and ii caponetts and ii ducklins, which I send all by Peter, my cooke. I wolde your brother's cooke were lyke him in Christian behavour and yet a yowng man and mery. Geve him a shilling because he had goode wyll to cary them on foote.

AB.

33. *Anne Bacon to Anthony Bacon*, 25 December [1592 or later][251]

Holograph. LPL 653, fo. 366r–v. 1p.
Endorsed (fo. 366v): lettre de Madame

I have sent *even invita*[252] ii hoggsheds[253] of my howsehold bere, which I cowlde very yll spare having but litle store for ii places. I much rather

---

[247] *Sub . . . anguis* [Latin] 'A snake lurks under every stone'. Anne seems to be conflating various proverbs here. Virgil records the line *'Latet anguis in herba'* ('A snake lies hidden in the grass') in his *Eclogues*, whereas Erasmus records the adage *'Sub omni lapide scorpius dormit'* ('Under every stone sleeps a scorpion') in his *Adagia*. See Virgil, *Eclogues*, 3.93; D. Erasmus, *Adages: Iı to Iv100*, ed. R.A.B. Mynors, *Collected Works of Erasmus*, XXXI (Toronto, 1982), p. 344.
[248] *Cogita tu ipsi* [Latin] 'Take heed of yourself'.
[249] *Vale et bene vale* [Latin] 'Farewell and goodbye'.
[250] *hisce diebus* [Latin] 'these days'.
[251] **25 Dec [1592 or later]** Rudolph Bradley was appointed as vicar of Redbourn in October 1592, so this letter could not have been written before 25 December 1592, but equally could date from a later December.
[252] *even invita* [Latin] 'reluctantly'.
[253] **hoggsheds** hogsheads. A hogshead was a large vessel for holding liquids.

desyred your aboad. I do not heare that Mr Trott[254] or eny other such gentleman is with yow, elce I wolde have sent yow a peece or two brawn, but I know your selff eates none and I do not mean Barnes shulde make it scambling[255] breakfast meate.

I harde avowched that Mr Bradley[256] did not preach this day. Ether he is excommunicat or two careless of his charg, specially among such a people who lyke eny save a faythfull and paynfull preacher. Now belyke Robin Hoode and Mayde Marian are to supply with their prophan partes, for leave is geven.

Well yf yow stayed here tyll after, yow had ~~ben~~ spent your tyme ^no dowt^ more comfortably and profitably ^every way^. Sneaking Smith babbells he wyll come and see yow and so moe[257] but yow know and I hope consider the best for yow. God bless yow and be with yow.

Avoyde and cura[258] yow sharpen not the gowt; ne te acrius tractet.[259] I send iiii pewter candlesticks. Gorhambury 25 December.

I am sory my men must loose the exercises of religion for carieng to morow. And besyd I am bownd to have my servants to go to the howse of God with me. For goode example too.

Your mother,
ABacon.

34. *Anne Bacon to Anthony Bacon*, 22 January 1593[260]

Holograph. LPL 649, fos 15r–16v. 2pp. Damaged.
Endorsed (fo. 16v): lettre de Madame dattee du 23eme de janvier 1593

I pray God direct your wayes to please him in all things and send yow health of body to able yow to performe goode things. Consider wysely your own state. Troble not your rest, nor breake it unseasonably in no wyse. Looke not for nedefull health yf yow leave not untymely watching and disordrying your naturall qwiett sleepe by occupieng your head owt of time and tune. Use not ^yet^ company at meales

[254]**Mr Trott** Nicholas Trott was a barrister at Gray's Inn and a long-term creditor of the Bacon brothers. See *History of Parliament*, III, pp. 531–532.
[255]**scambling** makeshift.
[256]**Mr Bradley** For more details about Bradley, see the Introduction, p. 26.
[257]**moe** Deride or mock, presumably to mock Anne.
[258]*cura* [Latin] 'you must take care'.
[259]*ne . . . tractet* [Latin] 'it should not tear you more sharply'.
[260]**22 January 1593** The dating of this letter is somewhat confusing as Anne wrote the date as 22 January 1592, whereas it is endorsed as 1593; presumably Anthony's secretary was here following the European practice of the year beginning on 1 January, not the English practice of starting the year on 25 March.

to make sytt long and to procure commers to your hurt. Eate not fruther²⁶¹ toyes after your meales to provoke superflous drinking; that use wyll brede but rawnes of stomack and make yow ˆlongˆ wearish. I pray be godly wyse to consider; be not to ready nor open in talk. *Sub omni ˆlatereˆ latet anguis his diebus.*²⁶² Because I hard yow mislyked your too strong drink, well may yow do so still and by observation yow shall finde it best for yow not to sharpen your gowt humour. Yet this present I sende yow ˆbereˆ brewed in September and above xvi weeks owlde or thereabowtes; I think it is not so heady as yours is and yet too strong alone for meate. I sende it throwgh by myn own cart, because it shuld not twyse trobled being so stale. Yf it come well to morow as I trust, anon after the settling in the seller,²⁶³ the vent wolde be qwyckly lyft upp and stopt strayte again. It is not lyke to work much because brewd so long and yf it had not ben styrred it wolde have lasted good tyll Easter, I think. Let it be well and after looke so for leaking or running after carriage and not ~~seet~~ sett too low behynde. Knight²⁶⁴ knowes well and wyll care. The other hogshed is of ordinary beere but ˆoneˆ a weeke owlde; not to be dronk these vi weeks onless²⁶⁵ cariag prevent by new working. The other hogshed I think may be dronk of after 3 dayes settling. Stale ordinary had I none but a cant²⁶⁶ in a pype vessell. Be your own taster; your men are ready to dysprayse your drink early upon no cawse (specially Jaqwes²⁶⁷ who can better skill of French water and wyne then Englysh beere) and to a syckly body it is not goode to dysprayse rashly and fondly, and be not to mixe in your tast, but judg aryght. The Lorde Jesus heale and helpe yow both and encrease his grace dayly in yow, and do well and wysely. 22 January 1592.

Your mother, ABacon.

Burn this.

---

²⁶¹**fruther** further.
²⁶²*Sub ... diebus* [Latin] 'A snake lurks under every stone these days'. See p. 111, n. 247.
²⁶³**seller** cellar.
²⁶⁴**Knight** Robert Knight. See p. 109, n. 239.
²⁶⁵**onless** unless.
²⁶⁶**cant** portion.
²⁶⁷**Jaqwes** Jacques Petit, Anthony's Gascon servant. See G. Ungerer, 'An unrecorded Elizabethan performance of Titus Andronicus', *Shakespeare Survey*, 14 (1961), pp. 102–109.

35. *Anne Bacon to Anthony Bacon*, 25 January 1593

Holograph. Latin and English. LPL 649, fo. 23r–v. 1p. Damaged.
*Endorsed (fo. 23v): lettre de Madame envyoie le maresihal et receue le 25eme de
janvier 1593*[268]

*Modo ˆpost meridiemˆ audivi oppidanos Albanenses elegisse denuo duo illos priores
burgessos, scilicet Conisbeum et Maynardum. Procull dubio ab initio ita statuerant,
videri tamen ˆvellentˆ captare benevolentiam tuam in offerendo. Sic astuti sunt et
dissimulantes egregie et plus experiendo senties. Profecto pro re ipsa non est ˆquodˆ
cures, pro modo tractandi, ne sis minus anxius, ˆnon tanti estˆ. Plures adhuc loci
sunt [. . .]. Cura ut bene valeas et animo et corpore, ne negligas statum tuum.
Deus propitius suo tempore te placido vultu respiciet. Interim sis bono animo,
prudens et cautus et nullo modo locum dato podagrae vell per cibum, potum, aut
intempestivas vigilias. Si semel solide convalescas, Deus dives est in misericordia et
ˆinˆ munificentia suis filiis. Hoc raptim.*

25 Januarii 1592.

Mater tua, ABacon.

I had written the above before my men returned. Truly I do nott
understande the inclosed writing. I pray yow sende in my name to the
Lord Treasurer by your brother. For I know not how to speak or write
to him in the matter. I send it herinclosed again. Shew your brother
this. It was sent in his lettre; it wold not be delayed.

[Translation]
Just after midday I heard that the townsmen from St Albans had
chosen once again those principal burgesses, namely Conisby and
Maynard.[269] Without doubt they had decided this from the beginning,
but they would wish to appear to capture your good will in making an
offer. They are so cunning and so good at pretence, as you will learn
more by experience. Undoubtedly you would not care for the thing
itself and not for the way of behaving. Do not be too anxious; it is not
of such great importance. There are still many places.[270] Make sure
you stay well, both physically and mentally, and do not neglect your
condition. God is on your side and in his time he will grant you his
favour. Meanwhile be of good spirit, be prudent and careful and do

[268] *lettre . . . de janvier 1593* [French] 'letter from the mistress, sent by the farrier, and
received on the 25th of January 1593'.
[269] **the townsmen . . . and Maynard** Humphrey Conisby and Ralph Maynard were
elected as MPs for St Albans in 1593, as they had been in 1586 and 1588–1589 and would
be again in 1597. See *Corporation Records*, p. 302.
[270] **There . . . places** Anthony Bacon was elected MP for Wallingford in Oxfordshire in
1593. See *History of Parliament*, I, p. 372.

not let your gout get the better of you, either by what you eat, drink, or through keeping late hours. Once you properly recover, God is rich in mercy and in generosity to his children. This in haste.

25 January 1592.

Your mother, ABacon.

36. *Anne Bacon to Anthony Bacon*, [5 February 1593][271]

Holograph. LPL 653, fo. 361r–v. 1p.
Endorsed (fo. 361v): lettre de Madame

Her Majestie, God his holy spirit be in her and direct her, is upon coming nere now to my Lord Tresurer's there to lodg this night. Mr H Clark[272] was to see me, and asking him whether he send not my pardons in therle of Lecester's tyme, he sayd he dyd and therle discharged it wylling withowt fyne.[273] His advise is I shuld bring to my Lord at my next going a ^some^ breff notes wherof and in what yeres and how and he sayth yf I wyll, he wyll follow this too as he dyd the other. He sayth he saved my profitt well ^then^. I pray yow show Mr Crew[274] thus much, for I wyll speak with my Lorde as soone as conveniently I may after her Majestie's going. I wold gladly have the writing to morow and I wyll sende for it as Mr Crew appoints me with the Lorde's goode

---

[271] **[5 February 1593]** The letter mentions both a pardon for alienation of land and a stay by the queen at one of Lord Burghley's houses. For the pardon for alientation, granted on 8 February 1593, see below, n. 273. It therefore seems that the letter must date from Elizabeth I's visit to Cecil House in London, which began on 5 February 1593; Anthony was still in France during the queen's 1591 progresses to the lord treasurer's properties. For Elizabeth's royal visits to Lord Burghley, see M. Hill Cole, *The Portable Queen: Elizabeth I and the politics of ceremony* (Amherst, MA, 1999), pp. 209–210.

[272] **Mr H Clark** Henry Clark was the receiver for Nicholas Bacon while lord keeper. See *Stiffkey*, II, p. 52.

[273] **Mr . . . withowt fyne** Nicholas Bacon I had acquired land from Ralph Rowlett by indenture on 23 July 1566, comprising the manors of Minchenbury, Abbotsbury, and Hores in Barley and the manor of Napsbury; Sir Ralph Rowlett's second wife had been Margaret Cooke, sister to Anne Bacon. A new indenture was issued between Henry Goodere and his wife, Rowlett's heirs, and Nicholas Bacon I on 1 May 1574, shortly before sentence for validity was passed on Rowlett's will. Nicholas Bacon did not obtain a licence to alienate these lands from Goodere, held in chief, which seems to be the cause of Anne's anxiety in this letter; **39** mentions the value of Napsbury and the Barley manors. A pardon was granted, for a fine of 20s., on 8 February 1593. See The National Archives, PRO 11/53, fo. 248r; C. Leighton (ed.), *Calendar of Patent Rolls 35 Elizabeth I, Part I to Part X* (Kew, 2000), p. 92.

[274] **Mr Crew** Thomas Crewe was a godly young lawyer. See A. Thrush (ed.), *The History of Parliament: the House of Commons, 1604–1629*, 3 vols (London, 2010), III, pp. 736–747.

wyll. The former sent by Mr Crew ^to^ Gorhambury I returned in next lettre to yow within 3 dayes after the receit.

Vale et cura ut bene valeas. Abstineto ab intempestivis horis in cena et in somno. Vigiliae debilitant vires et animi et corporis in valetudinariis noxi.[275]

37. *Anne Bacon to Anthony Bacon*, [*c.*5 February 1593][276]

Holograph. LPL 653, fo. 250r–v. 1p.
Endorsed (fo. 250v): lettre de Madame

Sonne, me thinke it were very nedefull that Mr Fuller[277] dyd see the notes. What thei be and in what maner and to have his certein cownsell with Mr Crewe's in what sort I were best to move my Lorde. As I remember it goeth in Mr Goodyere's name, but that was I take it to make the better and stronger assurance for his part as one of Sir Ralph Rowlett's herres.[278] To bedwarde. For hyndring your rest troble not your selff later but sure it were well to have his advyse, Mr Fuller's, set down plain for me. God bless us.

38. *Anne Bacon to Anthony Bacon*, [*c.*5 February 1593][279]

Holograph. LPL 653, fos 330r–331v. 2pp.
Endorsed (fo. 331v): lettre de Madame sans datte

Ever since I cam to my loging, save that I wrote a few wordes to my Lorde to that purpose as yow know, I have wayted at my Lord's chamber to have it delivered this night with promys for his so doing. For my Lord is both ill handled with the gowt and stomack syck with

---

[275] *Vale . . . noxi* [Latin] 'Farewell and take care in order that you are in good health. You must in future abstain from unreasonable hours in dinner and sleep. Sleeplessness weakens the strength of both body and mind in those who are invalids'.

[276] [*c.*5 February 1593] The reference to Henry Goodere suggests this letter was written close to 36, 38, and 39, as the pardon for alienation related to land acquired from Goodere and his wife. See above, p. 115, n. 273.

[277] Mr Fuller Presumably Nicholas Fuller, the lawyer and politician. He was admitted to Gray's Inn in 1563, so he may have known the Bacons through that connection, although he also acted for the godly in various trials in the early 1590s, which again may have brought him to Anne Bacon's attention. See *History of Parliament*, II, pp. 161–162.

[278] As I . . . herres Henry Goodere had been made a ward of Sir Ralph Rowlett, his maternal grandfather, on his father's death in 1546.

[279] [*c.*5 February 1593] This letter is undated, but the internal references to Burghley suggest that it was written at a similar time to 36. Burghley had been 'dangerously sick' in early January 1593 and was only making a slow recovery. See S. Alford, *Burghley: William Cecil at the Court of Elizabeth I* (New Haven, CT, and London, 2008), p. 316.

all and tyll ^now^ lettres owt of France cowlde not be deliverd to him wherabowt he now is. I dyd not use Mr Maynarde[280] but another whome I have used when occasion served and he promiseth yf it may well, he wyll this night. Mr Maynarde refuseth to deale with the person as unfitt, he sayth, for that or eny other ^such^ thing now. I desyred him to say nothing of my motion thus for that.

Your brother presumeth to much, he knoweth too well upon what late cause I have to geve not onely motherly but godly advise. His profession is not ^or^ owght not to be of vayn devises and unprofitable.[281] 'Be ye holy as I am holy', sayth God by his prophett.[282] Let him reade the 5 to the Ephesians towching unclean speachs and thowghts.[283] Trust in the Lord with all this hart, sayth the wysedom of God, and not in thin own. Read the 3rd of the Proverbes.[284] The apostle sayth, or rather the holy gost, 'yf eny man think him selff, let him be a foole in this world that he may be wyse'.[285] *Outre*[286] gwdance marres many or disgraces many goode gyfts. God geves grace to the humble.[287] God bless yow both and geve yow upright mynds to live in ^his^ feare and walk in his truth,[288] the sownde preaching wheroff consiseth not all in ~~wysdom of words~~ ^the wordes^ men's wysdom but in the power and evidence of the spirit,[289] which God graunt.

Your mother, ABacon.

Read not my lettres ether scoffingly or carelesly, which hath ben used to much. For I humbly thank God I know what I write and cownsell.

39. *Anne Bacon to Anthony Bacon* [*c*.5 February 1593][290]

Holograph until '*Vale in Jesu Christ*, AB', thereafter in another hand. LPL 653, fos 359r–360v. 2pp.
Endorsed (fo. 360v): lettre de Madame

Mr Crew coming hether to me, I thank him and even newly returned from my Lord Tresurer, I purposed to have come to yow to tell yow of

[280] **Mr Maynard** Henry Maynard, Burghley's chief secretary.
[281] **His profession ... unprofitable** See Titus 3:9.
[282] **Be ... prophett** See 1 Peter 1:16 and Leviticus 11:44.
[283] **Let ... thowghts** Ephesians 5:1–20.
[284] **Trust ... Proverbes** Proverbs 3:5.
[285] **The apostle ... wyse** 1 Corinthians 3:18.
[286] *Outre* [French] 'unorthodox' or 'improper'.
[287] **God ... humble** James 4:6.
[288] **walk ... truth** Psalm 86:11.
[289] **the wordes ... spirit** 1 Corinthians 2:4.
[290] [*c*.5 February 1593] Letter 39 seems to have been written after 38.

my Lord Tresurer's answer to me for pardon of alienation. For myne own opinion, I never looked but for such an answer which was it must nedes be compownded now, for nether my late Lorde's priviledg, ner my opteining the lyke of the erle of Lecester since my Lorde's death cowlde warrant him being put in trust by the Queen to geve away that which was here ~~and~~ ^as^ now it was; and that therle had it as an officer, but now none such. Reply was but hardely taken, he was so very earnest. He wylled to see the notes and then he wolde helpe to compownd as he might deale with the deputie for the Queen. It fell owt that as upon a sudden I saw her Majestye, so very gratiously saluted and asked of yow, seming to pitie your hard handling gowt. She hoped this spring wolde be better. To morow as opportunitee wyll serve I wolde again to my Lord Tresurer. I pray yow sende me the perfect value of the manours of the rent as bowght by your father. Apsbury I know is 16 li by yere. I take it that yours in Barly is above xl li. Yf yow sende to Mr Clark, this bearer shall go.

Vale in Jesu Christo.[291]
AB.

I remember very well that my Lorde Kepar's pryvilege was allowed of by the Erle of Leicestre in the former that I declared to my Ladye. But for what land it was, I is not now[292] remember nor no notes thereof be with me but all were delyvered to my Ladye. I thinke my Lorde of Leicestre might since chosen[293] whether he would have allowed pryvilege in that case or no.

40. *Anthony Bacon to Anne Bacon*, 25 March 1593

Draft. LPL 649, fo. 89r–v. 1p.
Addressed (fo. 89r): To the honorable and his verie good Ladie mother
Endorsed (fo. 89v): A Madame le 25me de mars 1593

Madame, I humblie thanke your Ladyship for your lettres and will not faile to remember and endeavour to followe your ~~Ladyship's~~ wise and kinde advise, as also to save a spetiall care not to goe too fast, both in respect of my self and your Ladyship's horse.

---

[291] *Vale in Jesu Christo* [Latin] 'Farewell in Jesus Christ'.
[292] **I is not now** Presumably 'is' was included by mistake.
[293] **might since chosen** Presumably there is a missing word here and it should instead read 'might since have chosen'.

It is verie trewe that Mr Mayor[294] and 3 of his brethren were with me one Frydaie laste and brought me their commission[295] ^under the broad seale^ by them ~~renew~~ lately renewed and increased by the puttinge in of Mr Raffe Coinsby,[296] Mr Harry Butler,[297] Mr Haydon[298] and my self placed next, the foure knights which, yf it had bene possible, I would verie willingly have refused, beinge as litle desirous as yet able to attend ~~thereunto~~ to suche matters. But your Ladyship knoweth ^verie well^ that it beinge done by my Lord Keeper's[299] appointment upon their motion, altogether without my knowledge, it can not be undone but upon my particular sewte, which upon conference with my brother I will advise yf I ^maie^ make to my Lord Keeper, without seeminge to disdaine that which my eaquals have ^accepted^.[300] In the meane time, I have excused my self unto them, as also to Mr Frewicke[301] and Mr Clark[302] who came likwise the next daie, that I could not be at their sessions ~~nor would not under~~ till it should please God to enable me with some furder strengthe and refused flatly to be a comissioner in this late jarre fallen out betwixt Mr Steward[303] and Mr Clarke of the one side and the mayor with the moste parte one the other side, which they did both earnestly require me ~~require them~~ to promise to accepte ^when^ they should have procured the same from the Lords of the Councell. And so assuring your Ladiship that neyther in suche, muche lesse in greater matters, I will not medle but by ~~dewtie~~ conscience and dewty ^and^ warranted by ~~good~~ the best allowance, I most humbly take my leave with remembrance of my humble dewty and beseche God to strengthen and comforte your Ladyship every waie.

Your Ladyship's moste humble and obedient sonne.

Redborne, this 25th of Marche 1593.

---

[294]**Mr Mayor** Francis Babbe was mayor of St Albans in 1593.

[295]**commission** Commission of the peace.

[296]**Mr Raffe Coinsby** Sir Ralph Coningsby of North Mimms, Hertfordshire. Coningsby was made a JP of Hertfordshire in 1591. See A. Thrush (ed.), *The History of Parliament: the House of Commons, 1604–1629*, 3 vols (London, 2010), III, pp. 628–629; J.R. Hankins, 'Local government and society in early modern England: Hertfordshire and Essex, *c.*1590–1630' (unpublished PhD thesis, Louisiana State University, 2003), p. 57.

[297]**Mr Harry Butler** Sir Henry Butler of Bramfield in Hertfordshire.

[298]**Mr Haydon** Sir Francis Heydon of Watford, Hertfordshire.

[299]**Lord Keeper's** Sir John Puckering was lord keeper from 1592 to 1596.

[300]**But ... accepted** Anthony Bacon was made a justice of the peace in 1594. See Hankins, 'Local government and society', p. 384.

[301]**Mr Frewicke** Henry Frowick had been steward of St Albans from February 1590. See *History of Parliament*, II, pp. 160–161.

[302]**Mr Clark** John Clark was mayor of St Albans in 1577 and 1592. See *Corporation Records*, p. 292.

[303]**Mr Steward** Henry Frowick. See above, n. 299.

41. *Anne Bacon to Anthony Bacon*, 15 April 1593

Holograph. LPL 649, fos 99r–100v. 2pp.
Endorsed (fo. 100v): lettre de Madame receue ce 16 avril 1593 le gantier.[304]
Addressed (fo. 100v): To my sonn Mr Antony Bacon at Grayes Inn

The g[l]over my neighbour upon going to London for his own busines tolde me of it sodenly after ^this^ Sabbath forenone sermon that he must go to London and that earely to morow. I am desirous to know how your health is, how matters after Parlement go to private folk *nempe*[305] Mr Moric[e],[306] your cosin Hoby,[307] and *si vis*[308] your brother too. God graunt us all faythfull harts in pietie and religion and wyse and discrete in godly practise. Yf eny lack wysdome, ask of the Lorde and receive *ut ait Jacobum apostolus*[309] for his geves[310] with all Christian fortitude to beare upp a goode conscience. I hast to the church again. God make yow able to heare publick instructions to your great comfort. I cowld wyllingly heare of Barly proceedings. For your state of want of health and ^of^ mony and some other things towching yow both οὐκ ἐᾳ με εὐδειν ἡσυχωσ.[311] God bles yow both with goode and godly encrease in Christ.

Easter *ut aiunt*[312] 15 April.

Your mother,
AB.

---

[304] *lettre . . . le gantier* [French] 'Letter from the mistress received 16 April 1593 by the glover'.

[305] *nempe* [Latin] 'namely'.

[306] **Mr Moric[e]** James Morice, an attorney of the Court of Wards and MP, instituted an attack in Parliament in February 1593 against Whitgift's use of the *ex officio* oath in the High Commission when questioning clergy on his expanded twenty-four articles; Morrice had described the oath as 'an ungodly and intolerable inquisition'. As a result, he was summoned before the Privy Council for his outburst, confined for eight weeks, and stripped of his lucrative position as attorney for the Court of Wards. Upon his release, Morrice visited Anne's sister Elizabeth Cooke Hoby Russell, and asked her to intercede on his behalf for a new position. She applied to her nephew Robert Cecil by letter in May 1593. See *Cooke Sisters*, pp. 174–175.

[307] **cosin Hoby** Edward Hoby, the son of Elizabeth Cooke Hoby Russell, Anne's sister. He had just been publically rebuked by the queen for insulting a fellow parliamentary committee member, Sir Thomas Heneage, and placed under house arrest.

[308] *si vis* [Latin] 'if you will'.

[309] *ut . . . apostolus* [Latin] 'as says the apostle James'. Anne is here recalling James 1:5.

[310] **geves** gifts

[311] *οὐκ . . . ἡσυχωσ* [Greek] 'do not allow me to sleep peacefully'.

[312] *ut aiunt* [Latin] 'as they say'.

42. *Anthony Bacon to Anne Bacon*, 16 April 1593

Draft. LPL 649, fos 103r–104v. 2pp.
Endorsed (fo. 104v): une lettre a Madame le 16 d'auvrile 1593

My dutie most humblie remembred. I assure my self that your Ladyship as a wise and kinde mother to us both will neyther finde it strange nor amise, yf tendringe first my brother's helth, which I know by myne owne experience to depend not a litle upon a free mynde and then his credit, I presume to put your Ladyship in remembrance of your motherlie offer to him the Sonneday yow departed, which was that to help him out of debt, yow would be content to bestowe your whole interest in Markes upon him.[313] The which unlesse yt would please your Ladyship to accomplishe out of hande, I have juste cause to feare that my brother wilbe put to a verie shrowde plondge,[314] eyther to forfeyt his revercyon to Harvie,[315] or els to undersell yt verie muche, for the avoydinge of both which great inconveniences, I see no other remedy then your Ladyship surrender in tyme. The formall drafte wherof I referr to my brother him self, whom I have not anie waye as yet made acquainted with this my motion, neyther meane to doe till I heare from yow. The ground wherof beinge onlie a brotherlie care and affection, I hope your Ladyship will thinke and accept of yt accordinglie, beseechinge yow to beleeve that beinge so neare and deare unto me as he is, that cannot but be a greef unto me, to see a mynde that hath givne[316] so sufficient proof of yt self, in havinge brought forth manie good thoughts for the general, to be overburdened and cumbered, with a ~~continuall~~ care of clearinge his particular estate. Touchinge my self, my dyet, I thanke God, hitherto hath wrought good effect, and am advised to continewe this whole month, not medlinge with anie purgative phissicke more then I must needs, which wilbe but thrise duringe my whole dyet; and so I moste humblie take my leave.

From Graise Inne this 16th of Aprill 1593.

---

[313]**yow ... upon him** Anne had conditionally granted Marks manor to Francis Bacon on 1 January 1584. They had jointly leased Marks to George Harvey in October 1584. See 'Money-lenders', p. 239.
[314]**plondge** plunge, i.e. dilemma.
[315]**to forfeyt ... to Harvie** On 26 April 1592, Francis Bacon had mortgaged Marks to its lessee, George Harvey, with £1,300 repayable on 30 April 1593. Harvey had written to Anthony Bacon regarding his repayment on 24 February 1593. See LPL 648, fos 153r–154v; 'Money-lenders', p. 240.
[316]**givne** given.

43. *Anthony Bacon to Anne Bacon*, 16 April 1593

Draft. LPL 649, fo. 105r–v. 1p.
Endorsed (fo. 105v): une lettre a Madame 16iesme d'auvril 1593

My humble dutie remembred for answear to your Ladiship's leter which I receyved this daye by the glover, havinge dispatched Spencer[317] in the morninge, maye yt please yow to be advertised that Sir Edward Hobbie was at libertie before the laste daye of the Parlament, but not without a notable publicque disgrace, layed uppon him by her Majestie's royall senseur, delivred emongest other things by her self, after my Lord Keeper's speeche, which summe saye was much inferior to his first in the begininge; the effecte of that which her Majestie uttered your Ladiship shall receyve here inclosed.[318] Diverse gentlemen that werre of the Parlament and thought to have retourned into the contrie after the ende thereof, are stayed by her Majestie's commandment for beinge privye, as yt is thought, and consentinge to Mr Weyntworth's matter.[319] The earle of Essex hath bin twyse verie earnest with her Majestie touchinge my brother, whose speeche beinge well grounded and directed to good ends, as yt cannot be denyed but yt was, I doubt not but God in his mercy will in tyme make yt an occasion of her Majestie's better opinion and lykinge.[320] I have not yet gonne throughe with anie for Barlie, neyther can conveniently, though I would, tyll the tearme. And so I humblie take my leave.

From Graise Inne this xvith of Aprill 1593.

Madame, havinge ended my letter and before the glover parted from my lodginge, my man Spencer aryved by whome I received your Ladiship's leter, which I communicated imediately to my brother, who hath written his owne answear.

---

[317] **Spencer** Presumably Edward Spencer. He was a nephew of Alderman Spencer and a servant of Anthony Bacon's. Edward Spencer and Anne had a series of disagreements between 1593 and 1594. For more details, see the Introduction, p. 33, and *Cooke Sisters*, pp. 219–223.

[318] **the effecte . . . inclosed** The enclosure no longer survives.

[319] **Mr Weyntworth's matter** Peter Wentworth had met with several other parliamentarians prior to the start of the session in February 1593 to discuss how to pursue the issue of the sucession in the Commons. He was subsequently sent to the Tower, where he died in 1597. See D. Dean, 'Peter Wentworth', *ODNB*.

[320] **but God . . . lykinge** Francis Bacon had angered the queen with his parliamentary opposition to her subsidies in March 1593. See *Troubled Life*, pp. 143–145.

44. *Anne Bacon to Anthony Bacon,* 17 April [1593][321]

Holograph. LPL 653, fos 318r–319v. 2pp.
Endorsed (fo. 319r): lettre de Madame recue ce 17ime avril

For your brotherly care of your brother Francis' state yow are to ^be^ well lyked and so I do as a Christian mother that loveth yow both as the chyldern of God. But as I wrote but in few wordes but yesterday by my neighbour, the state of yow both doth much disqwiett me, as in Greeke wordes I signified shortly. I am sure ye both do or shulde remember what I sayde to and of yow both at my coming hether, speaking of myn own syckliness and styll long wishing strength and ^so lyke^ of but short continuance, that I was in mynde allmost to make none of ^yow both^ myn executors, as well for my buriall, as I dyd wyll, as also that those that greatly abused and spent yow both and with whome yu[322] were so besotted to ^my^ very hart's greeffe shulde beare eny stroke in my appointed matters ^and howse^ after my death and truly but for evydence I am still in the same mynde. And how God wyll dispose my mynde herin as yet I know not. Goodes shall I leave none as mony or plate; as I may with God his leave, I wyll geve to my servants before as I am able. I have ben too ready for yow both till nothing is left. And surely thowgh I pitieth your brother, yet so long as he ^pities not him selff but^ keepeth that bloody Peerce,[323] as I towlde him then, yea, as a coch companion and bed companion, a prowde, ^prophane^, costly fellow, whose being abowt him I verely ^feare^ the Lord God doth mislyke and ^doth^ less bless your brother in credit and otherwyse in his health. Surely I am utterly discoraged ^[to] make a conscience^ further to undoe my self to maytein such wretches as he is. ^That^ Jones[324] never loved your brother in dede but for his own creditt, lyving upon your brother ^and thankles bragg[ing]^, thowgh your brother wylbe blynd to his own hurt and picking such vyle[325] his wycked cowntry men to supply ^in^ his absence. The Lorde in mercy

---

[321] **[1593]** This letter must date from 1593 as it responds to **42**.
[322] **yu** you.
[323] **bloody Peerce** There is some debate over the identity of Peerce. He has previously been identified as Antonio Pérez, the former secretary of Philip II, who befriended the Bacon brothers after his arrival in England in 1593, but that is based on a mistranscription. It is certainly 'Peerce' in the manuscript, presumably the same character labelled 'Percie' in **45**. It seems likely that this is Henry Percy, a servant of Francis Bacon's. For Percy, see *Bacon Letters and Life*, I, p. 244. For Pérez's time in England, see G. Ungerer, *The Correspondence of Antonio Pérez's Exile*, 2 vols (London, 1974–1976).
[324] **Jones** Presumably Edward Jones, who wrote to Francis Bacon on 16 August 1593. For his letter to Francis, see BL, Additional MS 28167, fos 5r–6v. For more on Jones, see *History of Parliament*, II, pp. 382–383.
[325] **vyle** abase.

remove them from him and evell from yow both, and geve yow a sownde judgment and understanding to order your selffs in all things to please God in tru knowledg and in his tru feare unfeyned, and to harken to his worde which onely maketh wyse in dede. Besydes your brother towlde me before yow twyse ^then^ that he entended not to parte with Markes and the rather because Mr Mylls[326] wolde lend him 500 li and as I remember I asked him how he wolde come owt of dett. His answer was meanes wolde be made withowt that and mentioned Jenings[327] and Cornellis.[328] It is most certein tyll first Edney,[329] a fylthy wastfull knave, and his Welch men, one after another. For take [o]ne and they wyll still swarm ill favoredly ^did so land him as in a train^. He was a towardes yowng gentleman and a sonne of much goode hope in godliness, but truth he hath norished most synfull prowde villans wyllfully.

[*Left-hand margin*] I know not what other answer to make. God bless yow both with his grace and goode health to serve him with truth of harte.

Make no errors in your phisyck tyme. Gorhambury, 17 April. ABacon.

[*fo. 319r*] Yf your brother desyre a release to Mr Harvy, let him so reqwyre it him ^selff^ and but upon this condition by his own hande and bonde I wyll not. That is that ~~he~~ ^he^ make and geve me a true note of all his detts and leave to me the hole order of the receit of ^all^ his mony for his lande to Harvy and the just payment of all his detts thereby. And by the mercy and grace of God it shalbe performed by me to his qwiett discharge withowt cumbring him ~~and~~ and so his credit. For I wyll not have his cormorant seducers and instruments of Satan to him committing fowle synns by his cowntenance to the displeasing of God and his godly tru fre[n]ds. Otherwyse I wyll not, *pro certo.*[330]

AB.

---

[326]**Mr Mylls** William Mills, clerk of the Star Chamber since 1572–1573. See A. Pollard 'Council, Star Chamber, and Privy Council under the Tudors', *English Historical Review*, 37 (1922), p. 534.

[327]**Jenings** This is most likely to be Gabriel Jennings of Collye Rowe in Dagenham, as Francis Bacon had borrowed £200 from him in 1590. See 'Money-lenders', p. 239.

[328]**Cornellis** Michael Corneillis, merchant and creditor to Essex. See CP 58/31.

[329]**Edney** Francis Edney was granted £200 in Francis Bacon's will. See *Bacon Letters and Life*, VIII, p. 543.

[330]**pro certo** [Latin] 'for certain'.

45. *Anne Bacon to Anthony Bacon,* [18 April 1593][331]

Holograph. LPL 653, fos 301r–302v. 2pp.
Endorsed (fo. 302v): lettre de Madame

I received somewhat late yesterday all sent by the glover. All the notes savour of discontent myxed. God turn all to the best. Your continuance in dett still, I feare still. Often and diverse surveies[332] and no goode effect marreth, I dowt, the bargain. But looke yow, yf trobles threaten, purchasers wylbe lowe. *Mora trahit periculum.*[333] I send herin your brother's lettre.[334] Constru the enterpretation. I do not understand his enigmaticall fowlded writing. O, that by not harkening to holsome and carefull goode cownsell and by continuing still the meanes of his own great hindrance he had ^not^ procured his own early discredit, but had joyned with God that hath bestowed ^on him^ goode gyfts of naturall wytt and understanding. But the same goode God which hath geven them to him wyll I trust and hartely pray to sanctifye his hart and the right use of them to glorifye the gever with them to his own inwarde comfort.

The scope of my so called by him circumstances, which I am sure he must understand, was not to use him as a warde; a remote phrase to my playn motherly meaning and yet, I thank the Lorde and the hearing of his worde preaced,[335] not voyde of judgment and conceving. My playn purpose was and is to do him good, but seing so manifestly that he is robbed and spoyled wyttingly by his base exalted men, which with Welch wyles praye upon him and yet beare him in hande the[336] have other mayntenance, because their bowlde nature wyll not acknowledge, I dyd desyre onely to receave the mony to discharge his detts in dede and dare not trust such his riotus men with the dealing withall. I am sure no preacher nor lawyer nor frende wolde have mislyked this my doing for his goode and my better satissfieng. He perceaves my goode meaning by this and before too, but Percie[337] had wynded him. God bless my sonne. What he wolde have me do and when for his own goode as I now write, let him return plain answer by Fynch.[338] He was his father's first chis[339] and God wyll supply yf

[331] [**18 April 1593**] **45** was presumably received the day after **44**.
[332] **surveies** surveys.
[333] *Mora ... periculum* [Latin] 'Delay brings danger'. This was a common proverb: see P. Collinson, 'Thomas Wood's letters', in P. Collinson (ed.), *Godly People: essays on English Protestantism and puritanism* (London, 1983), p. 89.
[334] **I send ... lettre** The letter is no longer extant.
[335] **preaced** preached.
[336] **the** they.
[337] **Percie** See p. 123, n. 323.
[338] **Fynch** John Finch. See p. 103, n. 202.
[339] **chis** The Middle English 'chis' is akin to choice or dear (*OED*).

he trust in him and call up upon in truth of hart, which God grant to mother and son.

[Left hand margin] I sende the fyrst flyte of doves to yow both and God bless yow in Christ.

AB.

46. *Anne Bacon to Anthony Bacon*, [*c.*22 May 1593][340]

Holograph. LPL 653, fos 328r–329v. 2pp.
Addressed (329v): To my sonne Antony Bacon

God in mercy looke upon yow and geve yow a goode issue of your phisick. Baylye Waggoner towlde me from yow, yow had not yet sent to my cosin Kempe[341] for the 15 li and that Mr Crew wolde not receive the 4 li till I was wylling to say whylest I had it and the copieng and the ^law^ cownsellors had had fees all ready of him. But as he wyll. I wolde Mr Crew these holy dayes[342] mowght have but seene what spoyle Carter makes with his coales burning but most of all hurting the steimmes with burning the spray so nygh them. Fynde fawt, no amendment but my lease doth allow all. I wolde his lease were a litle neerer lookt into for he seemes to make the uttermost spoyle and so dryve to forfait when it is at worst. Cross is gon to be maried, I know not now where eny lyeth and am loth to look more my selff. Yow shall do well not to make William Dell eny hope of enterteinment. He is but a nawghty subtill felow thowgh he speaks fayre and to say troth, your kind lyveries be for men of better credit. For his lewde towng and behavour hath got him but litle credit in the parish. I met homeward hether Humphrey *Lanio*[343] in your cloak; me thowght a butcher dyd scase[344] become and much less such a troblesom fellow and ill favored as Dell. Thomas Knight hath sent yow a feasant hee tooke on Saturday last; I cowlde not ^send^ it sooner. I was content and but hardely to lett Hamlett tary at Shafforde for his wyffe's sake and bidding him trust whether I lyved or departed, he greenned upon me and sayde he had better hope; then so from whence yow know best. His alehowsing and trading to London weekly hath made him careless of all there, besyde the liberty he hath suffred to let vyle vagabond and their nawghty packs both ^haunte^ lodg abowt the woodds and

---

[340] [*c.*22 May 1593] This letter seems to have occasioned Anthony's response in 47.
[341] cosin Kempe Bartholomew Kemp's wife was the daughter of Nicholas Bacon I's sister. Kemp served as a treasurer to Nicholas Bacon I while he was lord keeper and was later a Chancery clerk. See *History of Parliament*, II, pp. 390–391.
[342] these holy dayes The rogation days prior to Ascension Day.
[343] *Lanio* [Latin] 'Butcher'.
[344] scase Anne was here using a sixteenth-century spelling of 'scarce'.

made that walk a common passage to my howse continually, so that the gate and grownd is seldom withowt them rownd abowt. I prepare and new wash the faschions with ii payre of shetes of Gorhambury fyttest to cary, and 4 pilloberes,[345] a sqware cloth diaper, a doson lyke napkins. Send me worde when and what elce yf yow nede by Bury. Write not your selff, but burn this.

[*Left-hand margin*] It may be Ewarde[346] is come to yow. He went away on a sudden, lyke as he is a whet and tipsy verlett. Yow shall have a goode perish catch of him. He pickt a qwarell for this nonce[347] it seems. My two cheffe servyce horses are syck. God helpe me.

47. *Anthony Bacon to Anne Bacon*, 22 May 1593

Draft. LPL 649, fos 132r–133v. 2pp.
Endorsed (fo. 133v): une lettre a Madame 1593

My most humble dewtie remembred. I have receyved xv li of my cosen Kempp, for the which, as also for that your Ladyship sente me by Badtforde, I humblie thanke your Ladyship. ~~For the foure pounds I cannot as yet get~~ Mr Crewe ^as yet^ ~~to take that~~ will needs make me his pursbearer and yet moste willinglie undertakes anie paines in your Ladyship's or your sonnes' busines. The gentleman is ~~of~~ justlie of your Ladyship's minde that the same cuninge *compagnon*[348] Carter will make as great havocke as he can and then give that over. As for Deall, I have given him no kinde of promise but willed him onlie to live honestlie hereafter, howsoever he had bene heretofore, yf he desired my favour and good will. The provicion of linninge[349] which it hath pleased your Ladyship to specefie in your letter semes to me ~~verie~~ sufficient ~~which yf I may receyve~~ The time ~~for~~ ^of^ sendinge of yt I referr to your Ladyship's discrecion. In what sorte Edward camm to me, how sorrie he is of your Ladyship's displeasure and readie to acknowledge and repaire his faults and what answeare I gave him, I hope Mr Wybo^r^n and Mr Wilplet[350] will trewlie and

---

[345]**pilloberes** pillowcases.
[346]**Ewarde** Presumably Edward Spencer. See p. 122, n. 317.
[347]**for this nonce** for this purpose.
[348]*compagnon* [French] 'companion'.
[349]**linninge** linen.
[350]**Mr Wilplet** There is some uncertainty over the identification of Mr Wiplet (also spelled Welplet in **56** and **104**). It may refer to Andrew Willett. His father, Thomas Willett, was the rector of Barley in Hertfordshire from 1571 to 1598, after which his son almost immediately filled the position. Andrew Willett dedicated a verse to Anne Bacon in his *Sacrorum emblematum centuria una* (London, 1592), sig. FIv. Or 'Wiplet' may instead mean Humphrey Wilblood (see p. 104, n. 207) as, phonetically, the spelling is relatively similar.

indifferentlie advertice your Ladyship, ~~without whom~~ ^who may be assured that wyth owte your^ good lykinge, how necessarie soever such a one is nowe ^for me^ and like to be more and more hereafter, I meane to passe with him and recover some other when and where I may, and so I most humblie take my leave.

From Graise Inne this 22th of May 1593.

Your Ladyship's moste humble and obediente sonne.

48. *Anne Bacon to Anthony Bacon*, 25 May 1593

Holograph. LPL 649, fos 121r–122v. 2pp.
Endorsed (fo. 122v): Lettre de Madame receue ce 25 may 1593 le baille[351]
Addressed (fo. 122v): To my sonne mister Anthony Bacon at Grayes Inn

It is but cownterfayt whatsoever he moveth yow and Mr Wyborn to write.[352] In dede as I might I kept him from his former starting to the town to tiple which liberty he will craftely seeke and loves to well. He is but an irefull pevish fellow yf he be looked into and checked for his loose demeanour from which I restraind him. And how your horskeper and others ryght emboldened him I know not, but sure I am he purposely wrangled to be gon diverse tymes. But that he was for a soldiour I had parted with him or[353] this and I care not for his servyce. Let him go lyke a prowde ignorant verlet. Let him be talking and stepp abroade ^unseasonablely^ and cloake ^it^ with lyes. He is lyke him selff. I trust to have some honest man for my horses never prosper since he came to them. He wylbe ready to borow and pay at leasure. That which he had of me fownd him well in my service but he had a secret nawghty vent and so wyll still, warrant yow, yf he once may after a while dissembling get a litle credit. God send yow encrease of his grace and favour and health. How doth Barly? The linnen sometyme next weeke. Pierre weepes for new cloths. I wyll pay for it and let his apparell be made here, except his cote or elce made more large, the last was but spoyled by Redborn taylour, made so scant, and taylours now so abhominably scant, both men's and boye's hose before, that their fylthiness is ready to be sene upon every stepp, going or stooping. A most beastly and sinful custome now. So ungodly becomes England under the holy and pure gospell. Yf yow wolde have your horse here

---

[351]*Lettre . . . le baille* [French] 'Letter from the mistress, received 25 May 1593, by the bailiff'.

[352]**It is . . . write** This is likely to refer to Edward Spencer, considering the references in this letter and in **47**.

[353]**or** before.

in the soyle, sende worde how to be ordered in writing and how long. Onselow mendes slowly, yf he do. God helpe me.

[Left-hand margin] Your mother, AB.

49. *Anthony Bacon to Anne Bacon*, 28 May 1593

Draft. LPL 649, fo. 135r–v. 1p.
Endorsed (fo. 135v): une lettre a Madame 1593
Incomplete address (fo. 135r): To the right.

My most humble dutie remembred. Mr Crewe, as I thinke, will weyght upon your Ladyship ~~on day~~ ^toward the ende^ of the next weeke, till which tyme your Ladyship may deferre, yf yow thinke good, the delivrie of thwrit[354] ^that^ I send yow here inclosed, which Mr Crewe recevied from my cosen Kemp. Your Ladyship's lininge[355] will stande me in noe lesse steade here before I goe to the Bath,[356] then at the Bath, concyderinge my brother takes his provision with him to Twitnam.[357] For the time of my departure, I cannot presentlie set yt downe ^but^ my next, havinge once spoken withe Earle, I shalbe able particularlie to advertice your Ladyship eyther the continewance or alteraition of that my pourpose. Good Mr Wyborn, ^I thanke him^, was here with me this afternone, whose companie I was bould to request to the Bath, yf I went, which I thanke him he did not denie though not flatlie resolved. Thus beschinge God longe to preserve your Ladyship, I most humblie take my leave. Graise Inne 28ᵗʰ May 1593.

Your Ladyship's most humble and obedient sonne.

50. *Anne Bacon to Anthony Bacon*, 31 May 1593

Holograph. LPL 653, fos 363r–364v. 2pp.
Endorsed (fo. 364v): lettre de Madame

Grace and health in Christ.

I have sent yow some linnen, the parcells herin closed; parte of myne from London and part from Gorhambury, as the ii payr of fyne

---

[354]**thwrit** the writ.

[355]**lininge** linen.

[356]**the Bath** By the late sixteenth century, there were five baths within the city of Bath in Somerset. See J. Eglin, *The Imaginary Autocrat: Beau Nash and the invention of Bath* (London, 2005), pp. 26–27.

[357]**Twitnam** Twickenham Park was Francis Bacon's chosen retreat in the 1590s; he had a personal lease from 1595, although it had previously been leased by his half-brother Edward Bacon since 1574. See 'Money-lenders', p. 243.

shetes and the v pilloberes,[358] almost all I have. For Edward I leave to yow; God send yow a better servant of him then I have had, but I have had but his carcase a goode whyle. But yet yf necessite do constrian[359] I wyll use his soldior's servyce yf he be not at Bathes, thowgh against my wyll. Upon a soden he is but an ignorant irefull wranglour, yf fawt be fownde, howsoever he deserveth and loveth shipps[360] conningly. He wyll peradventure dissemble a while and now he may talk and tiple and have his nose over the manger ^idlely^ . Sorie, some what a ^wit^,[361] he cam for his clothes yesterday. I denied not for the value, for his best he had ^in^ my service and mony in his purse, yf he typled not it way. But that I denyed him was to make him know his pevish pride. For greeved yet with the loss of my speciall noble horse ut ita dicam,[362] and Onslow not well, in talk in justly of his carelessness he both lyed and wrangled disdaynfully with me. Wherupon loth to troble my selff I bad with these wordes, 'A man master wolde go ny to breake thy head for this speach, but I byd the gett the owt of my syght lyke a lyeng prowde verlett'. Wherupon glad belyke he went immediatly to the stable and took his cloake and sworde and jetted away lyke a jack. He was here both christianly and too well used here. I wryte this to tell yow the trowth howsoever he lyeth. Yet yf your necessitee compelleth, yow take him, as yow think goode, and kepe him in order for your servyce. God geve yow much goode of the Bathe. Yowng Mr Alexander here doth say they dyd him no goode and some think yf your gowt be hote the heate of that water doth rather farther the gowt then the patient. I trust yow have well consulted and considered before.

To Mr Crew hereafter.

[*Left-hand margin*] And the Lorde in mercy be with yow and geve goode and blessed success in Christ our Lorde and health and hope.

ultimo[363] May 1593 Gorhambury. Your mother, ABacon.

I hope your horse comes to yow sownde and well.

---

[358] **pilloberes** pillowcases.
[359] **constrian** constrain.
[360] **shipps** In the sense of his own affairs or fortunes.
[361] **wit** aware, understanding.
[362] ***ut ita dicam*** [Latin] 'so to speak'.
[363] ***ultimo*** [Latin] 'last'.

51. *Francis Goad*[364] *to Anne Bacon,* June 1593[365]

Holograph. LPL 650, fo. 206r–v. 1p. Faded.
Endorsed (fo. 206v): De Monsieur Gode a Madame mere de Monsieur 1594[366]
Addressed (fo. 206v): To the right worshipful my Ladie Backen, this be delevred at Gras Enn.[367]

Madam, my duty rembred. I thought yt my duty to write to your Ladiship for in that I havinge founde divers and sondry tymes your good kindnes towrds[368] me and beinge her[369] I cold do no lese then in part to your Ladishipe the stayt of this rwuenese[370] kingdom.[371] For the Kinge him selfe,[372] he ys in good helth and sencs my cominge owyer not annye thinge don agayn. The ienymye[373] her hath byn a partinge on a pese, but not nothinge doun but adiuys by the King's inmyes to intrape him by som on[374] way or other. The which yf the[375] cold bringe to pas then that ys al the hayfe so longed shouted at. Her was apounted theor of inne ametinge[376] of al the nobilite of the Kinge's sid, but as yt not don but brocken of that is quyt and yt is thought nothinge but treson. So that the Kinge ys cominge downe hether with his powres and to help them her or eyls the Spannerd is lyck to get al her. In Peckerdie,[377] yf he do not com in tym, this wars ys nothinge but to consume men and tresur withowt getinge of ether honnor or credite. Her was 2000 as brafe Ingles men,[378] when I cam owyer, as is

---

[364]**Francis Goad** Described later by Anne as 'a Christian Captain', Goad was resident at Essex House in April 1596, so seems to have been part of the earl of Essex's wider circle. See **148**.

[365]**June 1593** Francis Goad dated his letter in the New Style, so depending when during the month he wrote the letter, it could have fallen in May 1593, according to the Old Style of dating.

[366]*De ... 1594* [French] 'From Mr Goad to the mistress, mother of the master, 1594.' This is incorrectly endorsed as 1594, as Goad himself gave the year as 1593.

[367]**To the ... Enn** Goad also began an additional address on fo. 206v, which he then crossed through: 'To the right honorabyle'. By 'Gras Enn', Goad was referring to Gray's Inn.

[368]**towrds** towards.

[369]**her** here (used throughout the letter).

[370]**rwuenese** ruinous.

[371]**the stayt of this rwuenese kingdom** Goad described Henri IV's struggles to claim the crown of France, prior to his abjuration of Protestantism the following month, on 25 July 1593.

[372]**The Kinge himselfe** Henri IV of France.

[373]**ienymye** enemy.

[374]**on** one.

[375]**the** they.

[376]**ametinge** a meeting.

[377]**Peckerdie** Picardy.

[378]**brafe Ingles men** brave Englishmen.

in Ingland and now not 100 to be sen and yt newer cam to sarwys and
to consom annnye man but manye ded for want, and som rayn awaye
and the pesenttes hath kiled manye awon.[379] This ys howr Majestie's
men and tresur consumed. In that the Kinge's consel ys most of them
papes[380] and known to be as pencheners unto the Kinge of Spayn. In
my openyon, look not for beter wares her then yow her[381] of by my
leters. So longe thing as so handled as the be. Yt is God that must
remedi yt and a godlye consel and not consel of papest to set a Kinge
in his kengedom to gowerrn a prodistant King.

[fo. 206v] For as fast as we and his frend do to his good, the rest of his
consel binge papes[382] seike to undieue yt so that yt ys to be ferred[383] he
may continue as he doute but not get the thinge which is his right.
This with my duty to your Ladishipe, I comyt you and yours to the
Almight[y]. Amen.

Your to command,
Francis God.

In Depe[384] the [ ] June[385]
styl nowe 1593.

I do pray God blese our good prencs and grant us pese and that thowse
in Ingland wold but rember the benifet the hayf by hour Majestie's[386]
and the pese the resefe by God and hour. Yf you war her to se the
mesorye of this contry yt wold mack annye Cristen hart to rwe yt; not
bred nor drinck to get her in the contry but water and yf yow do fynd
in on places bred in 20 myl not annye but what ys in gret castel and
tounes as Depe or such lick. The Lorrd deliwer Ingland from yt and
sen[d] yt. I do newer se the lick, I pray to God. Amen. Yf yt shold
com yt will be grevs unto us for mor then we thinck for be cawse of
our long pese.

---

[379] **manye awon** many a one.
[380] **papes** papists.
[381] **her** hear.
[382] **binge papes** being papists.
[383] **ferred** feared.
[384] **In Depe.** In Dieppe. Francis Goad also wrote to Anthony Bacon from Dieppe in May
1593. See LPL 649, fos 114r–119v. In one of these letters he asked to be remembered to the
'good Lady yowr mother'. See LPL 649, fo. 116r.
[385] **the [ ] June** The date is missing from this letter. Perhaps Goad intended to add the
date just before dispatch.
[386] **the hayf by hour Majestie's** they have by her majesty's.

52. *Anthony Bacon to Anne Bacon*, 2 June 1593

Draft. LPL 649, fo. 190r–v. 1p.
Endorsed (fo. 190r): une lettre de Madame 1593

My dutie most humblie remembred. I have receyved all the linninge[387] accordinge to your Ladyship's note, for the which I render your Ladyship most humble thanks. My journie to the Bath ~~is~~ must be ^deferde^ for a monthe at the least and I knowe not whether for altogether this yeare, upon ~~occasion~~ most importante and necessarie occasion, that toucheth me nearer then myne health. Your Ladyship shall receyve a booke,[388] which the printer therof de Piux[389] brought unto me this morninge, accompanied with Mr Castor,[390] one of the Frenche ministers, who both requested me to conveye the same unto your Ladyship as a remembrance and token from good Mr Bezea,[391] who God be thanked is as well as one of his yeares can be. ~~yf~~ To whom yf it please your Ladyship to wright anie thinge they have promised ^me^ to attend heare ^upon Friday next^ for the same. My brother goeth this daye to Twitnham, and ~~would~~ will nedes boroughe Mr Crewe, of one who in that respect shall not be able to wayght on your Ladyship. The Earle of Essex wrote me this daye that her Majestie is thoroughlie appeased and that shee standeth onlie ~~to~~ ^uppon^ the exception of his yeares, for his present preferment,[392] but I doubt not, saithe my Lord, I shall over come that difficultie verie soone and that her Majestie will shewe yt by good effects, and so I most humblie take my leave.

From Graise Inne, this 2th of June 1593.

---

[387]**linninge** linen.

[388]**a booke** Anne was presented with the most recent edition of Theodore de Bèze's meditations on the Penitential Psalms: T. de Bèze and G. Buchanan, *Sacratiss. psalmi Davidis* (Geneva, 1593). It also contained George Buchanan's psalm paraphrases. Bèze had already dedicated the French edition of his meditations to Anne in 1581 and the English translation of the following year bore the same dedication. See **18**; T. de Bèze, *Chrestienes meditations sur huict pseaumes du prophete David composees et nouvellement mises en lumiere par Theodore de Besze* (Geneva, 1581); T. de Bèze, *Christian meditations upon eight Psalmes of the prophet Dauid*, trans. J.S. (London, 1582).

[389]**de Piux** Jean le Preux, the Genevan printer.

[390]**Mr Castor** Jean Castol, assistant pastor of the Calvinist French Stranger Church in London from 1582 to 1601.

[391]**Mr Bezea** Theodore de Bèze. According to Percival Wyborn, Bèze often sent correspondence to England via the French Stranger Church. See H. Robinson (ed.), *The Zurich Letters*, 2 vols (Cambridge, 1842), I, p. 190.

[392]**that shee ... preferment** Anthony is here reporting the earl of Essex's efforts to advance his brother, Francis, to the position of attorney-general.

53. *Anthony Bacon to Anne Bacon*, 8 June 1593

Draft. LPL 649, fo. 187r–v. 1p.
Endorsed (fo. 187v): une lettre a Madame le 8me 1593

My duty most humblie remembred, with like thankes to your Ladyship for increasinge my ˆsmalleˆ store of lynninge.[393] Accordinge to your Ladyship's wyse councell I have begone, ~~and~~ thanks be to God therfore, and meane to continewe to ineure my self as much I can to ˆtheˆ open ayre. Mr Crewe is not yet returnd from Twitnham which is the cause I keepe Sir Jhon Broˆcˆket's[394] letter to shew unto him. Mr Castor,[395] the Frenche minister, and the printer of that booke which Mr Bezea sent your Ladyship cam to me at the same ˆtymeˆ that Bashford arrived, to know yf your Ladyship would wright or commande any thinge to Mr Bezea, who ˆbothˆ, to be plaine with your Ladyship, gave me at their first cominge, and now likwise, to understande that Mr ˆBezeaˆ expected more then a leter from your Ladyship. In consideration whereof, as also to revive my ancient acquaintance with the good ould father,[396] I was bould to sende him in your Ladyship's name and myne owne ~~a girdle of gould~~ a present ˆnot of bare monieˆ ~~to the valewe of xx marke~~ but otherwise imploied to the valewe of xx marke, accompanied with a leter of myne owne to him self, and two more to two other of my espetiall frends at Geneve. And so I most humblie take my leave beschinge God longe to preserve your Ladyship. Graise Inne the 8ᵗʰ June.

Havinge ended my leter, Mr Crewe arived after super from Twytnham, who, after I had redd Sir Jhon Brocket's leter, said ~~he never~~ that he looked for as muche at his handes and yet seeinge yt hath pleased your Ladyship to make choice of him, your Ladyship must now expect what his cosen will doe of him self or by his precurement. Maye yt please your Ladyship to excuse Bashford for staieinge for my only occasion.

---

[393]**lynninge** linen.
[394]**Sir Jhon Brocket's** Sir John Brocket (*c.*1540–1598), a Hertfordshire county gentleman and neighbour of Anne Bacon's. See *History of Parliament*, I, p. 486.
[395]**Mr Castor** See above, p. 133, n. 390.
[396]**to revive . . . father** See **16** and **17**.

54. *Anthony Bacon to Anne Bacon*, 15 June 1593

Draft. LPL 649, fo. 188r–v. 1p.
Endorsed (fo. 188v): une lettre a Madame mere le Monsieur le 15me de juin 1593

My deutie most humblie remembred. Maie it please your Ladyship to hould me excused, yf by reason of the good companie, which I have not wanted ˆnether can nor thus houseˆ, both at dinner and souper, namelie since my brother's returne hether, whose cheefest ease and comforte ˆduringe his sicknesˆ is by companie, as also in respect of the arrivall of a gentleman from beyonde sea whom ˆit pleasedˆ her Majestie to ~~appoint~~ ˆcommandˆ ˆmy Lord Tresorer to directˆ to repaire and remaine here with me,[397] I be so bould as to desire your Ladyship to spare me, yf yow cann, one hogshedde of the same beare I had laste and three others of a later brewinge, as also the standinge cuppe[398] double guilte, which ~~it my pleased~~ my ˆlateˆ father ~~to~~ lefted me.[399] The earle of Essex, I thanke his Lordship, sent me yester daie thre warrantes for three bucks and writt unto me he would not faile to be with me this eveninge to see my brother and my self, and to speake withe gentleman, who ~~I send~~ parteth this ~~daie~~ ˆmorningeˆ in my coatche to my Lord Tresurer at Tyballs.[400] ~~and so I most~~ Yf your Ladyship likwise could spare me two geldings to accompanie my coatche which I shall have occasion and meane, God willing, dalie to imploie, they should be ~~most~~ no lesse welcome then they are necessarie. Your Ladyship shall not neede to doubt but that I will have a speciall care of them and so I most humblie take my leave. June 15th.

[397]**as also ... with me** Anthony Standen, the English Catholic, had just returned to England after a twenty-eight-year Continental exile. A double agent, his cover with the Spanish had been ruined en route. He had arrived at Gray's Inn on 13 June. For Standen's return and his reception from Burghley, see P. Hammer, 'An Elizabethan spy who came in from the cold: the return of Anthony Standen to England in 1593', *Historical Research*, 65 (1992), pp. 277–295.

[398]**the standinge cuppe** A standing cup was a goblet with a base.

[399]**which ... lefted me** Nicholas Bacon's will specified leaving a standing cup to his brother-in-law, William Cecil. While the will does not expressly state that Anthony was left another standing cup, he did inherit half of all the household goods at Gorhambury on his father's death. See *Stiffkey*, I, p. 26.

[400]**Tyballs** William Cecil, Lord Burghley, had bought Theobalds estate in Hertfordshire in 1564.

55. *Anne Bacon to Anthony Bacon*, [15 June 1593][401]

Holograph. LPL 653, fo. 251r–v. 1p.
Endorsed (fo. 251v): lettre de Madame

Abowt beginning of the next weeke, sonne, I mean, yf it please God, to stepp to London to see and know how it is with yow for your health and business and not long after to send some beere. July wyll come on a pace for your brother's dett to Cornelis.[402] The Lorde God shew mercy to yow both and direct and bless yow as chyldern and kepe yow from evell every way. My fyne black hoby[403] for servyce is complayning, not well. God save the beast; I know not how to do for servyce yf it continue.

Gorhambury.

56. *Anthony Bacon to Anne Bacon*, 15 June 1593

Draft. LPL 649, fo. 189r–v. 1p.
Endorsed (fo. 189v): une lettre a Madame le 15 1593

My dutie most humblie remembred. ~~I~~ After I had dispatched my letter by Risbrough, my bayliffe of Barlie, I receyved your Ladyship's by Mr Welplet,[404] wherein perceyving your Ladyship's purpose to come one Mondaye or Tewsdaie to Wilssons Howse, I thought it my dutie to advertice your ^Ladiship^ that there is no place in London more dangerous nor where thinfection is more ryffe then ^in^ that parishe. Therfor beseche your Ladyship to see one weeke more paste. My brother, God be thanked, is almost red of his ague,[405] and my self will not faile to ~~let~~ ^certifie^ your Ladyship ~~understand ^by letter^~~ by letter or what soever it shall please your Ladyship to understande, eyther concerninge my brother or my self.

Graise Inne ~~juin~~ the 15th of *juin* 1593.

---

[401] **[15 June 1593]** This undated letter preceded **56**.
[402] **Cornelis** Michael Corneillis. See p. 124, n. 328.
[403] **fyne black hoby** A small or middle-sized horse.
[404] **Mr Welplet** See p. 127, n. 350.
[405] **red of his ague** rid of his acute or high fever.

57. *Anne Bacon to Anthony Bacon*, 26 June 1593

Holograph. LPL 649, fo. 153r–v. 1p.
Endorsed (fo. 153v): lettre de Madame, 1593
Addressed (fo.153v): To my sonne

Sonnne, goodeman Grimwell[406] of Barly came this morning hether, very sadd upon a speche he had harde yow were abowt to lett his ferm to another, yet hopeth better both for your promiss and the receit of some mony upon it. Goode sonne, kepe your worde advisedly spoken, it is a Christian credit. Be not sodenly removed nor beleve hastely, but know whome and how. Sure yf that disposition be fownde and observed in yow once it wylbe wrowght upon to your hindrance in estimation and profitt. Besydes that the grandefather, father and sonne have there continued. I think once upon a sale of woodd ^in your absence^, I hard that the Grimwells had dwelled there above a vi^xx[407] years. The man is willing to do as much as another. The same person that now wolde, I wot not what ^reversion^, in your absence was backwarde and rather hindred wood sales and other things. He wolde fayn have had goode^man^ Finch with him to yow but I can in no wyse now spare him, mowyng and other businesses come on. It is here marvelous hote and dry and grass burn away, God helpe us. I pray yow comfort Grimell's hart and kepe just promises justly and be not credulous lyghtly and so the Lorde bless yow and gwyde yow with his holy spirit in his feare. Be not to frank with that papist.[408] Such have seducing spirits to snare the godly. Be not too open; sit not upp late, nor disorder your body that yow may have health to do goode service when God shall appoint. Gorhambury 26 *Junii* 1593.

Your carefull mother,
ABacon.

58. *Anne Bacon to Anthony Bacon*, 3 July [1593][409]

Holograph. LPL 653, fo. 317r–v. 1p.
Endorsed (fo. 317v): lettre de Madame

I sende purposely. I can ^not^ tell what I ayled. But still I suspecte a dilatory bargayning; to have goode assurance is requisite but your tytle

[406]**Grimwell** Anne spells the name of this Barley tenant variably, even within this letter. For Grim[w]ell, see also **32**.

[407]**vi^xx** One hundred and twenty. For a discussion of the use of Roman numerals in medieval and early modern England, see A.G. Petti, *English Literary Hands from Chaucer to Dryden* (London, 1977), p. 28.

[408]**that papist** Presumably Anthony Standen. See **54** and **60**.

[409]**3 July [1593]** The discussion of the sale of Barley estate and Marks manor suggests that this letter dates from 1593.

and case made weaker by it, I think is not wysely or skillfully handled. I wolde have no speach of dowte at all; let not my man this bearer understande eny thing by your selff or your men. For thowgh honest and pretely spoken for his kinde yet he ^is^ *satis linguae et non insulsus.*[410] Surely I suspect there is some drift to fetch Barly from yow, but yow wyll, I trow, not so discredit your selff; and possible some have hereby pried wylbe mistrusted there too. I pray be ware and wyse in your own doings and not too open. The worlde is full of false semblance. Yow have ben very long absent and so must of brobalitee[411] be yet to seek in your own state and sycknes is dangerous.

What yow mean to bring, trunks or such. Robert Knight knowes the cariag dayes. To leave your loging withowt one to lye I feare were not saffe. Yf it will stande yow to stay my man till next day, as yow have cause do, other wyse I appoint his return *eodem die Deo propitio.*[412] I pray yow shew your brother. I wolde have the two kallenders very saffly returned ^hether^[413] and Mr Wyblud's lettre *ad archiepiscopum*[414] and all Redborn evidence with all the apertinance[415] Marcks lease and all saffly deliverd to my cosin Kempe, with a note therof to him and another to me. Yf my man know of your coming, charge him with secresy. I have prepared for yow as well as I can the chamber next the great parlour as fittest for your ease being no better in your lymms.

The ^Lorde^ make yow better and better dayly. Take care of your all writings and bewraying[416] unadvisedly. Yf I wyst yow came not this weke; I wolde make a jorny but for ii dayes to speake with a frende. *Fac certiorem et valete eo citius scirem.*[417] God be ^with^ us in mercy in all our doings and goings. I thank God that the learned men did visit yow, as tokens of his favour. Make profitt of it.

3 July.   Burn this well marked.

Mater tua,[418]
ABacon.

---

[410]*satis . . . insulsus* [Latin] 'talkative enough and not stupid'.
[411]**brobalitee** probability.
[412]*eodem . . . propitio* [Latin] 'the same day, God willing'.
[413]**the two . . . hether** This may be a reference to the puritan apologia, *A Parte of a Register*, published in 1593. See discussion in the Introduction, pp. 26–27.
[414]*ad archiepiscopum* [Latin] 'to the archbishop'.
[415]**apertinance** appurtenance.
[416]**bewraying** betraying yourself.
[417]*Fac . . . scirem* [Latin] 'You must make more certain and you must be effectual so that I might swiftly know'.
[418]*Mater tua* [Latin] 'Your mother'.

59. *Anne Bacon to Anthony Bacon*, [early July 1593][419]

Holograph. LPL 653, fo. 322r–v. 1p.
Endorsed (fo. 322v): lettre de Madame
Addressed (fo. 322v): To my sonnes

Si valetis, ut cupio est.[420] I cam, I humbly thank God, well hether and before I think your brother was risen, *sed non in laudem nec pro valetudine.*[421] For I was ˆatˆ Ailbons[422] befor 9 of the clock and rode but a convenient pace. I sende purposely to know how and what is or whether owght ˆisˆ by me to done.[423] I have charged to come a way next morning *si Deus voluerit*[424] by 3 of the clock both for his health and for that his leasure was scant now to have come. It is hote here early or elce I am very fainty.[425] For I feele it so. Yf yow have eny thing dispatch by v or six of the clock at farthest. For my man riseth very early two mornings ˆtogetherˆ to avoyde heat and dust and goeth on foote, not used but upon such reqwest of me. Looke well to your selff, servants and loging and the God of mercy be with[426] yow and kepe your mynds in the knowledg and love of him and his holy law.

These be the last partriches kylled yesterday, thinking ˆonceˆ my man shulde have come this morning but it cowlde not be.

Valete in Christo ut filii altissimi.[427]

I pray yow make no spech of your comming since it is no better with yow. Yf yow write to me for eny thing secretly it shalbe don, God wylling.

Your mother.

Shew your brother.

---

[419] **[early July 1593]** This letter is undated, but the internal evidence suggests that it was sent after **58**. Anne mentioned making a journey in **58** and she also complained of the heat that summer in **57** and **61**. Furthermore, Anthony was also planning to visit in July 1593, as revealed in **55** and **61**.

[420] *Si . . . est* [Latin] 'If you are strong, that is my wish'.

[421] *sed . . . valetudine* [Latin] 'but not for praise nor for the benefit of health'.

[422] **Ailbons** St Albans.

[423] **to done** to be done.

[424] *si . . . voluerit* [Latin] 'God willing'.

[425] **fainty** Inclined to faint, sickly.

[426] **with** Repeated.

[427] *Valete . . . altissimi* [Latin] 'Farewell in Christ as the sons of the most high'.

60. *Anthony Bacon to Anne Bacon*, 18 July 1593

Draft. LPL 649, fos 223r–224v. 2pp.
Endorsed (fo. 224v): Lettre a Madame le 18me de july 1593

My most humble dutie remembred with the like thankes to your
Ladiship for your kinde remembrance and care of me and myne estate
every waye, which howe weake and meane soever it be, or maie seeme
to be in the eye of the world, ~~ether~~ both for health ~~or~~ and wealthe, yet
so longe as it shall please God to strengthen the same with his grace
and to blesse me with the inwarde comforte of a Christian and honest
minde, in the course of my lyfe I have juste cause with a thankfull
patience to attend his good pleasure for the betteringe of mine estate
with temporall and externall blessing. Concerninge Mr Standen, as
~~he hath~~ I have saide here to fore, so maie it please your Ladyship
to rest assured that his companie neyther hath nor shall with God's
helpe prejudice me eyther in mynde or bodie and therfore I judge it
^in^ no wyse conveniente that your Ladyship should shewe by letter or
otherwise anie discontentment of his aboade here, so longe as it shall
please her Majestie to like therof. Nether have I nede, I thanke God,
to trouble my Lord Tresorer in demandinge his Lordship's helpe
by loane of anie somme to satisfie my debtes; the effects of whose
good will towards me, accordinge to his Lordship's often protestations
and not altogether without my deservinge, I would eyther request to
some good purpose or els not at all, especiallie consideringe the more
free I keepe my self, the mor bould I maie be with his Lordship in
my brother's behalf, whose benefite and ~~preferment~~ ^advancement^ I
have and shall alwaies esteeme as mine owne. Our most honourable
and kinde frende the Earle of Essex was here yester daie three howers
and hath most frendlie and freelie promised to set up, as they say, his
whole rest of favour and credit for my brother's preferment before Mr
Cooke, whensoever the now Atournie shallbe removed to the ^place^
of the Rowles.[428] His Lordship tould me likwise that

[fo. 224v] he had alreadie ~~tould~~ moved the Queene for my brother and
that she tooke no exceptions to him but said that she must first dispatch
the Frenche and Scotishe Ambassadors and her busines abroad before
she ~~medle with~~ ^thinke of suche^ home matters, and so I most humblie
take my leave.

Twitinham this 18th of Julie.

---

[428] **for my brother's . . . Rowles** Gilbert Gerard, master of the rolls, had died in
February 1593. It was correctly assumed that he would be replaced by Sir Thomas Egerton,
the current attorney-general, leaving that position vacant. Edward Coke became attorney-
general in April 1594.

61. *Anne Bacon to Anthony Bacon*, 31 July [1593][429]

Holograph. LPL 653, fos 338r–339v. 2pp.
Endorsed (fo. 339v): lettre de Madame
Addressed (fo. 339v): To my sonne Anthony Bacon at Gray's Inne

I pray God to bless your coming and allweies in Christ. I make litle speech of it. Have regarde to your easy cariag this veri hote weather; best alone yow shall finde it. 4 horses as yow wylled. Yow will not ryde fast for your selff and the horses being grass and will qwickly take hurt in this heate; one specially very fast which Mr Selwin[430] wyll lyke and use ^well^. Me thowght your coch d[y]d jogg and shake uneasely. Be carefull yow do not be bowlde at the fyrst. Leave goode order for your chamber and loging in safety. No more brute of the town suspition. God kepe us sownde in mynde and body.

I send Mantell's[431] subtile and combersome lease to be consydred. The three yeres' terme endeth the day or two at most after Bartolomew.[432] He takes all tyll then. I wolde know surely yf I do take the remeintyth after that day. Whether I hinder my right for this somer's ^hole^ comodites, which is to me the hole yere's profitts. At this present thus it standeth. Theris unpaid to me the last halff yere of the Annunciation[433] and now this sommer frutes ^due^,[434] which is an C markes, in all one C li. I pray yow speak to your brother to sende sownde and sure advyse and make a goode agreement, yf he can, with down payment, yf he can, *quia indigeo*,[435] or elce what I must and may saffly do after Bartolomew. Goode cownsell. The Lorde be with us in mercy and kepe yow both from synn and evell.

[*Left-hand margin*] Your mother, ABacon.   Gorhambury *ultimo Julii*.[436]

---

[429]**31 July [1593]** Anne sent this letter to Anthony at Gray's Inn. As he had moved to Bishopsgate Street in April 1594, the letter probably dates from the previous summer. Furthermore, the summer of 1593 was a particularly hot one, as testified to by Anne's and Anthony's letters.

[430]**Mr Selwin** Edward Selwyn, an old friend of the Bacon brothers.

[431]**Mantell's** Hugh Mantell, Anthony's steward at Gorhambury.

[432]**Bartolomew** The feast of St Bartholomew the Apostle was on 24 August.

[433]**Annunciation** See p. 107, n. 226.

[434]**this sommer's frutes due** See p. 107, n. 227.

[435]***quia indigeo*** [Latin] 'because I require it'.

[436]***ultimo Julii*** [Latin] 'last day of July'.

62. *Anne Bacon to Anthony Bacon*, 14 August [1593][437]

Holograph. LPL 653, fos 303r–304v. 2pp.
Endorsed (fo. 304v): lettre de Madame
Addressed (fo. 304v): To my sonne Mr Antony Bacon

I was and am very sori when I understoode by Mr Trott your returned payn of the gowt more paynfully. I pray the Lorde sende yow the best cownsell and goode success with all. As I wrote before unto yow, beware of issues never withowt danger and be well advised. I am of an opinion that yow with a constant order ^do not^ prevent taking colde in the affected lymmes and that yow kepe your selff to close and too much owt of the ayre which maketh yow apter to be towched. For it is not almost possible but yow must be tender with keeping in and ^in^ your bed so continually. The gowt is named *pulvinarius morbus*[438] because it lyketh softness and ease. Goode sonne, call upon God to take patiently his correction and using ordinary goode means have comfort and hope yet of better and endevour it as yow may, ~~with~~ yea with some travell of body more then heretofore. Yow eate late and slepe litle and very late, both enemies to a sownd and short recovery. Make not your body by violent and uncessant pullyng and phisick practise unmete and unable to serve God, your prince and cowntry, but procure next care of tru godliness, your health of body, and make not night day nor day night by disorder^ly^ discowrsing and watching to hinder ^and decay^ both mynde and body. God bless yow, cownsell and comfort yow. I had gotten Mr Wyborn's goode ^wyll^ to have come unto yow as I wrote before, but this ^great^ chang of your health and other syck too there makes him ^and^ me dowt of eny opportunitee now, so he stayeth, I am sory, and wyll shortly return to his own howse. Mr Trott continueth frendly wylling to take paine and care for your matters. I desyre to know how it proceadeth with Barly; come not to uneqwall nor unusuall conditions in no wyse. It may be God wyll sende helpe for mony borowing and yet not known, and I wyll prove all my frends rather with his grace and ayde.

[*Left-hand margin*] He took small rest here and interteynment in goode part and hasted early hence. Kepe yee your howse in Christian order exercyse.

14 August.   Your mother, ABacon *Χηρα*.[439]

---

[437] **14 August [1593]** This letter mentions the sale of Barley, which was concluded in September 1593.
[438] ***pulvinarius morbus*** [Latin] 'the cushioned disease'.
[439] ***Χηρα*** [Greek] 'widow'.

63. *Anthony Bacon to Anne Bacon*, 15 August 1593

Draft. LPL 649, fos 262r–263v. 2pp. Damaged and faded.
Endorsed (fo. 263r): A Madame mere de Monsieur et une autre a Monsieur Wyborn, ce une autre a Jian Finche, le 15 aout 1593.[440]

Madame, I can but give your Ladiship moste humble and hartie thanks for your continuall care and remembrance of me and my estate testified aswell by your Ladyship's lettres as by my good frend Mr Trott's particular relation unto me. Whereupon groundinge my selfe, as upon moste fare foundation, I have according to good and sounde advise I sett doune and sente to Alderman Spencer and his councell that which in conscience and equitie accordinge to my trewe meaninge and worde ought to satisfie him.[441] Whom I have plainlie assured that yf he meane to leape over the limites of conscence[442] and equitie for his profitt, I, with juste reason for my credit, will rather imploie my nearest and dearest frends then ascervile[443] my self to unusual and unreasonable inconveniences. His answerre I looke for to morrowe whereof I will not faile to advertice your Ladiship. My brother is still at the coarte in reasonable good health, God be thanked, the dangerous and unlooked for changes. France and Scotlande trouble much and posses her Majestie's minde,[444] who in worldlie discource seemeth to have as much neede, nowe as ever, of God's mightie and mercifull protection by Christien sinceare and timelie councell. And with remembraunce of my ~~moste~~ humble dewtie to your Ladiship, I take my leave.

Twicknam Parcke this 15th of Auguste 1593.

---

[440]*A Madame ... 1593* [French] 'To the mistress, mother of the master, and another to Mr Wyborn, and another to John Finch, on 15 August 1593.' The draft of Anne's letter is written on the verso folio (262v), along with the draft of a letter to John Finch; on the recto side is a draft letter to Percival Wyborn, in response to some spiritual counsel which he had attempted to give to Anthony.
[441]**I sett ... him** Anthony had begun negotiations with John Spencer for the sale of Barley. See 'Money-lenders', p. 241; *Wealth of the Gentry*, p. 102.
[442]**conscence** conscience.
[443]**ascervile** asservile, i.e. to make subservient.
[444]**Fraunce ... minde** Presumably Henri IV of France's abjuration of the Protestant faith on 25 July 1593.

64. *Anne Bacon to Anthony Bacon*, 20 **August [1593]**[445]

Holograph. LPL 653, fos 333r–334v. 2pp.
Endorsed (fo. 334v): lettre de Madame
Addressed (fo. 334v): To my sonne Mr Antony Bacon

Sonne the Lorde in mercy all weyes ^be^ with yow. I am desyrous to know the ende of Barly matter; I pray do wysely herin for your selff and be not readely removed from the best advyse and determynation, but ^ever^ in goode things be constant with circumspection and judgment. I send yow v partriches from Thomas Knite. Dell, under pretence for yow, makes revell ~~and~~ ^in^ my grownd here and leaves allmost none. He every yerre hath new scollers[446] and such as by and with him learne to steale and spoyle the game, and where yow have two, he geves and selle 1/2 doson at least. I know him nowght and a great lyir and very bowlde shameless ^and flattring^ fellow for his own turn. I pray cowntenance him not to the dislyke of your honest neighbours and your own discredit. When I am in heaven, do as God shall gwyde yow, but known nawghty persons[447] use not, nor enterteyn not for eny tattler. Experience wyll teach yow to your cost, I warrant yow, yf yow be hasty that way.

The Lorde bless yow both and thowgh yow answer not *more solito.*[448] When yow were beiond sea, my particulers written, yet I hope yow allow and wyll follow the advyse to your own goode for health and other wyse. And so I commend yow to the love of God in Christ, who bestow goode health upon yow with dayly encrease. I am very sory yow have no learned man. It may be Mr Wyborn, yf he can, will hereafter. Let your servaunts and hole howse exercyse godlynes with prayours and psalmes reverently, morning and evening.

Gorhambury 20 August.

Your mother,
ABacon.

---

[445] **20 August [1593]** This letter has been dated to 1593 because Anthony responded to its points with **65**.
[446] **scollers** scholars.
[447] **nawghty persons** See Proverbs 6:12.
[448] *more solito* [Latin] 'as usual'.

65. *Anthony Bacon to Anne Bacon*, 20 August 1593

Draft. LPL 649, fos 264r–v. 1p.
Endorsed (fo. 264v): A Madame mere de Monsieur le 20me d'aoust 1593

My moste humble dewtie remembred. I could not sende your Ladyship anie certaine advertissement whether I were to breake of or proceed with Alderman Spencer before this daie, when it pleased him nowe the thirde time to come hither and parted but a litle before your man's arryvall, and nowe what hath passed and beene agreed betwixte us, your Ladyship shall understande by Mr Trott's lettre.

As for Dell, he never had promisse of anie favour from me further forth, then he should shewe himself dewtifull to your Ladyship and honest to his neyghbours, but speciall warnings not to spoile the game, and threatinings yf he did, which I hope he will not so soone sett so light by. Towchinge ~~may~~ ^my^ not answeringe particularlie your Ladyship's lettres as some points maie require it, so in matter of advice and admonition from a parent to a childe, I knowe not fitter nor better answerre then signification of a dutyfull acceptance and thankes, unlesse there were juste cause of replie, which howe reasonable soever it be, manie times is more offencive then a respective silence. Yester daie after my longe reste forced by my goute, I had a verie shrewd fitte of the stonne,[449] which I have now paste over, havinge voided three, the leaste as bigge as a barlie corne, by which discharged, God be thanked, I am muche eased. And so I moste humblie take my leave.

Twicknam Parcke this 20 of August 1593.

Your most humble and obedient sonne,
Anthony Bacon.

---

[449] **fitte of the stonne** Attack of kidney stones.

66. *Nicholas Trott to Anne Bacon*, 20 **August 1593**

Copy. LPL 649, fos 248r–249v.[450] 2pp.
Endorsed (fo. 249v): [Lettre a] Monsieur Francois une et une autre a Madame mere de Monsieur. Le 2[0] l'aoust 1593.[451]

Madame my ~~humble~~ dewtie in humble sorte remembred this Mondaie 20 of this Auguste. Alderman Spencer has bene here, my selfe beinge present at his conference with Mr Anthonie your sonne, who by remonstrans and reason hath removed him from dyvers unreasonable demands of bonds and assurances; the rest is referred to a second consideration of Mr Francis to whome the books are to be sent to morrowe, and by reason of the inclyen and yeldinge of the Alderman I thinke will ende in agreement of the bargains. It is agreed upon both parties that it shall not be needfull to send to Sir Nichlas[452] Bacon before the bargaine profited and exquited[453] and the Alderman requireth not with anie earnestnes that he make any assurance reposinge himself uppon such securitie, as without him the lawe will make notwithstandinge for gaininge of time and speedier paiement. Mr Anthonie is determined to sende to Sir Nicholas whom the rest is profited. Thus committinge your Ladyship to the protection of the Almightie. 20 Auguste.

Your Ladyship's trewe servant,
Nicholas Trot.

67. *William Cecil, Lord Burghley, to Anne Bacon*, 29 **August 1593**

Copy. LPL 649, fo. 276r–v. 1p.
Endorsed (fo. 276v): Lettre de Monsieur le Grand Tresorier a Madame mere de Monsieur. Escripte de sa propre main le 29me d'aoust 1593.[454]

Good Madame, I thanke yow for your kinde letter; and for your sons, I thinke your care for them is noe lesse then they both deserve, beinge so quallified in learninge and vertue, as yf they had a supplie of more

---

[450] **fos 248r–249v** This letter is written on the verso of folio 249; the other half of that piece of paper forms folio 248 and on the recto side is written a letter by Nicholas Trott to Francis Bacon on the same day.

[451] *Lettre . . . 1593* [French] 'One letter to Mr Francis Bacon and one other to the mistress, mother of the master. The 20 of August 1593'. The endorsement is partially damaged.

[452] **Nichlas** Nicholas.

[453] **exquited** Trott's use of legal terminology in this letter is somewhat confused; he may have meant to use the word 'executed', as a bargain is executed in law.

[454] *Lettre . . . 1593* [French] 'Letter from the master lord treasurer, to the mistress, mother of the master. Written in his own hand on the 29th August 1593'. This endorsement must refer to the handwriting of the original letter, of which this is a copy.

helth, they wanted nothinge, but none are, ore verie fewe, *ab omni parte beati*,[455] for suche are not elect, but subjecte to ~~temptation~~ tentations,[456] from the highe waye to heaven. For my good will to them, thoughe I am of lesse power to doe my frends good then the worlde thinketh, yet they shall not want the intention to doe them good; and so, God continew yow in his favour, by your meditations, and that I as your olde frende, maie be the partaker of your good wishes and prayers.

From my howse at Theobalds, the 29 of August 1593.

Your Ladyship's lovinge brother in lawe,
W. Bourgley.

68. *Anthony Bacon to Anne Bacon*, 6 September 1593

Draft. LPL 649, fo. 314r–v. 1p.
Endorsed (fo. 314v): une lettre a Madame mere de Monsieur le 6me de septembre, 1593.

My moste humble dutie remembred. Maie it please your Ladyship to be advertised, that yester daie Mr Alderman Spencer, and one of his councell ~~of~~ Mr Altham of Grayse Inne,[457] cominge hether expreslie for that purpose ^we made an ende^ by the sealing and delivered ~~unto him suche~~ ^of^ wrytings which were his ~~done~~ acknowledged ~~by Mr of the~~ here before a master of the Chancerie, so that nowe nothinge resteth but my brother Bacon's[458] joyninge, which beinge done the Alderman is bounde to paie me imeadiatelie 15 hundred pounde more besides the ^fourteine hundred^ pounde he hath alreadie delivered; but yf ^my brother^ make difficultie, I am not to receyve it till the ende of the next tearme, at which time likwise he is to paie ~~me~~ me the other ~~500~~ ^five hundred^ pounde, which makes in all ~~3000~~ 3400 pounde, whereof I am to paie ~~130~~ thirtene hundred pounde to Mr Trot, who moste frendlie and kindlie hath promised me to lende it my brother for the redemeinge of ^Marks out of^ Mr Harvei's hands. I pourpose out of hande to sende to my brother Bacon to knowe his finall resolution, whether he will doe willinglie like a kinde brother without anie prejudice to him or his, that which yf he refuse I shall performe without him by lawe with the helpe of some further tyme. And havinge hard his answere, I meane, God willing, according to

---

[455]*ab ... beati* [Latin] 'blessed in all respects'.
[456]**tentations** Temptations, often used in the sense of an 'experimental trial'. See *OED*.
[457]**Mr Altham of Grayse Inne** James Altham (d. 1617) of London and Oxhey, Herts. See *History of Parliament*, I, p. 341.
[458]**my brother Bacon's** Nicholas Bacon II.

good advise both of phisistions and other of my frends, to goe downe to
the Bath, but in as much as I have bene advertised that the waie hether
is verie ill for a coatche, I am to besiche your Ladiship to spare me,
yf yow maie, your lytter. As for horses and guydes, the Earle of Essex,
I thinke, his Lordship hath promised to furnishe me. I have likwise
speciall neede to use a cooke yf your Ladiship could convenientlie
~~spare~~ ^for beare^ Richard; for rather then your Ladiship should be
anie waie discommodated by want eyther of the one ^or^ of the other
I will take ~~some other~~ otherwise the best order I cann. In the meane
tyme I am to crave pardone at your Ladiship's hands yf I cannot doe
my dewtie in persone, as I desire, till yt shall please God I be retournd
from the Bath, in as tru[th] as before my goinge I shall have ^dailie^
earneste occasion ether to wryte ^unto^ or ~~to~~ heare from my Lord of
Essex and my brother in courte, besides my owne unfitnes to make
anie postinge journey. And so beinge verie sorie ^to have understood^
that your Ladyship have ~~understood~~ bene ^somwhat^ ill at ease, and
besechinge God to strengthen and comforte your Ladyship everie
waie, I most humblie take my leave. Twitnam Parcke, this 6th of
September 1593.

~~Your moste humble~~
Your Ladyship's most dewtifull and lovinge sonne.

69. *Anthony Bacon to Anne Bacon*, 21 September 1593

Draft. LPL 649, fo. 312r–v. 1p.
Endorsed (fo. 312v): Lettre a Madame mere de Monsieur le 22me de septembre 1593

My moste humble dewtie remembred.

As I thought it my parte by my last letter, ~~havinge~~ ^first to^ advertised
your Ladyship of my purpose to goe to the Bath and then to present
my humble and trewe excuses, that I could not absent my self from
~~this place~~ hence for that litle tyme I am to remaine here, by reason of
the continuall occasions I have eyther to sende unto or ^to^ heare from
the earle of Essex and my brother in court, so havinge understood by
your man Winter to my great greef the continuance of your Ladyship's
sicknes, I am most humblie to besiche your Ladyship to let me
knowe whither my presence maie be anie waie serviceable to your
Ladyship before my departure, beinge no lesse redie then bounde to
preferre the performance of such a dewtie before the respects above
mentioned. Maie it please your Ladyship therefore not to make anie
difficultie to commande my personall attendance, for your Ladyship's

service and contentment, otherwise with your Ladyship's good leave, I continue my ~~resolucon~~ purposed journey so soone as I have hearde from my brother Bacon. As for the litter, I humblie thanke your Ladyship ~~I have no need hereof~~ ^it shall not need^, havinge otherwise accommodated my self. The service of Richarde ^the cooke^, seinge it pleaseth your Ladyship to spare him, I shall be willinge to imploie and will sende for him after I have harde out of Suffolk.[459] My brother cam yester night from the courte unlooked for in my Lorde of Essex's coatche and is returnd hether againe this morninge. I cannot tell in what tearms to acknowledge the deserte of the Earle's unspeakable kindnes towards us both, but namelie to him nowe at a pinche, which by God's helpe shortlie will appeare by good effects. Surlie, Madame, I must nede confesse, ~~that the noble~~ besechinge God to give us the ^grace and^ means to be thankfull therefore, the Earle declareth him self more like a father then a frende unto him and doubte not, but yf that he that should be first[460] doe but seconde the earle, that those gifts which God hath bestowed of my brother shall lie no longer fallowe. And so besechinge the Almightie, to give your Ladyship spirituall strength and comforte, wherebie yow maie suppporte with a Christian patience and bodlie visitation whatsoever it shall please him in mercie to laie upon yow, I most humblie take my leave.

Twicknam Parcke this 21th September 1593.

70. *Anne Bacon to Anthony Bacon*, [*c.*23 September 1593][461]

Holograph. LPL 653, fos 203r–204v. 2pp.
Endorsed (fo. 204v): lettre de Madame

Yesterday Godram[462] was here from yow, he sayd, and that yow wolde come and see me, which in no wyse I wolde, as it is now with us both;

---

[459]**after . . . Suffolk** Anthony's half-brother Nicholas Bacon II had inherited Redgrave manor in Suffolk from his father.

[460]**yf . . . first** Namely Lord Burghley, lord treasurer and uncle of Anthony and Francis Bacon. See **67**.

[461][*c.*23 **September 1593**] The dating is provided by Anne's reference to the earl of Essex's departure for the Isle of Wight. See below, p. 150, n. 466.

[462]**Godram** Thomas Gotheram, a servant of Anthony Bacon's. Gotheram had previously been a 'yeoman ordinary' serving Nicholas and Anne Bacon; he was described in Francis Bacon's will as one 'bred with me from a child'. See *Stiffkey*, II, p. 54; *Bacon Letters and Life*, VIII, p. 543. For Gotheram's reports on Gorhambury during Anthony Bacon's European sojourn, see *Troubled Life*, pp. 76–77. By 1609, he held copyhold land in Redbourn. See HALS X/C/7/A.

it much disqwiet me then eny comfort. My howse is trobled inowgh with my sycklines, now in a quarttans[463] in myn owlde age. I pray troble not your selff and me; yf yow had ben in health and made a stepp, I wolde not have mislyked, but I pray yow looke to your selff and pray for me. Doctor Smyth[464] coming did very much satisfye me to know how to order my selff and then rest in the goode wyll and mercy of God, as I humbly thank for his grace I endevour to do. My ansier, yow know. I am sory my wyll is such a poore wyll, not able to dispose 300 li amongst my frends and others I owght, but it is not long of me, having that I have continually kept howse and lyved owt of dett. I never purchased nor bowght eny matter of value, by yow specially and also your brother, but not the thyrde part.

This morning, I being in bed after my fytt that night, one came from my syster Russell,[465] whome I thanked and prayd her to make no mention of me and, as before by Doctor Smyth, I prayd her not to see me for she shall ˆlooseˆ her labour and I wolde not be cumbered with her loging here. My purpose was to kepe my howse and my selff qwiett. My fytts, thowgh very paynfull, yet not extreme, I humbly thanke. The colde seemes to be less sore and shorter and was this last. I sende of purpose. I heare the earle of Essex is gon to the Ile of Wyght.[466] I wyshed your brother had traveled with him for exercyse with but a man or two. Surely yow kepe not a right regarde of your lymms that yow are so never withowt gowt. Yow troble your head and break your slepes, I feare, with *supervacuum*,[467] and want of digestion by want of due rest wyll encrease the gowty humour. I can say no more but God heale yow well. I wyll send yow worde from me except yow sende to me. How your detts are discharged and that from your brother, I desyre to know. God bless yow both. This bearer can enferre of our parish state but wealie.[468]

Your mother, AB.

Gorhambury.

[463]**quarttans** Quartan fever, i.e. a fever that recurs every fourth day.

[464]**Dr Smyth** Richard Smith was a physician to the queen and also to Nicholas Bacon I. He attended the autopsy of Nicholas Bacon I and was a mourner at his funeral. See *Stiffkey*, II, pp. 34, 49, 57, 61.

[465]**my syster Russell** Elizabeth Cooke Hoby Russell. For more on Anne's relationship with her sister, see the Introduction, pp. 27–28.

[466]**I heare ... Wyght** The earl of Essex left for the Isle of Wight on or just before 23 September 1593, as Anthony then revealed in a letter to Anthony Standen that the earl 'hath made a starte' on his journey there. See LPL 649, fo. 298r.

[467]*supervacuum* [Latin] 'unnecessary things'.

[468]**wealie** poor and unproductive (concerning the land).

71. *Anthony Bacon to Anne Bacon*, 23 September 1593

Draft. LPL 649, fo. 313r–v. 1p.
Endorsed (fo. 313v): Lettre a Madame mere de Monsieur le 23me de septembre 1593

My moste humble dewtie remembred. Seinge it hath pleased your good Ladiship to dispence with me at this present ~~for the performance~~ of my personall attendance, I thought it my parte ^to acknowledge^ by these fewe ^lynes^ your Ladyship's ^kinde^ care of my well doinge, and withall to beseche yow to rest assured, that wheresover I be, I shalbe no lesse mindefull and redie ^in harte^ then I am bounde by dewtie, to carrie a continuall remembrance of your ^Ladyship^ in my dailie prayers. Upon my brother's returne, I purpose, God willinge, to begine my journie to the Bathe, which ~~by God's grace~~ yf it doe me noe ^present^ good, yet by God's grace, I ~~shall~~ ^will^ take suche order and advice, as it shall doe me noe harme. Touchinge your Ladyship's cooke, as I made the moition before I knewe of your Ladyship's sicknes, so I praie your Ladyship ~~give me leave~~ to beleve that I would not for anie good, God is my witnes, discomadate your Ladyship ^anie waie^, especiallie seinge I maie provide my self otherwyse, as my brother can certefie your Ladyship. One ~~want~~ ^hinderance^ onlie remaineneth, ~~with which~~ ^towards my of my journie^ wherein with your Ladyship's good leave and favour I am to crave your ~~supplie~~ ^Ladyship's assistance^. Yf it standeth with your lykinge to wit a couple of ^your^ gueldings, which I dare assure your Ladyship, uppon my credit, shalbe so well used and looked unto, as that they shalbe as ~~freshe~~ ^lustie^ and servicable ^God willinge^ at their returne, as yf they had stoode all the while in the stable. And so with remembrance of my moste humble dewtie, and offer of my presence and service, eyther nowe or hereafter whensoever yt shall please your Ladyship to command the ^same^, I commit yow to God's mercyfull and saffe protection.

Twicknam Parcke, this 23 of September 1593.

72. *Anne Bacon to Anthony Bacon*, 18 October 1593

Holograph. LPL 649, fos. 340r–341v. 2pp.
Endorsed (fo. 341v): lettre de Madame 1593
Addressed (fo. 341v): To Mr Anthony Bacon my sonne at Twycknam

I pray God kepe yow saffe from all infection of synne and plage. Yt hath pleased the Lorde to put me in remembrance on both sydes of me by taking two of the syckness, very necessary persons to me, a wydow, specially the goodeman Fynch[469] whose want I shall have cause to lament dayly. His careful, skillful and very trustye husbandyng my speciall rurall busynesses every way procured me, and that even to the ^very^ last, much qwiett of mynde and leasure to spende my tyme in godly exercises, both publick and private. I confess I am so hartely sory for his death as I cannot chuse but moorne my great loss therby and now in my weakysh, syckly age. But the Lorde God doth it to humble his servants and teach them to draw neerer to him in hart unfeynedly, which grace God graunte me to be effectuall in me, I humbly besech ^his Majestie^. Surely, sonne, one cannot value rightly the singular benefitt of such a one in these dissolute and unfaythfull dayes, but by wyse consyderation and goode experience. It may be yow know it er this by sombodye's posting in joylitee;[470] but be wyse and ware in tyme to your own goode estimation and be not redely caried ether to beleve or do upon unthrifte pleasing and boasting speaches, ^and but mockeryes in ded^ to make them profitt of yow and to beare owt their unknown to yow disordred unruliness among their peradventure pott felloshipp companion.[471] There wylbe craving of yow and I wott not what. Promiss not rashely, be *tui juris*.[472] Yow shalbe better esteemed, both of wyse and unwyse, before that *puniens experientia docebit tuo malo*.[473]

It is sayde that Thystleworth[474] is visited. Some talk how Finch shulde take it there in bayting his horse, but now he is gon. So was the wyll of God who bless yow and sende yow much goode of all your bodely phisick and make yow strong to do his holy wyll to your comfort. *Sis tardus ad loqwendum et promittendum ne sero peniteat*.[475] Commende me to your brother. Looke well to your ^howse^ and servants for late and night roads now towarde wynter.

18 October 93.

Your sad mother, ABacon.

[469]**goodeman Fynch** John Finch. See p. 103, n. 202.
[470]**joylitee** jollity.
[471]**peradventure pott felloshipp companion** Presumably Anne means 'without doubt drinking companion'.
[472]*tui juris* [Latin] 'of your own right', i.e. be master of your own affairs.
[473]*puniens . . . malo* [Latin] 'punitive experience shall teach you to your cost'.
[474]**Thystleworth** Twickenham Park, Francis Bacon's chosen retreat in the 1590s, was more commonly known as Thistleworth or Isleworth Park up to the mid-sixteenth century. See p. 129, n. 357, and D. Lysons, *The Environs of London*, III (London, 1795), p. 442.
[475]*sis . . . peniteat* [Latin] 'Be slow in speaking and promising lest you repent when it is too late'. See James 1:19.

73. *Anthony Bacon to Anne Bacon*, 19 October 1593

Draft. LPL 649, fos 337r–338v. 2pp.
Endorsed (fo. 338r): Lettre a Madame ˆmere de Monsieurˆ le 19 d'octobre 1593.
Addressed (fo. 337r): To the honorable his very good Lady and mother
the Lady Anne Bacon widdowe.[476]

My most humble dewtie remembred. I thought it my parte to advertice
your Ladyship, that on Saterdaie laste I undertooke a journey to
the courte, with resolution to have donne my most humble dewty
to her Majesty. But havinge ˆpasedˆ three partes of the waye betwixt
Colboroughe and Eaton, I was so sadonily surprised by an extreame fit
of the stone that I was faine to take the nexte harboroughe[477] at Eaton.
Where findinge my self so weake as that it had chargued rather in me
a very great presumption then a dewtyfull minde to have presented
my self, thoughe it had bene possible, to her Majesty in so painfull a
plight, I commited the signification of my uttermost endevour and my
unlooked for pange ~~to the right honorable my very to the relation of~~
to the Earle of Essex ˆrelationˆ to her Majesty, who hath very
gratiouslie accepted thereof as your Ladyship should have seene by
the Earl's owne letter, but that I know your Ladyship could not read
my Lord's hande, it beinge as hard as any cypher to those that are not
thoroughlie acquainted therewith. It was no finalle comforte likwyse
ˆto meˆ to understand from my Lady Russell[478] that her Majesty about
~~her Majesty~~ a seven night ~~befo~~ agoe openly in the parcke[479] ~~vouch~~
before divers vouchsaffed of her self without any other occasion to
make mention of me and to moane muche my infirmity, protestinge
with oth[480] that yf I had but half as muche health as honestie and other
sufficientcie, shee knowe not througheout ~~not~~ her realme where to
finde a better servant and more to her lykinge. In returninge I met
with my Lord Tresurer[481] in his coach, whom havinge saluted out of
myne a foote man ˆthe highe wayeˆ, his Lord tooke that dewty very
kindlie and promised to joyne with the Earle in the rapportinge to her
Majestie my dewtyfull endevour. And renderinge

---

[476]**To . . . widdowe** This address is followed by a brief note in French, '*l'Monsieur par le present*' ('the master by the present'). This may mean 'by the present letter', although the incomplete nature of the phrase not only makes the meaning unclear but also makes it unclear whether this note was intended to be included in the letter.

[477]**harboroughe** harbour.

[478]**Lady Russell** Lady Elizabeth Cooke Hoby Russell, Anthony Bacon's aunt.

[479]**the parcke** St James's Park. Elizabeth I had gates and bridges erected to facilitate her walks in the park. See A. Somerset, *Elizabeth I* (New York, 1991), p. 364.

[480]**oth** oath.

[481]**Lord Tresurer** William Cecil, Lord Burghley.

[*Left-hand margin*] most humble thankes in my behalfe for her gratious remembrances of and good speeches of me, this I wryte not ~~upp~~ to your Ladyship upon any vaine glory but ^to that ende^ that your Ladyship may aswell be ^made^ partaker of my comforts ~~as~~ ^as advertised^ of my ~~paine as~~ crosses.

[*fo. 337v*] Touchinge the decease of goodman Finche, next after your Ladyship and his wyfe and children, I thinke noe body hath loste more nor consequently have greater cause to regreat him then my self. Yet God forbid that the ~~greatnes of the~~ ^remembrance of so great a^ losse in respect of your Ladyship's contentment and the necessary use of his service should make me so farr forget my self as to grudge or repine at God's unsearchable justice or to enter thereupon into any distrust of his mercyfull providence, which never leveth destitute of comfortable supplies those that have resource and truste thereunto. Lastlie it may please your Ladyship to rest assured that ^eyther^ to anye to succeed in ^Finche^ his chardge or to medle with ought ^els^ that concerneth your Ladyship's livinge ^without your leave^, I am so furr[482] from that rashnes or presumption as that I have more neede to be drawne on ~~by~~ ^to^ suche cares then ^of^ cavats to keepe me from hasty promises. And so I most humblie take my leave.

Twicknam Parcke, this 19th of October 1593.

Your Ladyship's moste humble and obedient sonne,
Anthony Bacon.

74. *Anne Bacon to Anthony Bacon*, [late October 1593][483]

Holograph. LPL 653, fos 201r–202v. 2pp.
Endorsed (fo. 202v): lettre de Madame
Addressed (fo. 202v): To my sonne

I purposely send to know how yow do, and what your brother, and determyn for coming hether. I cannot as I wolde provyde but sustentatyve meat; I wyll as I can provyde. Besyde the loss of the man Fynch, I have also a great want of the use of that howse, for yll was my dayry and powltry at all tymes, in season or owt. Herabowts is not the lyke; for the cawse of it, certeintee and reasonable price. He is with God, I trust. Even but yesterday it is advertysed abroad for very too

---

[482] **furr** far.
[483] **[late October 1593]** The death of John Finch was reported to Anthony on 18 October 1593 (**72**).

trew that a mayde hath ^a^ sore come foorth on her[484] at Buttler's[485] to
the encrease of much discomfort to the wydow and here yf yow come
yow must be very carefull for your men from stray^ng^ eny where, nor
not to Redborn. For Gooderam, I wyll tell yow more when yow come,
yf yow wyll beleve; a riotous, prowde, crafty fellow, all to get credit by
yll.

My fitts encrease and I weaker tyll the tyme God hath appointed. I
wyll have no resort hether because I wolde be qwiett in my sycklines
and surely all your servaunts must kepe goode order and due tymes
here. I know Hynds untymely starting last tyme; it was no marvell,
thowgh your horse miscaried, had yow known all, and marred myn
too. I do determyn to watch better over them and for stealers commers
to mocke me. I wolde prepare my selff to the Lorde's goode wyll. God
bless yow and shew mercy unto me, I humbly besech hym.

Your mother, AB.

Let not my lettre be sene, but to your brother, and teare it.

75. *Anthony Bacon to Anne Bacon*, 2 November 1593

Draft. LPL 649, fo. 399r–v. 1p.
Endorsed (fo. 399v): A Madame le 2me de novembre 1593
Addressed (fo. 399r): To the honorable his very good Ladye and mother
the Ladye Anne Bacon widowe at Gorhamburie in Hertfordshire

Madame,
My most I thanks most humbly thanke your Ladishipp for your
letter and sending your man Bashforde to visite me, who purposeth,
with God's helpe, so soone as possibly I can, to doe my dewtie to your
Ladyship, but the sonest I doubt wilbe much as ten daies to morrow
or next Mondaie come senight.[486] My brother, I thinke, will goe to
St Albon's soner with my Lord Keeper,[487] who hath kindly offred
him rome his owne lodginge there, as he hath also accomodated
him in his of a ^alredy of late, resigned unto him the use of his^
chamber in the courte. God forbid that your Ladiship shall trouble
your self any what more with anie extraordinary care in respect of
our presence, which yf we thought should be the leste cause of ^your^

[484]**a sore ... her** A plague sore.
[485]**Buttler's** Butler's manor in Redbourn. See 'Catalogue of field names', pp. 28–29. For
the local use of the name 'Butlers', see W.J. Hardy, 'Some old lawsuits connected with St
Albans', *St Albans Architectural and Archaeological Society Transactions* (1892), pp. 16–17.
[486]**senight** Sennight meant a period of seven days, i.e. a week.
[487]**Lord Keeper** Sir John Puckering. See p. 119, n. 299.

discontentment, we would rather absent our selves then occasion ~~yow~~ anie waie your Ladyship's disquietnes. As for Gotheram, I have bene and shalbe allwaies redye to heare dewtyfully your Ladyship's motherlie admonitions touchinge him or any other man or matter and to respect them as I ought. And so with remembrance of my humble dewtie I beseche God to preserve and comfort your Ladiship.

Twikinam Parcke, this 2 of November 1593.

76. *Anne Bacon to Anthony Bacon*, [late 1593][488]

Holograph. LPL 653, fo. 256r–v. 1p.
Endorsed (fo. 256v): lettre de Madame

Gragg bringing malt hether, I was playn with him. He had don evell to broak such a husband for wydow Finch, as his wyff made a way her selff an infamous note to him for ever in this lyff. He for his cowllour answerd yow had seene him and lyked him well. It was a base office, I sayde, to make yow the autour of it, who knew all but by him. I spake with her since and towlde as she was of yeres and experience to consider well another mariag and regard of him gon, of her own comfort, and her chyldern's thereby, ˆso I ment not but shortly to advise herˆ ~~I perceaved~~ and prayde her to pray to the Lorde to advise and cownsell her. I perceaved she was browght to some good opinion of him, wherof I was sory and towlde her for myne own part I cowlde never lyke such a fowle, blotted husband for her, nor such a neybour so nere as Butlers and therfore in my tyme, as it pleaseth God, I wolde never consent to her lenger continuance in Buttlers, for feare of diverse inconvenience, but that it were best for her, yf she ˆsoˆ mattched, to go away and dwell with him to avoyde obloqwy.[489] Surely, sonne, I verely think it were very hurtfull for yow to have such an infamed so nere a tenant. Besydes of trowth he is cownted but a loose lyver, in dett, hath many chyldern and one of Gragg's worthy prayses, forsooth: a good fellow, that is as much as a riotus pott companion and qwareling lyke with all. They wyll prease yow but consent not to your own harm hereafter. I thowgt[490] it good to declare thus much unto yow in tyme.

---

[488] **[late 1593]** This undated letter must have been written after the death of John Finch in October 1593 (**72**). From Anne's reference to Anthony's guests, it seems to have been written in response to Anthony's discussion of his forthcoming visit to St Albans (**75**).
[489] **obloqwy** Verbal abuse.
[490] **thowgt** thought.

Take heede to your selff.[491] For all your gests, I wolde I had fitt for them and yow. So God bless yow more and more.

Peero[492] must return to day.

ABacon *mater*.[493]

Gorhambury Thursday.

77. *Anne Bacon to Anthony Bacon*, [late 1593][494]

Holograph. LPL 653, fo. 332r–v. 1p.
Endorsed (fo. 332v): lettre de Madame

I thank yow, sonne, for your payns to make good agreement betwixt the wombe and frute therof. My neighbour Smyth[495] came to me to desyre yow also to make an indifferent ^ende^ for both parts betwixt wydow Finch and him. He sayth he made sodenly a foolysh bargain and can be content with some loss to warn him. I wolde not hynder her but yet not extremytee. God encrease your health with his favour.

Your mother, AB.

78. *Francis Bacon to Anne Bacon*, 4 December 1593

Copy. LPL 649, fo. 433r–v. 1p.
Endorsed (fo. 433v): Mr Francis Bacon to my Lady Anne Bacon 1593

Madame, I receyved this afternoone at the court your Ladyship's lettre after I had sent back your horse and written to yow this morning. And for my brother's kindnes, it is accustumed; he never having yet refused his securitye for me, as I on the other syde never mad[e] any difficultie to do the like by him according to our severall occasions. And therfore yf it be not to his own disfurnishinge, which I rekon all one with myne owne want, I shall receyve good ease by that hundreth poundes; speciallie your Ladyship of your goodnes being content it

---

[491] **Take . . . selff** See Deuteronomy 4:9. There is evidence that Anne was particularly interested in St Basil's homily on this biblical verse: see *Cooke Sisters*, p. 32.

[492] **Peero** Little Peter. See p. 110, n. 242.

[493] *Mater* [Latin] 'mother'.

[494] **[late 1593]** This undated letter is difficult to assign to a specific chronology. However, again, it must have been written after the death of John Finch in October 1593 (**72**) and his widow was the subject of concern for Anne Bacon at this time (**76**).

[495] **My neighbour Smyth** Presumably Richard Smyth, a copyhold tenant at Westwick Pray, part of the Gorhambury estate. Smith also acted as a juror for the Gorhambury manorial court in 1596. See HALS XI/2; X/B/3/A.

be repaied of Mr Boldroe's[496] dette, which it pleased yow to bestowe upon me. And my desire is it be paied to Knight[497] att Graies Inne, who shall receyve order from me to paye two fieties[498] (which I wish had been two hundredths) where I ow and wheare it presseth me most. Sir Jhon Foskeu[499] is not yet in court; both to him and otherwise I willbe mindfull of Mr Downing's[500] cause and libertie with the first opportunitie. Mr Nevell,[501] my cosin, though I be furder distant then I expected, yet I shall have an apt ocasion to remember. To my cosen Kemp I am sending. But that would rest between your Ladyship and my self as yow sayd. Thus I commend your Ladyship to Godde's good providence. From the court this iiii of 1obre[502] 1593.

Your Ladyship's most obedient sonne,
FB.

79. *Anne Bacon to Anthony Bacon*, 1 January [1594][503]

Holograph. LPL 653, fo. 358r–v. 1p.
Endorsed (fo. 358v): lettre de Madame

The bearer herof William Finch of the Pray[504] to whome his father did appoint that ^farm^ lease, after his ^second^ sonne Richard dyd, refused and chose rather to dwell with him. Now his mother is very wylling to resyng over her yeares to him for more assurance and he is very desyrous and she too for to have yours and my goodewyll fyrst ^er the^ ~~the~~ doing it. It is good both for the mother and the sonne it be done presently, she being well contented to perform her husband's wyll herin. For this cawse he now comes to yow. The farm nedes reparation, sonne, and he hath allready ben at charg by this late

---

[496]**Mr Boldroe's** Presumably Francis Boldero. See **10**.
[497]**Knight** Robert Knight. See p. 109, n. 239.
[498]**fieties** fifties.
[499]**Sir Jhon Foskeu** Presumably Sir John Fortescue, who had been chancellor of the exchequer since 1589.
[500]**Mr Downing's cause and libertie** Presumably William Downing, a London notary. Downing was from a Suffolk family, which may explain the connection to the Bacons. In 1583, Anthony Bacon alienated land in Kent and Essex to William Downing. See *History of Parliament*, II, p. 52; 'Money-lenders', p. 239.
[501]**Mr Nevell** Henry Neville was married to Anne Killigrew, daughter of Katherine Cooke Killigrew, niece to Anne Bacon and cousin to Anthony and Francis Bacon.
[502]**1obre** An abbreviation for December.
[503]**1 January [1594]** This letter must have been written after the death of John Finch in October 1593 (**72**), so would seem likely to date from January 1594.
[504]**the Pray** Westwick Pray was part of the Gorhambury estate.

stormes. He, sonne, an honest plain man and they say thryving. God looke on yow with mercy and encrease goode health.

1 January.

Your mother,
ABacon.

80. *Anne Bacon to Anthony Bacon* [*c.*10 January 1594][505]

Holograph. LPL 653, fo. 365r–v. 1p. Damaged.
Endorsed (fo. 365v): lettre de Madame

I pray sonne, send not to Albons to Mr Lockey[506] towching Dorball as yet. I think that the same Winter[597] wylbe advised before he deale with him, and as for Winter's wordes, fond inowgh ~~inow~~ to me, it is the man's ^custom they say^. I make no ^great^ reaconing of such person's speches. I have such usage often where I owght not and have learned not to make a matter of every such and wolde ^not^ have Mr Lockey deale in eny thing concerns my selff. He is an open ^mowthed^ man with owt all discretion, full of foolysh babling. He wolde make all the town ryng of his foolyshnes. I pray yow defende not me this way; I nether lyke it ner nede. Prowde speaches common and I am acqwainted with them and do rather contemn then regarde. It were not yet to styrr for Dorbull. Yf yow cowntenance him, it wyll cawse the other not to be hasty. But I have and mean styll to harken.

81. *Anthony Bacon to Anne Bacon,* 10 January 1594

Draft. LPL 649, fo. 22r–v. 1p.
Endorsed (fo. 22v): Lettre a Madame mere de Monsieur le 10iesme de janvier 1593
Addressed (fo. 22r): To the honorable his very good Lady and mother the Lady Anne Bacon widdowe

Madame, seinge your Ladyship thinks it needlesse that Winter should be called to account or any waie delt with all for his undewteyfull demeanour and speeches, I am very well content to rest spare eyther imployinge of Lockey or any other

---

[505] [*c.*10 January 1594] Letter **81** was written in response to this one.
[506] **Mr Lockey** Richard Lockey, mayor of St Albans in 1589 and principal burgher until 1598. See *Corporation Records*, pp. 14, 32, 35, 39, 40, 55, 292.
[597] **towching Dorball . . . the same Winter** Presumably Winter is Anne's servant, described as 'your man Winter' by Anthony Bacon (**69**). The identity of Dorball/Dorbull is not known.

~~which yet should I have thought.~~ I have reason to thinke that Winter's insolency ~~beinge so ordinary as it~~ ^(beinge a thinge ordinary with him)^ is or shalbe ~~nowe knowne and spoken~~ so much knowne and spoken of by his own braggs. Thus that Lockey's knowledge and *entremise*[508] could ^have^ avoad[509] nothinge thereunto. So soone as Mr Trot's man, whom his master looked for yester daie, shallbe returned ^from my brother^ I will not faile to advertise your Ladyship. I signified yester daie to the widdowe Finche that I was glad to understand her purpose to performe her husband's trew will and meaning towards ^ther younger^ children and have promised her my helpe therein in case the eldest should be intysed by ~~advan~~ some advantage of lawe ~~should~~ ^to^ forget the dewty both of a sonne and a brother, vainely beinge ^otherwise^ so well provided for and lefte ~~other wyse~~ by his late father. And so with remembrance of my humble dewty, I take my leave.

Redborne, this 10th of Januarie 1593.

Your Ladiship's humble and obedient sonne.

82. *Anne Bacon to Anthony Bacon*, 31 January 1594

Holograph. LPL 649, fo. 9r–v. 1p.
Endorsed (fo. 9v): lettre de Madame 1593

One ende of matter drawes on another, I am afrayd. Yow shall oft be trobled wth brabling matters, yet being your neybours to do goode among them pleaseth God and for your credit. My neighbour Laceby is combred with William Dell's nawghty dealing,[510] but that fellow is shameless and a wrangle crafty makebate,[511] geven to decrease with a scoffing impudency. I never yet knew him other; Mr Downing hath ^had^ much a doo with him and so shall yow.[512] Laceby is loth to law with him, but the other loves of lyst[513] crafte in word and dede. God make yow able for his servyce and your cowntry and be carefull every way for it, both *sustinendo et abstinendo*.[514] I am hartely glad for your good

---

[508]*entremise* [French] 'mediation'.
[509]**avoad** Presumably 'avoided'.
[510]**My neighbour ... dealing** Presumably Robert Laceby, who held land directly abutting that of the Dell family in Westwick Row. See HALS XI/2.
[511]**makebate** Fomentor of trouble and strife.
[512]**Mr Downing ... yow** The mention of Downing suggests that Anne was here referring to the manorial court. See the Introduction, p. 32.
[513]**lyst** cunning.
[514]*sustinendo et abstinendo* [Latin] 'sustaining and abstaining'.

^and qwiett^ ending of the Finches' ^cawses^. God encrease his grace in yow to do much goode, both wysely and religiously. When I can, I wyll see yow, but be yow very ware to jorny ^hastely^ after your great payn, phisick and chamber keepin, this very harde and colde season.

Gorhambury *ultimo Januarii*[515] 1593.

Your mother.

83. *Anthony Bacon to Anne Bacon*, 1 February 1594

Draft. LPL 649, fo. 48r–v. 1p.
Endorsed (fo. 48v): A Madame le premier de fevrier 1593 par le petit garcon petit Pierre[516]
Addressed (fo. 48r): To the honorable his verie good Lady

Madame, I am bould to referre your Ladyship to the beginninge of Mr Crewe's lettre, which I send here inclosed concerninge my brother; the rest beinge particularities not worth your Ladyship's reding. There is great speache at this time bothe at the court and cyty of Doctor Lopus, his accusation and commitinge ~~for~~ upon highe treason; the grounde whereof is thought by some to have bene discouvered by Don Antonio before his late goinge over into France.[517] Where the Frenche King's affaires succeede of late very well, as I have bene advertised this day by Mr Castol,[518] the princepall Frenche minister in Monsieur de la Fontaine's[519] absence, who is gone as assistant to Sir Robert Sidney sent by her Majestie into France.[520] And so with remembrance of my most humble dewty, I take my leave.

Redborne, this first of February 1593.

[515] ***ultimo Januarii*** [Latin] 'the last day of January'.
[516] ***A Madame ... Pierre*** [French] 'To the mistress, on the first day of February 1593, by the little boy, little Peter'.
[517] **There ... into France** Roderigo Lopez was the Portuguese physician of Elizabeth I. He was arrested at the end of January 1594 for conspiring to poison the queen. Dom António, prior of Crato, was a claimant to the Portugese throne.
[518] **Mr Castol** Jean Castol. See p. 133, n. 390.
[519] **Monsieur de la Fontaine's** Robert Le Maçon de la Fontaine, the principal minister of the French Stranger Church from 1574. For more on la Fontaine, see G. Ungerer, *The Correspondence of Antonio Pérez's Exile*, 2 vols (London, 1974–1976), I, pp. 330–331, n. 2.
[520] **Sir Robert Sidney ... France** Robert Sidney had been sent on an embassy to Henri IV of France in early 1594, following the French monarch's conversion to Catholicism.

84. *Anne Bacon to Anthony Bacon*, 4 February [1594][521]

Holograph. LPL 653, fo. 336r–v. 1p.
Endorsed (fo. 336v): lettre de Madame
Addressed (fo. 336v): To my sonne at Redborn

I pray God hartely to geve yow stregth[522] to beare and his healing help to overcome saffely the whole cause of your present payn. Full payn, no dowt, by all lykelyod[523] of your thyck, trobled urin and other tokins incident, the master *calculus*[524] is yet behind. Yow must in eny wyse be speciall carfull yow take no violent things to break it, for the peece wyll so cutt yow and raw the[525] place, that the smart theroff wylbe intollerable and very dangerous. I know yow should anoynt yow beneth and also the ^place before^ avoyding with oyle of allmons, as I remember, and oyle of lynsell.[526] I am not sure whether also camomyll oyle myxt. Once your father dowted much the avoyding and was proved with small qwylls, ravens ^or crowes^ I think, to helpe to turn it in the passag, yf nede were. Mr Huick[527] was then present at the doing, very gently at tymes. Your father dyd drink for some few dayes allmon mylk with the fower colde seedes, as they call them.[528] I wolde Dr Smyth[529] were with yow to consyder. Yf yow wyll sende one fyttest of your men, I wyll wryte to him earnestly. It were good to delay for casting yow into a feever, lacking slepe, ^when^ holsome, smoth and thine diett for the tyme best. Theris a bath yf yow did prove in goode order, but two howers, not thin with water, but full with certein herbes soden and some mylk and sytt in it but upp to your and a litle above your loyns. Yf yow wyll lett me, I wyllingly wyll come and make it for yow with less toyle to yow then the poticary. I have learnt by experience both of your father and my selff.

---

[521]**4 February [1594]** Nicholas Faunt consoled Anthony on his attack of kidney stones on 31 January 1594. See LPL 650, fo. 52r.
[522]**stregth** strength.
[523]**lykelyod** likelihood.
[524]*calculus* [Latin] 'stone'.
[525]**the** Repeated.
[526]**lynsell** linseed.
[527]**Huick** Robert Huicke was physician to Henry VIII, Edward VI, and Elizabeth I. He attended the autopsy of Nicholas Bacon I. See *Stiffkey*, II, p. 36.
[528]**fower ... them** The seeds of cucumbers, melons, watermelons, and pumpkins were known as the four (major) cold seeds, *quatuor semina frigida*, and were thought to be helpful in treating kidney complaints. See J. Dubois, *Methodus medicamenta componendi* (Lyon, 1548), p. 154, sig. K5v.
[529]**Dr Smyth** Richard Smith. See p. 150, n. 464.

[Left-hand margin] I pray lett me heare and the Lord take care of yow and saffly ease yow.

4th February. AB, your mother.

When Morer[530] is come, I wyll come qwickly, *Deo propitio.*[531]

85. *Anthony Bacon to Anne Bacon*, 5 February [1594][532]

Draft. LPL 649, fo. 49r–v. 1p.
Endorsed (fo. 49v): Lettre a Madame mere de Monsieur le 5me de fevrier
Addressed (fo. 49r): To the honorable his verie good Ladie and mother, the Lady Anne Bacon, widdowe.

Madame,

Beinge not able my self to doe my dewtie to your Ladyship, I thought it my part to advertise yow that which a frende of mine hath particularly written unto me by the Earle of Essex['s] appointment, prencepally concerninge my brother and *obiter*[533] some other *occurrens*[534] wherein I assure your Ladyship I alter not one worde, thinking it best to set it downe as it hath bene delivered from my Lord, who said one Thursdaie that the Queen's Majestie had understoode that my brother had argued verie well in a case of importance in the King's Benche.[535]

That the Earle at the same instant cominge from the Queen, she tould him that my Lord Tresurer[536] had streytly urge[537] ^her^ to the nomination of Cook to be her Generall Atturnie,[538] ~~and~~ also to the nomination of a paire of Secretaries[539] (Sir Robert Cycill and Sir Edward Stafforde) and a paire of other officers in her houshold (all these to be one Candlemas daie placed or at the furdest the Sondaie

---

[530]**Morer** Robert Moorer described himself as a 'grocer' (see LPL 658, fo. 120r); the Bacons seem to have used him specifically for their medical purchases. He also supplied stage props, including rosewater and musk, for royal masques in 1572 and 1573. See M. Wiggins and C. Richardson, *British Drama 1533–1642: a catalogue: volume II: 1567–1589* (Oxford, 2012), pp. 90, 109.

[531]*Deo propitio* [Latin] 'God willing'.

[532]**5 February [1594]** The discussion of Francis Bacon's argument in the King's Bench and the attempts of Essex to seek his advancement to the position of attorney-general, together with the details regarding Roderigo Lopez's arrest, date this letter to 1594.

[533]*obiter* [Latin] 'incidentally'.

[534]*occurrens* [Latin] 'occurences'.

[535]**My brother ... Benche** Francis Bacon argued his first cases in the King's Bench in January 1594, arguing another on 5 February.

[536]**Lord Tresurer** William Cecil, Lord Burghley.

[537]**urge** urged.

[538]**Cook ... Generall Atturnie** Edward Coke was appointed attorney-general on 10 April 1594.

[539]**the nomination ... Secretaries** The position of secretary of state was vacant after the death of Francis Walsingham in April 1590.

followinge) but said the Earle, 'Mr Baccon shall ~~understand~~ ^finde^ by the event that howsoeuer the olde man and his sonne[540] doe beleve, the same now of them shallbe as yet'.

That Doctor Lopus for all the favorers he had was on Tewsdaie at nine committed to the Tower and the Wednesdaie followinge at seven of clocke in the morninge beinge examined before the Earle and Sir Robert Cycell confessed more then enoughe. They two returninge backe in coatche together, Sir Robert began of him self saying 'My Lord, the Quene is resolved, ere five daies passe, without anie furder delaie to make an Attournie Generall, I praie your Lordship let me knowe whom yow will favour and desire to preferre'. To which the Earle answered that he wondered Sir Robert should ask him that question, seinge it could not be unknowne unto him that resolutely againste all who soever, he stoode for Francis Bacon. 'Good Lord', quoth Sir Robert, 'I wonder your Lordship should goe about to spende your strength in so unliklie and impossible a matter', desiring that my Lord would alledge unto him but ^one^ only president of so rawe a youth to a place of suche moment. My Lord workinge upon the speeche of Sir Robert said that for the Attournieship, which was but an ordynary office of justice, he could not produce anie instants bycause he had never made any searche therefor, but that a younger then Francis Bacon of lesser learninge and of no greater experience seueth[541] and shoueth withall might and maine for an office of farre greater importance, state and chardge then the Attournishipp, suche a one the Earle said he could name unto him. To which Sir Robert replied that he well knewe my Lord noted him selff but admittinge that both his yeares and experience were but small yet wayinge the schoole ~~he~~ ^Sir Robert^ studied in, the great

[*Left-hand margin*][542] wisdome and learninge of his schoolour,[543] the paines and observations he daily passe in that schoole, he thought his forces and wisdome be sufficient to swaye that machinge,[544] alledginge withall ~~his father's~~ ^my Lord Tresorer's^ deserts, his continuall and painfull travails of so longe regiment, to merit a note of gratitude from her Majesty in the persone of his sonne in sum. ~~Touching~~ ^For the matter of^ my brother, he praied my Lordship to be better

---

[540] **the olde . . . sonne** William Cecil, Lord Burghley, and his son Sir Robert Cecil.
[541] **seueth** To chase or pursue (to sue for).
[542] **[*Left-hand margin*]** There is a small torn piece of a second folio still extant, which forms an extended left-hand margin and contains the remainder of this letter.
[543] **schoolour** Schoolmaster, i.e. his father, Lord Burghley.
[544] **machinge** scheme.

advised sayinge 'Yf your Lordship had spoken of the Solicitorsship[545] that mought[546] be of easier digestion to her Majesty'. 'Digest me noe digestinge', said the Earle, 'for the Attournship is that I must have for Francis Bacon and in that will I spende my uttermost credit, frendship and aucthority against whomsoever and that whosoere went about to ~~get the office~~ procure it to others, that it should test both meadiators and the sutors, the settinge one before they cam by it. And this be yow assured of Sir Robert', quoth the Earle, 'For now do I fully declare my self and for your owne part, Sir Robert, I thinke muche and strange both of my Lord your father and yow that can have the minde to seeke the preferment of a stranger before so near a kindsman, namelie consideringe yf yow waie in a ballance his parts and sufficiency in any respect with those of his competitor, exceptinge only five poore yeares of admittance, which Francis Bacon hath more then recompensed with the priority of his readinge, in all other respects yow shall finde noe comparison between them.' These speeches it pleased my Lord to confirme unto my brother upon Fridaie ^laste^ at Graise Inne and promised him to be present in the King's Benche at his next pleadinges, which was appointed this daie ~~leavinge my brother~~ and so he departed from ~~there~~ my brother's lodginge leaving him justly verie glad and comforted to see my Lord sticke so stoughtly and surely to him and to make it his owne case. And so with remembrance of my humble dewty I take my leave.

86. *Anthony Bacon to Anne Bacon*, 8 February 1594

Draft. LPL 649, fo. 47r–v. 1p.
Endorsed (fo. 47v): Lettre a Madame le 8iesme de feuvrier 1593 par petit Pierre[547]

Madame,
    Maie it please yow to be advertised that two or three daies after the conference betwixt the Earle of Essex and Sir Robert Cycell, my Lord Tresorer vouchsaffed, uppon what motive God knowth, to use a verie honorable compliment towards my brother in sendinge Mr Hickes, his secretarie,[548] to him at Greise Inne, with chardge to tell him from his Lord that he did with much joye and contentment congratulate

---

[545]**Solicitorsship** Edward Coke held the position of solicitor-general, which would be vacated when he became attorney-general.
[546]**mought** might.
[547]*Lettre . . . Pierre* [French] 'Letter to the mistress, on the 8 of February 1593 delivered by little Peter'.
[548]**Mr Hickes, his secretarie** Michael Hickes was one of Lord Burghley's secretaries from 1580.

unto my brother the first fruicts of his publique practise and requested ~~him~~ to sende ^him his^ case and the cheif pointes of his pleading to the ende he might make report thereof there where it mought[549] doe him most good. Mr Fant[550] and Mr Gosnall[551] ~~requested~~ ^have desired^ me to remember their humble dewty to your Ladiship, which they would have performed them selves in persone, but for the haste they made to be at my brother's pleadings to morrowe in a most ^famous^ Exchecker Chamber case where the Lord Keeper and the Lord Treasorer, yf he be able, the two Lord's Cheif Justices, with two other judges of eache benche, the Lord Cheif Baron and the rest of the barons are to it.[552] I beseche God to strengthen his understandinge and memorie with the vertue of his holie spirit to the ende that his words findinge grace before so manie princopall majestrats, he maie thereby hereafter be more enabled and encouraged to imploie his good gyftes to the best purposes; I meane to the advancement of God's glorie and her Majesty and country service. And so with humble thanks to your Ladyship that it please yow to spare me an other quarter of wheate, I take my leave.

Your Ladyship's most humble and obedient sonne.

Redborne, this 8 of Februarie 1593.

87. *Bartholomew Kemp to Anne Bacon*, 8 February 1594

Draft. LPL 649, fo. 30r–v. 1p.
Endorsed (fo. 30v): Lettre de Monsieur Bartholomew Kemp a Madame Bacon de 8issime de feuvrier 1593
Addressed (fo. 30r): To the honorable ~~his~~ and my especiall good Lady, the Lady Bacon at Gorhamburie, give theise

Good Madame, as I have alwaies founde your Ladyship bothe good and gratious unto me, even from my youth uppe hither unto, soe I moste humbly beseche yow not to forsake me and leave me in my greatest nede and necessity. I have had, as it is well knowne, theise two laste yeares ii great extraordenary charges, which I trust wilbe to the benefit of my wyffe and children yf God call me before them.

---

[549]**mought** might.
[550]**Mr Fant** Nicholas Faunt. See p. 99, n. 185.
[551]**Mr Gosnall** Henry Gosnold, a young laywer at Gray's Inn and a long-term friend of the Bacons. He was the son of Matthew Gosnold of Hempton. See A.F. Marotti, *Manuscript, Print, and the English Renaissance Lyric* (New York, 1995), p. 17, n. 50.
[552]**my brother's ... to it** For a report on Francis Bacon's performance, see p. 169, n. 558.

That is the revercion of mine office for my sonne[553] and the lease of my howsse at Eaton. Trewlie, Madame, theise two chardges did stande me in CCx li and upwarde, which hath made me the lesse able to paie yow, whereof I am sory. I knowe your Ladyship hath bene good unto many and althoughe I have not deserved this favour at your handes, yet I trust God will move your harte in this my necessity to graunt me fouer or five yeares days payement.[554] Which yf I shall obtaine of your Ladyship yow shall the more binde both me and mine unto yow and yours. And for the performance hereof I will put yow my good ~~securetie~~ suerty. Never the lesse, yf I cannot obtaine this favour at your Ladyship's hands, I will sell theise thinges againe and all that I have to satisfie your Ladyship, rather then I will marre your displeasure that hath bene heretofore so good and gracious unto me. I have neyther eloquence nor understandinge to perswade your Ladyship to graunte me this my poore sute in my greatest nede and necessitie. But it must come from him who gives unto those that be his assured ~~prosperity~~ adversity as prosperity and I trust he will incline your harte to graunt me this my poore sute. And hopinge of your Ladyship's good favour herein, I most humblie take my leave. From the Strande, this viiith of Februarie 1593.

Your Ladyship's moste bounden to commande,
Bartholomew Kempe.

88. *Anne Bacon to Anthony Bacon*, [between 8 and 12 February 1594][555]

Holograph. LPL 653, fos 340r–341v. 2pp.
Endorsed (fo. 341v): lettre de Madame

I sent yow my cosin Kempe lettre by goodeman Rolff. His maner of writing is very unkinde and allmost unchristian, knowing as he doth myn unmoveable purpose to that last use and that it was only of trust and upon a moneth's warning betwixt him and me. I never thowght it possible such dealing ^from him^. He hopes belyke of some delay

---

[553] **the revercion ... sonne** Kemp, together with his son Nicholas, was granted the patent of the office of clerk for writing presentations in Chancery in 1591. It is likely that he held the office prior to 1591, but the patent secured his son's succession to the post. See *History of Parliament*, II, pp. 390–391.

[554] **fouer ... payement** Presumably Kemp is asking to be granted a day when the payment must be made in four or five years' time.

[555] **[between 8 and 12 February 1594]** Anne stated that she was sending Bartholomew Kemp's letter, **87**, written on 8 February, with her letter. Anthony responded to this letter from his mother with **89**.

after my time. But I wyll by the grace of the Lord follow it to have ^it^ by law owt of hande. I pray yow sende me advyse by law how to begin and to proceade, for I cannot away with such dealing in such a matter and for such a use.

I mean also, God wylling, to send for my implements there upon Wensday next, yf Mr Yarts,[556] ^your man^, may go. I wolde have him ready ^here^ by ix of the clock with horse yf he may. Yf his leasure serve not, I wyll sende Lawrence and some other, because my cosin wylbe away abowt ende of the week at Wynsor and uncertein of his return ^to London^, yf not unwylling.

Cura ut bene valeas.[557]

Sende my lettre from my cosin, I pray.

89. *Anthony Bacon to Anne Bacon*, 12 February 1594

Draft. LPL 649, fo. 50r–v. 1p.
Endorsed (fo. 50v.): A Madame le 12me de fevrier 1593

Madame,

I receyved by goodman Rolfe my cosene Kemp's lettre to your Ladyship, the contents whereof were verie farre both from my expectation and contentment, ~~namedly from him~~ as well in respect of his undutyfullnes towards your Ladyship as of the carlesnes of his owne credit; which yf without declaringe my self sencelesse, I could finde anie trewe reason to induce me thinke that it proceded anie waie of necessity, I should be as redy to intreat your Ladyship in his behalf as I am now loth to dissuade ~~your Ladyship~~ yow from your resolution to recover your dew out of his hands. And yet under your Ladyship's correction, consideringe this tearme is nowe at an ende me thinketh it were ~~never~~ not amis to ~~differre~~ surchardge him with kindnes so farre forthe as to give him ^therefore^ some respit betwixt this and the next tearme, in case he should forget himself so extreamely as not to satisfie your Ladyship before.

Touchinge the service of my man Yates, he shalbe according to his bounden dewtie ready, ~~at the~~ ^God willinge^, one Wednesdaie next at the houre appointed.

---

[556] **Yarts** Edward Yates, a servant of Anthony Bacon's. Yates had served Anthony Bacon while he was in France and he returned to France extensively between 1594 and 1596. See *Troubled Life*, p. 129; G. Ungerer, *The Correspondence of Antonio Pérez's Exile*, 2 vols (London, 1974–1976), II, pp. 9–11.

[557] **Cura . . . valeas** [Latin] 'Take care of your good health'.

I am bould to sende your Ladyship hereinclosed a lettre of Mr Harey Gosnalls,[558] thinkinge it more convenient for my self and comfortable ^to^ your Ladyship that yow should understande rather by other relation then by ^my^ owne reporte that which concerneth him who is so neare and deare ~~unto your Ladyship and my self~~ ^to us both^. And so ~~most humblie~~ with remembrance of my humble dewty, I take my leave.

Redborne, this 12th of February 1593.

90. *Anthony Bacon to Anne Bacon*, 14 February 1594

Draft. LPL 649, fo. 51r–v. 1p.
Endorsed (fo. 51v): A Madame le 14me de feuvrier 1593

Madame,

I have perused this ~~which~~ ^coppie which^ it pleased your Ladyship to sende me and meane not to perswade your Ladyship to alter anie thing therein, by reason I cannot imagine whie or howe his present refuse and demande of furder delaie.[559] Possibly proceade of necessitie, as I would have tould him plainly my self yf he had ever spoken or sent unto me about it, that which I wrote unto your Ladyship, ~~for~~ to give him the respeit till the next tearme, was not upon anie intent or desire to pleasure the man havinge never deserved it at my handes, but ^for^ that I did thinke that your Ladyship could not conveniently begine anie suite againste him sooner. And so I most humblie take my leave.

Redborne, this 14th of Februarie 1593.

91. *Francis Bacon to Anne Bacon*, 14 February 1594

Copy. LPL 649, fo. 60r–v. 1p.
Endorsed (fo. 40v): La copie de la de Monsieur Francois Bacon a Madame touchant le fait de Mr Kempe le 14me de fevrier 1593.[560]

After remembrance of my humble deuty it is so that my cosen Kemp is gonne to Windsore and, as he appointed, not to retorne till the ende of the next weeke. He acquainted me of his going upon this occacion

---

[558]**to sende … Harey Gosnalls** For the report of Francis Bacon in Henry Gosnold's letter, see LPL 653, fos 187r–188v.

[559]**his … delaie** Bartholomew Kemp's delayed payment. See letters **87**, **88**, and **89**.

[560]***La copie … 1593*** [French] 'A copy [of a letter] from Mr Francis Bacon to the mistress, regarding the act of Mr Kemp, on the 14th of February 1593'.

that he brought to me and lefte with me a cuple of keys, sayinge that he thought your Ladyship would sende for certen apperell which by the meanes of these keys your Ladyship maight receive. So that by reason of his absence your Ladyship's lettre could not be delivered. And your servant Lawrence was of opinion, and so me thought he had reason, that suche thinges as your Ladyship sent for, beinge delivered and chardged by inventorie, could not be safelie redilivered without his presence. For your Ladyship's monie, my cosen Kemp tould me that rather then he would purchase your Ladyship's displeasure he would provide it, what shifte so ever he made. And so I thinke verielye he will. Therefore my intention is at his comming to deliver your Ladyship's lettre and to proceed as you have directed, except I heare otherwis from your Ladyship in the meane time. Furder, if your Ladyship withdrawe anie implementes of house from hence, which I take it were suche as served in Yorke Howse,[561] your Ladyship had ever ^an^ intention they should have bene bestowed of Markes[562] or Twicknam,[563] and indeed I want them, and finde howe costlie the buyinge of it newe is. Whereof I doe but remember your Ladyship; for I am faine, as they saie, betwene Graise Inne and Twicknam to rob Peter and paie Paul and to remove my stooffe[564] to and fro, which is chardgable and hurteth the stuffe. And therefore, Madame, they would doe wonderous well, yf yow thinke so good; and yf your Ladyship will give me leave to see what I want, the rest maie remaine where it shall please yow. But herein I referre my self to your Ladyhip's good pleasur. Besides my cosen hath in coustodie my resideiw of plate, which yf your Ladyship take all out of his hands ^which^ I praie yow let me receive. I have sent your Ladyship the key of your juell casket which I lately received from my cosen. I humblie thanke your Ladyship for your good counsell everie waie and I hope by God's assistance to followe the same. For my health, I shall have now some leysor[565] to use the benefit of the springe season for the confirminge therof and I am right glad to understande it is so well with my brother as it is. And thus I leave your Ladyship to the good favour of the Almightie, hopinge this springe will recover clearly from your quartaine.[566]

From Grayse Inne, this 14th of Februarie 1593.

Your Ladyship's most obedient sonne,
Francis Bacon.

[561]**Yorke Howse** Anne Bacon was bequeathed the remnant of the lease of York House in London in her husband's will. See *Stiffkey*, II, 26.

[562]**Marks** Marks manor. See the Introduction, p. 29.

[563]**Twicknam** See p. 129, n. 357.

[564]**stooffe** stuff.

[565]**leysor** leisure.

[566]**quartaine** Quartan fever. See p. 150, n. 463.

92. *Anne Bacon to Anthony Bacon*, 16 February 1594

Holograph. LPL 649, fos 39r–40v. 2pp.
Endorsed (fo. 40v): lettre de Madame 1593

I can very yll spare my howsholde men. It is a tyme of busines for
sowing and for carieng woodd, besyde other home workes. I wolde
not that eny belonging to me shuld take in others' manners. William
Dell v yeres since was bowlde so with Mr Reade and had lyke to have
sett him and well worthy by the heeles and so sent worde he wolde
ˆand I consentedˆ; do not for a byrde begin no qwarell. Yow are yet
unknown and not amongst the gentlemen and Justice. And your men
as others maye feede qwarells. As it is lyke Gooderam[567] wyll suff[er]
as bygg and bowld to hinder peace and qwiet. Be advised, I pray
yow, but myne must not. As for Carpenter, I am not fully agreed of
his dwelling, both for myn own uncertein and weaking body, as also
becawse he is geven to typling disorder and worse. So as I yet stay
dowtfull till more proffe; for dronkelyk hath he ben often, thowgh not
wylling to heare of it. I mowght have had him or this elce but all these
bybbers ar conttentious and furnish.[568] He hath also used idle stealing
with Dell as are of his scollers and in dede besyde such idle occupation
marrs their goode husbandry and make them but lease ill. I have kept
him well in and to his worke for the tyme. He hath hethertoo ben
with me and may not go eny where with owt my leave. Send him back
again in tyme, for he must ˆnotˆ lye abroade. Them ˆas lateˆ shall,
God wylling, comm to morow morning to yow but not tary, but so
as he be heere at ~~evening~~ ˆafternooneˆ cathesing,[569] becawse the next
day following all my folk are examined by Mr Wyblud[570] again. Yf yow
wyll eny feasonts here to sende to Grayes Inne, now at reading or for
your selff, apoint as yow think mete Thomas Knight. God encrease
your health with his blessed favour. Use gestation,[571] not violent body
exercyse and use your leggs, ayre, diett and rest in season and kepe
your joints from colde taking in eny wyse, and ryse not ˆin nyghtˆ,
drink not late nor especially ˆin theˆ night, as frendly to the gowte and

[567] **Gooderam** Thomas Gotheram. See p. 149, n. 462.
[568] **furnish** furnish themselves.
[569] **cathesing** catechizing.
[570] **Mr Wyblud** Humphrey Wilblood. See p. 104, n. 207.
[571] **gestation** The act of being carried, for example in a carriage or on horseback, was
regarded as a form of exercise. See *OED*.

very hurtfull for the gowty party. *Observa et bene vale et cura diligentissime ut quam optime valeas et sis homo frugi per crumena.*[572]

Gorhambury 16 February 93.

Your mother,
AB.

93. *Anne Bacon to Anthony Bacon*, 25 February 1594

Holograph. LPL 649, fo. 37r–v. 1p.
Endorsed (fo. 37v): Lettre de Madame receue 25me de feuverier 1593

I cary a continuall greef for your ^no^ intermiting syckness. The Lorde release it in his good tyme to your comfort. Beere I can very yll spare, but the carying in nowyse. My husbandry horses betwixt wood carieng, wherof yet I have not xx loads caried and now earnest sowyng, I can not spare to lett one dry, whylest season serveth, but as yll as I am want my drink this halt lent tyme. Yf it be for own drinking in dede, or your frends, sende me plain worde by the boy *statim.*[573] Yf for your howse, thowgh I can not in dede well spare, then of a newer for them. Let me know, I pray yow, but sende for it must nedes be or elce none at all in very dede. Let your men consider better and not be lavish. ^Idle^ Redborn men[574] have hunt here allmost dayly; yf I were not syckly and weak I wolde owt my selff with all kind of doggs against them and kyll theirs, but stopp I do and wyll. Wynter must of necessitie attende upon myn appointed servyce. Fyrst morning and evening he reade the chapter and prayers, with psalmes last of all. Now it is gardening allso which must be plyed. I look for his diligent now attendance. Owlde Smyth[575] do nawghty to leave ordinary ministery on the Sabbath for belly chew, and bading, and tellyng what he list in his cupps. I wylbe earnest with him for it. He shulde serve better example. I pray yow allow him not to do so ungodly even for hym self.

[*Left-hand margin*] This messenger must turn back strayt. God make yow hole and sownd. Send for bere or elce it can not be.

---

[572] ***Observa et . . . crumena*** [Latin] 'Observe and do well and take dilligent care so that you have the best possible health and that you are a thrifty man with your money'.
[573] ***statim*** [Latin] 'immediately'.
[574] **Redborn men** Redbourn manor. See p. 102, n. 197.
[575] **Owlde Smyth** Presumably Richard Smyth. See p. 157, n. 495.

94. *Anthony Bacon to Anne Bacon*, 6 March 1594

Draft. LPL 649, fo. 88r–v. 1p.
Endorsed (fo. 88v): A Madame le 6me de mars 1593

Madame,

The cause of my over lately troublinge your ^Ladyship^ is to advertise yow ~~Ladyship~~ before my Lady Spolman's[576] departure that his Lordship havinge not ~~well Nicholas~~ particularized unto me the contents of his ^~~Lordship's~~^ lettre unto your Ladyship maie perhaps looke for some ^further^ answere then generalities of comendations or thanks from your ~~Ladyship~~ self. The consideration whereof, I submittinge unto your Ladyship's good ^will and^ pleasure, I humbly take my leave.

Redborne, this 6th of March 1593.

95. *Bartholomew Kemp to Anne Bacon*, 13 March 1594

Draft.[577] LPL 649, fo. 63r–v. 1p.
Endorsed (fo. 63v): Lettre de Monsieur Kempe a Madame le 14me de mars 1593
Addressed (fo. 63r): To the honorable and my verie good Ladie, the Lady Anne Bacon, widowe, at Gorhamburie

I am verie sorie that I did so muche offend your Ladyship by my laste lettres. I will rather sell all that I have then offend yow willinglie. Trewly, Madame, yf it had not bene with me as it is at this present for want of monie, I ~~have~~ would never thus often have troubled your Ladyship with my rude lettres to forbeare the same. And I doe knowe and am fullie perswaded that yow would have doone more for me then the forbearinge of one hundred poundes for some fewe yeares, had it not bene that your Ladyship appointed the same, as I knowe verie well, to the performance your will. Nowe, good Madame, this is my humble seute unto yow and I hope God will prolonge your yeares that it would please yow that upon bandes with good severtie[578] unto suche as yow shall appoint that I might paie the same within one monthe next after God shall calle yow to his mercie. And this I trust in God willbe not hard matter to obtaine of your Ladyship bycause

---

[576]**Spolman's** Presumably Lady Eleanor Spelman, wife of Sir Henry Spelman (c.1564–1641), of the Barbican, London, and Congham, Norfolk. Henry Spelman was a friend of Nathaniel Bacon's. See *Stiffkey*, III, p. 207.

[577]**Draft** The corrections suggest that the letter may be in draft form, which raises the possibility that Anthony Bacon helped Kemp craft the letter to his mother.

[578]**severtie** Presumably either 'severity' or 'surety'.

you have alwaies voued the sayd to the excecution[579] of your will. And I hope yow will thinke to paie the same within one moneth after the same, your decease, noe great time bycause yow ment it to that use. And thus leavinge this my sewte to your good Ladyship to dispose of as it shall please God to move your heart. ~~I am able~~ I remaine alwaies redy to doe yow and yours the best service that I am able. From Eaton this xiiith of Marche 1593.

Your Ladyship's most bounde to commande,
Batholomew Kempe.

96. *Anne Bacon to Anthony Bacon*, 25 **March 1594**

Holograph. LPL 650, fo. 130r–v. 1p.
Endorsed (fo. 130v): lettre de Madame 1594

I besech God of his mercy in Christ, gwyde yow and govern yow and take continuall care of yow. Looke well to your selff and sytt not up late and beware of joints colde and sinowes. *Cura ut valeas ad Deum et patriam.*[580] Commende to your brother. I hope he wylbe a Christian master and be carefull to please God and depende upon ^him^ with goode hope.

I sende yow this lettre from Sir Jhon Brakett[581] for vew of hors. Yf Edward were able, he shulde appere; I have now none other ready for it. Take saffe order for your howse and provision. Yow learned in Terence long ago, *sic luxuriantur famuli cum absunt domini.*[582]

Bene vale in Christo.[583] Gorhambury. 25 *Martii* 94.

Sende me back the lettre by the boy.

---

[579]**excecution** execution.
[580]*Cura . . . patriam* [Latin] 'Take care of your health with regard to God and your commonwealth'.
[581]**Sir Jhon Brakett** Sir John Brocket. See p. 134, n. 394.
[582]*sic . . . domini* [Latin] 'in this way the servants grow indulgent when the masters are absent'. Terence's original line is, in fact, '*perstrepunt, ita ut fit domini ubi absunt*' ('chattering away, as happens when the master is absent'): Terence, *Eunuchus*, trans J. Barsby (London, 2001), p. 381 (3.5.600).
[583]*Bene vale in Christo* [Latin] 'Farewell in Christ'.

97. *Anne Bacon to Anthony Bacon*, [late] March 1594[584]

Holograph. LPL 650, fo. 127r–v. 1p.
Endorsed (fo. 127v): lettre de Madame, mars 1594

One of the prophetts, Naom I think, ^sayth^ that the Lorde hath his
way in the hurle wynde, the storme and tempest and cleudes[585] are the
dust of his fete.[586] The wynde hath had great power. It hath thrown of
a nomber of tyles, some frute trees and one or two other pales,[587] posts
and all, and stone pinacle, and, that I am soriest for, hath blown upp a
shete of lead on one syde of the gate where the diall stands; but in my
conscience your French cartall[588] Jaqwes[589] and all had before loosened
it with hacking leade for pelletts. I pray burn this; let them not see
it, but hurtfull they ^were^. I desyre to know how yow did and do. I
pray be carefull to be well to your own comfort and goode desyre of
your frends, with avoyding coldetaking continually and preventing by
warines; *sustine et abstine*[590] and be cherefull and slepe in due tyme. I
lyked nothing my cosin Kemp's lettre I sent yow. I wyll not grant. My
time in God's hande and not at his appointment; he ever stoode upon
a moneth's warning in my lyffe. Some unknown tryck theris; it wyll
not serve with me dowtless and shall Elsdon and Brocket[591] thus dayly
and mock still. Yf God geve me strength I wyll to London for these
two cawses, by his mercyfull gwyding.

                                                                    AB.

---

[584] **[late] March 1594** In February and March 1594, Anne was in dispute with
Bartholomew Kemp and she seems to make reference to **95** in this letter. As it is endorsed
March 1594, it would seem to date from after 25 March, when the civil new year began.
[585] **cleudes** clouds.
[586] **Naom . . . his fete** Nahum 1:3.
[587] **pales** fence posts.
[588] **cartall** cartaller, i.e. challenger, one who challenges defiantly.
[589] **Jaqwes** Jacques Petit. See p. 113, n. 267.
[590] ***sustine et abstine*** [Latin] 'sustain and abstain'.
[591] **Elsdon and Brocket** Presumably Elsdon is the 'Mr Elsdon' mentioned in **29**, although
nothing more is known of his connection to the Bacons. It is likely that Brocket is the Thomas
Brocket referred to in **144**; he is presumably one of the many Hertfordshire Brockets, but
again little is known about his association with the Bacon family.

98. *Anne Bacon to Anthony Bacon*, [late] March 1594[592]

Holograph. LPL 650, fos 128r–129v. 2pp.
Endorsement (fo. 129v): lettre de Madame mars 1594

I sende to know whther[593] yow kepe your jorny to morow. Mr Spencer[594] spake for horses. I promysed two. I mean to send one to bring them next day early back. They be grass horses, and but poore and faynt to kepe your coch horse pace, and I have no better, nor moe[595] almost, nor mony for moe.

My selff, my horses and my mony is as goode as spent all. I thank God for all his goodeness, past and present. Yf yow had your health, my care shulde be much less for whatsoever. It was towlde me the Mayor[596] of the town and some of company with yow; surely, sonne, onely for their own credit. An truly and much misordred town, all for their own profytt marvelous greedy. I hard their offred forsooth great to have yow Justice amongst them. Take it not yet sonne, *si sapis*,[597] it is but to charge yow and make a partaker of all their undiscrett and wrangle bra[w]les. Your father cowlde never have their goode wyll, because he wold reprove and hinder their riots and disorders sondry weies betwixt Albons and Redborn. Gorhambury is besett and the worse for the yll prophaness and unruly lycentiousnes of those beggerly towns.

Take goode order how yow leave your ^howse^ in your absenc. They wyll make havock and revell abroad when yow are gon and make lyberall expences of your back and other things. And also for the safty of your howse. The Lord in mercy be with yow both. Feare God, look to your health and mare your bodyes[598] with vain discowrsing late. Be not liberall of spece; yow know how to use all the Lord Treasurer and others. Be ware and wyse and still my sons *ad consilium* ^*reti*^*neor*.[599] The blessing of God be with yow; kepe yow from sinn and evel. Look to your servants ^with^ your brother.

[*Left-hand margin*] From my cosin Kempe, nothing but down payment. I am fully still and shalbe resolved. Let him not unkindly and so to

---

[592] **[late] March 1594** The reference to Bartholomew Kemp's payment suggests this dates from late March 1594, as opposed to March 1594/5.

[593] **whther** whether.

[594] **Mr Spencer** Edward Spencer. See p. 122, n. 317.

[595] **moe** more.

[596] **the Mayor** John Moseley. See *Corporation Records*, p. 292.

[597] **si sapis** [Latin] 'if you are wise'.

[598] **mare your bodyes** Presumably Anne meant to write 'mare not your bodyes'.

[599] **ad ... retineor** [Latin] 'I am restrained to counsel'.

his discredit compel me to law. I never was for myn own necessitie
[. . .].[600]

99. *Anne Bacon to Anthony Bacon*, [late March 1594][601]

Holograph. LPL 653, fos 254r–255v. 2pp.
Endorsed (fo. 255v): lettre de Madame

God geve yow grace well to do and geve yow goode understanding to
discern and follow that which best pleaseth him and is goode for your
self every way. Yow sende for ii loads of bushes and ii quarters wheate;
yf had stayed,[602] I had ben more wylling. But truly for my corn, the
last yere's cropp was but small and my owld well nigh spent and in
dede, as I towlde yow, having no mony for the poore, I have wylled
corne to them. So that I may not nor wyll not by the grace of God be
wanting to that use. In trowth I can hardly spare ii quarters but ii yow
shall have for this present, which is three in all and trust to it I wyll
geve no more tyll I se the wyll of God. For my lyff afterwarde, I leave
to ^in^ the worlde ^and^ to your disposition. I marvell yow send to me
for bushes. Yf yow wyll have eny yow must appoint with my consent,
and Crosby's[603] discretion where, and not above ii loade; they are yll to
comeby and scant besyde. Yow must provyde cariag of your own. My
folk cannot by no means intend it. I am to make provision of ^work^
for my howse and to plow; inowgh ^labour^ for myn own beasts and
servants. Goodram must not ^make^ my men his underlyngs to check
and commande for their honest hart to yow and to me, and yf Crosby
forgett, I must remember myn own busines in time. He is not ^yet^
throwghly acqwainted with my doings and this I am sure of by my
^own^ example, none that serveth me with a sownd and a Christian
^hart^ but are most wylling to accompt yow their master and ready to
shew it. But fawners for their own turn to charge yow, beware how yow
trust them too well with lyght affection and later costly experience. Yf
Mr Faunt wolde tary all night, I desyre him to forbeare. It is my syck

---

[600] **[. . .]** The rest of this sentence is obscured by the binding.

[601] **[late March 1594]** This letter is difficult to date from the internal evidence. However, Anthony asked for a quarter of wheat on 8 February 1594 (**86**) and this letter refers to his request for a further two quarters, which Anne stated meant that he had had three quarters of wheat from her in total. The letter also mentions Brocket and horses, which suggests that it was written around the time that Sir John Brocket and Anne were corresponding regarding this matter (**96**). It also makes reference to a visit of Anthony Bacon's, which may be that mentioned in **98**.

[602] **yf had stayed** if you had stayed.

[603] **Crosbye** John Crosby, a servant of Anne Bacon's, later bought Windridge manor from Anthony Bacon in October 1599. See *VCH, A History of the County of Hertford*, 2 vols (London, 1908), II, p. 399.

day, thowgh every day syckly after a sorte. Yf Brockett spake not with yow ˆto the materˆ, Goodram knowes I ment the lettre shulde have ben delivered to him. It is but hollow handling. Commende me to Mr Trott and shew not your men my lettre or the contents to misconster.[604]

Your mother, AB.

100. *Anne Bacon to Anthony Bacon and Francis Bacon,* [before April 1594][605]

Holograph. LPL 653, fos 246r–247v. 2pp.
Endorsed (f 247v): lettre de Madame
Addressed (fo. 247v): To both my sonnes at Gray Inn

The Lorde of grace and health bless yow both in your phisick and allweyes and worke in yow both a goode ˆand ferventˆ desyre and a right use of the heavenly phisick to strengthen yow against all dangerous infection of mynde and bodie. Beware of synn in your selffe and yours; 'Beware of the concision', *ut ˆait apostulus*ˆ[606] and subtill seducers. And beware also of your speches towching matters God suffreth for a ponishment of our carnall securitee to be qwickned with workers of iniqwitee[607] under pretence, therfor nede of provident wysdome and patience and requisite silence.

Agews[608] hardhandling and somtime ending after langwishing be here abowts some what rieff. Litle Peter is payned with red swelling in knee and neerer plaices but not syck much yet, I thank God. Mr Wyborn came down a litle towched in foote but now I dowt with plain *podagra.*[609] He wysheth him selff well at London. Yf yow be content so, I wolde pearce 1 vessell of your owlde claret wyne. I offer the whyte wyne but learned men and some others ask for claret. I towlde yow at first what Franklin wolde do; dryve ˆofˆ conningly and then slipp the coller lyke a crafty worldelyng. I disprayse none upon mallice, I thank God of his grace, but upon experience of their much evell doings. I do with a Christian judgment take hede of them and avoyde dealing with them so familiarly. Well take hede of Goodram. He jornieth to

---

[604]**misconster** misconstrue.
[605]**[before April 1594]** This undated letter must have been sent before Anthony left Gray's Inn, given the address.
[606]**ut ait apostulus** [Latin] 'as the apostle says'. See Philippians 3:2.
[607]**workers of iniqwitee** For this common scriptural expression, see particularly the Psalms (6:8, 29:3, 36:12, 53:4, 59:2, 64:2, 94:4, 125:5, 141:9), as well as Proverbs (10:29, 21:15), Job (31:3, 34:8, 34:22), and Luke 13:27.
[608]**Agews** Agues, i.e. ague fevers.
[609]**podagra** [Latin] 'gout', specifically gout in the feet.

harken of your sale and receipte to pay his riotus and ungodly, I know it, expences and after kick his heele at yow on less yow make him to bowlde with yow for his credit. He is owt of dowt but *mala mens et malus tuis*[610] for all his owtward fawning with tryfles to make yow pay deere. Looke to that and such lyke in time and for yowng Robert Bayly; he did grow lyke his father, litle goode fayth and very wylde and ignorant and irreligious. *Cogita et ne quid temere.*[611] Yow may hinder your credit with the better with interteining unadvised the worse. My cownsell hath ever ben for your goode, both to your brother and yow; ^*dies docebit*^.[612] For the wyne, write your mynd, elce wylbe a spech to procure folk to sende for it liberally which is not my custome but upon some neighbourly occasion *et hoc rare.*[613] In your phisick, kepe a constant wyse coorse that goode may follow wyth God his blessing. Avoyd sutch, watch now. All for now both.

[*Left-hand margin*] Let your brother read this as myne and be godly advised of spech and cherefull. God is wyser and stronger then men and wyll reign for ever. Yf cawse shulde be yet let which wyll hurt. Let your brother wysely kepe the Lord Tresurer and Syr Robert's favour. *Propter rumorem, dissimulatore loco et pie et prudentia. Vale.*[614]

101. *Anne Bacon to Anthony Bacon*, April 1594

Holograph. LPL 650, fos 187r–188v. 2pp.
Endorsed (fo. 188v): lettre de Madame avril 1594

Having some spech with Mr Henshew[615] after yow went hence towching your howse taken in Bishopsgate ^Strete^,[616] he very soberly sayde 'God geve him well to be there, for this last plage that strete was much visited and so was Colman Strete; large and wyde stretes both', and asking him what ministery there, he answerd itt was very mean. The minister there but ignorant and as commonly with all careless and he thowght yow shulde fynde the people therafter geven to voluptousnes, and the more to make them so having but

---

[610]*mala . . . tuis* [Latin] 'a bad mind and bad for yours'. Anne was here recalling Terence's line '*Mala mens, malus animus*': Terence, *Andrian*, 164.

[611]*Cogita . . . temere* [Latin] 'Think and do nothing rashly'.

[612]*dies docebit* [Latin] 'the day will teach', i.e. time will tell.

[613]*et hoc rare* [Latin] 'and this rarely'.

[614]*Propter . . . Vale.* [Latin] 'Close to the report, the dissembler in place and conscientious and with foresight. Farewell'.

[615]**Mr Henshew** Possibly Thomas Henshaw, London lawyer and MP for Whitchurch in 1597 and 1601. See *History of Parliament*, II, p. 293.

[616]**your howse . . . Strete** For the move, see H. Berry, 'Chambers, the Bull, and the Bacons', *Essays in Theatre*, 7 (1988), pp. 35–42.

mean or no edifieng instruction. The Bull Inne there with continuall enterludes[617] had even infected the inhabitants there with corrupt and lewde dispotions;[618] and so accownted of he was even sory on your behalff. I promiss yow, sonne, it hath runn in my mynde since with greeff and feare for yow and yours to dwell so dangerously every way. I marvell yow did not fyrst consider of the ministery as most of all nedefull ^consydering your state^ and then to have so neere a place haunted with such pernicious and obscean playes and theaters able to poyson the very godly and, do what yow can, your servants shalbe entyced and spoyled. Goode Lorde, thowght I, how yll falleth it owt ^for^ the choyce of the best exercises and commoditees in places to dwell ^for my chylderen^, for no ministery at Twyttnam nether. Surely I am very sory yow went from Grayes Inne, where was very good ayre and Christian company in comparison, to charge and venture your selff, your lymms no better. But your men ~~over~~ overrule yow and seeke them selffs and not yow in dede when yow overtrust. God bless yow and kepe yow from evell.

AB.

102. *Anne Bacon to Anthony Bacon*, [before 3 June 1594][619]

Holograph. LPL 653, fo. 362r–v. 1p.
Endorsed (fo. 362v): lettre de Madame

I had thowght to have come to see yow but this Aprilllyke shoower lett it. It is lyke the gowt worketh with the weather. Have patience and looke upp to God and wysely and warely order your selff. I feare your last drink is to strong for ordinary drink, not yf ^yow^ can betwixt meales, nor after supper to bedward or in the night. Your father was so cownselled and folowed it well but upon some extremitee and wolde say he fownde goode of it and wolde wash his mowth with a garglyng glass.

---

[617]**The Bull . . . enterludes** The Bull Inn was on the west side of Bishopsgate Street and regularly staged plays from at least 1577. See G. Wickham, H. Berry, and W. Ingram (eds), *English Professional Theatre, 1530–1660* (Cambridge, 2000), p. 295.

[618]**dispotions** Presumably 'dispositions'.

[619]**[before 3 June 1594]** This undated letter is difficult to place in an exact chronology. Thomas Newton was imprisoned repeatedly between 1592 and June 1594. For Newton, see LPL 650, fo. 347r. The 'backgon bishop' described by Anne is John Aylmer, the bishop of London, so the letter must have been written before his death on 3 June 1594.

My man sayde as he came away forenoone he mett Mr Kempe[620] coming to yow with one cheined. Yow know how to use curtesye and yet *ne quid nimis*[621] but with gravitee. He belongeth to the bishopp and dyd hurt in Mr Dyke's[622] and Mr Cooke's[623] tyme and was ^then^ as the official now in maner. They be byting vipers, the hole pack of them. They can flatter and his too their venum. Be wysely ware of them and such and promiss not to do much for them. For thei are all for them selff and hindrerers of goode men and matters pryvy or apert[624] *ut vulgo dicitur*.[625] Had I thowght he had come to yow I wolde have desyred some motion to him for poore Newton, prisoned by such as he and others now in place. The Lorde pull them owt of ther dwelling in his goode tyme and their backgon bishop.[626]

Burn this, thowgh I wryte tru. Beware of liberall speeches the[627] captious dayes.

AB.

Your brother, Sir Nicolas, towlde my cosin Kempe, as he lately towlde me, that one tyme at ende of his gowt (I am not sure of the tyme) that he sett leaches to his leggs, which drew so much blood with some exercyse upon it that he hath fownde much ease ever synce. Take hede, I pray yow, how yow do all your phisick practises. I did but write this by the way. Yow may know better of my cosin Kempe him selff.

---

[620]**Mr Kempe** David Kempe had served as the archdeacon of St Albans between 1560 and 1581. See J. Le Neve, *Fasti Ecclesiæ Anglicanæ 1541–1857*, comp. J.M. Horn *et al.*, 12 vols (London, 1962–), I, p. 14.

[621]*ne quid nimis* [Latin] 'nothing to excess'.

[622]**Mr Dyke's** William Dike had previously been installed by Anne as assistant curate of St Michael's parish, close to Gorhambury. For more on Dike at St Michael's, see *Cooke Sisters*, pp. 178–179.

[623]**Mr Cooke's** Erasmus Cooke was the vicar at St Michael's from 1591 to 1607. For more on Cooke at St Michael's, see *Cooke Sisters*, pp. 179–180.

[624]**apert** open.

[625]*ut vulgo dicitur* [Latin] 'as is commonly said'.

[626]**backgon bishop** John Aylmer was bishop of London from 1577 to 1594. The archdeaconry of St Albans was under the diocese of London until 1845.

[627]**the** these.

103. *Anne Bacon to Anthony Bacon*, [before 3 June 1594][628]

Holograph. LPL 653, fo. 335r–v. 1p.

Yf the rolls must be searched, I pray yow cause yow it to be done. I have no body of skill to do it. It wolde not be much spoken of. Your brother must think to borow. I am at this time greatly ^greved^ because Mr Wyblud[629] is committed by that godles Bishop[630] to the Gatehowse for refusing to pay unlawfull charge to a wycked fellow of Redborn that hath ^had^ Mr Wylblud's lyving by seqwestration this yere and[631] spent upon his malicious sutes that he neded not. Boner, I think, did not so far cruelly in such case.[632] I pray remember to search in time by some honest frend. I think the date of thindenture must be known for the yere wherin to search. Your brother had nede think of borowing mony, yf but for halff first and get further day for the other yf he can. I am determyned as I may with good cownsell follow for Mr Wylblud's wrong dealing, the Lorde assisting as I trust he wyll, to whome I ^commend^ the goode cause and injust ponishing of his most faythfull servants.

God bless yow both with perfect health and have care to fare well and do well.

AB.

104. *Anthony Bacon to Anne Bacon*, 4 June 1594

Draft. LPL 650, fo. 213r–v. 1p.
Endorsed (fo. 213v): A Madame le 4me de juni 1594

My most humble dewty remembred.

Your Ladyship's minde ~~God willinge~~ *et ultima voluntas*[633] shall by God's help and favour be dewtyfully and thoroughly performed, bothe in substance and ^all^ circumstances, according to your owne desire

---

[628] **[before 3 June 1594]** The dating of this letter is difficult to determine. The references to Francis' debt are inexact. The letter mentions Humphrey Wilblood, who was deprived of his benefice in 1592 and was licensed again in 1594 to officiate and teach in the archdeaconry, but was forbidden from preaching or acting as a schoolmaster. As with **102**, it must at least have been written before the death of John Aylmer, the bishop of London, on 3 June 1594.

[629] **Mr Wyblud** Humphrey Wilblood. See p. 104, n. 207.

[630] **godles Bishop** John Aylmer, bishop of London. See p. 181, n. 626.

[631] **and** Repeated.

[632] **Boner . . . case** Edmund Bonner, bishop of London, 1540–1549 and 1553–1559; known as 'Bloody Bonner' for his persecution of heresy under Mary I.

[633] *et ultima voluntas* [Latin] 'and last wish'.

and appointment. Thoughe I veryly hope that your Ladyship's time is not so neare as by a Christian and wyse foresight your Ladyship semeth to apprende. Touchinge Stretlie,[634] I beseche your Ladyship give me leave to followe Eclesiasticus' sute and ~~wyse and~~ charitable advise where he suithe sayinge 'Despise not a man that turnethe him self awaie from sinne, nor caste him not in the teethe with all but remember that we are all worthy blame',[635] which councell is directly confirmed by St Paule in the 6th to the Galatyans, the first and seconde verse in these wordes, 'Bretheren, yf a man be sodainly taken in my offence, yea which are spirtuall, restore suche an one with the spirite of meaknes concideringe thy ^self^ least thou also be tempted & c.'[636]

Mr Welplet[637] and Mr Aake, I thanke them, were here with one yesterdaie to whom I offred, yf it might stande them in any stead, my best endeavour in their particular businesses. And so I most humbly take my leave.

London this 4th of *Junii* 1594.

> Your Ladyship's most humble and obedient sonne.

105. *Francis Bacon to Anne Bacon*, 9 June 1594

Copy. LPL 650, fo. 217r–v. 1p.
Endorsed (fo. 217v): Copie de la lettre de Monsieur Francois Bacon a Madame, le 9me de juin, 1594.[638]

My humble dewtie remembred. I was sory to understand by goodman Gotheram that your Ladyship did finde anie weaknes, which I hope was but caused by the season and weather, which waxeth more hot and fainte. I was not sorry, I assure your Ladyship, that yow came not up, in regard that the stirringe at this tyme of year and the place where yow should lye, not beinge very open nor freshe, mought[639] rather hurt your Ladyship then otherwise. And for any thinge to be passed to Mr Trot, suche is his kindnes, as he demandeth it not, and therefor as I am to thanke your Ladyship for your willingnes, so it shall not be needfull

---

[634]**Stretlie** Possibly the Mr Stretley who became schoolmaster of the St Albans grammar school in 1597 at Anthony Bacon's instigation. See **188**.
[635]**Despise . . . blame** Ecclesiasticus 8:5. Anthony was here quoting the exact wording of the Geneva Bible.
[636]**Bretheren . . . tempted &c** Galatians 6:1.
[637]**Mr Welplet** See p. 127, n. 350.
[638]*Copie . . . 1594* [French] 'Copy of a letter from Mr Francis Bacon to the mistress, on the 9th of June 1594'.
[639]**mought** might.

but uppon suche an occasion as maie be without your trouble, which the rather be bycause I purpose to, ^God willinge^, comme downe, and it be but for a daie, to visit your Ladyship and to doe my dewtie to yow. In the meane tyme I praie your Ladyship as yow have done the parte of a good Christian and saint of God in the comfortable preparinge for your ende, so neverthelesse, I praie denie not your body the dew, nor your children and frends, and the churche of God, which hath use of yow, but that yow enter not into furder conceyte then is cause, and withall use all comfortes and helpes that are good for your health and strength. In truth I hard Sir Jhon Scidmore[640] often complaine after his quarten[641] had lefte him that he founde suche an heavines and swellinge, speciallie under his ribbes, that he thought he was buried under earthe half from the waste, and therefore that accident is but incident. Thus I commend your Ladyship to God's good preservation. From Graise Inne, this 9th of June 1594.

> Your Ladyship's most obedient sonne,
> Francis Bacon.

It maie be I shall have occasion, bycause nothinge is yet donne in the choyce of a Solicitor,[642] to visit the courte this vacation, which I have not nowe donne this month's space, in which respecte, bycause carriadge stuffe to and fro spoylethe it, I would be glad of that light bed of stryped stuffe which your Ladyship hath, yf you have not otherwise disposed it.

106. *Anthony Bacon to Anne Bacon*, 10 June 1594

Draft. LPL 650, fo. 214r–v. 1p.
Endorsed (fo. 214v): A Madame le 10me le juni 1594

My most humble dewty remembred.

The time is yet to come, Madame, God be thanked who knoweth the harte and searcheth the ~~raynes~~ reynes that I ever misdoubted or mistooke your Ladyship's motherly ~~affection~~ ^meaninge in your admonitions^ and advis which if I doe not ~~sturdley~~ ^allwayes immediately^ and verbally performe your Ladyship, I know, is wyse and kinde to thinke that the difference and delaie maie ^be justly

---

[640]**Sir Jhon Scidmore** Sir John Scudamore, Hertfordshire gentleman and husband to Mary Scudamore, a close confidante of Elizabeth I. For Mary Scudamore, see **114**.

[641]**quarten** quartan fever (see p. 150, n. 463).

[642]**the choyce of a Solicitor** The position of solicitor-general became vacant on the appointment of Edward Coke as attorney-general on 10 April 1594.

occasioned and^ proceed from any other cause rather then from want of deutifull respect.

Touchinge musique as ^I^ knowe the knowledge and my right use thereof to be Christian and comparable ~~so I am~~ so doe I contemne and abhore the ^sondry^ abuses thereof. I have signified unto my brother your Ladyship's mind and resolution to effectuate whatsoever shall be in reason founde requisite for Mr Trot's ^full^ satisfaction and assurance, who ~~freely~~ ^trulie^ Madame hath showde ~~so great~~ ^more real^ confidence and kindnes towards us bothe then I thinke all our brethren and uncles together would have performed, yf we had bene constrayned to have had recourse to them ~~upon nowe~~ in the like case. I purpose, God willing, to doe my dewtie unto your Ladyship after the tearme ^but^ not to remaine at Redbourne above ~~two~~ 3 daies ~~for the~~ by reason of some business which your Ladyship, ~~shall~~ ^with God's leave, shall^ understand by my self and so I most humblie take my leave.

London the 10th of June 1594.

107. *Anthony Bacon to Anne Bacon*, 22 June 1594

Draft.[643] LPL 650, fo. 212r–v. 1p.
Endorsed (fo. 212v): A Madame le 22me de juni 1594

My most humble dewtie remembred.

It is verie trewe Madame that amongst other speche with goodman Crosbie I let fale that yf your Ladyship could have conveniently spared a hundred pounde it should not have bene unseasonable ~~but as your in this my common,~~ but as in me incuringe this to Crosbie to mention it to your Ladyship, I preferred your Ladyship's conveniencie before myne owne desire and occasions, so am I nowe ~~as~~ ^verie^ redie to make a full point without ~~pressinge yo~~ proceedinge anie furder. As for this bearer I hope your Ladyship shall finde by his dewtyfull demeanour that he hath served a master that hath kepte and can kepe in good rule, more unrully then ever he was, otherwise I would be verie lothe that he should be nearer your Ladyship.

---

[643] **Draft** There are rough notes in the top right-hand corner of the letter ('Madame, may it please your Ladyship') and towards the bottom of the page ('To the honorable and').

I have understood by Mr Lawson[644] that he hath receyvd the 2 globes and astrulabe[645] of your Ladyship. I and[646] thanke you ~~Ladyship~~ therefore, as also for Lawson himself, who I hope with God's grace will omit nothinge, ~~that he~~ eyther in the ^dewtyfull honest^ cariadge of himself, or his faithfull care of ^and diligence^ in my busines, that he can conceave, maie procure and confirme your Ladyship's good opinion of him. I sent worde by him that the soonest leysure I looke for to come downe would be a 12 daies hence, before which time I will not faile to advertise your Ladyship more certenly. And so I most ^humblie^ take my leave.

London this 22 of *Junii* 1594.

Your Ladyship's moste obedient sonne,
Anthony Bacon.

108. *Anthony Bacon to Anne Bacon*, 12 July 1594

Draft. LPL 650, fo. 228r–v. 1p.
Endorsed (fo. 228v): A Madame mere de Monsieur le 12me de juillet 1594.
Address (228v): To the honorable and his very good Lady and mother the Lady Anne Bacon widowe.[647]

Madame, for answere (on my parte) to your Ladyship's lettre to us bothe, havinge asked councell and leave of him who onlie knoweth and guydeth the hartes, I founde my self imboldened withe warrant of a good conscience, and by the force of truthe, to remonstrate unto your Ladyship, with a moste dewtyfull minde and tender care of your Ladyship's soule and reputation, that howsoever your Ladyship dothe pretende and alledge for reason your motherlie affection towardes us in that which concernethe Lawson, yet anie man of judgme[nt] and indifferentcy must needes take it for a meere passion, springinge eyther from presumption (that your Ladyship ~~can your~~ can only judge and see that in the man, which never anie man yet hath seene ~~or for shame dare saie~~) or from a souveraigne desire to overrule your sonnes in all thinges, how litle soever yow understande eyther the grounde or the circumstances of their proceedings, or els from ~~lacke~~ want of charety, abandoninge your minde continuallie to most

---

[644]**Mr Lawson** Thomas Lawson. See p. 99, n. 184.

[645]**astrulabe** An astrulabe was an instrument used for making astronomical measurements.

[646]**I and** Presumably this is misordered and should read 'And I'.

[647]**To ... widowe** There is also another address at the bottom of fo. 228v, in reference to another letter, stating 'To his right honorable and very good Lord'.

strange and wrongfull suspitions, notwithstandinge all most humble submissions and indeavours possible on his parte to procure your Ladyship's satisfaction and contentment. This my remonstrance as I have just cause to feare that ^it^ will at the first ~~by~~ sight be offencive to your Ladyship, yet have I noe lesser reason to hope that Almighty God, ~~that~~ ^who^ knoweth with how dewtyfull intente and to what ende I have made the same, will ^in his mercie^ dispose your Ladyship's harte not to yelde to your cradle which you counte ~~for gre~~ as it were so heynous an offence, but to truthe and charety, whereupon intirely reposinge my self as infallible grounds[648]

[fo. 228v] I remaine ~~as~~ ^more^ redie to receive and indure your blam[e] for performinge ~~that dewty~~ which for filliol respecte this my bounden dewty, than your thanks or likinge for soothinge or allowinge by sylence so dangerous humours ^and uncharitable ~~and~~ misconceyptes^ in your Ladyship. And so I most humbly take my leave.

Londres ce 12me du juillet 1594.[649]

109. *Anne Bacon to Robert Cecil*, 13 July 1594

Holograph. CP 27/33, fos 59r–6ov. 2pp.
Endorsed (fo. 6ov): July 1594. Lady Bakon to my master. In favour of North.
Addressed (fo. 6ov): To the right honorable Sir Robert Cecyll of her Majestie's Prevy Cowncell

This bearer, Syr Robert, as he sayth is lately a ranger in Enfeild, wherupon as being at your command is desyrous to belong unto yow.[650] He is by his sayeng reteining unto my Lady of Warwyck,[651] yet now placed in the forrest service under your government. His sute is that it wolde please your Honour to accept of his service and maketh me his mein[652] upon no acqwaintance at all but becawse his wyffe's syster is maried to a substantiall man in this parish where I dwell, which made him, he sayde the ~~Bo~~[653] bolder, which I would not deny

---

[648]**infallible grounds** Repeated on fo. 228v.
[649]***Londres ... 1594*** [French] 'London, on the 12th of July 1594'. This is repeated on the bottom left of fo. 228r.
[650]**This ... unto yow** Enfield Chase, a royal hunting park, had been under Robert Cecil's control since 1587, as master forester of Enfield. See R.W. Hoyle, '"Shearing the hog": the reform of the estates, c. 1598–1640', in R.W. Hoyle (ed.), *The Estates of the English Crown, 1558–1640* (Cambridge, 1992), p. 208.
[651]**Lady of Warwyck** The countess of Warwick, Anne Dudley. See also **140**.
[652]**mein** intermediary.
[653]**Bo** This seems to be smudged, which Anne may have meant to indicate a deletion.

him, both becawse I ^at least^ take it to be an ordinary that rangers retein to the liewtenant and because he is a comely man and taken to be in goode case.[654] His maner of speech to reqwyre me to write was thus, which did seeme to me discrete, that he might ^but^ know your pleasure yf he might be so bowlde to move that sute ^unto yow^, because of him selff he wolde not take upon him in respect of your Honour and place, and then yow as it were accepting and lycencing him therto, he wolde procure the cowntess to speak for him for the accomplyshing. At the fyrst sight and behavour every way and also his brother in law's neybourhod, I wylling move yow in his behalff as he reqwyred, leaving yt to your own lyking.

For my maner health upon late leting blood, I feele a goode releeving of faynt heate and burning, but leave and leave again very much elded.[655] I am in goode comfort in the Lorde's mercy, when sooner or later as pleaseth him, and can be content to have some venyson when you can.

God healpe both my poore sonns. Francis hath ben tossed *inter spem curamque*[656] to appose another maner ^of man^, ~~if~~ and he everyway; let them learn to depende upon· God and in his feare and favour wayte upon him with goode hope. For sure is he. They feele the smarting want of a father now in their ripe age. Fare yow well, goode nephew, with God his gratious assistance, with good encrease of his love towarde yow. Gorhambury, 13 July.

Your aunt, ABacon.

110. *Anthony Bacon to Anne Bacon*, 27 July 1594

Draft. LPL 650, fo. 198r–v. 1p.
Endorsed (fo. 198v): A Madame le 27me de july 1594

My moste humble dewtie remembred.

I have receyved the two bonds and the coppie of your Ladyship's lettre to Mr Boldro which having communicated to Mr Crewe, his advis is that your Ladyship should not enter any accion[657] against her till Lawrence his retourne, and that afterwards yf your Ladyship receyve noe satisfaction from her, nor her suerties ~~yea would,~~ he will

---

[654]**in goode case** in good circumstances.
[655]**elded** aged, grown old.
[656]***inter spem curamque*** [Latin] 'between hope and care'. See Horace, *Epistles*, 1.4.12.
[657]**accion** Action, specifically a lawsuit.

doe what your Ladyship shall appoint him. In the meane tyme, the
bonds as also the paper of the imposte[658] shalbe well kepte.

Touchinge Stretly, I referre me to Mr Bradlie[659] himself, whether
he ~~receyved not good~~^ wer not^ satisfied before ever I tooke him into
my howse, and whether that ever since he hath ^given^ any offence,
eyther inwards or behaviour, but rather shewed ~~a full resolution~~ a
manifest change and resolution to spende his tyme well, uppon which
condition and not otherwise I have accepted his service, which hath
and maie stande me in some steade. The man hath good and ^very^
worshipfull frends in Leystershire, whereof some have alredy and
more will yf need be answere for his good demeanour. Maie it please
your Ladyship therefore ~~in consideration~~ consideringe Mr Bradly hath
had full satisfaction and that he hathe caried himself honestly ^and
studiouslie^ since he hathe bene with me and that he hath good
serviceable partes in him, and that I have good pledges for him, your
Ladyship would be content that I maie use him ~~according as he now~~
thinkinge ~~as~~ him as he nowe is and not as he was, till I finde cause to
the contrarie.

Touchinge my brother, we are both resolute that in case he be not
placed betwixt this and next terme never to make any ^more^ words
of it. And so I most humbly take my leave.

111. *Nicholas Trott to Lady Anne Bacon*, 3 August 1594

Copy. Latin, with Greek words and Greek transliteration. BL,
Harleian MS 871, fo. 8or–v. 1p.
Addressed (fo. 8or): To the honourable my veri good Ladie, the Ladie
Bacon at Gorhamburie

*Magna me verecundia totum hunc annum exercuit, illustris Domina, cum te inter
Christiana studia et infirme valetudinis molestias rerumque familiarum curam
ad cogitationes de me homine tantillo et equilio meo disscendisse audirem cum
vero tantum tibi liberalitatis superfuisse viderem ut tuis impensis bene et sollicite
curatum, alio multo meliore comitatum ad me transmiseris, dolebam sane me
singulari tua tuorumque beneficentia supra meritum et conditionem meam auctum,
nova hac munificentia cumulari. Puero certe meo qui sua negligentia primo hanc
molestiam creavit et futilitate sua consilium meum de eo vendendo prodidit iure
succenseo. Spencero etiam subirascor qui tibi errorem meum hac in re, non satis
amice detulit. Sed cum propter rerum borealium expectationem mihi alio hac estate*

---

[658]**imposte** A tax or duty.
[659]**Mr Bradlie** Rudolph Bradley, the vicar of Redbourn parish. See the Introduction,
p. 26, and p. 111, n. 251.

excurrere non liceat et lentas in deliberando moras itineris celeritate reparandas videam et proinde nos citis et dispositis equis usuros iudicarim. Consultum non putavi ἱππουσ ἀέριουσ toto hoc anno alere. Sed tuam una cum meis divendere. In quo video quantum contra viri grati officium commiserim. Sed ignoscas precor simulque existimes. Nullum quantumvis generosum asturconem mihi gratiorem nec κειμήλιον ullum carius eo animo a quo profectus sit unquam futurum. Dominus Franciscus nondum ad vos rediit sed cum Deus Optimus Maximus hanc illi remoram immiserit, non dubito timentibus eum in ˆomniaˆ melius cessura. Morbum istum seu potius molestiam (nam morborum et precipue illius cui is maxime obnoxius est) propria et efficacissima medicina sunt ἁμαρροιδεσ nihil est quod inutiliter pharmacis exasperet et corpusculum tenue intempestive vexet. Quod etsi is pro sua prudentia optime videat, a me tamen si opus est admonebitur. Dominum Antonium sua negotia diutius hic detinuerunt varia usum valetudine. Quod etsi non ignoro tibi pro materna caritate solicitudinem et dolorem afferre, non dubito tamen prudentiam tuam ea solatia que res ista intus habet Christiane explicare. Nihil dicam de iis artibus virtutibusque quibus equales vincunt. Id illis relinquo quorum iuditium est intelligentius et testimonium minus suspectum nec mihi sumo ut te feminam omnium quas novi doctissimam prudentissimamque admoneam. Ea tantum cum bona venia memorabo quibus me ipsum consolor primum ethnici philosophi bona quedam prima esse dicunt ut sanitatem pacem &c illius modi quedam secunda ex infelici materia expressa ut in morbo patientia, in bello fortitudo, et cum prima illa optabiliora fortasse sint secunda tamen ista laudem habere maiorem. Et bene Tertullianus vitam tranquillam rebus ad desiderium fluentibus et ventis leniter ad votum spirantibus Mare Mortuum appellat per quod raro ad felicitatis portum navigatur. Salvator etiam noster qui ad coelum preivit et nobis viam stravit, notas quasdam apposuit ut nos non aberrare sciremus, molestas afflictiones et morbos. Sed ista meliora domi nascuntur ego certe erga te et tuos, quos meritissimo vestro unice amo et colo, nullum unquam officium fidelis grati et diligentis amici pretermittam. Deus te servet incolumem.

Ex hospitio Grao 3 August 1594.

Dominationi tue devictissimus,
Nicolaus Trottus.

[Translation]

I have been vexed by great shame this whole year, distinguished lady, after I heard that you, amidst Christian pursuits and the problems caused by ill health and the concerns of family matters, have condescended to think of me, a person of such little consequence, and of my wretched horse. When I saw that so much generosity remained in you that you at your own expense sent it over to me, carefully and well cared for and accompanied by another much better horse, I was most sorry that I, who was enriched above my merits and status, as the result of your outstanding kindness and that of your family, had

now been overwhelmed by this new act of generosity. I am angry
with my boy, to be sure, because his negligence caused this problem
in the first place and his stupidity made known my plan to sell it.
I am also rather angry with Spencer who reported my mistake in
this matter to you in a less than friendly manner.[660] But since it is not
possible for me to rush elsewhere this summer because I am waiting
for the things from the north,[661] and since I see that the prolonged
delay in deliberation must be repaired by the speed of the journey, I
accordingly judged that we must use swift and well-disposed horses. I
did not think it wise to feed 'airy horses'[662] for the whole of this year,
but to sell off yours together with mine. In this I see what a great error
I have committed against the duty of a grateful man. But I beg you to
forgive me and at the same time to consider that no ambling horse,
however noble, will ever be more pleasing to me, or any heirloom
more valuable, than that affection from which it came. Master Francis
has not yet returned to you but since Almighty God has brought
about this delay for him, I am sure that everything will end better for
those who fear him. This illness or rather discomfort, for of illnesses
and particularly of this one to which he is especially prone, a proper
and most efficacious medicine is haemorrhoids;[663] there is nothing that
exasperates more and unreasonably vexes the frail body than useless
drugs. But even if he should discern very well in accordance with his
good sense, he will nevertheless be admonished by me, if necessary.
Master Anthony has been detained here for longer by his affairs while
he has experienced varying degrees of health. But even though I am
aware that this causes you anxiety and grief in accordance with your
motherly love, I am nevertheless sure that your good sense will unfold
in a Christian fashion the solace which this matter contains within it. I
will say nothing about those skills and virtues which overcome those of
your equals. I leave that to those whose judgement is more intelligent
and whose testimony is less suspect and I will not assume to remind
you, who are the most learned and prudent woman I have known.
I will just remember with your good leave that with which I console
myself; firstly the pagan philosophers say that certain moral qualities

[660]**I am ... manner** Edward Spencer told Anthony Bacon on 31 July that he had
informed Lady Bacon that Trott's horse was 'brocke-winded'. See LPL 650, fo. 231r.

[661]**I am ... north** Trott attempted to gain the position of secretary to the council of the
north in early 1595. See *History of Parliament*, III, p. 531.

[662]**airy horses** Trott wrote the Greek for 'airy horses' in his letter. If it was his intention to
use the word 'airy', then presumably he meant it in terms of being 'impractical' or 'fanciful'.

[663]**This illness ... haemorrhoids** Gout and haemorrhoids were thought to be
connected conditions, unable to occur at the same time. The presence of haemorrhoids was
therefore thought to cure gout temporarily. See M. Berdoe, *An Essay on the Nature and Causes
of the Gout* (Bath, 1772), p. 25.

come at the first, like good sense and peaceableness and others of this kind, some are secondary, which are forced out by unhappy matters, such as endurance in illness, bravery in war, and although these first ones are perhaps more desirable, however the second ones are more praiseworthy. And Tertullian rightly applies the term 'Dead Sea' to a peaceful life with things flowing as one wishes and with winds that blow gently towards one's desires as one breathes, whereby one rarely sails into the port of happiness like this. Our Saviour, too, who has preceded us to heaven and paved the way for us, set out certain marks, such as troublesome afflictions and illnesses, so that we would know not to go astray. But these things are brought forth better at home; towards you and yours whom I love and adore most deservedly, I certainly will never omit any duty of a loyal, pleasing, and diligent friend. May God keep you safe.

From Gray's Inn 3 August 1594.

Yours most completely to command,
Nicholas Trott.

112. *Anne Bacon to Francis Bacon*, 20 **August 1594**

Copy. LPL 650, fo. 255r–v. 1p.
Endorsed (fo. 255v): Copie de la lettre de Madame a Monsieur Francois Bacon le 20me d'aout 1594[664]

I was so full of ~~paine~~ backe paine when yow came hether that my memorie was very slipper.[665] I forgot to mention of Rame.[666] Yf yow have not, I have not receyved Franck[667] last half yere of midsommer; the first half so longe unpaide. Yow will mare your tenants yf yow suffer them. Mr Brocquet is suffred by your brother to cosene[668] me and beguile me without cheke. I feare yow came too late to London for your horse; ever regarde them. I desire Mr Trot to harken to

---

[664] *Copie . . . 1594* [French] 'Copy of a letter from the mistress to Mr Francis Bacon, on the 20th of August 1594'.

[665] **slipper** forgetful.

[666] **Rame** Francis Rame had a long association with Anne's natal family in Essex. He had been appointed deputy steward of the manorial court in Havering, Essex, by Anne's father, Anthony Cooke, in 1563, a position which he continued to hold until 1605. Anne's reference to Rame probably relates to the Gorhambury manorial court, as Rame also acted as its steward on occasion during the late 1590s. For more details about Rame, see M.K. McIntosh, *A Community Transformed: the manor and liberty of Havering, 1500–1620* (Cambridge, 1991), p. 316. For Rame as steward at Gorhambury, see HALS X/B/3/B.

[667] **Franck** Presumably 'Franck's'.

[668] **cosene** To cheat or defraud.

some honest man and Cooke[669] too as he maie. Yf yow can heare of a convenient place I shalbe willinge, yf it so please God. For Lawson will drawe your brother *quocunque vult ut timeo valde*[670] and that with false semblance. God give yow bothe good healthe and heartes to serve him trewlie and blesse yow always with his favor.

I sende yow pigeons taken this daie and let bloode. Looke well about yow and yours too. I heare that Robert Knight is but sicklie; I am sorie for it. I doe not wright to my Lord Tresurer bycause yow liked to staie. Let this lettre be unseene. Looke verie well to your healthe. Supp not, nor situpp late. Suerlie I thinke your drinkinge to bedwards hindrethe your and your brother's digestion verie muche. I never knew anie but sicklie that used it, besides ill for head and eyes. Observe well yet in tyme. 20 August Gorhambury.

In Christo,[671]
ABacon.

113. *Anne Bacon to Anthony Bacon,* 7 September 1594

Holograph. LPL 650, fos 331r–332v. 2pp.
Endorsed (fo. 332v): lettre de Madame le 8me de septembre receue 1594
Addressed (fo. 332v): To my sonne Mr Antony Bacon

I sende yow herein Crossbye's lettre[672] because yow may better understande by hym ^the^ words of the shryff to him selff. Yf the state be browght in question, I am sory of the last act yow so earnestly reqwired, whertoo I was hardely[673] drawn, as yow know, for dowt of danger. Dowtless your brother Nicholas[674] hath don somewhat in thexchequour. Yow thowght it cowlde not come to his eare so sone, but yow see ^yow^ are deceaved. Yow shall do well to send for the ^your^ atorny and myne, Marsh[675] I do mean, yf he shulde strein[676] upon the manners to troble me and my tenants. I have browght my selff in goode case by your means. Mr Crew is not in citie I heare; it is the

---

[669]**Cooke** Presumably Erasmus Cooke, the vicar of St Michael's in St Albans. See p. 181, n. 623.
[670]**quocunque ... valde** [Latin] 'wherever he chooses, as I very much fear'.
[671]***In Christo*** [Latin] 'In Christ'.
[672]**I sende ... lettre** This is no longer extant.
[673]**hardely** with difficulty.
[674]**your brother Nicholas** Nicholas Bacon II.
[675]**Marsh** Possibly Thomas Marsh, who attended St Albans grammar school as a boy and was admitted to Lincoln's Inn in 1584.
[676]**strein** distrain.

worse. The shryff threateneth to strayn[677] before the next audite which is before Michaelltyde,[678] which is not iii weeks hence at uttermost. Yow had not nede to slack this, as Brocket's matter is to my hindrance. Some mony I had nede of for to ^have^ pay the sute ^by his cosins^. I have not of myne own at this present for my howse and other chargs vi li in mony; I am ready to borow x li of my neyghbours, yf I can. I sende purposely. I pray yow let me know certeinly what way yow take to helpe it with spede. Yf it once came in Cheqour sute, one troble wyll follow another. Prevent therfore.

I wolde fayn have gon to London for phisick next weeke but I perceave I cannot, being weakish to ryde so farr and the way is but yll for a coche for me, besyde the wett wether. I wyll desyre Mr Moorer[679] to be with me here for that time. Yf yow prove your new in hande phisick, God geve yow goode of it. My Lord Tresurer abowt 5 yeres past was greatly preased by the graunt[680] vaunts of ^a^ soden startupp glorious stranger, that wolde nedes cure him of the gowt by boast, but quod my Lorde, 'Have yow cured eny; let me know and se them'. 'Nay', sayde the fellow, 'but I am sure I can'. 'Well', concluded my Lorde and sayde 'Go, go and cure fyrst and then come again or elce not'. I wolde yow had so don but I pray God bless it to yow and pray hartely to God for your goode recoverye and sownde. I am sory your brother and yow charge your selffs with superfluous horses. The wyse wyll but lawgh at yow both being but truable[681] besyd your detts ^for^ long jornyes and private persons. Earles be earles.

[Left-hand margin] The heavenly preacher sayth, 'Ech thing hath his opportunite and due season'.[682] Well may yee do as blessed in the Lorde. 7 Sept 94.

[fo. 331v] Your vain man Stretly by his slewth and prowde qwarell piking conditions setts all your howse at Redborn owt of qwiette order by generall complaint as I heare. Lately yowng Moorer was smot in the eye by him. I pray God yow heare not of some mischeff by him. But my sonns have no judgment. They will have such abowt them and in their howse and wyll not in tyme remedy it before it break owt in some manifest token of God, his displeasure. I cannot cease to warn as long as I am a mother that loveth yow in the lorde most deerly and

---

[677] **strayn** distrain.
[678] **Michaelltyde** Michaelmas. See p. 107, n. 225.
[679] **Mr Moorer** Robert Moorer. See p. 163, n. 530.
[680] **graunt** grand.
[681] **truable** trouble.
[682] **ech . . . season** Ecclesiastes 3:1.

as Seneck by phisophy[683] onely cowlde say, *in amico admonendo mallem successu et quod tamen nollem, quam fidem deesse.*[684]

Your mother,
ABacon.

114. *Anne Bacon to Anthony Bacon*, 5 December 1594

Holograph. LPL 650, fos 333r–334v. 2pp. Severe damage to right-hand side of letter.
Endorsed (fo. 334v.): Madame le 5me de decembre 1594
Addressed (fo. 334v): To my sonne Mr Antony Bacon at Byshoppe gate.

This very colde frost and snow yet seasonable and healthfull to heale and s[no]w compelleth me, sonne, to sende to know yow do feele your gowty body ha[rd]. I remember well this tyme of the yeare, and in such hard freesing and sn[owy] wether, your father was greevously tyred and payned with the gowt here at Gorhambury and scant able to endure coch jornyeng to London, but two da[yes] next most before ^that^ Christide, and kept his howse all the tyme and after neere ter[me]. It was the same yere my Lady Skidmor[685] now went to her Majestie, being sent for ^at^ soden, and I fayn to go with her ^from hence^ to Hampton Coort. For all the gowt, se[e and] look well to your selff and sitt not upp in the night; yow wyll undoe your selff and make your lymns stark and your body bothered. Your father never w[ould] for eny payns so ponish and spoyle him selff. Be not to tender but [carefull] and avoyde occasions to call the gowt. My cownsell in this is mos[t needful] and allweyes hath ben both at your being abrode and at home, but to li[ttle] regarded, the Lorde knoweth.

For Mr Spencer,[686] your man, I think he had had a goode wyll to tary at London both in respect of his [. . .] the Lord Mayor and also becawse in dede he was sad that his hawlk[687] was [. . .] for here withowt that he had no cowntenance nor cowlde tell how to occup[. . .] For I putt him to nothing but restrayned him of unfitt being abroa[de . . .]

---

[683]**phisophy** philosophy.
[684]*in amico ... deesse* [Latin] 'In warning a friend, I would rather lack success, although I would not wish it, than fidelity'. Seneca, *Epistulae morales ad Lucilium*, 25.2. Anne Bacon's husband, Nicholas, used the same *sententia* in a letter in 1578 to Francis Walsingham, when trying to persuade him against military intervention in the Netherlands. See Huntington Library, HM 1340, fo. 94r, 24 July 1578.
[685]**Lady Skidmor** Lady Mary Scudamore. See S. Adams, 'Mary Scudamore', *ODNB*. See also **105** for mention of her husband.
[686]**Mr Spencer** Edward Spencer. See p. 122, n. 317.
[687]**he ... hawlk** Edward Spencer had been in dispute with Anne in August 1594 regarding his sparrowhawk. For more details, see *Cooke Sisters*, p. 220.

A yowng man and so many vyle creatures, hawnting abowt eve[. . .]
onley because I was lyke then to have sooner departed. I was will[ing
you have] one discrete man of yours against all events; otherwyse I
needed [nor] cared for eny. I have used him well here and so must he
nedes sa[yth. Beseeching] God I may hope of some lenger continuance
and yet I trust looke [. . .]

Forcye of Butlers was yesterday here with ^me^ to desyre my goode
wyll to con[tinue] your tenant there, becawse, sayeth he, 'My wyff
is marvelous ^loth^ to chang her dwe[lling]. For I have', sayth he,
'A howse of myne owne but she greatly desyres to be [here.]' He
had, he sayd, ben with yow to move yow but fully his interest tyme
is but short and [he] nede to know what to trust too. I think with
goode conditiones for payeing rent, and for hurting your wooddes
and providing for others inconven[iences], I think in respect of his
wyff, who serveth most for butter and my mylk her[e] when no other
tenant nor neybour can or wyll so certeinly, it were better to [keep]
the same, then to chang, thowgh but for vii or ix yeres. Truly [. . .] an
yll tenant there were a fowle comber diverse wayes. By proffe the[re]
yow shall fynd by experience. Geve no liberty to lett or sell, for I wyll
not [consent] to that. The grownde in occupieng there is demeins[688]
and neerer to anoy[ther] grownde and howse, yf he be not an honest
man and a kynde tenant with all. He [is honest] as ^it^ here reported
yet and carieth him selff with creditt; his wyff wolde be [. . .] for her
long aboad and borne and well alied here. I commend it to God yow
[be not] mysled.

For otees[689] to sow your grownd for that portion, I am very wylling,
as I en[deavour] to power in all. Now I know by my and your officer
it is your own request, I consent and so shulde it be betwixt us, for
restoring as the Lorde sy[gnifieth]. There is a love betwixt Jaqwes,
your *gallum*,[690] and Susanne, my mayd lately, bewrayed[691] by [a letter]
him to her sent lately by pot boy once with me. In dede I did justly
as somewhat [. . .] not the best I missed some thynges [. . .] she hath
ben plyed with lynes, I know not from whome. Yow shall do well to
have an eye watching ov[er] and *quod a me scis nescias omni modo.*[692]

[Left-hand margin] Of this more hereafter. I parted with her after a
sorte, before my last going to London. Be very close but observe. I
pray burn my lettre. Your men and your brother's prye in every matter
and lysten. I pray send back or burn this to be sure. The Father of our

---

[688]**demeins** demesne, i.e. land held by free tenure.
[689]**otees** oats.
[690]*gallum* [Latin] 'Frenchman'. See p. 113, n. 267.
[691]**bewrayed** 'betrayed' or perhaps 'defiled'.
[692]*quod . . . modo* [Latin] 'to be ignorant in every way of what you know from me'.

Lorde Jesu Christ be your mercyfull Father to both of yow and gwyde your hartes with holy spirit evermore.

Gorhambury 5 December 94, your loving and careful mother for yow. ABacon *Xηρα*.[693]

115. *Anne Bacon to Anthony Bacon*, 9 December 1594

Holograph. LPL 650, fos 329r–330v. 2pp.
Endorsed (fo. 330v): Lettre de Madame le 13me de decembre 1594 receue
Addressed (fo. 300v): To my sonne Mr Anthony Bacon

I pray God mitigate your gowt disqwiett paynes, both this stark colde wether here and allweyes. Why I send this sodenly is of some occasioned charite, which I thowght to make known to yow and I wolde do it thowgh very nedefull speedely. The miller, Preston, this morning made pitious moans that the whele of the wheat mill, the principall, was broken very much by the frost and remediles[694] this hungry ~~ty~~ present tyme and so his customers (my selff for one) compelled to seeke to others to his great undoing, being hyghe rented and having wyff and chyldern. Wherupon, I know not who putt it in his mynd, he earnestly begged the whe^e^le of the unoccupied water ment to come to the howse and yet unprofitable. Me thowght he had reason with him for this present great necessitee ^and also^[695] that all ^there^ unoccupied. So having made yow fyrst prevy and the matter well considred of by Crosby and others of skill ^I purpose^ to lett him have it owt of hand, yf it be thowght it may ^be^ conveniently done, for goode continuance of his customers and no harme in removing an idle wheele that but rotteth and ^to no use^. And this afternoone it was towld me the cockshote doore, but very lately fast nayled upp and stregthned[696] since the last pilfering thence, was newly broaken upp again and a pipe stolne owt above an ell long. Sure hereafter it were good to take all down and save the remeins of lead pipes.

Very harde colde snow here, both for men and cattell. I trust it wyll, with the Lorde's mercy, staye the infection abroad. For my going hence, I yet mean it becawse I am but unable to go to the church and to avoyd ungodly, unruly Albons rovers, besyde cownterfayt soldiors and roags.

---

[693]*Xηρα* [Greek] 'widow'.
[694]**remediles** Remediless, unable to be put right.
[695]**and also** This addition is marked, presumably incorrectly, to be inserted after the following 'that'.
[696]**stregthned** strengthened.

I think I shall go upon a soden very nere the tyme, *si Deus ita volet*,[697] who kepe us ˆinˆ his safty. I trust they wyll not[698] mum nor mask nor synfully revell at Grayes Inne. Who w[ere] ˆsometimeˆ cownted fyrst, God graunt they waxe not dayly and deprove[699] to [be cownted] last. The Lorde in mercy ~~bef~~ be with us and geve us tru repentant harts with amendment.

My swelling is lately encreased. I humbly thank God for all yf yow and your brother take ˆcareˆ to please the Lorde in your studies and all your actions. I shalbe be comforted ether to lyve or to dye, sommer or later, as God shall call.

Bene vale in Christo.[700] *5to Decembris.*[701] Gorhambury.

Your mother ABacon,
Χηρα.[702]

116. *Anne Bacon to Anthony Bacon*, 23 January 1595

Holograph. LPL 650, fo. 33r–v. 1p.
Endorsed (fo. 33v): Lettre de Madame a Monsieur le 23me de janvier 1594 / Lettre de Madame a Monsieur touchant Mr Francis Bacon le 24me de janvier 1594.[703]

After curteous and familer speches upon the cawse of my comming hether and the unlooked for differing,[704] to that point ˆSir Robertˆ[705] sayd 'Indede her Majesti was not well then'. I sayde yesterday I went to see yow,[706] much more to my comfort yf your health wolde lett yow be and see further, God having inabled your mynde. 'It is true', quod he, 'He hath goode partes, but gowte and such be too naturally drawn from parents'. 'Well', *inquam*,[707] 'The eldest of my but two in all sonns is visited by God and the other me thinks is but strangely used by man's

---

[697] *si Deus ita volet* [Latin] 'if God is so willing'.
[698] **not** Repeated.
[699] **deprove** disprove.
[700] ***Bene . . . Christo*** [Latin] 'Farewell in Christ'.
[701] ***5to [Idus] Decembris*** In Roman dating, this was 9 December.
[702] ***Χηρα*** [Greek] 'widow'.
[703] ***Lettre . . . janvier 1594*** [French] 'Letter from the mistress to the master, concerning Mr Francis Bacon, on the 24th January 1594'. This is the second endorsement given to this letter.
[704] **the unlooked for differring** The deferring by the queen over the appointment of the solicitor-general.
[705] **Sir Robert** Sir Robert Cecil.
[706] **yow** Anthony Bacon.
[707] *inquam* [Latin] 'says I'.

dealing, God knowes who and why. I think he is the very fyrst yownge gentleman of some accompt made such ^so long^ a common spech of – this time placed and then owt of dowt – and yet nothing done. Inowgh to overthrow a yowng and studious man, as he is geven in dede, and as fytt by judgment of wyser, both for yeares and understanding, to occupy a place as well as the Atturny. The worlde marvells in respects of his frends and his own towardnes.' 'Experience teacheth that her Majestie's nature is not to resolve but to delay.' 'But with none so', quod I. 'Why' *inquit*,[708] 'She is yet withowt officers of 3 whyte staffs[709] together, seldome ^seene^.' 'But', sayth he, 'I dare say my Lorde[710] wolde gladly have had my cosin placed or[711] this.' 'I hope so my selff', ^*inquam*^, 'but some think yf my Lorde had ben earnest, it had ben don.' 'Surely', sayth he, 'My Lorde even on last Tewsday moved the Queen that the terme day was neere and reqwyred a Sollicitor for her servyce and she strayt shulde say it was a shame the place was so long unfurnished. "No shame, Madam", *inquit ille*,[712] "But a lack." "I may not name any" sayth Majestie, "Nor other dare, for feare of yow and my Lord of Essex." "I trust", sayth my Lord, "yow are not withowt a nomination, but rather now to conclude." "Is there none, I pray yow", *inquit* Majestie, "but Francis Bacon fitt for that place ^Solic[ito]r^." "I know not", *inqu^it^ ille*, "How your Majestie may be altered but the judgess and others have and do take him sufficient with your favour and it is expected of all this terme."' Wherto she have no grant, and this sayth, and protested, Sir Robert, that my Lord did very playnly and in goode fayth.

Then upon my words that him selff was Secretary in place but not nominate,[713] 'As for that,' sayth he, 'I deale nor speake no more of it, but as long as none is placed I wayt still, thowgh I may think my selff as hardly used as my cosin. And I tell yow playnly, Madam, I disdayn to seeme to be thowght that I dowted of the place and so wolde I wysh my cosin Francis do so long as the rome vacant and beare her delay so accustomed. Let him not be discourage,[714] but cary him selff wysely. It may be,' sayde he, 'her Majesti was to much preased at the first, which she lyketh not and at last come of her selff.'

---

[708] *inquit* [Latin] 'says he'.

[709] **3 whyte staffs** Officers of the royal household had white staves of office.

[710] **my Lorde** William Cecil, Lord Burghley.

[711] **or** before.

[712] *inquit ille* [Latin] 'says he'. As this is second-hand reported speech, this is again William Cecil, Lord Burghley.

[713] **that . . . nominate** Robert Cecil was appointed secretary of state in July 1596.

[714] **discourage** discouraged.

This in maner was the speech and parting to the coorte. Truly his spech was all kindly owtward and dyd desyre to have me think so of him.

AB.

117. *Anne Bacon to Anthony Bacon*, 23 February 1595

Holograph. LPL 650, fo. 69r–v. 1p.
Endorsed (fo. 69v): 23 de feuvrier 1594

Grace and health.

Surely I appoint my men to return at my tyme. I dyd not think that Lawrence cowlde have sene yow then at all; his tarieng was but a day and I needed things ~~for~~ to be bowght, and to attende my impost,[715] and horsemeat charge is ^dere^. I saw him not but at his return synce. He hath much a do to pay all this hard yere and his ferm left so decayed and the grownd so pilled[716] bare. Yow do well to kepe promiss with your brother for the pale wood[717] valu, but have it hence with toyling doble cariag and halff purloynd at London in the working. The small *noxia*[718] reyning so ryff here in this ayre and every wheare threatening more syckness. I wryte now to him to geve place to reason and his purse and to skyllfull advyse, so I tell him playnly. Crossby I am sure wyll helpe to bye it commodiously for him. For hence cariag wyll not ner must be to his greater charg and toyle. Wolde to God *filii mei charissime*[719] wolde have more judgment with their knowledg to their fuller commendation *in actionibus suis*.[720] The Father of heaven bless yow both and gyde yow with his holy spirit and restor[e] yow to better health of body that yow might have experience to further knowledg and more right understanding to discern for your selff, ^*uteris*.^[721] Yow have a ^nother^ horse I weene; surely to your needless charg except yow were able to use them. Corn, all grein, very deere here; much more there, besyd Hynd's lewd costly neyligence.

I am very desyrous the coort keeping her[e] shuld ^be^ to the satisfieng of the tenants and in order for the leete,[722] which hath ben

---

[715] **impost** A tax or duty.
[716] **pilled** stripped.
[717] **pale wood** Presumably fencing wood.
[718] *noxia* [Latin] 'harm'.
[719] *filii mei charissime* [Latin] 'my dear sons'.
[720] *in actionibus suis* [Latin] 'in these proceedings'.
[721] *uteris* [Latin] 'you will be profited therby'.
[722] **the leete** Court leet, the manorial court. For more information, see the Introduction, p. 32.

hetherto observed, and that Mr Downing shulde be at the coorte
keping this one coort more in my tyme. Hereafter as yow wyl[l], and
they matters, thowgh small, are not to be don *obiter*.[723] Yf Mr Crew can
not in due tyme at Easter, yf Mr Downing cowld not, I wolde entreat
Mr Ramme[724] to do it, ^yf I do lyve to it^, for this once finall coort,
as I think. I am the Lorde's, my sure trust is whensoever Christ, my
saviour, elce as I may willingly. I wolde gladly have had a note of all
implements had from hence and from me. I have often desyred it and
I marvell not made ^and sent me^ or[725] this.

God encrease yow with encrease of his dayly favour.

Your mother,
ABacon.

118. *Anne Bacon to Anthony Bacon*, 24 February 1595

Holograph. LPL 650, fos 84r–85v. 2pp.
*Endorsed (fo. 85v): De Madame a Monsieur le 25me de fevrier 1594 en l'endroit
de Fausset.*[726]
Addressed (fo. 85v): To my sonne Mr Anthony Bacon

Had I known as much yesterday I wolde have written this now by
my man allredy sent to day morning, withowt leave of much tariang;
solito luce.[727] Goodman Furcey and his wyffe after two of the clock this
afternone (and yet before I had eate eny thing, being allmost afrayde
becawse of my after swelling, but as it pleased the Lorde, upon whome
I depend and wayte, his mercy in ^his^ due tyme appointed), they
were both but sad in ded, sayeng thei were not satisfied with the lease
making, standing so tyckley[728] upon my lyffe. I promiss yow when I red
that circumstance of 21 yeres yf my lyff and 3 yeres did continue so
long, I understoode not what was granted, then eny thing or nothing
in effect. Farr other wyse then your fyrst grant for ii yeres after my
departing and the^n^ one more at my reqwes[t] late with yow. Besyde
the yeare they have of their former lease in your father's tyme ended
at Michaell[729] to come 1596 ^which is their own^ and so 4 yeres in all

---

[723] *obiter* [Latin] 'incidentally'.
[724] **Mr Ramme** Francis Rame. See p. 192, n. 666.
[725] **or** before.
[726] *De ... Fausset* [French] 'From the mistress to the master, on 25th February 1594,
about the position of Fausset'.
[727] *solito luce* [Latin] 'as is customary, in the light', i.e. to return during daylight.
[728] **tyckley** uncertainly.
[729] **Michaell** Michaelmas. See p. 107, n. 225.

wherby he myght lett his ^own^ howse for iii or 4 yeres. This kinde of lease I looked for, which being ^not^ attended to cunningly for my understanding and very unprofytably for them, I playnly refuse to sett to my hande and graunt. Be my lyff as in God[730] hand, so at his goode pleasure. They (rather being discomfited yf they can not have ^it^ as yow fyrst as before rehersed did promiss and I verely did take your tru meaning) do desyre your favour and the lease restored them again and ^to^ abyde the wyll of God and that yeare and 2 they yet enjoy, ^certeinly^ by your father and me. It stands upon so many yffes and difficulties that they both did rather moorn then be owght glad. What law may be alleged I know not, but sure small commoditee to them, but great uncertentee, which is not goode for all parties. They are both very desyrous I shulde see the cowntinpanes[731] in your hands now left to my use. So the Lorde bless yow with dayly blessednes in body and sowle. Sytt not late up nor comber your head with busines late. It wyll spoyle both your health and understanding vigour. 24 February Gorhambury.

Your mother,
ABacon.
Xηρα[732]

119. *Anthony Bacon to Anne Bacon*, 25 February 1595

Draft. LPL 650, fo. 101r–v. 1p.
Endorsed (fo. 101v): A Madame le 25me de fevrier 1594

Madame
    I received yesterday a lettre of your Ladyship's by your man Woodward and a nother this day by goodman Fawcett.
    For the first, the other day my brother comminge to se mee, I advized him with confirmation of my office to employ some honest faithfull man as I ~~tooke~~ take Groome to be and Robert Large[733] his owne care unacquainted in such matters upon ^Groome^ his squill[734] and fidellitie rather then his manadgement or anie of his servants overseeing or provision; which my brother allowinge, I have sent for

---

[730]**God** God's.
[731]**cowntinpanes** Presumably the counterpart, the completed copy of the lease, retained by the grantor. It can also be used more generally to mean a copy.
[732]*Xηρα* [Greek] 'widow'.
[733]**Robert Large** Various members of the Large family served the Bacons. Anthony also mentions employing a John Large in his buttery in December 1596 (**178**) and his brother, Francis, left John Large £20 in his will. See *Bacon Letters and Life*, VII, p. 543.
[734]**squill** Presumably 'skill'.

Groome, who with Crosbie's direction ~~may and~~ I doubte not but will save him much.

For the time of keeping the court, as it hath ben, so shall it be allwaies of your Ladyship's pleasure and appointment, thinking it were convenient that Mr Downinge, if his bussinesse permitt him, performe that office ^alone^, seeing Mr Crewe cannot be there in due time to joyne with him; otherwise I cannot thinke of any man fitter to be extraordinarely emploud then Mr Rame.

~~For your Ladyship's~~ For your Ladyship's second lettre, maie it please you to be advertised that Mr Crewe being to departe to morrow morninge towards the presentlie[735] circaite I could ~~to~~ not ^resolve nor^ advise ~~upon~~ any ~~other~~ ^better^ order for your Ladyship's satissfaction and his certaintie, then according to your Ladyship's lettre, to lett his oulde terme stand ^by disnulling the newe^, with promise to ~~make~~ secon[d] your Ladiship, who maie make him a sufficient lease, if it please you, during your life by a particular assurance ^from my selfe^ of 2 yeares after. Which trulie, Madame, if ~~it please you will to remember~~ my memorie doe not over much faile mee was all that ever your Ladyship assured ^and I graunted^, having stoode with himselfe at (^considering your Ladyship maie as I hope and wishe live many^) the first ~~upon~~ for one yeare ~~after his oulde terme. And I grant it~~ And this ~~under~~ correction proceeding kindlie from your Ladiship and trulie from my selfe ought increase to content ^them bothe^ and maie well further but can no way hinder his creditt ~~for~~ ^nor^ the disposition of his owne to ^nere sorie^ uses. And so with remembrance of my most humble dutie, I take my leave.

This 25th of February 1594.

Your Ladyship's most loving
and obedient sonne.

120. *Anne Bacon to Anthony Bacon*, March 1595

Holograph. LPL 650, fos 117r–118v. 2pp.
Endorsed (fo. 118v): lettre de Madame receu en mars a Redbourne 1594

I came yesterday home, I thank God, well thowgh very weary, by that missing the right way we roaved and made it lenger. I fownd a very syck and soare altred man. One might by him see what is *mutatio ~~dextrae~~* ^*manus*^ *Excelsi*[736] in correcting. He hath ben as yow know a strong

---

[735] **presentlie** This seems to be an error, as presumably it should be 'present'.
[736] ***mutatio dextrae manus Excelsi*** [Latin] 'the change wrought by the ~~right hand~~ hand of the Almighty'.

armed man and active in such exercyces of strength as shooting, wrestling, casting the barr, and whyllst he was with me I never used footestoole to horsback. But now, God healpe him, weake in voyce, his flesh consumed, his hands bones and synewes, but his belly upp to his very chest swoln and hoved upp and as hard with all as thowgh one towched wenscott.[737] I thank the Lord that put me in the mynde to visitt him with a Christian desyre to comfort his sowle, which I trust Mr Wyblud's[738] spirituall cownsell and comfort with harty prayour was a means to it; God, I trust, working with his admonitions in the syck body to the reviving of his sowle. He hath his memory perfect and well and glad of godly exhortation. God grant him, and my selff allso, his continuall swete comfort and feeling mercy to the ende. Amen.

For your[739] going, yow spake of, to London and wyll have be ii bedds hence for your servants, let me know in tyme. I wolde yow had here taried tyll that remove. Yow shuld have spared much wast expences which yow nede not and have ben better provyded. Surely yf yow kepe all your Redborn howsholde at London, yow wyll undoe your selff. Mony is very hard to come by and sure frends more hard and yow shalbe still in other folks' danger, and not your own man, and your detts wyll pinch yow, thowgh yow may hope. But your continuall syckliness with all is a great hindrance and yf yow make shew of a howse keping in the cytie

[*Left-hand margin*] yow shall qwickly be over charged, much disqwieted and browgh[740] not over theres[741] but over shulders.[742] Therefore at the begining be very ware and wyse as it ˆisˆ sayde. *Tibi ipsi sapere disce*,[743] one sayde; he sayde he had rather be envied for goode state, then pitied for harde case.[744] Consult them and *ne quid temere*.[745] I cowlde not chuse but advise as heretofore. God gwyde yow to take the right and best cowrse.

---

[737]**wenscott** Wainscot, i.e. oak.
[738]**Mr Wyblud's** Humphrey Wilblood. See p. 104, n. 207.
[739]**your** Repeated.
[740]**browgh** brought.
[741]**theres** the ears.
[742]**not over theres but over shulders** A reference to the proverbial 'over head and ears', i.e. completely immersed.
[743]*Tibi . . . disce* [Latin] 'Learn to be wise for yourself'.
[744]*Tibi . . . hard case* These seem to be loose allusions to Pindar, although it is strange that Anne choose to write in Latin and not the original Greek: *Pythian Odes* 2.72; 1.163.
[745]*ne quid temere* [Latin] 'do nothing rashly'.

121. *Anthony Bacon to Anne Bacon*, 7 March 1595

Draft. LPL 650, fo. 149r–v. 1p.
Endorsed (fo. 149v): A Madame le 7me le mars 1594

Madame,

These few lines shalbe first to remember my most humble duti[e] then to render your Ladyship like thankes for that which it pleased you to send mee by my man John Wharton;[746] and withall to advertize your Ladyship that if it please you to make your impost provision of Gascoigne wine, ~~a frend of myn~~ the same marchant ~~of~~ who furnisheth my selfe will provide your Ladyship of ~~as good~~ the best that is come in this fleete, which is but mene in comparison of the yeares past.

My brother (thankes be to God) beares it out very well, having not seene him looke better. ˆI my selfe doe but attend the helpe and fittnes of the season with sound advice not to assaile by violence but to undermyne by some safe phisicke my infirmity. The ˆˆwinterˆˆ bruntes wherof (God be thancked) I have better borne and passed then I hoped for, considering my extraordinary discontinuance of ~~phisickes and~~ artificiall succour.ˆ And so I humbly take my leave beseeching God long to preserve your Ladiship.

Your Ladiship's most lovinge and obedient sonne.

122. *Anthony Bacon to Anne Bacon*, 15 March 1595

Draft. LPL 650, fo. 150r–v. 1p.
Endorsed (fo. 150v): A Madame le 15me de mars 1594
Addressed (fo. 150v): To the honourable his very good Lady and mother the Lady Anne Bacon

Madame,

I thought meete to advertise your Ladieshipp for this bearer, your Ladieship's servant's good and encouragement, that he hath begunn verie honestly to husband my brother's garden expanses, and may well affirme, though to my no lesse grief then the fellowe's ˆjustˆ commandation, that ˆthe care and affection ofˆ all my brother's me[n] together could not have stood him in halfe so much stead for such a purpose.

---

[746]**John Wharton** Presumably the religious writer and London schoolmaster who also signed the petition to the Privy Council against James Burbage's new theatre in 1596, along with Anne Bacon's sister Elizabeth. See SP 12/260, fo. 176r.

May it please your Ladieshipp according to that I mentiond in my last, to lett me knowe whether I shall take up any Gascoigne wine for your Ladieship's provision, by reason that the best of bad will quicklie be bought upp.

I am bold to send unto your Ladieshipp a taste of a Lenten Spanish daintie, which an honest merchante presented unto me the other day.

The good Earle of Essex hath bene ~~pulld~~ assald with certain fittes of an ague, but God be thanked he ~~hath at the last~~ ^is now quit so ridd of it^, and so I most humblie take my leave.[747]

123. *Anne Bacon to Anthony Bacon*, 1 April 1595

Holograph. LPL 651, fos 108r–109v. 2pp.
Endorsed (fo. 109v): De Madame le premier jour de avril, 1595

I mean yf God wyll to come hether again before Easter. But your going farther hence than my ablenes wyll endure to travell, ether by water or by lande, and know not when I shall see yow eny more, I pray God to go before yow and ^to^ be with yow, ever to heale yow, to healpe yow and to cownsell and comfort yow continually with his fatherly love in Christ Jesu our Lorde.

Amen.

I wrote yesterday to my Lady Wasyngham[748] and by her to the cowntess.[749] She tooke yt well and thanked me. The cowntess is very nere her travayling tyme.[750] I besech God of his goodeness make her a joyfull mother with dayly encrease of God his blessing upon her and hers.

Beware in ^eny wyse^ of the lord H. *Οουαρδε*;[751] he is a dangerous intelligencyng man. No dowt a subtill papist inwardely and lyeth in wayte. Peradventure he hath some close working with *Στανδον*[752] and

---

[747]**and so . . . leave** An alternative subscription has been drafted on 150v: 'Your most loving and deutyfull sonne, Anthony Bacon'.

[748]**Lady Wasyngham** Ursula Walsingham, widow of Sir Francis Walsingham, Elizabeth I's principal secretary until his death in 1590.

[749]**the cowntess** Frances Walsingham, the countess of Essex. Her second husband was Robert Devereux, the earl of Essex. She was the daughter of Francis and Ursula Walsingham.

[750]**her travayling tyme** The labour and birth of her child. The baby boy, Henry, was baptized on 14 April 1595, but died a little over a year later on 7 May 1596. For Frances' pregnancies, see P. Hammer, 'Robert Devereux, second earl of Essex', *ODNB*.

[751]*Οουαρδε* [Greek transliteration] 'Howarde', i.e. Lord Henry Howard.

[752]*Στανδον* [Greek transliteration] 'Standon', i.e. Anthony Standen.

the Σπανιαρδε[753] καιτοιουτοισ.[754] Yow can not espy; be not to open. He wyll bewray[755] yow to diverse and to your Αουντε Ρουσσελ[756] among. The duke had ben alyve but by his practising and styll soliciting hym to the Duke's undoing[757] and the Εαρλε of Αρουνδελε.[758] Avoyde his familiaritee as yow love the truth and your selff. A very instrument of the Spanish papists. No creature know or see this I wryte, ˆI pray yowˆ, but burn it, your own hands, and remember, for ˆheˆ pretendyng curtesy, works micheff devilyshly. I have long known him and observed him,[759] his workings have be stark nowght. *Procull esto*.[760] I am sory, I can not speak with Dr Fletcher.[761] For your horses I wolde certenily know. It is not lyke yow wyll over hastly. Sende me worde what tyme yow gess becawse of myne absence, yf God let me lyve, but vessells and cariag must surely be provyded. For in dede I have none for malt. Yf yow tell Crossby your mynde, I wyll pay for it when I have received rent. Gryst[762] is ˆveryˆ deere, my thinks, but he denieth. Yf yow had taken your physyck here in your well warmed ˆhowseˆ it had ben better, I think. God be your gwyde in all your weyes and take hede of cold taking upon remove and after physick call for your own neccessaries. Your men forgett yow and yow smart for it. Use your leggs ~~at~~ as yow may dayly; they wyll elce be the feebeler and the synewes stark and strengthless. It is true. I feare theris no ordinary preaching ministery at ~~Full~~ Chelsy.[763] I can not tell how to lament ˆitˆ, but both my sonnes me thinke do not cast for it where they dwell. Great want can not be. We had nede watch continually to be well armed against

---

[753] **Σπανιαρδε** [Greek transliteration] 'Spaniarde', i.e. Antonio Pérez.

[754] **καιτοιουτοισ** [Greek] 'and such men'.

[755] **bewray** betray.

[756] **Αουντε Ρουσσελ** [Greek transliteration] 'Awnte Roussel', i.e. Anne's sister Elizabeth Cooke Hoby Russell.

[757] **The duke ... undoing** Thomas Howard, the fourth duke of Norfolk and elder brother of Henry Howard, was executed in 1572. Suspicions about Henry Howard's role in his brother's treasonable activities led to his arrest in 1571.

[758] **Εαρλε of Αρουνδελε** [Greek transliteration] 'Earle of Aroundele'. Philip Howard, the thirteenth earl of Arundel, was placed under sentence of death for his Catholic sympathies in 1589. Although the sentence was never carried out, Arundel remained under the threat of execution until he died in the Tower in October 1595.

[759] **I ... observed him** Howard's suspected Catholic sympathies had led to him being placed under house arrest at the Bacons' Suffolk house in July 1585.

[760] **Procull esto** [Latin] 'Stand at a distance'.

[761] **Dr Fletcher** Richard Fletcher, the bishop of London from 1595 to 1596. In May 1595, Rudolph Bradley, the vicar of Redbourn, asked Anthony Bacon to intercede with Fletcher regarding a prebendaryship for him. See LPL 651, fo. 139r.

[762] **Gryst** Corn to be ground.

[763] **Chelsy** It appears that Anthony had left Bishopsgate Street and was residing in Chelsea during the spring and summer of 1595, before moving into Essex House in August. For other references to his time in Chelsea, see **131**, **133**, **134**, and **136**.

evell dayes[764] imminent to be feared. For of all sorts we waxe worse and worse.[765] London waxeth streight laced, urging subscription; that ^slavish^ pleasing wyll not salve his harde cured sore. Burn this.

The God of mercy, health and peace compass yow abowt with his heavenly favour whersoever.

Primo Aprilis[766] 95.

Mater tua[767] AB. *Bene vale in Christo nunc and semper.*[768]

[*Left-hand margin*] λυπη μου μεγαλη εστι υπο του Εσσεξ και σφοδρα φοβουμαι μη εν καιρω υπαρχει μοιχεια αισχροτατη και πικρα και μεστη των κακων.[769]

124. *Anne Bacon to Anthony Bacon*, 1 April 1595

Holograph. LPL 651, fo. 107r–v. 1p.
Endorsed (fo. 107v): De Madame, le premier de avril, 1595
Addressed (107v): To my sonne Mr Bacon

Sonne,

Woodwarde towlde me yow reqwired a hogsehead of beare. I wyll, yf it please God I come well and in tyme home to morrow. I wyll send yow one by the cart of my best ordinary beere.

The rest ~~March~~ remaining is March,[770] I pray yow lett me have another hogshead for it. I shall lack elce and lett one be ready with a carr to receave it of the carier on Fryday in goode tyme, thowh he tary a litle, because of doble jumblying. I think well used yow may drink it after v dayes settling at least, but that as yow see being above iiii moneths owlde after it is broched it wyll last above a fotenigh bycawse of cariag.

[*Left-hand margin*] This bearer I have newly taken into my s[ervy]ce. AB.

---

[764]**evell dayes** See Ephesians 5:16.
[765]**we waxe worse and worse** See 2 Timothy 3:13.
[766]***Primo Aprilis*** [Latin] 'the first of April'.
[767]***Mater tua*** [Latin] 'Your mother'.
[768]***Bene . . . semper*** [Latin] 'Farewell in Christ, now and ever'.
[769]**λυπη . . . κακων** [Greek] 'I feel great grief about Essex and am very afraid that, in due course, a most shameful and grievous adultery, full of evils, will arise'. There is an additional Greek sentence written on the edge of the paper, but it is impossible to make it out.
[770]**March** The March brewing.

125. *Anne Bacon to Anthony Bacon*, 3 April 1595

Holograph. LPL 651, fos 105r–106v. 2pp.
Endorsed (fo. 106v): De Madame le 4me d'a[vril] 1595
Addressed (fo. 106v): To my sonne Mr Anthony Bacon

I thank yow for your horses. I sende yow a hogshead of November
bere, me thinks goode, and a barrell also of the same bruing, which
I did cawse the bruyar then to ^torne^ of the fyrst toppe of the same
bruing and so stronger, becawse at that tyme it was thowght yow wolde
come to Redborn and I ment it to yow. It is so strong as I wolde not
drink it ordinaryly to my meales, but do yow use it to your most goode.
In eny wyse when these two vessells be emptie, let them be returned
by the cart. I can not want them in dede and they be strong. Besyde
diverse others vessells of myn sent to your sondry places. I did at one
tyme sende vi together, yf not seven, to Redborn and I payde vii s for
headding and hooping and seasoning of them, howsoever they made
yow pay afterwarde. I dyd so in trowth. I pray remember Groome's
yll handling and ende it well for all nowghty Godram and his tipling
mate. I wrong my men lyving well and Christianly in their honest
vocation to suffer them to be ill entreated and my selff contemned. I
mean not so. Crosby purposeth to be with yow on Monday, yf God
wyll and yow corn ready. Gorhambury 3 April.

Mater tua,[771] AB.

Yesterday seing my sister Russell at the Blackfries howse after the
sermon,[772] I fownde her ver[y] much greeved and her wordes charging
my Lord Tresurer of very unkinde dealing in a matter very chargeable
to and a slyte ende procured, she sayde, to her hurt *cum lachrimis per
illum*.[773] I saw her so lamenting I sayde I wolde writ to Sir Robert Cecill.
'No, no', *inquit*,[774] 'It is to late, he hath marred all and that against my
cownsells lyking at all.' But not yow nor your brother; *vosmet inter
miscere*.[775] Never be aknown of it, I pray yow. Shew your brother this
and let him not take knowledg, lest yee both sett on work, and for that
Ὁουαρδε,[776] once again be very ware, as of a subtile serpent. Burn all.

[771]*Mater tua* [Latin] 'Your mother'.
[772]**seing . . . the sermon** When staying at her Blackfriars house, Elizabeth Cooke Hoby
Russell regularly attended Stephen Egerton's sermons at St Anne's, not only with her sister
Anne but also with her daughter-in-law, Lady Margaret Hoby. See J. Moody (ed.), *The Diary
of Lady Margaret Hoby, 1599–1605* (Stroud, 1998), pp. 119, 120, 124, 134, 136.
[773]*cum lachrimis per illum* [Latin] 'with tears on account of him'.
[774]*inquit* [Latin] 'says she'.
[775]*vosmet inter miscere* [Latin] 'do not get embroiled'.
[776]Ὁουαρδε [Greek transliteration] 'Howarde', i.e. Henry Howard.

Ne famuli quidem.[777] Be not hasty to remove. Your drink well used and not sett abroch all at once ~~but~~ (^above the barr fyrst then^ by degrees lower once or twyse) wylbe better and last lenger, ^sayth the bruyer^. Yok Howse[778] lease is not here, as I sayde to my cosyn Kempe. Mr Bayly[779] hath seene every place purposely to satisfye my Lord Keeper. I do not remember that ever I saw eny lease from the Bishop sealed, but by parley and trust betwyxt both. *Bene vale.*[780]

The bruyar who is now here sayth that your beer ^now^ sent, well handled, wyll drink well a moneth's space. Lett not your servants begyle yow *clam aut aperte.*[781] Use your leggs and eyys[782] in eny wyse and dayly, least they fayle yow when yow wolde. Neglect not in tyme and serve the Lorde with all your hart and *omnia ad salutem tempestive.*[783]

126. *Anne Bacon to Anthony Bacon,* 8 April 1595

Holograph. LPL 651, fo. 89r–v. 1p.
Endorsed (fo. 89v): De Madame le premier jour d'avril 1595[784]

I sende between your brother and yow the fyrst flight of my dovehowse, the Lorde be thanked for all; ii doson and iiii pigeon, xii to yow and xvi to your brother becawse he was wont to love them better then yow from a boy. Marvelous harde, snowy, hayly and strong, wyndy wether here and great scarsytie. I have had more toyle in my body few dayes since I cam last hether the[785] in above twyse as long at London. I wysh my selff ther again and peradventure, yf God wyll, I wyll before Easter as now mynded. I am glad your bere was sent so soone. To day upon occasion of a mayd sending to Redborn, but none of my servants, I heare Mistress Read and He[n]rie are mallcontent for certein implements, specially as the[y] say in the best reserved chamber for your frends, noble or not noble: a carpett and other things fyled with byrds hunting or hawks or doggs. Mr Lawson was

---

[777] *Ne famuli quidem* [Latin] 'Not even servants'.

[778] **Yok Howse** See p. 170, n. 561.

[779] **Mr Bayly** Presumably John Bailey, 'a gentleman wayter' under Nicholas Bacon I, who also received a legacy from the latter after his death. See *Stiffkey*, I, pp. 54, 66.

[780] *Bene vale* [Latin] 'Farewell'.

[781] *clam aut aperte* [Latin] 'secretly or openly'.

[782] **eyys** eyes.

[783] *omnia . . . tempestive* [Latin] 'everything at the proper time for health'.

[784] *De . . . 1595* [French] 'From the mistress, the first day of April 1595'. There seems to be a discrepancy between the date which Anne gave on the letter and the date of the endorsement. Anne sent two other letters on 1 April (**123, 124**), so it seems as if Anthony's secretary may have been incorrect in this endorsement.

[785] **the** then.

the nobleman lodg there, I weene, and lyke inowgh for he is *totius vanae gloriae*[786] and make yow bleared styll to endure all and pay for all; and further it was reported that Morice was discontented for your resining[787] to Mr Reade, he not made prevy before. Thus they talk and some think elce now yow are gon, and one that tames the bit is become a tipler and wylbe oversene with drink, but an yll servant in your howse and ^the frute of idleness^. Large was here this day. I towlde him it was honesty and ^Christian^ duty to dwell at home with his ^wyff^. I wolde, I sayde, be loth that my sonne ^shulde^ beare the blame of his being an yll husban[d] and leave his first calling to labour ~~and~~ ^and so leeve over to^ be a good thriving fellow. I used him so styll thowgh other civill ^servyce^ wayting among. It is commonly spoken that Fynch of Woodende[788] ^and Goodram^ are joint companions in all yll fellowshipp. Use them therafter and take no luck by such. Yow and your brother have taken much discredit by not judging wysely and rightly of those yee both of yow overcredit to your wylling hyndrance. I pray the Lorde geve yow good understandyng by his worde and spirit and health to serve him in truth to your goode estimation with encrease of his blessed favour. Let not your men be prevy herof. As your goode mother, I thus certefie. Think of it.

Gorhambury 8 of April 1595.

Mater tua,[789] AB.

Use your leggs betymes for feare of loosing in disuse.

Goode Rolff[790] was here to day to speak with me, very sadly sayde thus to me that h[e] had before now and lately again did here that his ferme shuld be lett from him. Wherupon his ancient wyff and he both were much greeved. I towlde ^him^ I never harde eni litle of it and thowght it was nothing so. It wyll be worst, I wys,[791] for yow to mak a chang for Humphrey. He hopes yow wyll at least lett him tary iii yeares lenger after his present state fynished. Scamblers[792] are easily had every where, but discrete, honest, suffucent farmours wolde be continued. They serve the cowntry and cowntenance their landlorde in deed. Gooderam wyll prove stark nowght yf yow suffer to lett the

---

[786] *totius vanae gloriae* [Latin] 'entirely vain glorious'.

[787] **resining** resigning.

[788] **Fynch of Woodende** Wood End was in Redbourn, where many members of the Finch family were resident. In 1609, both John and William Finch held land in Wood End. See HALS X/C/7/A.

[789] *Mater tua* [Latin] 'Your mother'.

[790] **Goode Rolff** Goodman Rolfe was a tenant at Burston. See p. 104, n. 205.

[791] **I wys** certainly.

[792] **Scamblers** parasites or spongers.

grownd from Pleadalls Ferm.[793] Yow are marvelously abused by him and misled. Some in my howse are often with him. I wyll looke better to them for it. Yet by them I heare ˆofˆ there his nowghty doings, both for him selff and yow. God be with yow and make yow able to every goode dutye and gwyde yow all weyes to your comfort. God knowes when I shall see yow. I am therfore more carefull to advyse yow to beware.

Remember Groome, I pray yow. Brockett wyll make jeste of us both. Kepe not superfluous servants to marr them with idleness and undoe yow. Let Larg lyve at home; best for him, a maried man. Nobody see this, but burn it or send it back; and so commend yow to the Lorde.

127. *Anne Bacon to Anthony Bacon,* [*c.*20 April 1595][794]

Holograph. LPL 653, fos 252r–253v. 2pp. Damaged.
Endorsed (fo. 253v): lettre de Madame
Addressed (fo. 253v): To my sonne

I am not wylling Mr Crew shulde come hether against the time, in dede I have yet no cooke and Thomas Witherton syckly and my selff peradventure wyll stay at Mr Cooke's howse.[795] I can therfore spare such tyll the holy dayes[796] be spent. Yf he wyll come after on Tewsday Wensday to vew as I wrote to yow, he shalbe hartely welcome, but not for myne own unwoleness to go to and froe before that time. Then yf yow and he wyll welcome, yf he tary 3 or 4 dayes and bring some frende yf he wyll.

Osborn and his wyff are well gone hence, yet she to brew yf qwiettly and orderly. In very truth, sonne, my servants of that sorte with Edwarde and such lyke brake ~~of~~ owt of order with me last sommer. But I have it as I myght not, greving liberly to their hurt and my discredit, because I wolde ˆyow shuldeˆ every way be well and comfortably here. Truly your often geving to such and where no desert was, made them serve more frowardly. Osborn's wyffe learnd her brewing with me and I payde well for her learning, specially since her mariag, with

---

[793] **Pleadalls Ferm** Playdells manor was part of the manors of Gorhambury, Westwick, and Praye from 1533/4. See 'Catalogue of field names', p. 86. For the description of the farm and surrounding lands in a 1569 survey, see HALS XI/2.

[794] **[c.20 April 1595]** This letter is difficult to date from the internal evidence. It mentions the 'holy days', but also the putting out of horses to grass, which may suggest that Anne is refering to Easter. She also mentions her dispute with Edward Spencer, from the summer of 1594, which means that this letter may date from around Easter 1595.

[795] **Mr Cooke's howse** Erasmus Cooke, the vicar of St Michael's parish in St Albans. See p. 181, n. 623.

[796] **holy dayes** Easter Sunday fell on 20 April 1595.

more comber to her and troble and almost doble charg in every thing, besydes which I was loth then to mention, certein other things ^were gon^ besyde one your best shertes. But I use her well inowgh and she brewes in diverse places and with me shortly. But I pray yow in my tyme, lett my servants loke to me. Yow shall soone inowgh fynde them lyke themself and for them selfs.

I hope yow wylbe very care[797] of your health and that constantly. I had worde yow wolde not your horse to the grass; as yow appoint, it shalbe. I pray yow let me know what tyme yow mean to jorny, yf it please God whose mercy and favour go with yow and bless the meanes to your recovery. In no wyse but as of necessite, kepe no superfloous expences. Remember yow have yet ^not^ visited God his howse nor seene our Soverein after your long absence. Be wyse and the Lorde geve goode success. How doth your brother and what?

128. *Anne Bacon to Anthony Bacon*, 26 April 1595

Holograph. LPL 651, fo. 110r–v. 1p.
Endorsed (fo.110v): De Madame, le 28me d'avril 1595
Addressed (fo. 110v): To my sonne Mr Antony Bacon. If the *Βρυιαρ*[798] go on with his sute (the cheet) he wyll frey[799] yow at nede. But *Περι εστι*.[800]

I humbly thank God I came well hether and fownde my howseholde well, saving that Jhon Knite was from home, after he had ben with the rest for a fashyon at church, came not home tyll x of the clock at night, much to my myslike. Be not offended, sonne, but in dede Redborn resort, which he hath haunted secretely and unseasonably above these 3 quarters yere, hath appayred[801] him much. Goodram and he and James your man and Woodend Fynch companons of late in yll and it lyghteth so upon Goodram. For as here it is spoken in my howse, the shryff hath seased Goodram's cattell and cotes.[802] I pray yow sonne, let not ungodly once abuse and cary ^yow^ to frende[803] synne. O that your health wolde suffer yow to heare publick preaching. I hartely wyshed yow had harde Mr Ege^rton^[804] the two

---

[797] **care** careful.
[798] *Βρυιαρ* [Greek transliteration] 'bruiar', i.e. brewer.
[799] **frey** Presumably in the sense of agitating and bothering, drawing on a sixteenth-century form of 'fray'.
[800] *Περι εστι* [Greek] 'he is superior', i.e. he is at an advantage.
[801] **appayred** injured.
[802] **cotes** Usually meaning sheep-cotes, i.e. small buildings for sheltering sheep.
[803] **frende** befriend.
[804] **Mr Egerton** Stephen Egerton, vicar at St Anne's, Blackfriars. See p. 209, n. 772.

^last^ weke exercyces. Surely your knowledg and judgment wolde much encrease thereby to discern aright; which gyft proveth my sonnes me thinks specially in their own matters and calling ^do want^, thowgh wyse otherwyse in diverse things *ore tenus*,[805] but *aliud semper agentes suo magno sumpto et incommodo*.[806] Do ^not^ cowntenance such nawghty ^un^godly spendalls.[807] Your cowntenancyng Goodram so soone made him careless to badd. Yf I had my xv pownds, I wold gladly bestowe yt for your credit and goode but it greveth my conscience knowing your great want, the more for such that yow shulde partetake to releve and mayntein their synfull expence.

I thank yow for your horses; that left here shalbe well looked, but horses wyll with horse play lyte and strike one anoter unhapply; myne own doble one so lately. Thother when in dede he is throwgly well. I dare say that ^iuke^[808] beast Hynde hath spoyled yow in hors since your commyng over above 200 marks every way.

Looke well to your selff inwardely and owtwardely and peace of God and love in Christ Jesu be with yow ever. Lett not your men see my lettres; it were *magna injurya*.[809]

Gorhambury 26 April.

Your mother, ABacon.

129. *Anne Bacon to Anthony Bacon*, 6 May 1595

Holograph. LPL 651, fo. 142r–v. 1p.
Endorsed (fo. 142v): De Madame le 7me de may 1595
Addressed (fo. 142v): To my sonne Mr Anthony Bacon in Bishipps Gate Strete, with some spede

Your beere, God wylling, wilbe ready to be caried on Fryday at furthest, sayth the bruyer. Yf ^it^ tary lenger, it wylbe the worse, he sayth. It is don as yow appointed the qwantite. Yow promised certeinly to me to take order for the cariag. I looked to ^have^ know[810] from yow for it when vessells were sent. I cannot, nor wyll not, take the care of cariag. Send worde with spede therfore or elce it shalbe layde in to seller

---

[805] *ore tenus* [Latin] 'verbally'.
[806] *aliud ... incommodo* [Latin] 'always doing something else to their own great expense and inconvenience'.
[807] **spendalls** spendthrifts.
[808] **iuke** slippery.
[809] *magna injurya* [Latin] 'greatly harmful'.
[810] **know** known.

ˆsaffly principleˆ.[811] Folke now apply seing the former season hath ben so fowle. I pray therfore write whom yow wyll to cary and sende owt of hand. I think Mr Crossby wylbe with yow on Fryday, yf can dispatch your busines, he sayde.

The less yow use Goodram the better. He wasteth beastly trusting to your foolysh pitie, but now sett not sinn in him nor others to your hurt. *Ne te plura mala damna sequantur.*[812] Discern and not ˆtoˆ be too easely ~~caried~~ ˆled awayˆ. Your age reqwyreth now a godly, wyse constancy in ~~yo~~ in all your proceadings.

The Father of Heaven, bless yow more and more in Christ Jesu.

Gorhambury 6ᵗʰ *Maii* 95.

Your mother,
ABacon.

Memento[813] Brocket, Grome.

130. *Anne Bacon to Anthony Bacon*, [before 8] May 1595[814]

Holograph. LPL 651, fos 165r–166v. 2pp.
Endorsed (fo. 166v): de Madame le may 1595
Addressed (fo. 166v): To my sonne Mr Bacon at Bishops gate. This was ment to be sent with the beere.

Gratia et amor Dei in Christo.[815]
Your beere, well handled I trust, is ment to be sent tomorow early. The bruyar hath ben careful him selff. I had no bruing, I dare say, this twelve moneth more diligently attended upon of my servants. Yf the cariers do their part and afterwards well watched and looked to in the seller, it is thowght for your own speciall use it wyll last tyll nye Michaeltyde,[816] both for qwantitee and qwalitee. As yow appointed it is brued; viii hogshed in all of the cheefest beere, ii hogshedds marked with an S on ech syde of the wheele mark. The third somwhat less strong being a seconde is marked lyke wyse with chalk wyth a smaller whele mark and one only S bye it to know it ryghtly; thother v alyke. God geve yow the right use of all his ˆgyftsˆ to God's glory and your

[811]**principle** at first.
[812]*Ne te . . . sequitur* [Latin] 'Lest more bad losses may follow you'.
[813]*Memento* [Latin] 'Remember'.
[814]**[before 8] May 1595** Letter **129** notes that the beer must be sent by Friday 9 May. This letter mentions that it will be sent the next day.
[815]*Gratia . . . Christo* [Latin] 'Grace and the love of the Lord in Christ'.
[816]**Michaeltyde** Michaelmas. See p. 107, n. 225.

own further advancement and tru comfort. The rowelled[817] horse I had no mynde to indede nor the horse Mr Spencer roade on. Lawson thrust in here his and others, smutled[818] and spoyled beast. The horse is ful[l] of wyngalls,[819] a token of very spoyling in ryding and dress^ing^. Grass is here yet but poore and scant and I must turne shortly my two service geldings of necessitee. I wyll not chang my ^own^ fayely[820] husband's horse[821] for yours, both heavie and stumbling and never broken for ^such a^ toward ho[rse] when yow fyrst had him. Diverse of my folk now sy[ckly]. God encrease your health, I pray God, and be mercyfull to us both.

[Left-hand margin] I thank yow for your comly mastive. It is suspected he wyll hunt after shepe and is to owlde. I durs not prove him yet.

Your mother, ABacon.

131. *Anne Bacon to Anthony Bacon*, 12 May 1595

Holograph. LPL 651, fo. 156r–v. 1p.
Endorsed (fo. 156v): De Madame le 12me de may 1595

Grace and health.

I hope your beere is well where yow appointed. I ment a lettre to yow then, but it was afterwarde by the carier ^sent^. Hangings I wolde ^not^ sende with the new working tonned drink[822] for hurting. The two upper chambers be not ^to^ be altered, they are no sute but odde ones most. As nere as cowld I chose the best and fyttest for your chamber here. Yf yow wyll those iiii odd romes too. And one ^of them^ of the great chamber hanging at your howse in your father's tyme of Barbary. Yf yow wyll have them to eny goode purpose sende me worde by this bearer. So yow sende wythall by him a right note of the former implements yow ^have^ had allready from hence, which I looke for and often have justly reqwyred heretofore. For your horse I wyll take him thowgh in ^dede^ spoyled ^*ut antea levissi*^[823] in comparison as freely as I gave him to yow; and yf I put not the beast to my cart and put a way ^one^ of my 4 now, for moe[824] wyll I not kepe. I wyll sell

---

[817]**rowelled** Pricked by rowels, the small spikes at the end of a spur.
[818]**smutled** smutted or dirtied.
[819]**wyngalls** A windgall is a soft tumour on the leg of a horse.
[820]**fayely** Presumably 'faithly', i.e. faithful.
[821]**husband's horse** A reliable, trustworthy horse.
[822]**new working tonned drink** This is a reference to the beer, mentioned in **130**. The description 'new working' is another expression for a new brewing; 'tonned' refers to the storage of the beer in casks.
[823]*ut antea levissi[mus]* [Latin] 'as before very nimble'.
[824]**moe** more.

him as well as I can and when I am able bestow a nagg in his stede.
I pray dispatch this my man. I send him of purpose to yow, and for
none other business, and I nede his service here at home, besyde the
charge of tareing. Remember the note to be sent elce I can sende no
more hence. *Vale in Christo quam optime.*[825]

Beware of ἐνρι Ὀουαρδ[826] and such. Ἀμυνου εστι κινδυνοτατοσ
και κακω[ν] δολων ανηρ.[827] God kepe the Earle[828] from such poyson
and snaring και σεαυτον ομοιωσ[829] but *matris monita nihil estimantur.*[830]
I think for my long attending in coorte and a cheeff cownsellour's wyffe
few *preclarae feminae meae sortis*[831] are able or be alyve to speak and judg
of such proceadings and worldly doings of ^men^.

But[832] God bless yow and make yow able to heare wholsome, publick
doctrine for your better understanding every way. I am sory yow
at Chelsey and your brother at Twycknam do want that pretious
commoditee for cheff health and comfort.

Gorhambury 12 *Maii* 95.
Your mother, ABacon.

132. *Anne Bacon to William Cecil, Lord Burghley*, 22 May 1595

Holograph. BL, Lansdowne MS 79, fos 79r–80v. 2pp.
Endorsed (fo. 80v): 22 May 1595. Lady Bacon to my Lord. One Mr
Holme returned one of Ireland from Mr Travers
Addressed (fo.80v): To my singuler goode Lorde, the Lord Tresurer of
Englande

This morning, my singuler goode Lorde, I was so bowlde as to desyre
Mrs Whyte,[833] whose very kinde curtesy I allweies find, that she wolde
in passing by this way upon eny occasion do so much as to see me
that by her I might do my humble dutie to your Lordship and know
of your goode health to my comfort.

---

[825] *Vale . . . optime* [Latin] 'Fare you right well in Christ'.
[826] ἐνρι Ὀουαρδ [Greek transliteration] 'Henri Howard', i.e. Henry Howard.
[827] Ἀμυνου . . . ανηρ [Greek] 'Take care, he is most dangerous and a man of evil cunning'.
[828] **the Earle** The earl of Essex.
[829] και σεαυτον ομοιωσ [Greek] 'and yourself likewise'.
[830] *matris . . . estimantur* [Latin] 'your mother's warnings are estimated as nothing'.
[831] *preclarae . . . sortis* [Latin] 'distinguished women of my sort'.
[832] **But** There is a large gap between 'but' and 'God'. It may be that Anne had initially planned to add additional words in the space before dispatch.
[833] **Mrs Whyte** Presumably Burghley's sister Anne, the widow of Thomas White.

This afternoone even abowt 3 of the clock came Mr Holmes, the learned man that went over with Mr Travers into Ireland and reqwested of me ii or three lynes that he might have access to your goode Lordship for the matters of her Majestie's yowng colledg there, he sayde.[834] I fynde such favour in your Lordship that for such a one and such cawse I do not readily deny to troble your Lordship thus. Rejoysing in dede, my Lord, of your goode continuance and ablenes for the great benefitt of our lande and specially of the advancement of the gospell herin, *domi forisque*,[835] to your great harte's solace. God encrease it more and more.

I came hether to take a litle cownsell for my much disordred body synce my quartan,[836] sondry weyes to ease some payns, diverse at this present and not able to go but with payn in one of my feete and other wyse. I have great cawse to acknowledg the mercy of God towarde ^me^ in granting me tyme and meanes to more mortification, which by his grace I besech him I may dayly ^endevour^ to be better and better prepared for a better lyffe. The Lorde prolong yours with feeling encrease of his love and goodness in Christ Jesu.

I humbly take my leave, with thanks from my hart for your honorable comforts. Flete Strete. 22 May 95.

In the Lorde *ex animo*,[837]
ABacon
Χηρα.[838]

133. *Anne Bacon to Anthony Bacon*, 31 May 1595

Holograph. LPL 651, fos 225r–226v. 2pp. Damaged along right-hand side.
Endorsed (225v): De Madame le 3me de juni 1595
Addressed (225v): To my sonne Mr Anthony Bacon at Bishopps gate street. *Ne subito relinquas aut concedes alicui edes urbanas.*[839]

Sonne yow had a mynde to have the long carpett and the ancient learned philosoph[ers'] pictures from hence, but in dede I had no

---

[834]**This ... he sayde** Matthias Holmes was a fellow of the newly founded Trinity College, Dublin; Walter Travers was provost of the college.
[835]***domi forisque*** [Latin] 'at home and abroad'.
[836]**quartan** Quartan fever. See p. 150, n. 463.
[837]***ex animo*** [Latin] 'from the heart'.
[838]***Χηρα*** [Greek] 'widow'.
[839]***Ne subito ... [a]edes urbanas*** [Latin] 'Do not quickly relinquish or concede your town house to anyone'.

mynde therto, yet have I sent, very carefully bestowed and layde in a
hamper for safty in cariage. For the carpet, being withowt golde, yow
shall not, I think, have the lyke at this time in London, for the right,
and not paynted, cowllers;[840] which is to common in this age in moe[841]
things then carpetts, and such. It is for all not of late bowght, worth
20 li to bye. Such implements as your father ˄left˄ I have very diligent
looked to and kept; yow have now bared this howse of all the best. A
wyffe wolde have well regarded such things, but now they shall serve
for use of gaming or typling upon the table of every common person,
your own men as w[ell] ill as others, and so be spoyled as at Redborn.
I wolde think that Jhon your taylour shude be fittest to looke well
to your furnitre.[842] God I humbly besech him encrease in yow dayly
spirituall stoare, also the comfort of bodily health and other comforts
of this lyff to his own good pleasure to whose fatherly love in Christ I
commend yow.

I wysch the hamper were not opened tyll your selff were at Chelsey
to see it don before yow; for the pictures are put orderly within the
carpett. Yow have one long carpett allredy; I can not think to what use
this shulde be. It wylbe an occasion of mockery that yow shulde have
a great chamber, called and carpeted. *Haud inane est quod dico*.[843] Draw
no charge till God better enable yow, but observe narowly both for
your health and purse. Surely your vi s beere is no ordinary drink for
your howse no tyme of the yere specially, and usually to strong for yow,
but *podagra*[844] wyll bestur him. Seing God hath geven yow some goode
abilities, I wolde I trow[845] watch over my diett and every thing to put
them in ure[846] by health to God his glory and your own more creditt
getting publickly. Yf her Majesti have resolved upon the negative for
your brother, *ut audio*,[847] truly save for the brute a litle, I am glad of
it. God in his tyme hath better in stoare, I trust. For consideryng his
kynde of health and what ˄comber˄ perteins to that office, it is best
for him I hope. Lett us all pray the Lorde we make ˄us to˄ profitt by
his fatherly correction dowtles in his hande and all for the best and
love to his chyldren that wyll seeke him fyrst and depend upon ˄his˄

---

[840]**cowllers** colours.
[841]**moe** more.
[842]**furnitre** furniture.
[843]***Haud . . . dico*** [Latin] 'What I say is not foolish'.
[844]***podagra*** [Latin] 'gout'.
[845]**trow** trust.
[846]**ure** use.
[847]***ut audio*** [Latin] 'as I hear'.

goodenes, godly and wysely. Love thee lyke brethern what soever and be of goode corage in the Lorde with goode hope.
Vale et cura diligenter ut quam optime valeas et sis tui juris et prudenter age.[848]

ultimo Maii[849] 95.

Mater tua,[850] ABacon Χηρα.[851]

134. Anne Bacon to Anthony Bacon, 16 June 1595

Holograph. LPL 651, fo. 206r–v. 1p.
Endorsed (fo. 206v): De Madame le 18me de juni 1595

How matters went at Gorhambury yow understoode by Mr Crew. I offred him a litle golde and he wolde take none. Yf it were once the goode wyll of God, your being here or elce where shulde be very comfortable. Your continuall lack of health and other no small hyndrances thereby have gon very nere to me. But now I ^endevour to^ cast my burden upon the Lorde[852] ^and^ to wayte upon his gratious providence both for my selff and myne in his own goode tyme, not omitting goode meanes.

The weather ^here^ very boystrus with wynde, hayle and rayn. I feare yow feele theroff. I wolde, yf it please God, be a few dayes at London the next terme. I think yow wylbe gon to Chelsye before. I pray God yow take not hurt there this unseasonable weather and others enjoy your ^consumming^ charges and *illis sit bene cum tibi sit male.*[853] Do what yow can to expell the gowt by diet and seasonable sleeping. Use not your selff to be twanged a slepe, but naturally it wyll grow into a teadious custome and hynder yow much.

Jhon ^your man^ had thowght to have wayted on yow very shortly, but his fever is now every day again. He never feltt him throwghly well, but now works a fresh and looks thinn and pale, wherof he is sory for gladly wolde he return.

I think the great well chayn must be searched and amended. I have delivered goodeman woodd mony for Spanish iron for it.

The God of all grace be with yow and direct yow with his holy spirit allweies.

---

[848] *Vale ... prudenter* [Latin] 'Farewell and take diligent care of your health and you should live independently and act prudently'.
[849] *ultimo Maii* [Latin] 'the last day of May'.
[850] *Mater tua* [Latin] 'Your mother'.
[851] *Χηρα* [Greek] 'widow'.
[852] **cast ... Lorde** See Psalm 55:22.
[853] *illis ... male* [Latin] 'to them it may be good though to you it may be bad'.

βεουαρε of Ιακουεσ and αδελφοσ σου of κελλεττ. Σουσαν
ˆΛηστηρ and Λονηττˆ is gon to London and, as I desyred, Mr
Κρευε.[854] Λοοκε σπουδαιωσ,[855] owt of some ˆdowtˆ did maynteyn
her nawghtines. Do it wysely and closely but I think none abowt yow
ˆwyllˆ do it trustely. Burn this *sat cito*,[856] yet reede and marke. God kepe
yow both in his love in Christ ever.

Remember *ut sis tui juris et ˆenitere utˆ expergiscaris cum podragra cum omni prudenti cura.*[857]

Μάτερ *tua*,[858]
ABacon.

Gorhambury 16ᵗʰ *Junii.*

Comburatur hoc ne.[859]

135. Anthony Bacon to Anne Bacon, with return postcript by Anne Bacon, 18 June 1595

Draft, Anthony Bacon holograph from 'Your Ladiship's moste loving';
Anne Bacon holograph from 'I send yow the lettre'. LPL 651, fo. 207r–v. 1p.
Endorsed (fo. 207v): De Madame le 18me de juin 1595
Addressed (fo. 207v): To the honorable this verie good Ladie and mother the Ladie Anne Bacon
Additional address by Anne Bacon: To my sonne Mr Anthony Bacon in Byshopps gate Strete. Part not with your London howse *temere ne forte peniteat tei.*[860]

Madame,
These fewe lynes shalbe first to remember my most humble dewtie to your Ladyship, with the like thankes for the carpet and pictors which it pleased yow to sende me, wherof your Ladyship maie be asseured there shalbe speciall care had.

---

[854] *βεωαρε ... Κρευε* [Greek, transcription and direct, and English] 'Beware of Jakwes and your brother of Kellet. Sousan Lester and Lonett is gon to London and, as I desyred, Mr Krewe'. Jacques is presumably Jacques Petit, Anthony's servant. John Kellet was a freeman-apothecary who treated Francis Bacon. Susan Lester may be the maid, Susan, mentioned in **114**.
[855] *Λοοκε σπουδαιωσ* [Greek, transcription and direct] 'Looke carefully'.
[856] *sat cito* [Latin] 'very quickly'.
[857] *ut ... cura.* [Latin] 'it is in your control and strive to wake up the gout with all prudent care'.
[858] *Μάτερ tua* [Greek transliteration and Latin] 'Your mother'.
[859] *Comburatur hoc ne* [Latin] 'Let this be burnt lest'.
[860] *temere ... tei* [Latin] 'rashly lest perhaps you may repent'.

I am likewise to advertise your Ladyship that Mr Crewe and Mr Downinge, God willinge, will waight of your Ladyship on Wednesdaie next to keepe the courte; which is thought to be necessarie, for the certen knowledge by Mr Tille. Hawgood houldeth a good quantity of copiehold.[861]

And so I most humblie take my leave, and commit your Ladyship to God's best protection.

This oth[862] of June 1595.

Your Ladyship's moste lovinge and obdient son, Anthony Bacon.

[Postscript by Anne Bacon]
I sende yow the lettre that yow may your selff see how wysely ^and heedefully^ warning was geven by the writer. It made much dowt and disapointed much.

136. *Anne Bacon to Anthony Bacon*, 8 July 1595

Holograph. LPL 651, fo. 267r–v. 1p.
Endorsed (fo. 267v): De Madame le mois de juillet 1595
Addressed (fo. 267v): To my sonne Mr Anthonie Bacon in Bishopgate strete

I thank God I came well, thowgh weary, heather and thank yow for your horses. The not delyvery of my lettre, sent by the carier, returned me by myn own horses unlooked for then, and becawse I had written before dowtfully referring to another lettre to be sent afterwarde. ~~They~~ ^My men^ not hearing as they looked, fearing I had not ben well, came on, wherin the[863] shewed their honest and dutifull care and regard of me, which pleased me much.

I sende yow oakwood straberies gathred this morning by this bearer and other[s]. His name is Dawyes, diligent in the garden as the tyme will, for he came but lately and is also a zealous Christian servant; I thank God for him. I pray yow, sonne, see him and speak with him your selff. He returneth not tyll nigh a weeke, he sayth. He readeth the ordinary morning and evening prayour to my howse, even hartely ^reverently^. The Lorde God in mercy be with yow all weyes. Looke to your charges at Chelsey; small thankes for your great charges. Be

---

[861] **Hawgood copiehold** The Hawgood family were the copyhold tenants of Megdells Farm in Westwick until 1643. See HALS XI/2 and 'Catalogue of field names', p. 76.

[862] **oth** No date is given in the draft, only on the endorsement.

[863] **the** they.

an enemy to the gowt and watch over it with all goode observation and use your lymms in tyme, for God sake. Supp not, watch not late and slepe naturally *in utramque aurem*.[864] Call no *convivas*[865] till God better enable yow in his ˆownˆ gratious tyme ˆ*sed interem cave et enitere prudenter*ˆ.[866] Fare yow well in our Lorde Jesu Chris[t].

Gorhambury 8 *Julii*.

Your moother, AB.

Mr Purveiour[867] and Groome.

137. *Anne Bacon to Anthony Bacon*, [before 21 July 1595][868]

Holograph. LPL 653, fos 320r–321v. 2pp. Damaged.
Endorsed (fo. 321v): lettre de Madame

I sende to know how yow and your brother do, and I sende my horse Loss[869] yf yow wyll have him st[a]y, but I have no sadle to remein with yow for him. I have but v for myne own use. Yf I had ben able I wolde have bowght moe.[870] Yf yow kepe Loss, let him well used in dede. I have not such another for frende or a preacher. Mantell is scant sownde. Nether my horses ner my men are acqwainted with undiscrete[871] travell; he is taken from the grass. It wylbe chargeable keping him in and to put him abroade yow may qwickly be ridd of him. Do as your necessary business reqwireth and beware, sonne, yow procure to your sellf tangled matters t[o] no purpose but your nedeless charg. I wolde yow were well ridd of that owlde, booted, polling papist.[872] He wyll use discoorses owt of season to hinder your health,

---

[864] *in utramque aurem* [Latin] 'on either ear'. This is a classical phrase meaning to sleep soundly on both ears, free from cares. See D. Erasmus, *Adages III iv 1–IV ii 100*, trans. D.L. Drysdall, in *Collected Works of Erasmus*, XXXV (Toronto, 2005), p. 467.

[865] *convivas* [Latin] 'companions'.

[866] *sed . . . prudenter* [Latin] 'but meanwhile take care and struggle onwards wisely'.

[867] **Purveiour** Purveyor, figure in charge of provisions.

[868] **[before 21 July 1595]** This undated letter is difficult to place in an exact chronology, but it is likely to have been written before Antonio Pérez left for France on 21 July 1595. See below, n. 872.

[869] **Loss** Loss was the name of the horse. See also **149**.

[870] **moe** more.

[871] **undiscrete** indiscrete, unsound.

[872] **owlde, booted, polling papist** This is likely to be a refence to Antonio Pérez. Born in 1540, Pérez was then fifty-five years old, hence Anne's description of him as old; her account of him as polling suggests that she believed Pérez was prone to cheating, perhaps in reference to his Catholicism. It could also be a description of Lord Henry Howard, likewise born in 1540; Anne feared Howard was a 'subtile papist inwardly'. For Howard's suspected

the want wheroff is your great hindrance. Take ˆheedeˆ therefore every way and be ware and wyse. When yow are throwgh[ly] sownded then *adieu*.[873] Some do think that your brother and yow make to great a note of the *Εαρλεσ*[874] favour. Do well and committ your wayes to the Lord [and] seeke cowsell at him. Beware of emulation and be not frank to open your mynd to every body. Yow shalbe better estemed. The Lorde direct yow in all things. Mark what I write and but to your brother to nobody. Welldon, that in an ill tyme for her[875] maried her ˆCarpenter's wydowˆ, suffreth willingly his shepe to marr my last felled spring and hath with crapping hindred it above a yere's growth. He is ˆaˆ nawghty makebater[876] with his neighbours. Fyrst he and Ewer[877] cowlde never agree because his did still eate up his grownde and is styll offring occasion of qwarrells. Mr Downing hath ˆhadˆ somewhat to do with him,[878] with his ˆneverˆ challenging I wot not and ˆasˆ for his sonns, they be but riotus and hog that liberty, yf one be not typsye which is too trew and stub[bor]n with all. I heare Weldon braggs yow have graunted him a 100 li loade of chalk, which I can not think yow so ˆbeˆ unadvised and lyeng with in another tenant's grownd. So yow may make matter of continuall stryff and the other may chuse doing his dutie.

[Left-hand margin] I wis[879] yow shall dwell ˆhereˆ in a harde soyle and ˆbyˆ harde harted neighbour but for their own profitt conning. Be not hasty, *tacuisse numquam*.[880] ABacon.

Catholicism, see **123**. Anne has written over 'polling' with what seems to be the word 'yet', so it seems as if she particularly wanted to emphasize the papist's cheating nature.

[873]*adieu* [French] 'farewell'.

[874]*Εαρλεσ* [Greek transliteration] 'Earles', ie. the earl of Essex's favour.

[875]**her** here.

[876]**makebater** Fomentor of trouble and strife.

[877]**Ewer** William Ewer was recorded in 1569 as a copyhold tenant of considerable lands close to Gorhambury; he was acting as a juror in the manorial court in 1596. See HALS XI/2 and X/B/3/A.

[878]**Mr Downing . . . him** Presumably concerning the manor courts over which Downing presided.

[879]**I wis** certainly.

[880]*tacuisse numquam* [Latin] 'never having been silent'.

138. *Anne Bacon to Anthony Bacon*, 30 July 1595

Holograph. LPL 651, fos 310r–311v. 2pp.
Endorsed (fo. 311v): De Madame le 3me le aoust 1595
Endorsed (fo. 311v): To my sonne Mr Anthony Bacon geve theis

I most humbly thank God and much rejoyced when I harde by Crosby
yow do more exercyse your body and your leggs and that in your coch
yow go to the Earle ^your selff as occasion^. Surely, sonne, by the grace
of God yow shall fynde great healpe by bodily exercyse in season and
much refreshing, both to body and mynd and be more accompted
of. I wolde advise yow went sometyme to the French Church[881] and
have there (and bash[882] not your necessaries for warmeth) to heare the
publick preching of the worde of God, as it is his ordinance, and arme
so with prayour. For understanding it maketh the goode hearers wyse
to God and enableth them to discerne how to walk in their worldly
vocation to please God and to be accepted of men in dede, which God
grant to yow both.

Truly, sonne, the miller's last coming to yow was but a craft to
collour his halting, towching his secret consenting to steale, as cause
hath ben geven to suspect him not lately ^alone^ but long. He waxeth a
suttell fellow and hath a running head of his own. Now he goeth with
meale[883] to London and to some other places here abowt and wyll marr
the myll I dowt by his flitting. Wherfore shulde he have a nett? Him
selff confessed abowt the scowring of ^the mill^ but lately that there
was store of trowte and now allmost none, because Bun[884] and other
dyd lately robb as yow know. I took the miller's part in defending his
right dealing and so the Justices[885] have bownde Bun to goode abearing
tyll next sessions. But that ^same^ Bun sayde earnestly that the miller
cowlde join and beare with some and ^he^ cowlde abyde by it; and
so hath Mr Coltman sayde when I have blamed him but for angling.
Certeinly, sonne, where he bringeth yow two, I wolde they were moe[886]
for yow. He carieth to Mr $\pi\rho\epsilon\sigma\tau o\nu$[887] and others twyse as many but

---

[881]**French Church** The French Stranger Church, a Huguenot congregation, met in
Threadneedle Street in London. For Anthony's associations with members of the French
Stranger Church, see **52**, **53**, **83**, and **178**.

[882]**bash** discomfort.

[883]**meale** ground grain.

[884]**Bun** The 1569 Gorhambury survey reveals that a William Bunne held some copyhold
land on the manor. He also leased a cottage at Coptehall, according to accounts made on
Nicholas Bacon I's death in 1579. See HALS XI/2 and *Stiffkey*, II, pp. 38–39.

[885]**Justices** Justices of the peace.

[886]**moe** more.

[887]$\pi\rho\epsilon\sigma\tau o\nu$ [Greek transliteration] 'Preston'. Presumably the miller, Preston, mentioned
in **115**.

say yet not so to him. I mean to take his net from him. He is waxen so heady new fangled that the mille goeth to wrack and customers begyn to mislyke and forsake it, which hynder our living and discontinew it.

I wyll cause Humphrey[888] to be paid as yow order with Crossby. Surely set a syde my poore mortmain; but 200 li or little above. A small portion for my continuance. I thank the Lord ˆfor all.ˆ Spending mony goeth but from hande to mowth as they say with me. I gave your brother at twyse 25 li for his paling,[889] the rather to chere him since he had nothing of me. Crossby towlde me he looked very ill; he thowght he taketh styll inwarde greff I feare.[890] It may hinder his health herafter. Cownsell to be godly wyse ˆfyrstˆ and wyse for him selff too; and both of yow looke to your expences in tyme and oversee those yow trust how trustely, for I tell yow plainly it hath ben ˆlongˆ commonly observed that both your servants are full of mony.

My Lord Cheff Baron's mariag with your syster I never eny inkling of before Crossby towlde.[891] I pray at leasure wryte to me some circumstances of the maner and God bless it. I sende Wynter purposely becawse yow shulde not sende your boy.

Gorhambury *penultimo Julii.*[892]

Mater tua,[893] AB.

Nobody but your selff see my lettres, I pray yow.

[*Left-hand margin*] After harvest, some venison wolde do well here. God bless yow dayly with goode encreases.

139. *Anne Bacon to Anthony Bacon,* 2 August 1595

Holograph. LPL 653, fos 323r–324v. 2pp.
Endorsed (fo. 324v): lettre de Madame
Addressed (fo. 324v): My sonnes both

Sonne I had thowght to have sent unto yow on Fryday, yf your man had not come yesternight. The goode cawse was to know whether Mr

---

[888]**Humphrey** The butcher, as noted in **46**.
[889]**paling** paling wood, i.e. wood that will be made into fences.
[890]**he . . . greff I feare** Anne was here referring to Francis Bacon's continued quest for the post of solicitor-general.
[891]**My . . . Crosby towlde** Elizabeth Bacon, daughter of Nicholas Bacon I by his first wife, Jane, became the third wife of Sir William Peryam, lord chief baron of the exchequer, in 1595.
[892]**penultimo Julii** [Latin] 'next to last day of July'.
[893]**Mater tua** [Latin] 'your mother'.

Wyborn may be welcome to do goode unto my sonnes, living with owt publyck ministery and private and holsom conference to styrr yow upp to remember the Lorde, and serve him cheffely with yours. The other cawses were too. I have hard since I saw yow that yow have an issue abowt your shoulder or arme, wherof I was sory, as dangerous to beginn and more to shutte ^upp^. I never harde Mr Smyth[894] speak of it, and to use Archeloe[895] alone in such a case I feare is not saff for yow. He is very adventurous to promyss and very often his cownsell ^and warrant^ fownd nowght. God geve yow goode of your fysych[896] and to be wyse for your selff and send yow no nede of it with God's helping ^healing^ hande.

The last I have lately upon occasion harde that yow labour much for that Wolworth fellow, Lawson, and that by therle of Es[sex]. Yt were wysdome, I think, to use his favour in goode and pertinent matters for your selffs and your own farthering, and not to be teadious or overbowlde for such base personns, howsoever overvalyng yow, and ^who wyll^ to convey from yow your estimation for his own, which he hath already and wyll more doe as yow enable him.[897] Trust to that when the foxe seeth his opportunitee by your footing. Do not hinder your health and spend your goode tyme in discoorsing and yow and your brother, specially yow, be still occupied and entangled with state and wordely[898] matters above your calling, to make yow the more unfit to be employed and then your gyfts phiyn[899] appere to your own credit. Exercise your selff in the knowledg of holy and profitable things to please God, and then men, and now that yow have a coople of subtill ~~renoldes~~ ^raynoles[900] Standon and he^ to besett yow. I humbly besech the Lorde yow may escape all their snarings and God encrease your health with his favour.

A few plumms draweth much here; peares not ripe nor goode.

Valete in Domino Jesu Christo.[901]
AB.

Gorhambury ii August v.

[894]**Mr Smyth** Richard Smith. See p. 150, n. 464.
[895]**Archeloe** For Doctor Archelow, see SP 53/10, fo. 51, p. 957.
[896]**fysych** physic.
[897]**him** Anne repeated this word twice, as it was initially cut off by the edge of the paper.
[898]**wordely** Presumably 'worldly'.
[899]**phiyn** thin.
[900]*raynoles* Given Anne's deleted spelling, it seems that she is attempting to write the French for foxes: '*renards*'.
[901]*Valete ... Christo* [Latin] 'Farewell in the Lord Jesus Christ'. It is interesting that Anne uses the plural form of farewell, when writing only to Anthony; as she uses the same form in **59**, it may be that she meant the blessing to extend to her other son, Francis.

140. *Anne Bacon to Anthony Bacon*, 5 August 1595

Holograph. LPL 651, fos 328r–329v. 2pp.
Endorsed (fo. 329v): De Madame le 7 d'aoust 1595
Addressed (fo. 329v): To my sonne Mr Bacon

For your bottles, I thank yow. The malmesy[902] I tasted a litle; very good. Humphrey shall, God wyllingly, be answerd but with a syght of his reconing; he asketh for 20 neats towngs[903] at once, not very seldome neyther.[904] For Mr Barbar, Crossby wyll go with in these 3 dayes to kepe your credit with him and such is a veri Christian duty. Owe nothing to eny sayth the Lorde in his worde, but to love one another.[905] I wolde I were able to helpe yow both owt of dett, but set a part my poore mortmein which I certeinly have vowed, for eny *Dei gratia*[906] I am not worth one C li. Yee and specially yow have spent me qwick. Nothing can therfore remain after I am dead. God bless yow. I had not sent now but for this cawse. By your message by Wynter the two cowntisses, systers,[907] wyll neighbour yow. Both ladies that feare God and love his worde in dede zealously, specially the yownger syster. Yet upon advise and some experience, ~~few~~ I wolde earnestly cownsell yow to be ware and circumspect and not be too open nor wylling to prolong speche wth the cowntess of Warwick. She after her father's fashion wyll search and sownd and lay upp with diligent marking *quae nec sentiu[n]tur aulica prope ad Reginam, et patrissat in illa re nimis. Hac causa nunc scribendi.*[908]

Another matter is that now the mariag of your syster is well by God his appointment I trust. Use not such ˆbrodeˆ langeges ~~of~~ ˆuponˆ mislyke of unkindness; your men and others yow peradventure yow mark not may hurt yow very much. Surely yf such phrase as yow wrote in your lettre or such deriding shulde come to his eare it wolde be very hurtfull to yow more then one way, which yow nede not being never abroad amongst them. Your syster's nature is but unkinde and at that

---

[902]**malmesy** Malmesey, a sweet wine.

[903]**neats towngs** Ox or cow tongues.

[904]**Humphrey . . . neyther** As Humphrey is noted in **46** as the butcher, this letter refers to his bill for meat.

[905]**Owe . . . another** Romans 13:8.

[906]*Dei gratia* [Latin] 'with God's grace'.

[907]**the two . . . systers** The countess of Warwick, Anne Dudley, and her sister, Margaret Clifford, the countess of Cumberland.

[908]*quae . . . scribendi* [Latin] 'those things which seem not courtly near to the queen, and in this matter she takes too little after her father. This is the cause of my writing now.' The countess of Warwick's father, Francis Russell, the earl of Bedford, had been the father-in-law of Anne Bacon's sister Elizabeth, after her marriage to John, Lord Russell, heir to the earldom.

tyme of her mariage cowlde not her selff think of such things. I pray harken to him with all curtesy. He is of marvelous goode estimation for his religious minde in following his law calling upprightly. *Cave igitur a verbis et factis et sermonibus in mensa coram. Vix illi fides in servis.*[909] I write more herof becawse others write your lettres and not your selff. I am sory your brother with inwarde secret greeff hindreth his health. Every body sayth he loketh thine and pale. Let him looke to God and confere with him in godly exercyse of hearing ^and reading^ and contemn to be noted to take care. I had rather yee both with God his blessed favour had veri goode health and well owt of debt, then eny offyce yet; thowgh the *Εαρλε*[910] shewed great affection, he marred all with violent coorses. I pray God encrease his feare in his hart and a hatred of synn in deed; halting before the Lorde and backslyding are very pernitious. I am hartely sory to heare how he sweareth and gameth unreasonably.[911] God can not lyke it. I pray shew your brother this lettre, but ^to^ no creature elce. *Memento mei et tui.*[912]

AB *mater tua.*[913]

[*Left-hand margin*] Gorhambury 5th August 95. With a humble hart before God, lett your brother be ^of^ good chere. Alas, what excess of bucks at Grayse's Inne and to feast it so on the Sabbath. God forgive and have mercy upon England.

141. *Anne Bacon to Anthony Bacon*, 15 August 1595

Holograph. LPL 651, fos 330r–331v. 2pp.
Endorsed (fo. 331v): De Madame le 15me d'aoust 1595
Addressed (fo. 331v): To my sonne Mr Anthony Bacon

I besech God his blessing may foloww yow and be upon yow whereever yow go. The cownsell to part with that London howse so well agred and ^made^ necessary was more cunning then ment for your goode, being gowty as yow be, but yow *nimis*[914] in such ^were things^ to your great hurt, credulous suffer wyllingly your self to be abused. God open your understanding both inwarde and owtwarde. For thother place, thowgh

---

[909] ***Cave igitur . . . in servi*** [Latin] 'Beware therefore in words and deeds and speeches openly at table. There is scarce any fidelity in servants in that place'.
[910] ***Εαρλε*** [Greek transliteration] 'Earle', i.e. the earl of Essex.
[911] **I . . . unreasonably** For Anne's reproach to Essex regarding his swearing, see **146**.
[912] ***Memento mei et tui*** [Latin] 'Be mindful of me and you'.
[913] ***mater tua*** [Latin] 'your mother'.
[914] ***nimis*** [Latin] 'overmuch'.

honorably offred, *crede mihi fili*[915] yow shall fynde many inconveniences not lyght.[916] Envy, emulation, continuall and unseasonable disqwiett to encrease your gowt; many paynes, great urging for sutes, yea importune to troble thearle and your selff. Peradventure not so well lyked your selff there as in your own howse. What, others allready offended not small ones, may mark and laye upp, I feare, having as yow have working heads abowt yow, some encrease of suspition and disagreement which may hurt yow privetly, yf not publikly, or both by all lykeliods.[917] These so tykle[918] tymes the Lord healpe. ^And^ I have not ^mentioned^ before your unavoydable cause of expence. The maner of your removes have and go to my hart and surely *penitebit te, expertus te malo timeo*,[919] besydes your stuff spoyled and lost and many by incommoditees.

I thank yow for your ment venison. It wylbe but troblesome to yow and chargable to me. Mony is gon with me and I am but syckly and sadd.

I commende yow to the grace of God and to goode health every way.

Gorhambury 15 August 95. *καλωσ φερε. και σοφοσ εστω εν καιρω*.[920]

Mater tua pia,[921]
AB.

142. *Anne Bacon to Anthony Bacon*, 20 August 1595

Holograph. LPL 651, fos 326r–327v. 2pp.
Endorsed (fo. 327v): De Madame le 21me d'aoust 1595
Addressed (fo. 327v): To my sonne Mr Anthony Bacon

I pray God yow have throwghly premeditate[922] and his goodness was the best resolution for yow, but I cannot put the troble, some feare, owt of my mynde yet. I am on auncient experience *non in obscuris*

---

[915] *crede mihi fili* [Latin] 'believe me, son'.
[916] **For . . . lyght** Anne was here referring to Anthony's proposed move into the earl of Essex's house on the Strand.
[917] **lykeliods** likelihoods.
[918] **tykle** uncertain and threatening.
[919] *p[a]enitebit . . . timeo* [Latin] 'It will be repented by you, I fear, having experienced to your hurt'.
[920] *καλωσ . . . καιρω* [Greek] 'Take it well, and be wise in due course'.
[921] *Mater tua pia* [Latin] 'Your tender mother'.
[922] **premeditate** premeditated upon.

locis sed in principum aulis ab adoless^cencia^.[923] ii verses have come to my remembrance thinking of your purpose, long forgotten but now fresh. The one rather a ^proverbiall^ cownsel then a verse, which is as I have sene it by ^fyrst^ syllable onely sett down thus. *Ni= Fa= pa= con=;*[924] *adde ^prima^ mia, ^seconda^ miliaritas, ^tertia^ rit, ^quarta^ temptum*[925] which hole joined together to returne *longum usus rerum docuit et docebit.*[926] The verse is *dulcis inexperto cultura potentis amici.*[927] Yow have hetherto ben estemed as a worthy frende, now shalbe accownted his folower; a base kinde of goode wyll ^and speech^. Before his servants did regarde yow; now yow must respect and be in their danger to your comber and charg ^and care^ to please. Every thing yow do shalbe spoken and noted abroad and yourself browght as it were into a kinde of bondag where now yet free. Many, many wylbe the unqwiet and hurtfull molestations. But I wyll make my moane unto the Lorde in whose mercy is my onely comfort and trust, who bles yow and gwyde yow in all things.

The last Sabbath as I was past the block going to the church, a man of Mr Thomas Sadler,[928] he sayde, mett me and

[Left-hand margin] tolde my men he had venison from his master for me, which I sent home with my cooke b[y the] party. It is very goode flesh and fayre kylled. I thank yow and him too.

[fo. 326v] Yow were before nere the French church;[929] now uncertein but to knitt upp this greff. ^For^ I mean no more of this to yow but to the Lorde God. It may be my Lady and her ^Ladie^ mother[930] may think some whatt of it. *Vale.*[931]

Your horse sent upp is in so goode lyking that two of your men's jorneing wyll utterly spoyle the beas[t]. Your want of health spoyles

---

[923]***non . . . adolesscencia [adolescencia]*** [Latin] 'not in obscure places, but in the courts of the princes from youth'.

[924]***Ni= . . . con=*** [Latin] '*Nimia familiaritas parit contemptum*' ('Too much familarity breeds contempt'). This is supposedly a saying of Publilius Syrus. For discussion, see M. Colker, *Petronius Redivivus et Helias Tripolanensis* (Leiden, 2007), p. 178.

[925]***prima . . . temptum*** [Latin] 'first, you must add *mia*; secondly, *miliaritas*; thirdly, *rit*; fourthly, *temptum*'.

[926]***longum . . . docebit*** [Latin] 'long experience of things has taught and will teach'.

[927]***dulcis . . . amici*** [Latin] 'those who have never tried think it pleasant to court a friend in power'. The line is drawn from Horace. Anne does not give the crux of the *sentenia*: '*expertus metuit*' ('The one who has tried it, fears it'). See Horace, *Epistles*, 1.18.86–87.

[928]**Mr Thomas Sadler** Thomas Sadler of Standon, Hertfordshire, was also sheriff of the county in 1595, as he had been previously in 1587.

[929]**French church** The French Stranger Church.

[930]**my Lady . . . mother** The countess of Essex, Frances Walsingham Devereux, and her mother, Ursula Walsingham. For a previous mention of these ladies, see **123**.

[931]***Vale*** [Latin] 'Farewell'.

yow many wayes. Pray for encrease of grace and health and use all goode means in due season, specially your naturall rest and due diett, with exrcising the legges and lymmes. Late suppers and late rest tak[ing] *fomenta podagrae cum sociis eius nocivis.*[932]

Gorhambury ~~19~~ ˆ20ˆ August.

Mater tua,[933] AB.
Tewsday.[934]

I send x pigeons to yow, taken some yesterday, some this morning. As many to your brother so.

Standen being there and Lawson and such, yow verely wilbe cownted a practiser and more mislyked and ˆsuspectedˆ. God kepe yow ˆsaffˆ from Spanish subteltyes and popery and καὶ μητέρα *quoque.*[935] אמן[936]

143. *Anne Bacon to Anthony Bacon,* September 1595

Holograph. LPL 652, fo. 20r–v. 1p. Damaged.
Endorsed (fo. 20v): De Madame mere de Monsieur le mois de septembre 1595

I sende yow 4 trowts and a pickrell[937] owt of the river taken in hast, sent in hast and this written in hast. Trowts must be boyled as soone as possible because they say a faynt harted fysh. Let your cooke dress them presently; the viii of the clock before this messenger, *vicinus,*[938] come to your howse.

Large chydes Crosby I never ment before the next yere yf I lived. He wyll spoyle yowng Cresdon wood with his care, which in the nights er now hath had iii or 4 heads. I can not so sodenly put by Thomas Knight, who I am sure wyll looke to the yowng spring honestly and ˆincrease ren[t]ˆ. Larg is a whyning and crafty fellow. Nether did Fynch gon nor Crosby now, thowgh I have mislyked his often moving

---

[932]*fomenta ... nocivis* [Latin] 'hot fomentations to the gout with its hurtful companions'. Horace used the phrase '*fomenta podagram*' in *Epistles* 1.2.52.
[933]*Mater tua* [Latin] 'Your mother'.
[934]**Tewsday** Given Anne's alteration of the dating of her letter, she was either confused over the exact date or she sent the letter a day after it had initially been written, on Wednesday 20 August.
[935]καὶ μητέρα *quoque* [Greek and Latin] 'and even your mother too'.
[936]אמן [Hebrew] 'Amen'.
[937]**pickrell** a young pike.
[938]*vicinus* [Latin] 'a neighbour'.

me herin, bring me to theire beck in things to your hurt and myne. *Bene vale.*[939]

The Bisshop[940] is a grave and comely man and surely became his ^place^ well, thowgh ελισκοπαλλ,[941] and is learned. He used me courtiously and Mr Cook[942] and Mr Wyblud comfortably. *Cura et valeas.*[943]

Thursday on[944] of clock *post meridie,*[945] AB.

144. *Anne Bacon to Anthony Bacon,* 9 October 1595

Holograph. LPL 652, fo. 129r–v. 1p.
Endorsed (fo. 129v): De Madame le 9me d'octobre 1595 / Le Madame mere de Monsieur le mois d'octobre 1595.

Grace and health.

Lately by reason of my back payn and some things elce ^sending to the coort^, my Lady Stafford[946] sent me word that her Majesti marveled yow came not to see her being now so longe a tyme and wylled my messenger so ^to^ tell me from her and to advyse yow to think well of it at her Majestie's remove to Richmont,[947] which I do now. God geve yow ableness ^to^ and all good duties when it may please God that yow go; were no eny lyke wyse losse ruffs.[948] Your brother's here I lyked no thing. *De gesta coram illa satis scis, caute tamen cum officio et prudenter in vestitu ut unus gallice nunc parum ut potes per frigus, verum hac tibi relinquo, et te dei benignitati.*[949]

I send yow xii pigeons and a pullett. Dawys[950] browght me a few grapes; the poorest and the sowrest. Not worth the sending a bushe. I sende yow also a pigg and a pullett sent me by Cattlin's wyffe becawse

---

[939]*Bene vale* [Latin] 'Farewell'.

[940]**The Bisshop** Richard Fletcher, bishop of London. See p. 207, n. 761.

[941]ελισκοπαλλ [Greek transliteration] 'episkopall', i.e. episcopal.

[942]**Mr Cooke** Erasmus Cooke. See p. 181, n. 623.

[943]*Cura ut valeas* [Latin] 'Take care of your health'.

[944]**on** one.

[945]*post meridie* [Latin] 'afternoon'.

[946]**my Lady Stafford** Lady Dorothy Stafford, a gentlewoman of the queen's privy chamber.

[947]**Richmont** Richmond Palace in Surrey.

[948]**losse ruffs** Presumably the 'falling ruff', a type of unstarched, 'loose' ruff.

[949]*De . . . benignitati* [Latin] 'Regarding the behaviour in her presence, you know enough, but cautiously with duty and prudently, as far as possible during your cool reception, in clothing now not particularly like a Frenchman, but this I leave to you and you I leave to the kindness of God'.

[950]**Dawys** For this servant, see also **136**.

I stayed her husbande from going forth a soldiour. I thanks Thomas
Brockett and loke yow, I pray, for me in that and other curteyses.
Περι πραγματων του αδελφου ουδεν ακουω. Μηδεν ειπης
περι αυτου ενοπιον των θεραποντων σου αξιω σε.[951]

I sende your brother xii pigeons and a pullet. Geve ουιντερ[952] but
reasonably. *Cura ut bene valeas sede dormito tempestive. Alioqui certus frustra.*[953]
Yf now I had not great regarde of my diet and rest time I shulde be
payned miserably.

Your mother, ABacon.

But syns by the mercy of the Lorde I live yett lenger, I wyll wayte to
follow his goode wyll and procure as litle encrease of payn as I may,
that my lyffe may be comfortable to my selff and someway profitable
to other by his grace. *Iterum vale et sis memor* κυριασ σταφυρδ.[954]

Gorhambury 9 October.

Yf Woodwarde ^come again,^ enterteyn him not. He lately waxed
bragg and nowght ^I much dowt^ and cunningly got mony of yow by
mocking me. Let him walk lyke a unconstant varlett.

145. *Anne Bacon to Anthony Bacon*, 21 October 1595

Holograph. LPL 652, fos 128r–v. 1p.
Endorsed (fo. 128v): De Madame de 20 l'octobre 1595.
Addressed (fo. 128v): To my sonne Mr Anthony Bacon

Since it so pleaseth God, comfort one brother kindely and Christianly
and let me, mother, and yow both, my sonns, look upp to the correcting
hand of God in your wants every way, with humble harts before
him and with comfort and procure your health by goode means
carefully. Yf I did not warely *sustinere et abstinere,*[955] I shulde lyve in
continuall payn pitifully. For set syckness to speak of I have not now,
I thank God, but very combersom, troblous accidents to kepe [m]e
to exercise mortification. ^Remember^ her Majestie is, they saye, now

---

[951] Περι ... σε [Greek] 'About the affaires of the brother, I hear nothing. Do not say
anything about him in the presence of your servants, I beg you'.

[952] ουιντερ [Greek transliteration] 'Winter'.

[953] *Cura ... frustra* [Latin] 'You must take care and settle timely to sleep. Otherwise
certainly in vain'.

[954] *Iterum ... σταφυρδ* [Latin and Greek, direct and transliteration] 'In the meantime,
farewell and be mindful of Lady Stafurd', i.e. Lady Stafford.

[955] *sustinere et abstinere* [Latin] 'sustain and abstain'.

at Richmount. God preserve her from all evell and rule her ˆhartˆ to the zeallus setting forth of his glory; want of this zeale in all degrees is the very grownde of our home trobles. We have all dalied with the Lorde, who wyll not ever ˆsuffer him selffˆ be mocked. I send yow xii pigeons, my last flight, and one ring dove[956] besyde and a black cony[957] taken by Thomas Knight this day and pigeons too ˆhodieˆ.[958] Lawrence can tell yow my Lady Stafford's spech ˆwasˆ of yow, as she hath harde from her Majestie, marveling yow came not to see her in so long space; consider well and wysely. For I sent him ˆto herˆ to know of her Majestie's goode estate ˆto Nonsuch,ˆ[959] according to my dutie and to Mr Dr Smyth. He cam not home by London as I bad him.

Do what yow may for health *pie et diligenter*,[960] owt of qwestion where yow be yow must nedes disorder your tymes of diet and qwiet, want of which wyll styll kepe yow in lame and uncomfortable. I heare the $K\upsilon\rho\iota\varsigma$ $\mathrm{'}Oo\upsilon\alpha\rho\delta$[961] is *nimis sepe apud te*.[962] He is *subtiliter subdolus*.[963] *Cave et cave*[964] to burn this. The Lorde of heaven bless yow from heaven in Christ ˆour Lorde and hopeˆ.

Gorhambury 21 October. *Mater tua*,[965] AB. Burn, I pray, but rede well fyrst.

---

[956] **ring dove** wood pigeon.
[957] **black cony** rabbit.
[958] *hodie* [Latin] 'today'.
[959] **Nonsuch** Nonsuch Palace in Surrey.
[960] *pie et diligenter* [Latin] 'gently and diligently'.
[961] *$K\upsilon\rho\iota\varsigma$ $\mathrm{'}Oo\upsilon\alpha\rho\delta$* [Greek, direct and transliteration] 'Lord Howard', i.e. Henry Howard.
[962] *nimis s[a]epe apud te* [Latin] 'too often with you'.
[963] *subtiliter subdolus* [Latin] 'subtly treacherous'.
[964] *Cave et cave* [Latin] 'Beware and be careful'.
[965] *Mater tua* [Latin] 'Your mother'.

146. *Anne Bacon to Robert Devereux, earl of Essex,* 23 December [1595][966]

Holograph. CP 128/68. 2pp.
Addressed: Ad comitem Essexiae magnatem eximium[967]

σῷ Θεῷ καὶ ενώπιον του Θεου μονου.[968]

I crave leave and also pardon, my speciall goode Lord, for uttering my unfained Christian affection to your Honour, worthie Honour, in this simple maner which much rather I wolde have done by humble speache, yf my health and access to your own person myght conveniently have concurred. Therefore now this upon it is my goode Lorde I was moved to be thus bowlde. Lately in a place of a preching minist^ery^ in the citie freqwented as I may and the lecture finished, I sayde to a cowrte frend of mine a parte, one I am sure must and doth love yow well and then was there, 'I wysh many times', quod I, 'that her Majestie's selff did heare such wholsome and frutfull doctrine as we do heare and enjoy under her.' 'That were', quod they, 'happiest for her and comfortable to us all.' 'Surely,' quod I, 'her want theroff and also of catechising in that high place causeth great want of the right knowledg of synne and therby great carelessnes for synne. Yet is there one noble man that in his yowth doth remember his creator and loveth both the worde of God and goode preachers and goeth beyond his ancients in avoiding swearing and gaming with such common corruptions there.' 'Whome mean yow', *inquit.*[969] 'Even one', *inquam,*[970] 'To whome I am so much bownde that I owe to wysh him dayly encrease of godlines, with blessed success in his worldely state', and named indede the Εαρλε of Εσσεξ.[971] 'Is it he yow meane', *inquit,* 'wolde to God he did so. But he sweareth as much as others.' 'Wo, I am for it, sory,' *inquam,* 'I am to heare it, but yet I trust not ordinarily, nor great greavous othes.'[972] 'Alas,' *inquit,* 'He is a terrible swearer', which words me thowght stroke my hart in respect of the Εαρλε. 'Loe', *inquam,* 'The hurt of no catechising in coorte. For by expownding well

---

[966] **23 December [1595]** This undated letter is difficult to place in an exact chronology. Anne complained about Essex's swearing in August 1595 and April 1596 (**140**, **148**), hence the letter has been placed in the intervening December. Anne also complained about her attacks from quartan fever in May 1595 (**132**), although that does little to help the dating, as she admitted in September 1593 that she suffered from such conditions regularly: 'now in quarttans in myn owlde age' (**70**).

[967] *Ad . . . eximium* [Latin] 'To the great distinguished earl of Essex'.

[968] σῷ . . . μονου [Greek] 'To thine Lord and in the presence of God alone'.

[969] *inquit* [Latin] 'says he/she'.

[970] *inquam* [Latin] 'says I'.

[971] **Εαρλε of Εσσεξ** [Greek transliteration] 'Earle' of 'Essex'.

[972] **othes** oaths.

the law and commandments of God, sinne is layde open and disclosed
to the hearers and worketh in them by God his spirit more hatred of
evell and checketh our pronness[973] naturall, to all synn. By the lack
wheroff, even our cownsellors, both owlde and yowng, are pitifully
infected with that contagion to their own danger and lamentable
example of others, what degree so ^ever^.' And so we parted, which
God redress it ^wyth^ mercy cheffly there and elcewhere. I besech
yow, my goode Lord, let not this my mention^ing^ of religiouslyke talk
after a religious exercyse offende yow, nor ^provoke yow^ to caste in
undeserved displeasure who the other party shulde be. It may be the
Lorde God wolde have yow know it ^the mater^, thowgh by such a
poore weake meanes as this is.[974]

For I protest to your Honour that those words ('a terrible swearer')
did so terrefye me in your behalff, whose godly encreasinge a number
fearing God do hartely desyre, that my mynde cowlde not be well
qwieted, till I had committed ^it^ thus in scribling to your Honour,
my deere Lorde, and licence me, I pray yow withall, to add these few
textes for your remembrance, being diverse wayes drawn to forgett:

The fyrst is the charge the Lorde him selff joyneth with his own
commandement that he wyll not holde him gyltless that takes his
name in vain.[975] Our Saviour Christ also byddeth, 'Sweare not at all'
Mathew 5,[976] *cum*[977] the apostle James teacheth sayeng, 'Above all things,
my brethren, sweare not' 5,[978] *cum* the prophet Hoseas, soare accusing
that people in his time that by many horrible vices they brake owt, at
the fyrst front nameth by swearing &c cap. 3.ii.[979] To conclude with
the profecte Jeremye cap. 23, he complayneth saying to that people,
the Jewes, 'The lande', sayth he, 'is full of adulterers and by reason of
oathes the lande morneth.'[980]

I humbly desyre yow, my Lorde, not to note in me presumption
for this, but, as the Lorde knoweth, ^of^ a super abowndant care that
yow may please God and prosper in all goode things. For so yow have
geven ^me^ cause in my deerest, who neyther are, nor never shalbe
made prevy of this my doing, ner eny other whatsoever, by the grace of
Allmighty God, shalbe. For, for your owne sake alone, and before the

---

[973]**pronness** proneness.
[974]**thowgh ... as this** Anne is here referring to the biblical prescription, in St Paul's
first letter to the Corinthians (1 Corinthians 1:27), that God, through the Holy Spirit, may
use the weak to chastise the strong.
[975]**The fyrst ... in vain** Exodus 20:7; Deuteronomy 5:11.
[976]**Sweare ... 5** Matthew 5:34.
[977]***cum*** [Latin] 'together with'
[978]**Above ... not 5** James 5:12.
[979]**soare ... 3.ii** Hosea 4:2. Anne incorrectly notes this verse as 3:2.
[980]**The lande ... morneth** Jeremiah 23:10.

Lorde God alone, this I do in singleness of hart. I pray your Honour to accept it so and to use me so in silence and ^secrecy^, I pray yow hartely. I besech God to multiply his graces continually ~~upon~~ ^in^ yowr selff and upon your posteritee, his manifold blessings to grow upp as plants of rightousness, in the howse of the Lorde and to the honour of this their cowntry.

As my state of body ^is able^, so my scribling thus weak and blurred, unworthy your vew and troble to reade in so many carefull affayres, wherin the Lorde ever gwyde yow with his holy spirit. Fare yow well, my singuler goode Lord, it may be for ever. For thowgh I yet lyve, I feele sondry yll encombrance *post nuper febrem quartanam in languescente corpore.*[981] But I endevour to wayte upon Christ, my saving health and hope. From the confines of ruinated Verulam.[982]

23 Δεκεμβερ.[983] εν χριστω א ב αναυδρῳ.[984]

147. *Anthony Bacon to Anne Bacon,* 20 April 1596

Draft. LPL 656, fo. 262r–v. 1p.
Endorsed (fo. 262v): A Madame le 20me d'avril 1596

Madame,

I most humblie thanke your Ladishipp for your dainteyes, which though I dare not taste my selfe by reason of my diett, yett shall they be better imployed.

The losse of Cales[985] is to trew, whereby the enemy no doubt is wonderfullie puft upp to a most insolent pride and presumptuous hopes to annoy an[986] infest continuallie this state. The Duke of Bouillon,[987] heretofore called the viscount of Tureines, is come hither with verie lardge power and authoritie to treat and conclude for the

---

[981]***post . . . corpore*** [Latin] 'after the late quartan fever in my languishing body'. For 'quartan fever', see p. 150, n. 463.

[982]**Verulam** St Albans developed out of the ruins of the Roman town of Verulam, or Verulamium.

[983]**Δεκεμβερ** [Greek transliteration] 'Dekember', i.e. December.

[984]**εν χριστω א ב αναυδρῳ** [Greek and Hebrew] 'in Christ, AB, for the husbandless', i.e. 'Anne Bacon, in Christ, [who is] for the widow'.

[985]**losse of Cales** The siege of Calais, whereby the Spanish took the city from the French.

[986]**an** and.

[987]**Duke of Bouillon** Henri de la Tour d'Auvergne, the 4th vicomte de Turenne, became duc de Bouillon in 1591. He had converted to Protestantism in 1575 and entered into the service of Henri de Navarre. For the duc de Bouillon, see P. Hammer, *The Polarisation of Elizabethan Politics: the political career of Robert Devereux, second earl of Essex, 1585–1597* (Cambridge, 1999), p. 96; E. Delteil, 'Henri de la Tour, vicomte de Turenne humaniste et protestant', *Bulletin de la Societé de l'Histoire du Protestantisme Français*, 115 (1969), pp. 230–254.

French King's parte a straict league offensive and defensive betwixt the Queen's Majestie, the French king, the king of Scots, his brother the king of Denmarke, and the states of the Low Cuntries. This nobleman, the Duke, since his comming into England is fallen sick of an ague so that as yett he hath had no audience of her Majestie and this day hath vouchsafed, ^my Lord of Essex being absent^, to send for my coche to transport him from Billingsgate to a faire howse in Fanchurchstreet, where my Lord Tresurer is to visite him this day.

For the band wherin it pleased your Ladyshipp to stand bound with me, I have dew remembrance and care thereof. My brother hath within this seven nights spoken twise with her Majestie a full hower each time, whome she used at both times with grace and trust and sent me comfortable speches that she did remember me, trust me and would give me, ^soner then perhaps I loked for^, good proofe thereof.

Thus your Ladyshipp sees that ^though^ loyalltie, patience and diligence may for a time be shadowed and disgracde[988] by malice and envie, yett it pleaseth God, the ~~aucthor of them~~ founteines of all goodnes by his extraordinarie power, to make ^sometimes^ them shine to the Prince's eyes through the darkest mistes of cunning and misreportes. And so I most humblie take my leave.

148. *Anne Bacon to Francis Goad*, 27 April 1596

Holograph. LPL 656, fos 319r–320v. 2pp.
Endorsed (fo. 320v): De Madame Bacon a Monsieur Goad le 28me l'avril 1596
Addressed (fo. 320v): To Mr Goade, a Christian Captain

Mr Goade,

Yf I had ben able ^and not so late^ I wolde have gon a litle of the way to Essex Howse[989] with ^yow^ and so have byd yow fare well. As it is the dutye of all which love unfaynedly the glorie of God and the happy continuance of our Prince and ^of our^ deere cowntry, thowgh long tyme unthankfull, and presumptously sininng against our most loving God, and styll wayting for our conversion. So have I besydes ^a^ peculier just cawse to crave of the Lorde God, a speciall care of his fatherly protection of that noble valiant and religious Earle,[990] singuler goode Lorde to me in myne. And becawse I can by none other meanes, I from my very hart besech the blessed God to sende unto him all those blessings pronownced by God to be upon them

---

[988]**disgracde** disgraced.
[989]**Essex Howse** Both Goad and Anthony Bacon were resident under the earl of Essex's roof at this time.
[990]**Earle** The earl of Essex.

that love and feare him, both when he goeth owt, and whylest he is abroad, and at ^and after^ his retorne home. And that his gratious favour, mercy and truth may ever preserve him and prosper him with his hole charge and putt his strength into them for his own glory and great name ^sake^ and for our Lord and Saviour Christ's sake.

Amen.

It ^is^ written, as I remember, Mr Goade, in Alexander, the great history, that thowgh he were but yowng, yet he so sett forth with his army, that after he was owt of his own cowntry and pittched his campe in another lande, the inhabitance there marvelled and ^sayde that^ his army was more lyke to a senate then to a campe of warriours, so good was his conduct and their behavour for all they were chosen solidiours.[991] Now I trust, Mr Goade, that yea ^Christian^ capitains under the ministery ^of the gospell^, fyghting under Christ's banner for the defence of the gospell, wyll astonish much more the wycked miscreant enemies with your godly and tru Christian valliancy, abandoning blasphemy, swearing and cursed gaming, ^a fowle cheff and robber^ from among yow. That as it pleaseth ^the Lord him selff^ to say to his people, charging them to avoyd sinn and ungodliness, 'That I', sayth God, 'May walk among yow and be in the middest of yow to defend yow'.[992] I write this hartely, thowgh bowldely, and pray the Lorde to gwyde that worthy Earle, your grawnd worthy, and to prosper him and to preserve him form[993] all treacheries and from all maner evell, and be his continuall cownsellour and comfort and I pray yow humbly commend ^me^ to his goode Lordship.

[*Left-hand margin*] Fare yow well in the Lorde, *vel peri multo*.[994] 27 *Aprilis*. 96. A.B.

---

[991]**It is written ... solidiours** Anne was here drawing on her reading of *The Life of Severus Alexander*: 'And so, after showing himself such a great and good emperor at home and abroad, he embarked upon a campaign against the Parthians; and this he conducted with such discipline and amid such respect, that you would have said that senators, not soldiers, were passing that way.' See *Historia Augusta*, trans. D. Magie (Cambridge, MA, 1924), p. 279.

[992]**That ... defend yow** See Deuteronomy 23:14; verses 9–14 discuss the cleanliness of a military camp.

[993]**form** from.

[994]*vel peri multo* [Latin] 'or perish with the many'.

149. *Anthony Bacon to Anne Bacon*, 31 May 1596

Draft. LPL 657, fo. 15r–v. 1p.
Endorsed (fo. 15v): A Madame Bacon le 31me de may 1596

Madam, my most humble dutie remembred.

~~May it please your Ladyshipp to be advertised~~. Having intreated my good freind Mr Crew to make a stepp downe to Gorhamburie to peruse and bring me certaine evidences, I thought it my part first to advertise your Ladiship thereof and to know your plesure when the gentleman ~~may~~ ^might^ come, which the soner it may ^be^ the better, for my busines depending thereuppon. To ~~that~~ ^this^ purpose I have sent this bearer ^as allso cause^ ~~to bring upp 2 gellding for him and his man~~ Los[995] and my Galleway nagg ^to be brought^ for him and his man. And so I ~~hope~~ most humblie take my leave.

150. *Anthony Bacon to Anne Bacon*, 6 June 1596

Draft; second hand for 'Your Ladyship's in all filiall duties'. LPL 656, fo. 257r–v. 1p.
Endorsed (fo. 257v): Le Madame le 6me de juin 1596

Madame,

As from a mother sicklie and in yeares, I am content to take in good parte anie misconceite, misimputatione or causeles humorous threates whatsoever, onlie this I maie withe reason and must for mine upon the warrant of a good conscience remonstrate unto your Ladyship, that your sonne's poore credite dependethe uppon judgement and not uppon humour; and that your Ladyship cannot utter anie thinge in your passion to your sonne's lacke, so longe as God gives him the grace to be more carefull in dutie to please and reverence your Ladyship as his mother, then your Ladyship seemethe manie times to be towardes me as your sonn, and so I beseche God to preserve your Ladyship.

Your Ladyship's in all filiall duties.

---

[995]**Los** See p. 223, n. 869.

151. *Anne Bacon to Anthony Bacon*, 18 June 1596

Holograph. LPL 657, fos 168r–169v. 2pp. Very faded.
Endorsed (fo. 169v): De Madame Ann Bacon le mois de juni 1596

By the goode hand of the Lorde, I am come well to Gorhambury where I fynde my howsholde well and in goode order, I thank God. My syster, my Lady Russell's[996] coch is far easyer then ether of yours and her man, a comely man withall, dyd it with care and very wel, and your brother's footeman did very diligently go by me. Here be no straburie[997] nor fysh to send and for bere, sonne, I have none ordinary under 2 weeks at lest, above a monet[998] brued the fyrst week of May, which now caried after so long settling and in the heat of summer must nede be spoyled, which were great pitie this darth[999] tyme. Truli, sonne, as yet I know not when to brue by my provision, not this ii weeks at least, as well as for vessells. I have teerce[1000] of last March beere, but surely being yet unrype and caried this heat it wyll be utterly marred.

Payeng Mr Moorer's byll for my physick, I asked him whether yow did owe eny thing for physick. He sayd he had not reconed with since Michaell[1001] last. 'Alas, why so long?', *inquam.*[1002] I think I sayde farther 'it can be muted', for he hath his confectio[ns] from strangers, and to tell yow truly, I bad him secretly send his byll, which he semed loth but at my pressing, when I saw it came to above xv li or xvi li. Yf it had ben but vi or vii, I wold have made some shyft to pay. I towlde him I wolde say nothing to yow becawse hee was so unwylling. It may be he wolde take halff willingly, becawse 'ready mony made ^all weies^ a conning potecary',[1003] sayde covetous Morgan[1004] as his proverbe.

For Large, I cannot tell what yow wolde have me do for him. He fynds I do not recompence evell with evell. I have at tymes geven him, he knoweth, but he is but whyning and a companion to much with nawghty Gooderam, thowgh not at Redborn, but to his hurt. Let him ply his labours in God his name and not a busy body and secret qwarell pikar,[1005] as he is partly suspected. I use charite to him, thowgh

---

[996] **Lady Russell's** Lady Elizabeth Cooke Hoby Russell.

[997] **straburie** strawberry.

[998] **monet** month.

[999] **darth** dearth.

[1000] **teerce** tierce. A tierce is a cask, usually for holding wine.

[1001] **Michaell** Michaelmas. See p. 107, n. 225.

[1002] *inquam* [Latin] 'says I'.

[1003] **potecary** apothecary.

[1004] **covetous Morgan** Presumably Hugh Morgan, appointed Elizabeth I's principal apothecary to the royal household in 1583. See E.L. Furdell, *The Royal Doctors, 1485–1714: medical personnel at the Tudor and Stuart courts* (Woodbridge, 2001), pp. 90–91.

[1005] **qwarell piker** quarrel-picker, i.e. one who picks quarrels.

I lyke not his crafty soothing nature. With thanks for[1006] your horse. I besech, heade all your infirmities

[*Left-hand margin*] to your comfort. Be jelous over your health. *Intempestive horae occidant.*[1007]

Gorhambury 18 June.

Vale. Mater tua,[1008] ABacon.

152. *Anthony Bacon to Anne Bacon*, 23 June 1596

Draft. LPL 657, fo. 148r–v. 1p.
Endorsed (fo. 148v): Le Madame le 23me de juin 1596

Madam, my dutie most humblie remembred.

May it please your Ladishipp to beleive that my silence to your last lettre proceded rather of a respective forbearance to charge or importune your Ladyship, then any unthankfullnes or careles regard of your ^Ladiship's^ kindnes; the ^first^, God be thanked, possessing ^continually^ my minde, as much as the last, hath allwayes bene farre from me, assuring your Ladishipp that a kind, motherlie, free affection hath and shall ~~allwayes~~ ^ever^ carrie his full weight and due affirmation in my heart, referring unto your Ladiship's good will and pleasure what yow may spare to Mr Morer, who shallbe honestlie satisfied of the rest.

I most humblie thanke your Ladiship for your beare, not onlie for my selfe but in my cosen Bacon's[1009] behalfe, who I hope shall ~~employ~~ ^spend^ ^himselfe^, or cause to be employed uppon his spetiall frends that visite him, the 2 thirds of it.

I may not omitt with your Ladiship's good leave to certefie yow ^how^ unspeakeably my cosen is retorned cheared and satisfied with your Ladiship's honorable kindnes, which I know will ^not onlie^ confirme and seale that which is past betwixt him and me but being forty new effects in my cosen's mind, according to my occasions and his abilitie, and therfore, as in dewtie I ought, I render your Ladiship ^likewise^ most humble thanks for the same. And so I beseech God to preserve your Ladiship.

> Your Ladiship's most humble and dutifull sonne.

[1006] **for** Repeated.
[1007] ***Intempestive horae occidant*** [Latin] 'Untimely hours may torment you'.
[1008] ***Vale. Mater tua*** [Latin] 'Farewell. Your mother'.
[1009] **my cosen Bacon's** Presumably Robert Bacon, the son of Nicholas Bacon I's eldest brother. For a description of Robert Bacon's lineage, see **193**.

153. *Anne Bacon to Anthony Bacon*, 25 June 1596

Holograph. LPL 657, fo. 163r–v. 1p.
Endorsed (fo. 163v): De Madame Bacon le 25me de juni 1596

Of but halff a tonne I sende yow the best chosen hoggshed.[1010] There was a teerce[1011] last torned ~~of~~ ^wyth^ the same last March beere but wanting much of full; I wolde not send that, dowting. The other vessell is the newest in my howse of ordinary beere but to yow and syck I wolde not have spared it, season of the yeare upon hay seele.[1012] Care wolde be taken fyrst for the gentle and saff ^carieng and^ layeng it in the seller, becawse of the hoopes. Then that your March beere be in no wyse to soone broched before settlyng after cariag; I think not in a weeke at least. Thother ordinary after 4 or 5 days settlyng at the fyrst ~~peercin~~ broaching. It may seeme harsh, but well used after, better in drinking. I provided to have it caried immediately after the loading that it might take not hurt with stayeng by the way. The Lorde geving goode success, they wylbe at your loging by 8 or before 9 at least. Let it be attended upon. I sent warning by Rowland yf yow have eny swete empti vessells they shalbe welcom sent[1013] now. God and Father of our Lorde Jesus Christ, comfort and cownsell yow as his ~~deare~~ loved sonne in him and pray hartely dayly with reverence and understanding.

For the tyme abowt 4 of the clock a vehement glut of rayn, all my panns and other things wolde scant suffice to latch the rayn so very pouring down ^in^ every place. When I went but lately to London I saw all the gutters well clensed and the ponnes;[1014] twyse here a bryckleyer before Easter.

[Left-hand margin]
Goodeman Knite and Holt, who is from me alltogether, do join in carting, so I appointed them for more surty[1015] and ~~hasty~~ spede. Yf they wyll have eny thing for their cariag, I wyll leave it yf yow geve them some small reward, other wyse I wyll not in ^dede^. Even now at 7 of the clock it thundreth and rayneth for all the former storme. *Κυριε ελεησον.*[1016]

[1010]**hoggshed** See p. 111, n. 253.
[1011]**teerce** See p. 242, n. 1000.
[1012]**hay seale** 'Seal' is a term from Norfolk/Suffolk meaning season, thus 'hay-seal', meaning harvest time. It may be that Anne learnt the term from her Suffolk-born husband. See W. Holloway, *A General Dictionary of Provincialisms* (London, 1840), p. 149.
[1013]**sent** Repeated.
[1014]**ponnes** pans for cooking.
[1015]**surty** Presumably surety or security.
[1016]*Κυριε ελεησον* [Greek] 'Lord have mercy'.

154. *Anthony Bacon to Anne Bacon*, 25 June 1596

Draft. LPL 657, fo. 145r–v. 1p.
Endorsed (fo. 145v): A Madame Bacon le 25me de juni 1596

Madame, ~~my most humble dutie remembred.~~

I render your Ladiship most humble thanks for your vouchsafing me the ^better^ halfe of your Ladishipp's store of March beare, which shall not be broched[1017] this ~~fortnight~~ monthe.

For the weather, it hath bene here lamentable, stormie and unkindly for the season, the changes whereof as they were used for threatnings by the prophettes in antient time so ~~no dout but~~ ^God graunt^ they ^may^ worke more ~~in all good Christians minde amongst~~ ^in^ us as due and timelie apprehension of God's hevie judgements, imminent over us, for the deep prophane securitie that rayneth to much amongs us.

I will be bould *obiter*[1018] to certefie your Ladishipp first, that newes arrived at the court yesterday that the French king and the king of Spain by the entermise[1019] of a Florentine cardinall, sent into France of late from the Pope, have made a truce for 3 moneths.[1020] [. . . .] Next, that the great Turke is for certaine on horseback him selfe with 200 000 men and likelie to be a hevie scorge to Christendome.[1021] To theis 2 generall points I will ad a particuler which I know your Ladishipp willbe content to heare for my spetiall good Lord of Essex his sake, ^whome God in his mercie guid and protect^, to witt that the Countesse of Northumberland,[1022] ~~reputed~~ allwayes

[fo. 145v] reputed a verie honorable vertuous Ladie, is brought to bede of a goodlie boy, ^who God graunt may resemble and inheritt as well his mother and his noble uncle, her ^^most^^ worthie brother's vertue, as his father's antient nobilitie^. And so with the remembrance of my most humble dutie and my cosen's, I take my leave.

            Your Ladishipp's most humble and obedient sonne.

[1017]**broched** broached.
[1018]***obiter*** [Latin] 'incidentally'.
[1019]**entermise** intervention.
[1020]**that newes . . . moneths** It seems that this report was false.
[1021]**the great . . . Christendome** Mehmed III, sultan of the Ottoman empire from 1595, had taken personal command of the Muslim forces.
[1022]**Countesse of Northumberland** Dorothy Percy, the countess of Northumberland, was an elder sister of Robert Devereux, the earl of Essex.

155. *Anne Bacon to Anthony Bacon*, [late June/early July 1596][1023]

Holograph. LPL 653, fo. 325r–v. 1p. Damaged.
Endorsed (fo. 325v): lettre de Madame

I wolde see Mr Moorer's bill for this cawse. Me thinks xv li is a very great summ only for diett, drink and some few locull plasters. The man is veri honest and will be carefull both for the stuff and well doing. Yow shall do well not to ^have too^ much at once ^made^ ether to be cast away or taken not in season. Be not to busy with your eyes. I feare your diett drink is to strong and breedeth fumes. Be carefull [c]heffly for a religious mynde and use that phisick [and] then take goode care for your bodily health [t]hat yow may be now with God grace[1024] ^to^ serve God, your prince and cowntry to your own and the goode of others.

    God bless yow both. Be not styll in phisick nor temper not.

Your mother,
AB.

I am not loath to pay, specially him, but look yow the qwantitee be not much at once. It is the common maner of phisitions *nimis.*[1025]

156. *Anne Bacon to Anthony Bacon*, [c.2] July 1596[1026]

Holograph. LPL 658, fos 30r–31v. 2pp.
Endorsed (fo. fo. 31v): De Madame Bacon le mois de juillet 1596

I wolde know by Mr Crosby how your caried bere proveth. For the ordinary ever this I think ^well^. Thother after a week or 10 days I take; aske advise of home bruyar. For Mr Moorer, nether came the speech of your physyck eny whyll of him selff, but onely of myne own selff upon payment of my last physick things. I asked when he last retorned and was paid from yow. He sayde, becawse I preased him to shew, 'At Michaell tyde last,' *inquit.*[1027] Wher with I replied, somwhat offended with him, he differred so long for prises of such wares myght ryse more deere in that space and that it was ^crafty^ pollicie in your

---

[1023] **[late June/early July 1596]** This letter is undated, but other letters regarding Moorer's bills date from June and July 1596 (**151**, **156**).
[1024] **God grace** God's grace.
[1025] *nimis* [Latin] 'beyond measure'.
[1026] **[c.2] July 1596** Letter **157** is in response to **156**.
[1027] *inquit* [Latin] 'says he'.

father's tyme of muck lover Morgan to shyft ever to bring in his reconing in order yf he looked for price rysing, but I kept him to it for all that his murmuring ^every^ quarterly, as I dyd generally for all payments being put in trust by your father. Wheroff, after his death, I humbly thank God for his grace directing me, much qwiet and good credit to your father was noted and noysed, yet Morgan wolde say that mony present made the best potecary. Yf yow see and syng[1028] Mr Moorer's ^byll^, which he sayde, as I remember, came to 15 li, upon your hande, in part of payment I wyll sende x li, thowgh I promys yow I can but hardely spare it, my living now so abated as it is. But he must bring yow with all a discharg of his own hand and put so much owt of his book. What with last ii quarters' wages, your coale payment and now x li, besyde the woodds felled mony this yere all to yow, my sommer liveries, the butcher, the malt man, my physick ^to phisitian and potecary 20 marks (the physician all were farr at the coort^), and charges at London since the springe oneli, v li x s to Groome for your brother, and my howsehold charges, is above 220 li in mony layd owt. So that I can nott but be now but very scantly provide for sommer chargs, yf it please God I lyve. Crosby knowes well inowg.[1029] The Lorde that geveth all freely make us goode stewards of his diverse gyfts and multiply his merits in yow, manyfold wayes to your much comfort. I thank for your lettre. I humbly besech God ^to^ defende ^from all trechery and to^ geve goode success to the Earle and all his army ^power^.[1030] *Cura diligenter ut valeas.*[1031]

AB.

157. *Anthony Bacon to Anne Bacon*, 2 July 1596

Draft. LPL 658, fo. 3r–v. 1p.
Endorsed (fo. 3v): A Madame le 2me de juillet 1596

Madam, my dutie most humblie remembred.

So sone as I have sett a broch ether of those vessells it plesed your Ladyship to send me, I will not faile to advertise your Ladyship how I find them.

Touching Mr Morer, he himselfe after the 10 li received from your Ladyship for part of payment of my dett, came and tould me that

---

[1028] **syng** sign.
[1029] **inowg** enough.
[1030] **all his army power** A fleet headed by Charles Howard, the lord high admiral, had set sail from England for Cadiz in June 1596; Anglo-Dutch forces had won victory over the Spanish on 21 June, subsequently taking the city itself.
[1031] *Cura . . . valeas* [Latin] 'Take diligent care of your health'.

he had rased out so much out of his booke ^and a receipt signd with his owne hand^ for them, which I render your Ladyship most humble thanks, beseching your Ladyship to give me leave to observe but a little parenthesis in your Ladyship's lettre, where it pleges yow to specefie your charges, ~~sayin amo~~ saying that amongst them their were but 5 li 10 s to Grome for my brother. My meaning and desire in observing those words is onlie that your Ladyship may rest assured by mine owne sincere assertion that what soever your Ladyship hath or shallbe able and willing to spare to my brother hath bene and shallbe acceptable to my selfe, who I thanke God have ^hitherto^ ~~allwayes,~~ and ~~wil~~ by the assistance of his grace I hope shall alwayes, have a brotherlie feling and simpathy, aswell both of his good and furtherances, as allsoe of his harmes and hinderances.

For newes may it please your Ladyship to be advertised that the Duke of Bouillon's returne is now *in parle*[1032] and, in exchange of him, the Earle of Shrousberye's imployment to the French king, who is very much wrought and sought unto by the ~~Pope~~ Spanish faction to breake of the treatie latelie begonne with her Majesty,[1033] who ^hath^ receved lettres from the worthy Earle and my Lord Admirall dated the xx of the last moneth atesting, ~~that ther was helth ^by God's^~~

[fo. 3v] with thankfullnes to God, that there was helth under order and courage amongst them, which God in his mercie continew.[1034] And so I most humblie take my leave.

158. *Anne Bacon to Anthony Bacon*, 10 July 1596

Holograph. LPL 658, fos 28r–29v. 2pp.
Endorsed (fo. 29v): De Madame le 13me le juillet 1596

Now that Sir Robert is fully stalled in his long longed for secrettary place, I pray God geve him a religious, wyse and an upright hart befor God and man.[1035] I promiss yow, sonne, in my ^conjectural^ opinion, yow had more nede now to be circumspect and advised in your troblelous discoorsings and doings and dealings in your accustomed matters, ether with or for yourselff or others whome yow hartley

[1032] *in parle* [French] 'in talks', i.e. being talked about.
[1033] **Earle of Shrousberye's ... her Majesty** The Treaty of Greenwich between England and France was signed on 14 May 1596. Gilbert Talbot, the earl of Shrewsbury, was sent as a special ambassador to Henri IV, in order to ratify the treaty and to deliver the Order of the Garter to the French king.
[1034] **from the worthy Earle ... continew** See p. 247, n. 1030.
[1035] **Now ... man** Robert Cecil was promoted to the position of secretary of state on 5 July 1596.

honour, *nec sine causa*.[1036] He now hath great avantage and strength to intercept, prevent and to toy where he hath ben or is in, sonne, be it emulation or suspicion, yow know what termes he standeth in towarde your self and wold nede have me tell yow so, so very vehement hee[1037] was then. Yow are sayde to be wyse, and to my comfort I willingly thynk so, but surely, sonne, on thother syde for want of home experience by action and your teadious unaqwaintance for your ^own^ cowntry by ^continuall^ chamber and bedkeeping, yow must nedes myss of considerate judgement in your verball onely travayling. Yf all were scant sownde before betwixt the *Eαρλ*[1038] and him, frends had nede to walk more warely *in his diebus*[1039] for all doing elce ^may^ hurt, thowgh pretending goode. The father and sonne are ^affectionate^, joyned in power and policy.[1040]

The Lorde ever bles yow in Christ. Still I harken for Yates, I dowt somebody hindreth his comming to me. It were small matter to come speake with me. Yow know what yow have to ^do in^ regard towching the Spaniard.[1041] I reak not his displeasure. God graunt he marr not all at last with Spanish popish sutellty.

Alas, what I wrote towching the poor summ of 5 li to your brother, I ment ^but^ to lett yow know plainly. I wolde rather norish then eny litle way weaken nere brotherly love as appereth manifestly to yow both. God forbyd but that yee shulde allways love hartley *invicem*[1042] and kindely. God commandeth love as brethern,[1043] besyde ^a^ bonde of nature. This pescod tyme[1044] but bruing but hasty and somer drinking. In truth, yf I shuld purposely make a teerse[1045] somewhat strong for yow, I know not yow have it caried throwg; yt were pitie that yow and I both shuld be disapointed. *Annona cur[a]*.[1046]

Burn, burn in eny wyse. 10 *Julii*. AB.

[1036] *nec sine causa* [Latin] 'not without cause'.

[1037] **hee** he.

[1038] *Eαρλ* [Greek transliteration] 'Earl', i.e. the earl of Essex.

[1039] *in his diebus* [Latin] 'in these days'.

[1040] **The father ... policy** Namely William Cecil, Lord Burghley, and his son, Robert.

[1041] **the Spaniard** Antonio Pérez. See p. 123, n. 323.

[1042] *invicem* [Latin] 'each other'.

[1043] **God ... brethern** 1 John 3:14: 'We knowe that we are translated from death unto life, because we love the brethren: he that loveth not his brother, abideth in death.'

[1044] **pescod tyme** Early summer, the season for growing peas.

[1045] **teerse** tierce. See p. 242, n. 1000.

[1046] *Annona cura* [Latin] 'Take care with your provisions'.

159. *Anthony Bacon to Anne Bacon*, 13 July 1596

Draft. LPL 658, fo. 7r–v. 1p.
Endorsed (fo. 7v): A Madame le 13me de juillet 1596

Madam, my most humble dutie remembred.

I am at the earnest request of an honest merchaunt, an antient freind of mine, who hath bine long bedredd[1047] langueshing and now desireth greatlie (according to the advise of the phisitions) change of ayre, I meane Mr Robert Spencer, humbly to besech your Ladiship that yf yow have a litter and can spare it, yow would vouchsafe to lend and send it me, that I may pleasure him, ~~especiall~~ which I have so much the more cause now to doe, seing his pthisicall weaknes makes me ^justlie^ feare that this shallbe the last freindlie office I shallbe able to doe him, my prayers onlie accepted for the strength of his soule at the last hower of combatt. As for the due care and good usage of your Ladiship's litter, I will constitute my selfe suretie and answerable in his behalfe.

For occurents. Her Majesty is in daylie expectation and very carefull suspence for tydings of the Earle's procedings.[1048] The Christians under the Transilvanian Prince have very freshlie given important overthrowes to the Turke.[1049] The archrebell of Ireland, called Tyrone and created O'Neill, hath refused her Majestie's pardon, alledging frivolous excuses that he could not come and speake with Sir Edward More, who was to present him the same;[1050] his drift is onlie to delay to se what [....] else my lord of Essex shall have and accordinglie to reject or accept her Majestis grace. The uncardinallised Archduke of Austria[1051] is held better tack by the Count Maurice,[1052] second sonne to

---

[1047]**bedredd** bedridden.

[1048]**the Earle's procedings** The earl of Essex did not return to England from the Cadiz expedition until 8 August 1596.

[1049]**The Christians . . . Turke** One of the clashes that formed part of the Thirteen Years' War between the Austrian Habsburgs and the Ottomans. Sigismund Báthory, the prince of Transylvania, won the battle of Călugăreni, his most decisive victory, a year earlier, in August 1595.

[1050]**The archrebell . . . the same** Hugh O'Neill, second earl of Tyrone, delayed taking his pardon until 22 July 1596.

[1051]**Archduke of Austria** Archduke Albert VII of Austria became sovereign of the Habsburg Netherlands in 1598, held jointly with his wife, Isabella Clara Eugenia; he is referred to as 'uncardinallised' because, although he was appointed a cardinal, he was never ordained. L. Duerloo, *Dynasty and Piety: Archduke Albert (1598–1621) and Habsburg political culture in an age of religious wars* (Farnham, 2012), p. 30.

[1052]**Count Maurice** Maurice of Nassau, stadtholder of Holland, Zeeland, Utrecht, Gelderland, and Overijssel.

the late Prince of Orange, in the Low Cuntryes, then he was by the French king

[fo. 7v] at Caleys, the towne of Hulst houlding out bravely against him.[1053] And so with the remembrance of my most humble dutie, I take my leave.

160. *Anthony Bacon to Anne Bacon*, 13 July 1596

Draft. LPL 658, fo. 6r–v. 1p.
Endorsed (fo. 6v): A Madame le 13me de juillet 1596

Madam,

I most humbly thanke your Ladyship for your wise and loving admonition which, God willing, shalbe by me remembred and observed.[1054]

May it please your Ladyship to call to mind what ^speech^ late Queen Mary used, when she layd downe uppon the Counsell bord the purse where the privy seall was kept, for the which the ould Lord Pagett had bene so long so earnest a suiter and procured King Phillip to be his mediator,[1055] and so to consider withall what is befallen to that house ^since^. For mine owne part the reding and Christian meditation of the 36 and 37 psalmes shall, with God's grace, serve me for trew preservatives to keep me from emulating any worldly prosperetie or greattnes or fearing the effects of ~~man's~~ human power and malice, so long as it please God to comfort and strengthen the best part of ~~man~~ me, as hitherto in his mercy he hath done with extraordinary effectes.

Yates hath onlie stayed hitherto for a horse, beseching your Ladyship to thinke that no superiour, ^souverain ~~am~~ and not onlie excepted and yet [wi]th dutyfull^, or equall, muche lese my inferiour as servants bee, shalbe able to dissuade or withhould me from frowringe[1056] your Ladyship's contentment.

[1053] **then he was . . . against him** Albert took Calais from the French on 22 April 1596 and Hulst from the Dutch on 18 August; the latter was under siege from 31 June.

[1054] **I . . . observed** Letter **158** was only received by Anthony on 13 July, hence he wrote two letters to his mother that day; **160** responds to **158**.

[1055] **for the . . . mediator** Philip of Spain favoured William Paget's efforts to become a chief officer of state, suggesting that his wife, Mary I, should appoint Paget as lord chancellor. However, on 1 January 1556 Mary appointed Nicholas Heath as chancellor, leaving Paget to settle for lord privy seal. See G. Redworth, '"Matters impertinent to women": male and female monarchy under Philip and Mary', *English Historical Review*, 112 (1997), pp. 605–606.

[1056] **frowringe** forwarding. See T. Wright, *Dictionary of Obsolete and Provincial English* (London, 1857), p. 485.

That I wrote of this 5 li was onlie to exemplefie my inward desire and meaninge for myne done discharge and no waye to misimpute or misconster,[1057] whiche God knoweth is farr from me. And so referringe my selfe for occurrents to my former lettre whiche I had thought to have sent your Ladyship by express messenger, yf Lawrence had not come, I most humbly take my leave, with ~~my~~ like thanks for your Ladyship's fishe.

161. *Anne Bacon to Anthony Bacon*, 15 July 1596

Holograph. LPL 658, fo. 27r–v. 1p.
Endorsed (fo. 27v): De Madame Bacon, le 15me de juillet 1596

The truth is, sonne, the litter is unperfect to be used for a syck body and a very frende; owt of dowt it must needes fayle. It reqwyreth reparation, specially the lethers, scant strong, that cary it, and the saddell very owlde. Yates by my appointment hath narrowly vened[1058] all. Mr Dyke[1059] but a yeare past wolde nedes borow your father's owlde coch. I towlde him the weaknes of it, but nedes he wolde ventur and after vi myles jorny, his wyff and chyldern had lyke to take ^hurt^ and were compelled to make other provision by the way, with much comber.

I wold gladly yow had ii teerce[1060] of my beere but carriadg is the matter; myne own ^horse^ but 4, wherof one blynde and the rest but poore. My horses within these 3 yeres have much miscaried to my great comber, besyde the charges. Thomas Knite served me but lewdly. I am halff impotent now my selff and every thing decaies with me, which made me desyrous to have Yates my deputy in howse to oversee, taking him to be both honest and scillfull.[1061] This must I needes say of him, and truly that commended to me by yourselff, in your beyond sea aboad for your busines to be dispatched over by me then. I saw him do it with such a good harte to yow and carefull diligence, that the rest yow so sent, withowt exception, were nothing comparable. They all sowght themselff but he, me thowght, seemed to do all with love to your selff in dede. Yow know otherwyse but a stranger to me ner since your comming over. I thank yow for your lettres and good accepting.

[1057] **misconster** misconstrue.
[1058] **vened** weened, considered.
[1059] **Mr Dyke** William Dike. See p. 181, n. 622.
[1060] **teerce** tierce. See p. 242, n. 1000.
[1061] **scillfull** skilful.

162. *Anthony Bacon to Anne Bacon*, 29 July 1596

Draft. LPL 658, fo. 4r–v. 1p.
Endorsed (fo. 4v): Le Madame Bacon, le 29me le juillet 1596

Madam,

In lieu of my personall ~~dutie~~ attendance, and for your Ladyship's wellcome and assurance, I meane such as may be given ^and^ exspected ~~concerning accora~~ of newes that come so farre of and are subject to winde and wether, I send your Ladyship hereinclosed a lettre sent after midnight ^last^ from ~~principall councellor~~ Mr Secretary[1062] to an honourable friend of mine, who vouchsafed betimes this morning to bring it and leave it with me, which when your Ladyship hath perused ~~I besech,~~ may it please yow to returne it to me seulld without mentioning the sight therof to any whome soever. And so I most humbly take my leave.

163. *Anne Bacon to Anthony Bacon*, [before 3 August 1596][1063]

Holograph. LPL 653, fos 248r–249v. 2pp.
Endorsed (fo. 249v): lettre de Madame

Sonne, the Lorde allwey bles yow and be with yow, both allweyes in mercy and gwyding of yow. Peter hath desired me to write for his placing at Doctors' Commons[1064] for his preferment, otherwyse loth yet to part with him. I have written to Doctor Cesar[1065] and to my cosin Thomas Stanhopp,[1066] in stede of Doctor Stanhopp[1067] to whome I wyll never more write again ^but^ upon great occasion by God's sending. ~~His~~ For thowgh cosins, he is a love man to all, God his good minister before him, *experta loquor.*[1068] Her[1069] is a fylthy adulterer, yf not

---

[1062]**Mr Secretary** Robert Cecil. See p. 248, n. 1035.

[1063]**[before 3 August 1596]** This undated letter is difficult to place by the internal evidence. It must at least have been written before 3 August 1596, as Thomas Stanhope died that day.

[1064]**Doctors' Commons** The collegiate society of civil and canon laywers. As an informal association, it did not certify legal practice and, unlike the Inns of Court for common lawyers, it had no educational function. See B. Levack, 'The English civilians 1500–1750', in W. Prest (ed.), *Lawyers in Early Modern Europe and America* (London, 1981), p. 113.

[1065]**Doctor Cesar** Julius Caesar, the master of requests.

[1066]**Thomas Stanhopp** Thomas Stanhope, of Shelford, Nottinghamshire.

[1067]**Doctor Stanhopp** Edward Stanhope, chancellor to the bishop of London. Stanhope was also a kinsman of Anne's. See *Cooke Sisters*, pp. 181–182.

[1068]*experta loquor* [Latin] 'I speak having experienced'.

[1069]**Her** 'He' or 'here'.

fornicator too, according to his profession. Blackwell's wyffe is noted in strete as she goeth and pointed at as his harlot. Good sonne, write not to him at all in this nor be beholding to him for eny sute.

Yf these my lettres wyll not healpe Peter, let it go. *Noli te admiscere cum tali impio in re tam levi.*[1070] He is my man and therfore have I written. See, reade and seale, I pray yow. Forgett not that, but no more for yow; this is inowgh, yf God wyll.

Vale in Christo. Cura omni modo ut bene valeas et abstinendo et bene agendo.[1071]

Ner your brother to write nether to ~~writt~~ him. God gwyde him with his grace and send him ~~selff~~ health to serve God first and please man in his feare.

AB *mater tua.*[1072]

164. *Anthony Bacon to Anne Bacon*, 6 August 1596

Draft. LPL 658, fos 149r–150v. 2pp.
Endorsed (fo. 150v): A Madame Bacon, le 6me d'aoust 1596

Madame,

Having received the very same day your Ladyshipp departed from one Signor Lopus, a Spanish merchaunt much bound to my Lord of Essex, certaine dainteyes such as he hath presented to the countesse and my Lady Rich,[1073] I am bould to send your Ladyshipp the best parte of them, as allsoe a memorative note of such advantages as are accrued to her Majesty by the taking of Cadez; and will send your Ladyshipp, God willing, this next ^weeke^ a particuler trew relation of the whole action which, God be thanked, hath bene seconded with the taking of another place called Farrow,[1074] since for which speciall goodnes and blessing of God and the continuance therof there is appointed here prayer and thanksgiving. And so I most humbly take my leave.

[1070]*Noli ... levi* [Latin] 'You should not mix with such an impious man in such a lightweight matter'.
[1071]*Vale ... agendo* [Latin] 'Farewell in Christ. Take care in every way that you remain well both by abstaining and by behaving well.'
[1072]*mater tua* [Latin] 'your mother'.
[1073]**the countesse and my Lady Rich** Frances Walsingham Devereux, countess of Essex, and Lady Penelope Rich, her sister-in-law.
[1074]**the taking ... Farrow** After leaving Cadiz, the earl of Essex sacked Faro; he later donated the books which he seized from the bishop's library to Thomas Bodley's new library in Oxford.

165. *Anthony Bacon to Anne Bacon*, 11 August 1596

Draft. LPL 658, fo. 151r–v. 1p.
Endorsed (fo. 151v): A Madame Bacon le 11 d'aoust 1596

Madam,

I would not faile to certefie your Ladyshipp by goodman Forsett of the worthy Earle's most honorable, happie and safe returne,[1075] for the which God's name be praised and make both him and us thankfull.

I dout not but your Ladyshipp hath understood that my Lord Cobham was made Lord Chamberlaine on Sunday last.[1076] The Duke of Bouillon is daylie loked for and no dout will hasten his coming so much as he can possible to obteine of her Majesty the spedy employment of the greatest parte of her Majestie's armie, ~~returned~~ which my Lord of Essex, ~~hath brought home God be thanked~~ by God[1077] mercifull providence and devine protection, hath happely brought home in health, wealth and ^hartie^ courage for the recovery of Callis and to make inglishd.[1078] This is all, Maddam, that I have at this time worth advertising your Ladyship. And so I most humbly take my leave.

166. *Anne Bacon to Anthony Bacon*, 12 August 1596

Holograph. LPL 658, fos 167r–168v. 2pp.
Endorsed (fo. 168v): De Madame Bacon, le 11 d'aoust 1596[1079]

The Lorde Jesus *salus et vita vera nostra*.[1080] Restore yow from lymm lamenes to perfect health, yf be ^his^ blessed wyll that yow may, thank God, as the long creple dyd, skipping and leaping in the temple after he was cured of the apostles.[1081] Yelde not to much, but stryve against and use your lymms ^in due order^ more thowgh with some payn. Your unseasonable eatinge, resting and restles toyling with unorderly commers and commoners ^have and do^ spoyle yow.

[1075]**the worthy ... safe returne** Essex returned to Plymouth on 8 August 1596.
[1076]**my Lord ... last** William Brooke, Baron Cobham, was made lord chamberlain on 8 August 1596.
[1077]**God** God's.
[1078]**hartie courage ... inglishd** Anthony was here referring to Essex's plan to use the returned army for an assault on Calais.
[1079]**De ... 1596** [French] 'From Mistress Bacon, the 11 of August 1596'. The endorsement seems incorrect, as Anne dated her own letter 12 August.
[1080]**salus ... nostra** [Latin] 'our true health and life'.
[1081]**as the ... apostles** See Acts 3:8.

I thank for your lettres, fyrst and last. O that the Lorde of armies had ^his^ due prayses ^from hie and low^ geven to his holy name for the gratious success. For the Duke of Bollain sute for $K\alpha\lambda\varepsilon\sigma$,[1082] to speake lyke an unskillfull body and yet have observed somewhat, I dowt it wyll spende and spoyle our soldiour, whome God hath spared, and bring the plage into the lande, as Newhaven.[1083] The French might have prevented and now sett us a worke. The Spaniard in possession, the French a looker on and wee after good success contend with great cost and charg ^danger^ in a vain hope. God graunt wee may be truly thankfull to him and so ~~can~~ consult with him what is best for his glory and our state.

Impossible yet to take partriches. The corn slow going down by variable wether. Every pigeon I send yow as yow think good. Shawford com not yet with much care feeding and howse seasoning. Hamlett's lewd using.

God much bles the Earle and as he hath made him strong aganst his enemies, so to make him strong against $\kappa\alpha\rho\nu\alpha\lambda\ \kappa o\nu\kappa\upsilon\pi\iota\sigma\sigma\varepsilon\nu\varsigma$[1084] and prosper him in his feare and continuall favour. The Lorde God be ever with yow in mercy and comfort.

Gorhambury 12 August.

$M\eta\tau\eta\rho\ \sigma o\upsilon$,[1085]AB.

167. *Anne Bacon to Anthony Bacon, 30 August 1596*

Holograph. LPL 653, fos 354r–355v. 2pp.
Endorsed (fo. 355v): De Madame ^Bacon^ le 30me d'aoust 1596
Addressed (fo. 355v): To my sonne Mr Anthony Bacon geve theis

Snecking owlde Smyth, one your father never cownted but hollow, hath now begon contention and troble by his owlde crafty letting a lease of the thyrds, undermining wyse, not making forcly privie lyke a subtill miser. This bearer commes of purpose to yow for remedy being loth to law. And he hath lett it to Rocket,[1086] a head scraper of that their

---

[1082]$K\alpha\lambda\varepsilon\sigma$ [Greek transliteration] 'Kales', i.e. Calais.
[1083]**Newhaven** Soldiers returning from the Newhaven expedition in 1563 were credited with introducing plague into England. See J.F.D. Shrewsbury, *A History of Bubonic Plague in the British Isles* (Cambridge, 1970), p. 190.
[1084]$\kappa\alpha\rho\nu\alpha\lambda\ \kappa o\nu\kappa\upsilon\pi\iota\sigma\sigma\varepsilon\nu\varsigma$ [Greek transliteration] 'karnal konkupissens', i.e. carnal concupscience.
[1085]$M\eta\tau\eta\rho\ \sigma o\upsilon$ [Greek] 'Your mother'.
[1086]**Rocket** Thomas Rockett served as the official and registrar to the archdeacon of St Albans.

greedy snaphance[1087] ceort,[1088] trobling good and qwiet subiects. Yf it may lett not Rocket procead, but undoe it, being craftely in conscience wrasted,[1089] thowgh their litigious unspirituall may challeng advantage. Rockett in his claim coming on the grownde browght one with a halke[1090] under that cullour, with prowde wordes thowgh upon my sending to the Mayre to talk with him; 'Why he durst', he answerd, 'Forsooth it was but for company.' Thus styll besyde trobling the farme we shalbe combred with him. He is a prowde and for gain, full of qwarellpiking. I thowght good thus much by this greeved bearer. Do wysely and surely for thoficiall with all the pack of them seek only ungodly gain; litle good do it them. I write so even with a tru Christian hart by experience of their unlawfull dealings in my tyme.

Partriches yet will not to the net. Knite and one other of myn own men this hole week in full nights have ben styll abroad.

The Lorde of heaven rayse yow upp to more goode in your vocation and geve yow dayly encrease of godlines and health with his fatherly love to your comfort. Lett not prentyse for tryfles cowntenan[c]e such troblesom ~~de~~ deceaveable persons. Let him not see this. He can skill *uti foro*.[1091]

I pray yow remember coorte keping here according to order, which I carefully now; next coorte is lete also,[1092] which wolde not be neglec^t^ed. Mr Crew ether wyll not or owt of season or in hast. I saw not Mr Downing a great whyle; he can and wyll do it best. Mr Crew made prevy and present yf he wyll. It owght before Michalltyd.[1093] I may think of it.

168. *Anthony Bacon to Anne Bacon*, 7 September 1596

Draft. LPL 659, fo. 9r–v. 1p.
Endorsed (fo. 9v): A Madame Bacon, le 7me de septembre 1596

My most humble dutie remembered.

I render your Ladyshipp humble thanks for your patriges,[1094] which your man, ^it semes,^ was very carefull to bring in good sorte.

[1087]**snaphance** Suggesting a desperate or thieving character.
[1088]**ceort** archdeaconry court.
[1089]**wrasted** twisted.
[1090]**halke** Presumably 'hawk'.
[1091]***uti foro*** [Latin] 'to play the market', i.e. to adapt to circumstance or 'make hay while the sun shines'.
[1092]**next ... also** Court leet, the manorial court. For further discussion, see the Introduction, p. 32.
[1093]**Michalltyd** Michaelmas. See p. 107, n. 225.
[1094]**patriges** partridges.

The Duke of Bouillon on Sunday last, after dinner, vouchsafed to visite me, having ^with very kinde respect^ first sent a gentleman to know whither ^company^ should not be troobellsome unto me. He is this day departed, having receaved a cubberd of plate of 1200 li of her Majesty for a present. ~~The ambassadors~~ The ambassadors of the States are arrived to be joyned ~~in~~ with her Majesty and the French king against their common enemy, the Spaniard.[1095] It is spoken that the Scottish king and the king of Denmarke, his brother in law ~~shallbe~~ and other princes of Germany shallbe likewise invited thereunto. My Lord of Essex yesterday feasted ^here,^ my Lord Admirall,[1096] Mr Secretary[1097] and divers others of the nobilitie and, ~~at dinner~~ ere dinner was done, was sent for by the Queene, who for the most parte out of her selfe useth him most gratiouslie ~~allwayes~~ and I dout not but will more and more by God's goodnes so long as he continew his Christian zealous course, which he hath begonne since his returne, ~~in~~ not missing preaching, nor prayers in the courte, and showing trew noble kindenes towards his vertuous espouse intirely without any diversion. ~~And~~ The state of Ireland is more dangerous then ever, notwithstanding the false submission of Tyronne and acceptance of her Majestie's pardon. And so I most humbly take my leave.

169. *Anthony Bacon to Anne Bacon*, 30 September 1596

Draft. LPL 658, fo. 154r–v. 1p.
Endorsed (fo. 154v): A Madame Bacon le 30me de septembre 1596

Madam, I most humbly thanke your Ladyshipp for your lettre by Forsett and your daintyes by this bearer, who carrieth a lettre from me to ould Smith, wherein I have tould him roundly of his undutifullnes towards your Ladyshipp and my selfe and his unneighbourly dealing with goodman Forsett, whome, if he continew to trooble by the help of Rockett, I have signified unto him warninglie that nether of them both should gett any creditt or benefitt thereby, which I dout not but to make good if ether or both of them persist to vex goodman Forsett.

Uppon Sunday last her Majesty bestowed 2 white staves and made my Lord North, Tresurer, and Sir William Knolles, Comptroler.[1098]

[1095]**The ambassadors ... Spaniard** The United Provinces formally joined England and France in the Treaty of Greenwich on 21 October.
[1096]**Lord Admiral** Charles Howard was lord high admiral from 1585.
[1097]**Mr Secretary** Robert Cecil. See p. 248, n. 1035.
[1098]**her Majesty ... Comptroler** North was appointed as treasurer of the household and Knollys was appointed comptroller of the household on 30 August 1596. Both men were made privy councillors on the same day.

As Anthony was with in, it pleased the Earle of Shrowsbury[1099] to come and visite me ~~who hath~~ and to give me hirtie thanks for sending him my man Yates, of whome he hath hard so good testimony of those that know him in France;[1100] hereof I thought meet to advertise your Ladyshipp, having the rather taken this opportunitie to preferre ~~and place~~ him ^to so noble a man^ in place of spetiall creditt and trust in respect of your Ladyshipp's good opinion of him. And so in hast, as this bearer can wittnes, I most humbly take my leave.

170. *Anne Bacon to Anthony Bacon*, 1 October 1596

Holograph. LPL 659, fos 254r–255v. 2pp.
Endorsed (fo. 255v): De Madame Bacon, le 2me d'octobre 1596

Grace, peace and health be multiplied upon yow dayly. I send yow v partriches; they have in taking with 3 persons allmost as many nights as the number. I cowld hardly in dede have spared this bearer. Hast him away, I pray yow. I sende your brother 12 pigeons and all my two howses heare. Yf yow lyke to take for your selff 3 or 4, elce lett him have all.

Smyth,[1101] the carier, yesterday being Thursday, sent by his man a byll to me of above 7 li for coales and that since June. I cast ^my selff^ that June, July and August were the cheffe sommer moneths and he was paid all then. Surely, sonne, something or somebody goeth awrie for your reconing and experence[1102] perswade as yow wyll to your hindrance; yow did by your words to me name abowt v li and he now ^asketh^ above 7. Yf his reconing had ben right in dede, I had it not to pay him thence; Crossby was gon to a fayre. Yf yow sende me by this bearer a just warrant sygned, I wyll borow so much for so must I of necessitee; yet do and I wyll pay him upon Tewsday next, God wylling. I commend yow to the favour and blessing of the Allmighty. *Vale in Christo.*[1103]

Primo Octobris[1104] 1596.

AB.

[1099]**Earle of Shrowsbury** Gilbert Talbot, the earl of Shrewsbury. See p. 248, n. 1033.

[1100]**it pleased ... in France** Edward Yates was in France again, in the company of Charles Danvers. See p. 168, n. 556, and G. Ungerer, *The Correspondence of Antonio Pérez's Exile*, 2 vols (London, 1974–1976), II, p. 10.

[1101]**Smyth** Robert Smyth. See also **194**.

[1102]**experence** experience.

[1103]*Vale in Christo* [Latin] 'Farewell in Christ'.

[1104]*Primo Octobris* [Latin] 'first of October'.

171. *Anthony Bacon to Anne Bacon*, 2 October 1596

Draft. LPL 659, fo. 210r–v. 1p.
Endorsed (fo. 210v): A Madame, le 2me d'octobre 1596

Madam,

Thre houres after I had spoken with Miller, the carrier, and returned my humble thanks and just excuse for not writing my selfe, I receaved your Ladyship's by this bearer, and 5 partriges, for the which I humbly thanke your Ladyship.

The expense of coales I concesse[1105] ~~considering the season~~ ^for foure sommer moneths^ may justly seme ^over^ great, unlesse it please your Ladyshipp to consider first my sicknes, then the extraordinary moistnes of the season, the scituation[1106] of my lodging and the honorable helpes I have had to spend them since my Lord's returne, which I know your Ladyshipp ~~will not~~ would not have had me refused for tenn times as much, so long as ^not onlie^ it is knowen to the cheifest of this house, but thankfullie taken.

Her Majestie this day parted from Grennwhich and hath dined at my Lord Burrough's[1107] house by Lambeth and lodgeth this night at Micham[1108] and from hence to Nonesuch.[1109] Certaine number of Spaniards landed very latelie in Ireland,[1110] which hath bene foretould often and long enough agoe to have bene ~~presented~~ prevented, if any advertisements, how ^timelie and^ trew so ever were currante, unlesse they carried the stamp of the golden sheath. And so referring some other particurers[1111] worthey your Ladyshipp's ~~till~~ knowledge till ~~Sunday~~ ^some day of^ next weke, I comm[end] your Ladyshipp to God's hollie protection.

[1105]**concesse** confesse (i.e. confess).

[1106]**scituation** situation.

[1107]**Lord Burrough's** Thomas, Lord Burgh, appointed lord deputy of Ireland early in 1597.

[1108]**Micham** Julius Caesar, the master of requests, had a manor house at Mitcham in Surrey. It was certainly visited by Elizabeth I on 12 September 1598. For the entertainment in 1598, thought to be by John Lyly, see Leslie Hotson (ed.), *Queen Elizabeth's Entertainment at Mitcham* (New Haven, CT, 1953).

[1109]**Nonesuch** Nonsuch Palace in Surrey.

[1110]**Certaine . . . in Ireland** Spanish ships carrying arms and ammunition had landed in Donegal in Ireland in September 1596, although the main fleet which set sail in October was dispersed by bad weather.

[1111]**particurers** particulars.

172. *Anthony Bacon to Anne Bacon*, 8 October 1596

Draft. LPL 659, fo. 211r–v. 1p.
Endorsed (fo. 211v): A Madame A. Bacon le 8me d'octobre 1596

My humble dutie remembred.

According to my promise in my last by Mr Downing, I thought it my parte before the weeke ended to certefie your Ladyship of that which then I had no leisure to sett downe. To witt that my Lady Russell sent me worde I should be of very good cheare for that my Lord Tresurer had not onlie receaved satisfaction in that she delivered him from me, but thereby was ~~much~~ very well disposed to doe me all the good he could, which comfortable message of her Ladiship's I accepted with more thankfullness then I meane to relie uppon with confidence for τὶς πίστις ἀπίστῳ.[1112] In the meane time, I have cause to acknowledge it as a token of God's spetiall goodnes towards me that it hath pleased him to blesse my extemporall answer, which truth and innocency did dict[1113] unto me without meditation or affectation, so farre forth as that it hath dried upp the torrent of ^so mightie^ my Lord Tresurer's mightie indignation, at the least by show and his owne profession and so autenticall a testemony as my Lady Russell's.[1114]

For generall occurrences, to use the noble Earle's one judicious discription in his proper termes, 'Her Majestie's Councell have their hands and heads full; they see more dangers then they know how to prevent'. Ireland growing worse and worse and France, notwithstanding all externall formes and solemnities of amitie and league, internally discontented and consequentlie ^dangerously^ doutfull. And so I most humbly take my leave.

[1112] τὶς ... ἀπίστῳ [Greek] 'What trust is there in the untrustworthy'.
[1113] **dict** dictate.
[1114] **To witt ... Lady Russell's** To assuage the mistrust between the Bacon brothers and the Cecils, Elizabeth Cooke Hoby Russell visited her brother-in-law, Burghley, on 8 September 1596, to discover whether he held any ill will towards their nephew Anthony Bacon. She took his response directly to Anthony and then went back to Burghley with her nephew's defence. After her second meeting with the lord treasurer, Elizabeth again reported the conversation back to Anthony, urging him to write to his uncle. Anthony declined this suggestion, although he wrote to Elizabeth expressing his pleasure in her report of his uncle's goodwill, in terms very similar to those which he used in this letter to his mother. For a full reconstruction of these events, see *Cooke Sisters*, pp. 148–157.

173. *Anthony Bacon to Anne Bacon*, 22 **October 1596**

Draft. LPL 659, fo. 209r–v. 1p.
Endorsed (fo. 209v): A Madame An Bacon, le 22me l'octobre 1596

Madam,

I humbly thanke your Ladyship for your patriges[1115] and ^pigeons and^ would not let Anthony returne without these few lines, whereby I thought meet to assure your Ladyship that Ketterwell hath not made me any way acquainted with the putting out of his interest in the mill and therfore I may justlie, if it stand with your Ladyship's liking, charge him with undutifull forgettfullnes, ^or^ that which is worse, presumption.

The Earle of Shrewsbury is loked for daylie, who hath bene very royallie entertained in outwards; how ~~God k~~ whither from the harte or noe, God knoweth and time, ^the mother of truth,^ will better discern. For Ireland, the crosse advertisements from the Deputy on the one side and Sir John Norrice of the other; the first as a good trumpett sounding ^in his lettres^ continuallie the alarm against the enemye; the ~~other~~ last, serving as a treble vyall[1116] to invite us to daunce and be merrie upon false hope of a hollow peace, makes many feare ^rather^ the ruine then restoration of that state uppon that infallible ground;[1117] *quod omne regnum in se devisum dissipabitur.*[1118] And so I most humbly take my leave.

174. *Anne Bacon to Robert Devereux, earl of Essex,* 1 **December 1596**

Copy. LPL 660, fos 149r–150v. 2pp.
Endorsed (fo. 150v): De Madame Ann Bacon au Comte Essex le premier de decembre 1596

Hearinge, my singuler good Lord, of your honour's returne from the sea coastes this daie, and I goinge hence to morowe, yf the Lord so will, I am bould, uppon some speeches of some and withe some persone at the courte, where latelie I was, to imparte somewhat here of to your honour, bycause it concerned a partie there more nere to me then

[1115]**partriges** partridges.
[1116]**treble vyall** treble viol.
[1117]**For Ireland . . . ground** William Russell, first Baron Russell of Thornhaugh, was lord deputy of Ireland between 1594 and 1597, although this period was marked by disputes with Sir John Norris, the president of Munster.
[1118]*quod . . . **dissipabitur*** [Latin] 'that every kingdom divided against itself will be destroyed'. See Matthew 12:25.

gratious to her stocke.[1119] I will not denie, but before this great suspition of her unwiflike and unshamfast demeanour hath bene brought to me even into the contrie, but lothe to beleve, I laid it up withe secret sadnes in my brest. And trulie my good Lord I did not a litle but greatlie rejoyse in harte, that it pleased ^God^ of his mercie and goodnes, withe the ^late^ famous honor he gave yow in your late martiall exploite withe renowned good successe,[1120] he did also worke in yow such a change of your minde, before by reporte inclined to coorte carnall dalyance, that that honorable and Christian brute was carried aboute joyfulie to the much gladdinge of manie that unfaynedlie loved your Honour's trew prosperitye. But ^*proh dolor*^[1121] my good Lord, I perceived by some eye witnesses here, and which must needes heare and marke, that of late a backsliding to the foule ^~~incontinent~~ impudent^ doth plainlie appeare, and thoughe they did mervaill and muche blame your dishonorable and dangerous to your self course takinge, to the infaminge a noble mane's wyffe and so nere aboute her Majestie, yet she was utterlie condemned as to bad, bothe unchast and impudent, withe as it were an incorrigible unshamfastnes; the Lord speedelie by his grace amende her, or cut her of before some sodaine mischeef.[1122] Yt hathe alredie made her antient noble husbande[1123] to undoe his howse by fallinge, as one out of comforte. But yf a desperate rage, as commonlie, followthe, he will revenge his provoked jealosie and most intollerable injury, even desperatelie; and the more, bycause it is said he lovethe her, and greatlie, as withe greef, laborethe to winne her. Yt is great pittie she is not delivered to him and the courte to be clensed by sendinge awaie such an unchast gaze[1124] and common by-word, in respecte of her place and husbande.[1125] But yow, my good Lord, have not so learned Christe and hearde his ^holie^ worde in the 3d.4.5. verses of the 1 chapter to the first Thessulonians.[1126]

[1119]**it ... her stocke** Elizabeth Stanley, countess of Derby, Anne Bacon's great-niece and Lord Burghley's granddaughter.

[1120]**your late ... successe** The capture of Cadiz and the sack of Faro.

[1121]***proh dolor*** [Latin] 'alas'.

[1122]**cut ... mischeef** The reference must be to an unwanted pregnancy.

[1123]**noble husbande** William Stanley, earl of Derby.

[1124]**gaze** One that is looked at or stared at.

[1125]**Yt is ... husbande** For the affair between Essex and the countess of Derby, as well as the reaction of the earl of Derby, see P. Hammer, *The Polarisation of Elizabethan Politics: the political career of Robert Devereux, second earl of Essex, 1585–1597* (Cambridge, 1999), p. 385.

[1126]**3d.4.5. ... Thessulonians** Anne mistakenly attributes the quotation that follows to 1 Thessalonians 1:3–5, rather than 1 Thessalonians 4:3–5.

[fo. 149v] Yt is written 'This is the will of God that yea should be holie and abstaine from fornication, and everie one knowe how to keepe his owne vessell, in hollines and honor; and not in the luste of concupiscence, as doe the gentiles, which knowe not God.' And more, yf it please yow to reade and marke well, yt is a heavie thret, 'That fornicators and adulterors, God will judge'[1127] and that they shalbe shut out; 'For such thinges', saith the apostle, commonlie 'ˆcommethˆ the wrathe of God upon us.'[1128] Good Lord, remember and consider the greate danger hereby, bothe of soule and bodie, greve not the holie spirit of God, but honor God ˆthat honored yow and reward him not with such evellˆ for his greate kindnes towards yow. ˆGood my Lord, sinne not against your owne soule.ˆ

My Ladie Stafford[1129] said uppon occasion in her talke, the good vertuous Countesse your wyfe was withe childe.[1130] O honorable and valiant noble, make greate accounte of this God his blessinge to yow bothe, and make not her hearte sorrowfull to the hinderance of her younge fruite within her. For it was thought she ˆtookeˆ before to harte and that her last did not so comfortablie prosper.[1131] Yf yow be withe the Lord in deede, he wilb[e] with yow and make your verie enemies to reverence yow. Be stronge in the Lord,[1132] your and our good patient God, feare him and walke upritelie in his truth[1133] and for his promise in Christe,[1134] he will assist yow and looke favorablie uppon yow and yours, ˆprosper and increase his blessing uppon yow and yours;ˆ which mercie and grace, I humblie doe as I am most bound, calle upon him to graunte yow ever, my dere and worthy Lord in Christ Jhesu. With verie inwarde affection have I thus presumed, ill favoredlie scribled, I confesse beinge sicklie and weake manie waies.

[1127]**That ... judge** See Hebrews 13:4.
[1128]**For ... uppon us** See Colossians 3:6.
[1129]**Ladie Stafford** Lady Dorothy Stafford. See **144** and **145**.
[1130]**the good ... childe** The countess of Essex had a stillbirth in December 1596. For a list of all her children with the earl of Essex, see P. Hammer, 'Robert Devereux, second earl of Essex', *ODNB*.
[1131]**For ... comfortablie prosper** A son, Henry, born in April 1595, had only lived a little over a year, dying on 7 May 1596. For reference to the countess's pregnancy with Henry, see **123**.
[1132]**Be ... Lord** See Ephesians 6:10.
[1133]**walke ... truth** See Galatians 2:14.
[1134]**his ... Christe** See Ephesians 3:6.

Boni consulas te vehementer oro et quam optime vivas et valeas vir insignissime et quantum decet mihi charissime.[1135]

Primo Decembris.[1136]

In Christo ^ex animo^,[1137]
ABacona *Χηρα.*[1138]

175. *Anthony Bacon to Anne Bacon,* [1] December 1596[1139]

Draft. LPL 660, fo. 123r–v. 1p.
Endorsed (fo. 123v): A Madame Ann Bacon le Mr de decembre 96

My humble dutie remembred.

I thought it my parte to sende the inclosed, without delaie to your Ladyship. And withall to advertise yow that ^thoughe^ the noble kinde Earle ^had^ ~~havinge~~ not received my ~~lettre~~ ^pacquet^ by reason of infinite busines till this eveninge, yet it pleased his Lordship imeadiatelie ^after^ he had read your Ladyship's lettre and mine to returne me his answer to be sent unto your Ladyship, whiche I have bene bould to doe by his Lordship's owne footman, who ~~hath charge to attende me~~ by his Lordship's comandment attendethe here dailie to be dispatched where I thinke good. Uppon the perusinge my Lord's lettre, yf your Ladyship in your wisdome finde anie just occasion of replie, yt maie please your Ladyship that I maie be acquainted therewithe, to thende I maie be the better provided at his Lordship's next meetinge to performe my dutie to your Ladyship and his good Lordship. And so hopinge that God ~~that~~ hath blessed your Ladyship's Christian and yet most respective indeavours withe dere, kinde acceptance and affectuall impressions, I most humblie take my leave.

[1135]***Boni . . . charissime*** [Latin] 'Take this in good part, I earnestly besech you, and may you live in the enjoyment of good health and all felicity, most illustrious nobleman, and, as is becoming, most dear to me.'
[1136]***Primo Decembris*** [Latin] 'First of December'.
[1137]***In . . . animo*** [Latin] 'In Christ from the heart'.
[1138]***Χηρα*** [Greek] 'widow'.
[1139]**[1] December 1596** Letter **175** was written to accompany the earl of Essex's reply to **174**; **176** is a copy of Essex's letter.

176. *Robert Devereux, earl of Essex, to Anne Bacon,* 1 December 1596

Copy. LPL 660, fos 281r–v. 1p.
Endorsed (fo. 281v): Du Comte d'Essex a Madame Ann Bacon le 2/3 decembre 1596
Addressed (fo. 281r): To the honorable Ladie, the Lady Anne Bacon

Madame, that it pleasethe yow to deale thus freelie withe me in lettinge me knowe the worst yow heare of me, I take it as great argument of God's favour in sendinge so good an angell to admonishe me, and of no small care in your Ladyship of my well doinge. I knowe howe needfull these summons are to all menn, espetiallie ~~espetiallie~~ to those that live in this place. And I had rather withe the poore publicaine, knocke ~~and~~ my brest and ly prostrate, or withe the confesse, when I have donne all I can, I am an unproffitable servant, then pharisaycallie to justifie my self.[1140] But what I write nowe is for the truthe's sake and not for mine owne, I protest before the majestie of God, and my protestation is voluntarie and advised, that this charge which is newlie laide uppon me is falce and unjust. And that since my departure from England towardes Spaine, I have bene free from taxation of incontenentcy withe anie woman that lives. I never sawe or spake withe the Lady yow meane, but in publicke places, and others beinge seers and hearers, who, yf they would doe me right, could justifie my behaviour. But I live in a place where I am howerly conspired against and practised uppon. What they can not make the world beleve, that they perswade the Queen unto, and what they cannot make probable to the Queen, that they give out to the world. They have almost all the howse to serve them for instruments. Yea, the verie Oracles (I meane those that are accounted to be plaine and sincere) doe ^φιλλιπ π ιζ ειν^[1141] phillippisein, doe speake the largest language of the strongest faction.[1142] Plutarch taught me longe since to make profit of my enemies, but God teachethe it me muche better nowe. Worthy Ladie, thinke me a weake man, full of imperfections, but be

---

[1140] **And I had ... self** See Luke 18:9–14.
[1141] **φιλλιπ π ιζ ειν** [Greek transliteration] 'phillippizein'.
[1142] **the verie ... strongest faction** Essex was here quoting Aeschines, who reported that Demosthenes mistrusted the Delphic oracle because it had been 'philippized' (φιλλιπ π ιζ ειν), i.e. it had sided with Philip of Macedon. For Aeschines' quotation of Demosthenes, see *The Speeches of Aeschines*, trans. C.D. Adams (London, 1919), pp. 410–411. For Demosthenes' construction of the term 'to philippize', see P. Hunt, *War, Peace, and Alliance in Demosthenes' Athens* (Cambridge, 2010), p. 88.

assured I doe endeavour to be good and had rather mende my faultes then cover them. I wish your Ladyship all trewe happines and rest. ~~At~~

At your Ladyship's commandment,
Essex.

Burne, I praye yow.
i of December 96.

177. *Anne Bacon to Robert Devereux, earl of Essex, with postscript to Anthony Bacon*, 4 December 1596

Holograph copy. LPL 660, fos 151r–152v. 2pp.
Endorsed (fo. 152v): Le Madame Ann Bacon au Comte d'Essex et en hate sero a'Monsieur le 4me de decembre 1596[1143]

My honourful goode Lord, in ^your^ incessant and carefull affayres to vouchsaff me as one almost forgotten in the worlde, a lettre even with your own hande, is favor more then my poore thanks or il parts can reach unto. God doth diverse wayes make manifest his love towards yow, wherof his church here and our state do flow the swete benefytt to the prayse of his name, and your honorable fame, and the rejoysing in a goode conscience. Yet such excellent persons never want *emulatores malignos cum fastu.*[1144] But yet for all that, tru godly vertue in the Chris[t]en chyldern of God doth with the palme ryse and encrease styll, thowgh men stryve to suppress and oppress it, and they styll shall florysh in the coort of the God of glorious majestie and their seede shalbe blessed.[1145] *Ab imis precordiis,*[1146] as I am most bownde I besech the living Lorde to direct continually with his holy spirit your Lordship's hart to the love of him and of his eternall truth, and sanctifye yow throwgh ^it ever^ to lyve in his reverent feare and to approve that which is pleasing in his syght. And my good Lord, walk circumspectly for the dayes throwgh synn are evell *ut ait apostulus.*[1147] In peace, God graunt yow safty from all crafty treacyeries and subtile snare whatsoever, and in battell by sea or by land his mighty arme be your invincible puissance and make yow victorious, and sende his holy angell to pytch rownd abowt yow and your armies to watch over yow for your saffgard, and with fullnes of goode dayes and yeres in this

---

[1143] *Le Madame .. 1596* [French] 'From Mistress Anne Bacon to the earl of Essex, sent in haste, late at night, to the master, on 4 of December 1596'.

[1144] *[a]emulatores . . . fastu* [Latin] 'rivals malignant with pride'.

[1145] **But yet . . . blessed** Anne here drew particularly on Psalm 92:12–14, but also on Genesis 22:18.

[1146] *Ab imis precordiis* [Latin] 'from the deepest heart'. See Seneca, *De ira*, 1.4.

[1147] *ut ait apostulus* [Latin] 'as the apostle says'. See Ephesians 5:15–16.

268 THE LETTERS OF LADY ANNE BACON

lyff, preserve yow to his hevenly kingdom for ever.[1148] אמן.[1149] The God of peace geve yow peace all weyes[1150] by all means, my very singular goode Lord.

AB.

[Postscript to Anthony Bacon]
For dispatch I wrot late and yll. I wolde not send to yow, ^thowght it not best so,^ by his man, thowgh yow saw my Lord's lettre. I sende it enclosed. Send it back again. I sende by this bearer one Powle Roewly com to me. I think he wolde serve well in your buttry;[1151] he hath, he sayth, used that service. He seemes yet wylling and honest playn, readeth but poorely. Larg wylbe lavesh to pyck, thank and crafty filtching, besyde he hath an owlde father-in-law. Yow wylbe worse thowght of for calling to idlenes where h[e]r[e] your own to make bate.[1152] It is true.

[Left-hand margin] Three churches were here robbed in one night. Use not so much plate abroad to tempte the divell allwey as ready. Warn your brother to, I pray yow to, take hede in tyme for [. . .] sodenly. *Vale.*[1153] God bles yow with his grace and love in Christ.

178. *Anthony Bacon to Anne Bacon*, 6 December 1596

Draft. LPL 660, fo. 122r–v. 1p.
Endorsed (fo. 122v): A Madame Ann Bacon, le 6 de decembre 1596

Madam,
  I humbly thanke your Ladyship for sending me my Lord's lettre to your Ladyship, which I had not sene before bycause his Lordship writt it and sealed it at the court, as allsoe your Ladyship's replye, the sight of both which were very wellcome and comfortable unto me.
  Touching this bearer, though I dout not but in respect of his honestie and truth he deserve a better place then my buttry, yett having noe cause as yet to be discontented with John Large, I meane to employ him for one quarter, during which time I assure your Ladyship he shall have ~~much lesse time~~ ^many fewer howers^ to be idle then if he were at home.

[1148]**preserve ... for ever** See 2 Timothy 4:18.
[1149]אמן [Hebrew] 'Amen'.
[1150]**The God ... weyes** See 2 Thessalonians 3:16.
[1151]**buttry** Buttery, the place where household provisions were kept.
[1152]**make bate** make trouble.
[1153]*Vale* [Latin] 'Farewell'.

A For occurrents, Monsieur de la Fonteine[1154] tould me himselfe yesterday that he marveiled at so long and deep a French silence. Of the shipwrack much bruted, their is no certaine particuler confirmation.[1155] Ireland remaineth still in consumption and is like to pine away more and more unlesse better restoratives be sent thether in time. And so I most humbly take my leave.

179. *Anne Bacon to Robert Cecil*, 13 December 1596

Copy. LPL 660, fo. 129r–v. 1p.
Endorsed (fo. 129v): De Madame A. Bacon a Sir Robert Cecill, le 13me decembre 1596

Secretarie and honorable nephewe, I thanke yow for allowinge your ^olde^ aunte some speeche with some leysure at my laste beinge withe yow. Trulie me thinkethe I received refreshinge there but ever since. And I take my self bounde to my Lord, your father, for sendinge the cause to see yow bothe. God make yow stronge for your waightie causes to his glorie and to your owne rejoysinge in a good conscience.

And I praie yow, good Sir, since it pleased my Lord your father to use me so kindelie thereto, that yow will doe so muche as from me and for me to intreate his honour to remember still Mr Frowicke[1156] for his good by continuinge his Lordship's favour to him for his credit in well doinge. The gentleman withe his lawe and learninge lovethe trewe religeon and is well esteemed, thoughe otherwyse but of smalle livelihoode and manie children, even of the beste and wyseste and is lincked in kindred and alliance withe moste of the cheef hereaboute, who would be verie sorie, I knowe, to have him descredited by suche disordred and undiscreete *oppidani*.[1157] The towne is alwaie but unorderlie and unconscionable and careles of cheef dutie, bothe for good government or for providinge for their poore, whome they willinglie and wilfullie suffer continuallie, for lacke of good lookinge to, to straie everie where aboute, begginge likewayes, and makinge spoile of fences, and hackinge and stealinge woode, out of all measure, to striffe makinge by layinge open inclosieres, beside the

---

[1154] **Monsieur de la Fonteine** Robert Le Maçon de la Fontaine, principal minister of the French Stranger Church. See p. 161, n. 519.

[1155] **Of the . . . confirmation** Part of the Spanish fleet had been shipwrecked off Cape Finisterre in November 1596. For contemporary reports of the shipwreck, see CP 46/87: 01/12/96.

[1156] **Mr Frowicke** Henry Frowick of Lincoln's Inn, steward of St Albans from 1589 to 1617. See *Corporation Records*, p. 296.

[1157] *oppidani* [Latin] 'townsfolk'.

hurt they do tiplinge, taverninge and droncken idlenes and gameinge, which is almost this towne's proffession. God amend such vises there and generallie in this lande. And *exempli gratia*[1158] with in these 3 daies, the water conduit turrit made by my Lord for his howse here was the 3d time broken up and the cisterne leade and other thinges stollen quite awaie. The whole worke is nowe utterlie spoiled by them,[1159] no doubt, but complayninge prevailes not with suche wilfull, ignorant and evell base gouverners.

Lycence ^me^ a litle more for this once, good Mr Secretarie. After I had written the premiss and pawsed for my weake sight, the Lord lighten my soule's sight, this fell out to my muche unquyetinge uppon Wednesdaie laste.[1160] My few menn appointed for church and light horse roade them abroade, as by order they use to doe for excercise of the horses and their owne more fittinge to serve uppon commandment, my lance horse[1161] casteinge a shoe by the waie, his ryder went withe him to my farrier at Redborne by to shoe him. And beinge there at the Smithe's forge, comes firste a furious fellowe withe his dagger drawne and by violence wold needes take my principall beaste for a post horse,[1162] for all he was told whose he was and to what service and that he wanted a shoe, my man stryvinge still and callinge an officer to staie the horse, cam 3 more suche harebraine fellowes withe swordes drawne, swearing and madlie rageinge, and tooke him quite awaie scant withe 3 shoes well. My man not able to get a horse soone enoughe was faine to take my other light horse, a younge geldinge, to ride after for the other, and overtakinge him when a myle or more, got awaie my lance, and sendinge him home by his fellowe, he faine to make after him poste to Constable to recouver the light horse after this hurtfull post to the spoile, as is reported. They threwe downe meale sackes and tombled of the side cotes[1163] and their companie with savage rage. Yf ^Irelande^ had such soldiors, God healpe. Since Tilbory service,[1164] I have loste 3 great horses, and ^a^ spetiall geldinge, knowne and camended[1165] much at

[1158] *exempli gratia* [Latin] 'for example'.

[1159] **the water ... by them** Nicholas Bacon I had contrived to have water supplied by pipe to Gorhambury house from nearby ponds. See *Bacon Letters and Life*, VII, p. 169.

[1160] **Wednesdaie laste** 8 December 1596.

[1161] **lance horse** Presumably a medium-weight horse, such as would be used for jousting. Anne later in the letter referred to her 'other light horse', so this horse would have been one bred for agility and stamina.

[1162] **post horse** A horse kept at a post-house or inn for the use of post-riders, or for hire by travellers.

[1163] **side cotes** Long coats.

[1164] **Tilbory service** In 1588, English forces encamped at Tilbury in Essex in advance of the expected Spanish invasion.

[1165] **camended** commended.

the musters,[1166] nowe deade, and miscaried to my no smalle ^charg and^ greef. These 2 last I bought verie dere, bothe but younge beastes and scant yet thoroughly framed and nowe I feare spoiled. The losse of suche horses and my sonne's sicklie state will even goe verie nere my harte.

180. *Winter*[1167] *to Anne Bacon,* [before 15] December 1596[1168]

Holograph.[1169] LPL 660, fo. 141r–v. 1p. Torn and damaged.[1170]
Endorsed (fo. 141v): De goodman Wynter a Madame Bacon, le mois decembre 1596
Addressed (fo. 141v): To the honourable this verie good Ladie and Mistress, the Lady Bacon, delivered theise [. . .].[1171]

The Commyssion went in Sir Conwayes Clyfford's name, he saye at the Red Lyon[1172] at Mr Painard, and there it is reported there was 40 quarts of wyne dronke, so that som of them was thought to be verye merrey.[1173] It is thought it was his cocke that went before withe the comission. There was as it is reported dyver other Knights, whose names I cannot as yet inquyre out, but two of them, that is Syr George Gifford[1174] and Sir Rychard Bingham.[1175] They went from St Allbains the 8 dayes of december 1596, as it was thought, betwne[1176] the houres of

[1166]**at the musters** Men obliged to serve in the militia (local defence forces) had to gather periodically for inspection, which included presentation of their horses.
[1167]**Winter** Presumably this is Anne's servant Winter, described as 'your man Winter' by Anthony Bacon (**69**).
[1168]**[before 15] December 1596** It is unclear whether Anne knew the names of the rioters when she wrote to her nephew, and chose not to reveal them, or whether she learnt this information from Winter after receiving **180**. This letter was presumably written before **181**.
[1169]**Holograph** This is presumed holograph. It is certainly the original letter sent to Anne.
[1170]**Torn and damaged** For a copy, see LPL 660, fo. 234r–v.
[1171]**[. . .]** The ink at the end of this subscription is very smudged.
[1172]**The Red Lyon** Presumably the Red Lyon at Redbourn. See 'Catalogue of field names', pp. 92–93.
[1173]**The Commyssion ... mercey** Sir Conyers Clifford had been appointed chief commissioner of Connacht on 2 December 1596. He was accompanied back to Ireland by Sir Richard Bingham, the previous provincial president of Connacht, who had fled to England in September 1596 and had been suspended from office and imprisoned in the Fleet. See P. Hammer, *The Polarisation of Elizabethan Politics: the political career of Robert Devereux, second earl of Essex, 1585–1597* (Cambridge, 1999), p. 369.
[1174]**Syr George Gifford** Sir George Gifford, gentleman-pensioner, was knighted for his service at Cadiz. See *History of Parliament*, II, pp. 189–190.
[1175]**Sir Rychard Bingham** See n. 1173.
[1176]**betwne** between.

8 and ix in the morninge. It is reported that some of there behavyour was not very good, neyther at Barnett[177] nor withe there horses; by the waye sum report they kylled a horse withe a sworde or a dagger, they were so mad hedded, and abused there gwyde verye muche.

Thesise ar furder to certefye your Ladyship. I dyd speke with Nathiniel and Nycolas concernyn [. . .] sayth he wolde [*rest of letter has been torn away*].

181. *Anthony Bacon to Anne Bacon*, 15 December 1596

Draft. LPL 660, fo. 120r–v. 1p.
Endorsed (fo. 120v): A Madame Ann Bacon, le 15me decembre 1596

Madam, my most humble duty remembred.

I humbly thanke your Ladyship for vouchsafing me the sight of your lettres to Mr Secretary, which having perused and finding none ^of those riotours^ named, I asked goodman Crosbye whether he could not tell me any of thier[178] names, wheruppon he showed me a little paper mentioning Sir Coniers Clifford, who having bene heretofore a follower of my Lord of Essex and exceedinglye bound unto him for all that he hath, I knew his Lordship's censure of his folkes' outrage would be more waightie unto him then all ^of^ my Lord Tresurer's or Mr Secretary's threatnings. I therfore sent that little paper to my Lord of Essex who, very much moved, will put it as a spetiall item with shame enough in his next lettre to the said knight, thanking me for addressing my complaintes unto him without naming Sir Coniers Clifford to any other. Hereof I thought it my parte to advertize your Ladyship, whome ~~for~~ I meane not to trooble at this time with any generall ocurrences, but referre my selfe for them to my next. And so I most humbly take my leave.

---

[177]**Barnet** Barnet, then in Hertfordshire, is about ten miles from St Albans.
[178]**thier** their.

182. *Anne Bacon to Anthony Bacon*, 30 December 1596

Holograph. LPL 653, fo. 316r–v. 1p.
Endorsed (fo. 316v): De Madame Ann Bacon le 31 de decembre 1596
Addressed (fo. 316v): To my sonne Mr Antony Bacon at Essex Howse
with some spede

Becawse yow spake of brawn to my man, I have sent yow, lett quick.[1179]
I have not tasted of it my selff. I thank God for Mr Wyborn, but tyed
by the foote, as I may betwixt ryding and hobeling ^on foote^ this hard
frosly,[1180] God be blessed for it, I crawle to the chur[ch]. God make yow
able to go well and with ryght stepp.

   Fare yow well. Your brother, I heare, at court often. The grace of
God gwyde him and be with yow both ever.

Gorhambury *penultima Decembris*.[1181]

Mater tua,[1182] AB.

I thank yow for your deynties.

183. *Anthony Bacon to Anne Bacon*, 31 December 1596

Draft. LPL 660, fo. 124r–v. 1p.
Endorsed (fo. 124v): A Madame An Bacon, le 31me decembre 1596

Madam,
   I most humbly thanke your Ladyship for ^your^ seasonable provision
and am very sorrye to understand of Mr Wiburne's indisposition, but
thanke God ^your Ladyship^ doth hould out so well this ~~fear~~ trying
and persing[1183] wether. For my selfe, I prayse God, the state of my
bodye is as good as I looke for, considering that I daylye bere farre
more strong and healthy then my selfe to feele and complayne of the
rotten weather past and the late sodeine change.

[1179]**brawn . . . lett quick** Brawn is a pig's head, boned, rolled, and boiled, then either
pickled or potted. When Anne refers to the brawn as 'lett quick', she presumably means
that the pig was killed and let of its blood quickly.

[1180]**frosly** It may be that Anne meant 'frosty', but failed to cross the 't'. It is also possible
that she meant 'frosly' to signify 'untoward', with 'fros' as a variant of 'fro'. In either case,
it seems likely that she was referring to the inclement weather.

[1181]***penultima Decembris*** [Latin] 'next to last day of December'.

[1182]***Mater tua*** [Latin] 'Your mother'.

[1183]**persing** perishing or piercing.

It hath pleased God to call the Lord Mayor[1184] and Alderman Haughton,[1185] the 2 lustiest of their bench,[1186] both in shorte space. My brother, God be thanked, hath receaved gratious usage and speach this holly dayes[1187] of her Majestie, who I hope at the last will vouchsafe to exemplefie her good wordes by some princely reall effects. I thinke meet likewise to advertise your Ladyship that Mr Secretary of late hath professed very seriouslye an absolute ἀμνεϛια[1188] of all misconceits passed, with earnest protestation that to the Queene, to his father, or of himselfe he would be gladd and redye to doe me any kinde office if I would make proofe of him. This is soe much the more comfortable unto me that mine owne conscience doth wittnesse that it is onlye God's working and noe way mine owne seking by any base meanes or insinuation. And so beseching God to send your Ladyship ˆthisˆ new yeare and many moreˆ full measure of inward comforte and contentment, one grayne whereof is to be preferred befor quintalls[1189] of worldlye happines, I most humbly take my leave.

184. *Anne Bacon to Anthony Bacon*, January 1597

Holograph. LPL 654, fo. 45r–v. 1p.
Endorsed (fo. 45v): De Madame le mois de janvier 1596

Sonne, the Lorde well ease and heale yow of ˆyourˆ wofull to me payns. I am determined to have nether hawlk of my Lord Chamberlain[1190] nor Sir Edward Hoby.[1191] The Lord Chamberlain's ˆmenˆ hereafter ˆtoˆ challeng an autoryte[1192] by it, which I playnly denied in your absence. I wyll geve no such beginning in my tyme certeinly. Troble not them therfore. Sir ˆEdwardˆ Hoby is too to ˆI wot not whatˆ, I can not

---

[1184]**Lord Mayor** Thomas Skinner had only taken office as lord mayor on 29 October 1596. See 'Aldermen', in *Analytical Index to the Series of Records Known as the Remembrancia: 1579–1664* (London, 1878), p. 2.

[1185]**Alderman Haughton** Peter Houghton, a member of the Grocers' Company, was elected alderman of Castle Baynard in 1593. See *ibid.*

[1186]**bench** The bench of aldermen.

[1187]**holly dayes** The Christmas holidays.

[1188]ἀμνεϛια [Greek transliteration] 'amnesia'. It may be that Anthony intended the original Greek word to be used here – ἀμνησια – and that the slight differences are scribal error.

[1189]**quintalls** A quintall is a unit of weight equal to 100 lb.

[1190]**Lord Chamberlain** William Brooke, Lord Cobham, was lord chamberlain from August 1596 to March 1597.

[1191]**Sir Edward Hoby** Hoby was Anne's nephew, the eldest son of her sister Elizabeth by her first marriage, to Thomas Hoby.

[1192]**autoryte** authority.

~~tell what~~ skyll[1193] of him. I wyll nether byrde nor man ^of his^ come to my howse in my absence; to unorderly for me being away to lett him and his alone. Yf Mr Skippwith[1194] can not gett a hawlk, I know what I wyll do. I wyll have no revell in myne absence; send none, I pray, therfore. I wyll forbyd in dede. I wold yow cowld your selff, that were joy. Onely Mr Skippwith or none at all. Put not your selff ~~and~~ ner me to nedeless troble in so small a matter. For they shall not once again, I earnestly sett down, and ^so^ wyll make order. More sualter[1195] in it then yow are ware of. Herafter I wyll holde on in those things as I have begon, *Deo propitio*.[1196]

Mater tua,[1197] AB.

185. *Anne Bacon to Anthony Bacon*, 12 January 1597

Holograph. LPL 654, fo. 297r–v. 1p.
Endorsed (fo. 297v): De Madame Ann Bacon le 12me de janvier 1596
Addressed (fo. 297v): To my sonne Mr Antony Bacon at Essex Howse with some spede.

σ ω Θ ε ῷ ἠὺ[1198]

In hast for Mr Wyborne's hast away, I thank yow for your delicate wyne, as Mr Wyborn sayth, who tasted fyrst of it. Yf it please yow to send a rondelett,[1199] as Rowland, my man, sayd yow did meane ^and was reidi^, I pray yow in eny wyse send it upon Fryday next and that your man see it saffe sett in the cart for drawing. For in very dede the last was drawn at least 11 gallons; he that goeth with all must see it laden with charge to the carier, who be now more deere and careless. Upon Saturday ^next^, yf God wyll, I will looke for it and I wyll sett upp my selff saffe before I go hence. I have ben more comfortable this Christyd by the speciall favour of God to me and my howshold by Mr Wyborn's fatherly and holsome heavenly instructions, besyde the publick. But for the communion this next Sabbath, where I trust

---

[1193]**skyll** understand, comprehend.
[1194]**Mr Skippwith** Presumably one of the sons of William Skipwith of St Peter's Street in St Albans, elected MP for the town in 1571. The Skipwith and Bacon families were distantly related through marriage: William Skipwith's aunt was the sister of Sir Ralph Rowlett, whose second wife had been Margaret Cooke, sister to Anne Bacon. Letters of administration were granted to William's son Stephen on 27 June 1595, so his father must have died earlier that year. See *History of Parliament*, III, p. 392.
[1195]**sualter** swalter, i.e. time-wasting.
[1196]***Deo propitio*** [Latin] 'God willing'.
[1197]***Mater tua*** [Latin] 'Your mother'.
[1198]**σ ω Θ ε ῷ ἠὺ** [Greek] '[Greetings] to your Lord'.
[1199]**rondelett** A rundlet was a casket or vessel for carrying wine.

with my hole howsehold to be, with the blessing of God, I had gone
hence this week; on Wenseday ^next^ furdest I purpose, yf not before. I
have not sene Crossby yet towching your colliar,[1200] this day I looke for
him. He hath much busines, it shalbe browght. *Cura cura ut quam optime
valeas.*[1201] Yf Mr Wyborn had not dieted thin and in season, he shuld
have ben worse handled *cum podagra.*[1202] Gorhambury 12 *Januarius.*

ABacon.

186. *Anne Bacon to Anthony Bacon,* 20 January 1597

Holograph. LPL 654, fos 43r–44v. 2pp.
Endorsed (fo. 44v): De Madame le 21me de janvier 1596
Addressed (fo. 44v): My sonne Mr Antonye Bacon. *Cura ut tempestive edas
et dormias sanat crudos humoris.*[1203]

Salutem in Christo.[1204]

Si,[1205] my goode sonn, that by the handy work of the Lorde in ^us
both^, nether of us cowlde see one another being no further distant,
I thowght at my retturn hether to wryte as I cowlde to yow. Lett
us both know it is the Lord's fatherly correction to both and desyre
grace to make profitt of it to our inwarde healing. Thowgh my late
encreased pain in *superficie cutis*[1206] be soden and extraordinary to me
and may partly suspect some venom to be drunk with those block
wormes I tooke in drink 4 times, ~of them half a pint~ abowt ^half a
pint of them^, yet yow know the learned do call *senectus* ^*ipsa*^ *morbus,*[1207]
which synce my qwartan[1208] I fynde by diverse accidents to be tru and
very paynful, and I humbly acknowledg ^God's^ mercy that moveth
my mynde to take age, syckliness ^and infirmitees^ being naturall, as
well as yowth's health. And ^yf^ I use such goode means by cownsell
and diett as may make my unacqwainted payne more tollerable, and I
fynde much ease by ^thinn diet, wholsome and^ earlier suppers before

---

[1200] **colliar** coal merchant.
[1201] ***Cura ... valeas*** [Latin] 'You must take care, take care, so that you have the best possible health'.
[1202] ***cum podagra*** [Latin] 'with gout'.
[1203] ***Cura ... humoris*** [Latin] 'Take care to eat and sleep at the right times; this cures the raw humours'.
[1204] ***Salutem in Christo*** [Latin] 'Greetings in Christ'.
[1205] ***Si*** [Latin] 'since'.
[1206] ***superficie cutis*** [Latin] 'the surface of the skin'.
[1207] ***senectus ... morbus*** [Latin] 'old age itself a disease'. See Terence, *Phormio,* 4.1.9.
[1208] **qwartan** Quartan fever. See p. 150, n. 463.

vi, and clean usuall drink and never in the night and seldome in morning or betwixt meales.

Yf I shulde say true, your continuall, uncomfortable state of body dobleth what greeffs God sendeth me, besyde ^cherfull^ patience ^in your disease^ is necessary and the Lorde hath pitie of his chyldern. But lett your patience ^be growned^ upon humbling your selff and prayour and meditation to God to beare patiently his wyll, which is allweyes just and holy; and also upon goode hope ^and expectation^ of his fatherly comfortable restoring in his goode tyme, not ceassing by earnest and faythfull prayour to call upon him with confidence in his tender mercy in Christ our Lorde, and regarde your diet ^and healthy good order^ diligently and seasonably for eny. Yf your health did serve yow might do much goode even ^here^ among, but when the Lorde shall please, but *aude comit omni modo accuratissime.*[1209] So my God hath bestowed gyfts; labour to employ them *in tua persona*[1210] and I lament your continuall ^bodily^ impotency the more, becawse yow are therby, as it were, cast of and unabled for the comfort of the publick ministery, a greavous want, whereby yowr tru understanding judgment and knowledge are, and must nedes be, greatly hindered and weakned, and yow less able to discern aright betwixt spirituall and naturall flesh and the spirit. Labour therfore by harty prayour to God to heale yow every way to your comfort, and in the mean whyle be glad and religiously entertein the godly learned when they come to yow, that at length yow may have some privat conference and howseholde reading ^and^ prayour reverently and dayly as is commanded; ^the^ morning and evening ^sanctifyee^ in eny wyse, goode sonne. And never be afrayd to avow your Christian estimation of the godly preachers before ἑνρι ὁουαρδ,[1211] τεχνησ πληρον,[1212] or eny other. It is a goode report of yow and due, being continuall syckly; he is to much with yow. God kepe the goode Earle saffe.

[*Left-hand margin*] I feele, I thank God, the fury of my ^outward^ corruption somewhat abated and my stomack amending somwhat. I yeelde my selff to the goodness of my hevenly Father and yours. *Cura diligenter et timore.*[1213] Gorhambury 20 January. AB, *mater tua.*[1214]

[1209] **aude comit[er] . . . accuratissime** [Latin] 'act boldly, affably, and most carefully in every way'.

[1210] **in tua persona** [Latin] 'in your [outward] persona'.

[1211] **ἑνρι ὁουαρδ** [Greek transliteration] 'Henri Howard', i.e. Henry Howard.

[1212] **τεχνησ πληρον** [Greek] 'full of skill'.

[1213] **Cura . . . timore** [Latin] 'Take diligent care and with fear [of God]'.

[1214] **mater tua** [Latin] 'your mother'.

187. *Anthony Bacon to Anne Bacon*, 22 January 1597

Draft. LPL 654, fo. 295r–v. 1p.
Endorsed (fo. 295v): A Madame Ann Bacon, le 22me de janvier 1596

Maye it please your Ladyship to be advertised that my humble desire is that your Ladyship would signe a deede of mortgage ^of Cheedor,^[1215] wherein my brother and my self likewyse joyne, and for that purpose a master of the Chancery is appointed to attende your Ladyship at three of clocke as a witnes of recorde. The rent is to be continued still to your Ladyship till I have perfected the sale. And so likewyse of Napesburie,[1216] ~~yt beinge farr more advantagyeous for me to satissfie your Ladyship the rent~~ so that your Ladyship is no looser and I eased and inabled to satisfie pressinge debtes. And so I moste humbly take my leave.

188. *Anne Bacon to Anthony Bacon*, 25 January 1597

Holograph. LPL 654, fos 47r–48v. 2pp.
Endorsed (fo. 48v): De Madame le 27me de janvier 96
Addressed (fo. 48v): To my sonne Mr Antony Bacon at Essex Howse

Grace and mercy *matri et filio per Christum.*[1217]
 I verili think this sharpe weather doth stirr the gowt in yow paynfully. Your father, besyde other, in spring tyme felt often of it and sharpely. The Lorde heale yow in his mercy to your own comfort and others that love yow well in the Lorde. I heare that ther is disagreement in Abon town,[1218] wher owght not. By reason of continuall sycklines and therby lack of experience, yow may be missinformed and misled. Comber not your selff much with their envieing and undiscrete doings. There is fawt, as is thowght, in those that take them selff wysest and do take upon them. Some say that the Maior[1219] for his understanding proceadeth carefully and not contentiously, unprovoked and uncontemned. Mr Κλαρκε[1220] is an honest man and

---

[1215]**Cheedor** Nicholas Bacon I had purchased land with an annual rent of £30 in Cheddar in Somerset in 1553. See *Wealth of the Gentry*, p. 49.
[1216]**Napesburie** On 10 November 1593, Anne had given Anthony her life interest in the manor of Napsbury, which Anthony now wanted to sell. See 'Money-lenders', pp. 240–241.
[1217]*matri ... Christum* [Latin] 'to the mother and son through Christ'.
[1218]**Abon town** St Albans.
[1219]**Maior** The mayor in 1597 was John Saunders; his predecessor for 1596 was Robert Shrimpton. See *Corporation Records*, p. 292.
[1220]Κλαρκε [Greek transliteration] 'Klarke', i.e. John Clark. See p. 119, n. 302.

so hath ben cownted even in your father's tyme for an *oppidanus*.[1221] But when was it seene that an inholder shulde be made a Justice of Peace ^in^ his own ^such^ howse, thowgh against his wyll, must nedes be disorder and how in dede fitt to redress. They ^two^ band with too much note to do evenly. I pray yow lett ^not my^ writing be red of eny but your selff. Yow are to open *ut antea saepius monui, utinam monita matris plus sapuissent palato tua fortasse multo in meliore statu vixisse et tibi et tuis, sed omni in bonitate dei mei acquiesco, non sine bona spe.*[1222]

Theris a tinde[1223] of report that Streatly by your means shulde succede Mr Thomas.[1224] Surely, sonne, yf it shulde be so yow wyll sustein much discredit by him. I trust yow regarde more the great ~~charge~~ ^necessitie^ and duty of a religious sufficient scoolemaster, furnished with godliness ^with his teaching^ and wyse discretion, then carnall frendshipp to seek to place one that wanteth all these. He hath not been but ill spoken of and reconed *inpudicus et effrenis;*[1225] ^*forte gramma risui*^.[1226] Well, I deale playnly herin *coram deo,*[1227] who direct yow in this speciall. Your father rejoysed that God sent him such a man as the late was and did much encourag him, commending ^him^ in my hearing and to me *persepe*.[1228] I shulde be sory that yow, his sonne, shulde displease and dislyke many by a partiall choyce, to the hindrance of your good opinion for judgment and Christian, religious consideration by such a corrupt fantastyck person.

Brute[1229] goes here yow wolde sell Napsbury.[1230] I hope yow mean it not. The chiefest manor hereabowts. I wolde be sory to see but rather stay what I may for diverse respects. But yesterday, the Lord's day, being at the parish church, one asked ^by^ me the qwestion, who I looked not shulde heare or deale in such matters and sayde that

---

[1221] *oppidanus* [Latin] 'townsman'.

[1222] *ut . . . spe* [Latin] 'as I have warned often previously. If only your mother's warnings had been more to your taste, perhaps you would have lived in a much better position for you and for yours, but in all things I rest in the goodness of my God, not without good hope'.

[1223] **tinde** rumour.

[1224] **Theris . . . Mr Thomas** John Thomas, a Dutch Calvinist, had been appointed as master of St Albans grammar school by Nicholas Bacon I. When Thomas died on 13 January 1597, his successor was a matter of great local concern. John Clark recommended one Mr Stretley to Anthony Bacon. For more see W. Urwick, *Nonconformity in Herts. Being Lectures upon the Non-conforming Worthies of St Albans and Memorials of Puritanism and Nonconformity in All the Parishes of the County of Hertford* (London, 1884), p. 83, n. 1; *Cooke Sisters*, pp. 188–189.

[1225] *inpudicus et effrenis* [Latin] 'unchaste and unruly'.

[1226] *forte . . . risus* [Latin] 'as it happens his grammar is laughable'.

[1227] *coram deo* [Latin] 'before God'.

[1228] *pers[a]epe* [Latin] 'very often'.

[1229] **Brute** bruit, i.e. rumour.

[1230] **Brute . . . Napsbury** Edward Briscoe gave Anthony Bacon £700 for Napsbury manor on 10 May 1597; licence to alienate Napsbury to Edward Briscoe and his son and heir, also named Edward, was given on 2 September 1597. See 'Money-lenders', p. 245.

Mr Fuller[1231] had desyred a frend in these parties to harken owt some manor for him to buy ^and was desirous of it^. Thowgh I cowlde lyke of Mr Fuller better, ^*legis peritus*,^[1232] then other for him selff, I was, I promiss yow, much offended with the motion as a thing I greatly do and shall mislyke. Have yow no hope of posterite? Only my chyldern cownted in the worlde unworthy their father's care and provyding for them. Barly and Pinne, yf yow had kept them, wolde have ben above iv C markes a yere to yow.[1233] Do not, I pray yow, make your selff a by-word both here and to such as are but your halff frends by so selling to your great lack and encombrance to this howse many wayes. And to descent, your sonnes, yowng sonnes in latter tymes, are blessed posterite and ^it^ wolde be well issued ^for them^. I shulde have ben happy to have seene chylder's chylder but Frannce spoyled me and myne. God comfort us all, I humbly besech him, and look favorably upon ^us^ in Chris[t], his one dearly beloved אמן.[1234] Marke well *quo animo haec scribo*.[1235] And God bless yow wyth health and gratiously supply your wants.

Gorhambury 25 January.

Mater tua,[1236] AB.

189. *Anne Bacon to Edward Stanhope*, 14 February 1597

Copy. LPL 655, fo. 95r–v. 1p.
Endorsed (fo. 95v): De Madame a Mr Dr Stanhope, le 14ime de fevrier 1596
Addressed (fo. 95r): To Mr Doctor Stanhop give these.

Sir.

I cannot but marvell what ails yow, Mr Doctor, still to vex the godlie ministers of Christ and by your undeserved excommunication to hinder the glorie of God so pittifully.[1237] I understand yow have thus ungodlie delt with Mr Bradelie, the precher at Redburne, an honest man and carefull by his godlie paines to make the gainsaying and

---

[1231]**Mr Fuller** Nicholas Fuller. See p. 116, n. 277.
[1232]*legis peritus* [Latin] 'an expert of the law'.
[1233]**Barly ... yere to you** Anthony had sold Barley in 1593 to John Spencer. It is not known when he sold Pinner park and farm. For the sale of Barley, see p. 108, n. 232.
[1234]אמן [Hebrew] 'Amen'.
[1235]*quo animo haec scribo* [Latin] 'in which spirit, I write these words'.
[1236]*Mater tua* [Latin] 'Your mother'.
[1237]**I cannot ... pittifully** Rudolph Bradley, Anne's clergyman at Redbourn, had been declared excommunicate by Edward Stanhope. For Stanhope, see p. 253, n. 1067; *Cooke Sisters*, pp. 181–182.

waiward people[1238] to become the people of God. Besides that the cause, being God's cause, ought nerelie to touch anie Christian hart, I take my selfe bound, since he was there lawfully placed by me, to assist him and to further him in his ministrie to the advauncing therby of God's honor. For he is neither a proud man nor carelesse of his famelie, nor contentious, but to winne the hard harted to tollerating; yow can chardge him with no materiall just cause, I dare ansuer, if not to gentle among such alenolling[1239] and bad people most part, and yow would have them so still if yow bereave them of the meanes of trew conversion. By report, the enemies of God, of her Majestie and of our cuntrie are mighty and with cruell and fiery hartes preparing the readie ^to the pray^ and spoile of us all.[1240] We had need with most humble submission intreat the Lord of hostes to be with us and on our side by publick fasting and unfained humilation, and that troughout[1241] the land, and not presumptuouslie to beat back his faithfull and appointed servantes by his owne selfe, to stand in the gapp betwene God and us, to torne away his wrath so greatlie provoked daily by the fearfull contempt of his holie gospell, to hevelie and lamentablie manifested every where by our professed wickednes and most carnall securitie. I pray you, Sir, remember well your selfe and heap not thus God's displeasure uppon you, but incouradge the faithfull and painefull preachers of Jesu Christ that they maie labour comfortablie. Our life is uncertaine and riches speciallie gotten by partaking against God and increase of his trew honour will not availe in the day of his wrath, 'For he is a consuming fier' saith the holie prophet.[1242] I desire you hartely to remember and to your power to remedie this great undoing if[1243] her Majestie's people. Yf yow saw the grevous disturbance of a parish by disgracing and dissevering their godlie minister from them yow would, I am sure, both for conscience to God and your allegiance to our gracious soveraigne, avoid all occasions of such pernitious disquieting of the hartes of her good subjectes, who by the ghospell preached sincerelie amongst them love, dread and redelie obey her with willing hartes, and thatt of verie conscience pull awaye the good working meanes, yow kill their hartes and make them but sad and dull, either to serve God or her Majestie.

[1238]**gainsaying ... people** See Romans 10:21.
[1239]**alenolling** Presumably 'ale-swigging'.
[1240]**to the ... us all** See Ezekiel 29:19.
[1241]**troughout** throughout.
[1242]**For ... holie prophet** See Deuteromy 4:24; Hebrews 12:29.
[1243]**if** of.

It is to trew by to much experience, God help us. I commend yow and my selfe also to the grace of God in Christ.

Fleetstreete

> In the Lord, ABacon, your sicklie and
> auntient cosin, late Lord Keper's widow.

190. *Anne Bacon to Robert Devereux, earl of Essex,*
15 February 1597

Copy. LPL 655, fo. 215r–v. 1p.
Endorsed (fo. 215v): Le Madame Ann Bacon au Comte D'Essex le 15me le fevrier 1596
Addressed (fo. 215r): To my very good Lord, the Earl of Essex, worth[1244] noble

My very singuler good Lorde.

I humbly desire your Lordship to vouchsafe to read this lettre inclosed, bycause this very first advertisement is sent me from a good preacher thereabout, one Mr Dike, now at Hemsted parish.[1245] I am bould and tooke it my dutie to lett your Lordship understand the contents by his owne lettres; I could not well devide that cheife pointe, which I pray your good Lord to peruse bycause it concernes ^yow^ and yow could not have bene sure it came to me from the preacher indeed *sua sponte*.[1246] The Lord of heaven and earth prosper yow longe in the one with his continuall grace and favour and spare yow for the other everlastinglye.

> *A Fleetstreet.*
> *15 fevrier.*[1247]

In the Lord, as I have great cause, *ab imo pectore*.[1248]

> AB $X\eta\rho\alpha$.[1249]

[1244]**worth** Presumably 'worthy'.
[1245]**Mr Dike ... parish** William Dike, who had previously been installed by Anne as assistant curate of St Michael's parish, close to Gorhambury, had been living in Hemel Hempstead since 1591, apparently at the invitation of the clergyman there, as well as at the request of the parishioners. See *Cooke Sisters*, p. 183. Essex had already helped secure Dike the living of Hemel Hempstead in October 1594. See LPL 650, fos 287r–288v.
[1246]***sua sponte*** [Latin] 'of his own accord'.
[1247]***A ... fevrier*** [French] 'At Fleet Street. 15 February'. Presumably this subscription was not in French in the original version of the letter.
[1248]***ab imo pectore*** [Latin] 'from the innermost heart'.
[1249]***X\eta\rho\alpha*** [Greek] 'widow'.

191. *Anne Bacon to Anthony Bacon*, 1 March 1597

Holograph. LPL 656, fo. 49r–v. 1p.
Endorsed (fo. 49v): De Madame, le 2me de mars 1596
Addressed (fo. 49v): To my sonne Bacon

Sonne, Mr Dyke him selff wyll declare the matter to yow. He desyreth your carefull furtherance to helpe his sute to the Earle. The learned man hath great charge and yf my Lord may by his favorable ^letter^ further his sute, it wyll comfort him in his godly payns. Consider well and do discretely and yet hartely herin, yf yow may well. God make yow able to serve him in personall action with his dayly blessing.

Gorhambury *primo Martii.*[1250]

Your moother,
AB.

192. *Anthony Bacon to Anne Bacon*, 9 March 1597

Draft. LPL 656, fo. 5r–v. 1p.
Endorsed (fo. 5v): A Madame, le 9me de mars 1596

Madame, my most humble duty remembred.

My cosen Robert Bacon, havinge determined to imploie your Ladyship's meadiation and furthermore by lettre to my Lord Tresurer in the behalf of his nece, my cosen, Mrs Terrill,[1251] I could doe no lesse in acknowledgment of his confidence and spetiall kindenes towars[1252] me then accompainie him withe these fewe lines, and most humblie beseche your Ladyship to recomende this and his nece's sute unto my Lord Tresurer, ~~when I hope~~ whose Lordship, I hope, in wisdome will shewe himselfe no les willinge, then in honor and kindnes he is bounde to gratefie your Ladyship. And so I most humbly take my leave.

Your Ladyship's most humble and obedient sonne.

[1250]***primo Martii*** [Latin] 'first of March'.
[1251]**Mrs Terrill** Presumably the wife of Edward Tyrell, a ward of Nicholas Bacon I, who matriculated with Anthony and Francis at Trinity College, Cambridge, in 1573.
[1252]**towars** towards.

193. *Anne Bacon to William Cecil, Lord Burghley,* 10 March 1597

Copy. LPL 656, fos 95r–96v. 2pp.
Endorsed (fo. 96v): De Madame Bacon a Mr le Grand Tresorier, le 9me de mars 1596
Addressed (96v): To the right honourable, my singular good Lord, Lord Tresorer of England

My singular good Lord.

Now I humblie desire your honour to licence me to write in some what a more unaccustomed stile unto your good Lordship. I perceave by this gentleman, Mr Robert Bacon, my Lord that was his elldest brother's onelie sonne, that he hath made some meane allreadie unto your Lordship for the wardshipp of Mr Tyrell, to whose mother he is uncle.[1253] I confes trulie unto your honour that after he had requested me, being his allied aunt, to add my poore furtherance in this sort unto your Lordship for your obteining of the same, I was ever very willing and readie to trooble your honour thus much for him. Beseching your Lordship humbly and hartelie to be good Lord[1254] unto him in this his sute, proceding ^more^ from a naturall and kind affection for the good of the mother, warde, and thother chilldren, then for any profitt he meaneth to make by them. I dare assure your honour hereof for of long I have well knowen what trew, frendlie care he hath and had as a brother and as an uncle unto his kindred, discretlie and comfortably to his power, which naturall part manie omitt now adayes. Surelie, my ever good Lord, if it may please yow to lett him have that nere kin wardship and that intirelie without devideing of it, I am perswaded your Lordship shall not better bestow such a benefitt, in both respect of the widow and her other chilldren, as of the ward him selfe, who I know shall find him by the grace of God as a loving uncle-father in all kind dutie with wise usage and a good conscience, wherfore as may become me, I hartelie intreat your Lordship that he may gratiouslie obteine your honourable favour to the full obteining this, his naturall sute to so good and[1255] end, which I am sure he purposeth unfeynedlie, the Lord guiding him. Good Lord, excuse this my earnest maner in his behalfe, being the first matter he ever required of me. And gladlie would shew my hartie good will to him in respect he was so nere my

---

[1253]**I perceave ... uncle** For Robert Bacon's past efforts regarding this wardship, see *Cooke Sisters,* pp. 143–144.
[1254]**to be good Lord** to be a good lord.
[1255]**and** an.

Lord and under your Lordship's leave one that I take to be afitt[1256]
tutor every way. And I shall accompt my selfe as for your

[fo. 96v] other honourable acceptance of my constreyned bouldnes,
even for this onlie very matter very much bound unto your honour.
The God of all grace and comfort continew your good estate to your
godlie, hartie joy and comfort of many. Gorhambury 10 *Martii.*

In the Lord,
unfeynedlie allwayes,
ABacon.
Late Lord Keper's widow.

194. *Anne Bacon to Anthony Bacon*, 18 March 1597

Holograph. LPL 656, fos 47r–48v. 2pp.
Endorsed (fo. 48v): De Madame, le 19me de mars 1596
Addressed: To my sonne Mr Anthony Bacon at Essex Howse

υσ τ ε ρον π ρο τ ε ρον.[1257]

Grace and health.

I sent my seale ring fastened to a litle psalme boke in meeter by
my cosin Bacon.[1258] I think yow know. Sende it saff, I pray yow, yf not
well before, then by Thomas Knite, in eny wyse next weeke. I desyred
the bearer heroff, Robert Smyth, the carier, to go with this lettre hym
selff and to speak with yow. His byll for cariag and another for coales
are so confused and exceading that it to plainly appeareth yow have
none that careth for your profitt. I know not why your cariages shulde
be appointed by eny of your men whosoever to me and yf yow wolde
upon cawse have eny, then lett it be down orderly and sygned by your
selff. For his byll of xvi li browght me by him for coales is monstrous.
I had lyke to have torn it but that he browght it me him selff. Your
father nether in London nor here spent so many in two yeres and
was as ^well^ cherised[1259] in his gowte and syckness and better ^too^ in
goode order of expences, which yow want and so runn on in dett as
yow do. I turned back the coales byll by him again. Yow had of me

---

[1256]**afitt** a fit.
[1257]υσ τ ε ρον π ρο τ ε ρον [Greek] 'the later earlier'. This must refer to some element of the
letter-writing process, perhaps that a letter written later was sent first.
[1258]**I sent . . . Bacon** As the book is specified as a little volume, Robert Bacon seems to
have been given one of the smaller versions of Sternhold and Hopkins' psalter to take to
Anthony. See H. Hamlin, *Psalm Culture and Early Modern Literature* (Cambridge, 2004), p. 39.
[1259]**cherised** cherished.

for coales at London upon occasion of meeting the woman there, who sayde she cam for mony for coales, vi li abowt Hollantyde;[1260] when I saw yow ^last^ yow reqwyred of me viii li for coales, then by Crossby I was demanded ix li, one pound more then yow named, where with I was not content, but never the less, thowgh I may but ill being owt of mony and compelled to borow to pay this next quarter's ways, I have delivered Crossby the ix li and odd shilling. For the rest ^for coales,^ I wyll not nor can pay. Yf I may know from your selff what cariag yow have had in dede, and sende it noted by this Mr Smyth, it may be I wyll pay it. But to have horses sent hether and sent for I wot not by whome nor for whome, only by your bowlde oversawcy masters ^rather^ then servants, ~~for~~ I must not be appointed, nether wyll I alow it so. For no horse shall be hether or sent hence, of eny of my servants, but by my commandment. Elce I geve over my authorite to my inferiours, which I think is a discreadit ^to eny of accompt^ that knows rightly their place from God and pray for grace to use it well ^and^ in goode order. I may think much lack of kindenes and duty in yow and your brother that never write to me. I wolde know how my cosin Bacon did with my Lord Tresurer for the warde[1261] (but for him I wold not have written, nor of Mr Wolley's deall), nor where your brother tarieth the rest of this Lent and how it is with yow both. It greves me and I feare thaccess to yow styll of hollow ὁουαρδ.[1262] God kepe the Εαρλε[1263] from being seduced by such. I pray remember to pay your scrivener's dett. I looked for and yow owght in duty to have sent me or[1264] this your bond. I pray forget it no lenger, but let me have it shortly. Speak with Smyth your selff and take goode order with him.

[*Left-hand margin*] The Lorde geve good understa[nd]ing and goode health with his many blessings. *Sape tibi ipsi quoque ne forte.*[1265]

Gorhambury 18 *Martii.*

Mater tua,[1266] AB.

[1260]**Hollantyde** Shortened version of All-Hollantide or All Hallowtide, namely All Hallows' or All Saints' Day, 1 November.

[1261]**I wolde ... warde** See **193**.

[1262]*ὁουαρδ* [Greek transliteration] 'Howard', i.e. Henry Howard.

[1263]*Εαρλε* [Greek transliteration] 'Earle', i.e. the earl of Essex.

[1264]**or** before.

[1265]*Sape ... forte* [Latin] 'You must discern for yourself also lest perhaps'.

[1266]*Mater tua* [Latin] 'Your mother'.

195. *Anthony Bacon to Anne Bacon*, 24 March 1597

Draft. LPL 656, fo. 7r–v. 1p.
Endorsed (fo. 7v): A Madame, le 24eme de mars 1596

Madam,

Your Ladyship shall receave by Thomas Knight, according to your appointment, your seale and booke, for the which my cosen, Robert Bacon, rendreth by your Ladyship together, withe the remembrance of his dutie, most humble thankes, deferring to write unto your Ladyship till he be ~~more~~ assured by some good effectes, which my Lord Tresorer's sickness and exceding great business, ^he^ ~~taking~~ my cosen taking all thinges at the best, hath hetherto delayed. For Smith's bill, I tould him that what soever remained to be paid, I would satisfie. For ~~my catt~~ ^any cartte's^ bill notes, and I my selfe remember ~~it~~ nor he demaunded any thing of me, praying your Ladyship to thinke that what occasion soever I have yett, it shall be alwayes more contentment to me to receave nothing ~~fr~~ atall from your Ladyship, than how much soever with any disquietnes of minde or troublesome conceiptes, which springing many times more out of jealousie and motherlie apprehension, then out of truth, trooble your Ladyship more then they can profit me. My brother is well, thankes be to God, and some times heare, or therwhile at Twittnam. And so I most humblie take my leave.

196. *Anne Bacon to Anthony Bacon*, [before August 1598][1267]

Holograph. LPL 653, fo. 337r–v. 1p. Damaged.
Endorsed (fo. 337v): lettre de Madame

God bles yow with nedefull health, inwarde and owtwarde. Yow purge styll; me thinkes it shuld make nature nether to work digestion ner strength being so long still pulled. What custom of phisick hath done in yow God knows and yow me thinks feele. He helpe it in mercy.

I wolde gladly know when and how you sell Redborn. I think abowt 2 of the clock at furthest this day my Lady Pawlett wyll know certeinly for the lending me one C li as I lately wrote to her and she halff promised. But selling Redborn I wyll troble no more frends to borow,

---

[1267] **[before August 1598]** The internal evidence makes it difficult to place this undated letter. Redbourn was sold to Edmund Bressey in August 1598, so it was written before that date. Margaret Paulet did not die until 1602.

for yow and your brother must be all bownde for it. I have nothing to answer such detts.

Even as I had wrote thus farr, my Lady Paulett sent me worde by her kinsman that she was sory she cowlde not lend me a C li as I desyred but herafter yf L li wyll stande me, she wyll for that sum she sayth. I was glad I knew this so soone. I wyll ceass to troble eny moe,[1268] growing syckly as I do and being behinde hand. Do wysely for Redborn and be owt of dett as soone as yow can and that don geve your selff to serve the Lorde with all your hart and look to your health that God may bless yow with a good marriage to your comfort. Wee must trust in the Lorde but with well doing, with our fayth first fownded upon Christ ^and his worde^. I thank God my physick proved well.

Kepe the affected parts warme.

Your moother, AB.

Sende me plain worde.

197. *Anne Bacon to Nicholas Bacon II*, 3 **March 1600**

Holograph from 'in the Lord'. Chicago 4167. 2pp.
Addressed: To my lovinge sonne Sir Nicholas Bacon at Colford.[1269] Deliver this.

Sir Nicholas Bacon, I commende me unto yow, and to your Ladye, hopinge of your good health. I thancke God my owne health ys not verye good, but I beare yt with pacience. And I thincke my selfe beholdinge to yow for havinge care of payenge me myne anuytie in good tyme for I have neede of yt always before yt commeth to my handes. At this tyme yow have written to one Mr Cooke to paye me a hundered poundes at the Ladye Daye next,[1270] of whome I shalbe verye well content to receave yt yf he paye yt to me then, but if he dothe fayle me and yow then, at the daye, I hope yow will have care of me, to see me payed. And so with prayer to God for this tyme I leave yow to his protection. From my lodinge[1271] in Fleete Streete this third of Marche 1599.

Your Lordship's mother,
in the Lord,
very frend, ABacon Χηρα.[1272]

[1268]**moe** more.
[1269]**Colford** Nicholas Bacon II had purchased the Culford Hall estate in Suffolk in 1586.
[1270]**Lady Daye next** See p. 107, n. 226.
[1271]**lodinge** lodging.
[1272]**Χηρα** [Greek] 'widow'.

INDEX

All entries refer to page numbers, not letter numbers.
'n.' after a page reference indicates the number of a note on that page.

Abbotsbury (*see* Barley estate, Hertfordshire)
Albert VII, archduke of Austria 250–251
Albret, Jeanne d', queen of Navarre 85–86
aldermen (*see* London: aldermen)
Allen, Captain Francis 12–13
Altham, James 147
Anthony, servant of Anne Bacon 262
António, Dom, prior of Crato 161
archdeaconry court (*see* St Albans: archdea-
    conry court)
Archelow/Archeloe, Dr 227
Argentine, Richard 5
Audley, Thomas, lord chancellor 14, 67
Auvergne, Henri de la Tour d', fourth
    vicomte de Turenne, duc de Bouillon
    22, 238–239, 248, 255–256, 258
Aylmer, John, bishop of London 25, 180 n.
    619, 181–182

Babbe, Francis 119
Bacon, Lady Anne (*née* Butts) 288
Bacon, Lady Anne (*née* Cooke) *passim* but see
    especially:
  counsel: for the earl of Essex 18, 208,
      229, 236–238, 256, 262–265, 267;
      maternal counsel 7, 13–20, 22–23,
      99–108, 110–117, 123–125, 137–139,
      141–142, 144, 150, 152, 155–157, 171–
      172, 174–181, 192–196, 200, 202,
      204, 206–207, 209–215, 217, 219–
      235, 246, 248–249, 254–255, 257,
      268, 278–280, 286–288; religious
      counsel 17–19, 99–101, 120, 144, 178–
      179, 188, 196–198, 200, 206–208,
      213–214, 219–220, 225, 229, 236–
      240, 263–265, 267, 276–277, 280–
      282
  education 4–8, 95, 190–191, 217; Greek
      3 n. 8, 4–5, 7, 18–19, 38, 42, 55,
      85–86, 100, 108, 110, 120, 123, 142,
197–198, 202, 206–209, 213, 217–218,
220–221, 224–225, 229–230, 232–
236, 238, 244, 249, 256, 261, 265–
266, 274–275, 277–278, 282, 285–
286, 288; Hebrew 5, 7, 19, 100,
232, 238, 268, 280; Italian 5, 9 (*see
also* Bacon, Lady Anne: translations:
Ochino); Latin 5–9, 22, 42, 55–
58, 61–69, 76, 80–86, 89–93, 100,
102–107, 111–116, 118, 120, 124–126,
130, 138–139, 141–142, 144, 147, 150,
152, 157, 160–163, 168, 172, 174–176,
178–179, 181–182, 188–193, 195–196,
198–201, 203–204, 207–211, 214–221,
223–224, 226–238, 240, 242–243,
246–247, 249, 253–255, 257, 259,
262–263, 265, 267–270, 273, 275–
280, 282–283, 286 (*see also* Bacon,
Lady Anne: translations: *Apologia*)
  finances 28–31, 107, 123–128, 141, 150,
      157–158, 166–170, 173–177, 188–189,
      194, 214, 226, 228, 230, 239, 243,
      246–249, 252, 259–260, 271, 278,
      285–288
  health 89, 103, 137, 138, 148, 150, 155,
      177, 183, 188, 194, 198, 201, 210, 218,
      233–234, 238, 264, 270, 276–277, 288
  letters: delivery 41–44, 106–107, 110, 114,
      117, 120, 122, 125, 128, 131, 136, 139,
      142, 161, 165, 168, 170, 172, 178, 208,
      215–216, 222, 258, 260, 265, 267–
      268, 285; epistolary privacy 42–43,
      100, 106, 108, 113, 127, 138, 155, 174–
      175, 178, 181, 196, 207–212, 214, 221,
      226, 229, 235, 237, 249, 253, 267–
      268, 272 (*see also* Bacon, Lady Anne:
      education: Latin, Greek)
  marriage 6–9, 14, 57–59, 61–68, 71, 77–78,
      80–82, 85–86, 95, 162, 195, 202, 219,
      246–247, 279, 285 (*see also* Bacon, Sir
      Nicholas I; Haddon, Walter)

medical knowledge 34–35, 105–106, 109,
    112–113, 130, 142, 150, 162, 179–181,
    193–195, 203–204, 207, 218–219, 223,
    227, 235, 255, 276–278, 287–288
mistress of Gorhambury: estate manage-
    ment 31–34, 71, 103–106, 126–127,
    137, 141, 144, 151–152, 154, 156–161,
    171–172, 192–194, 196–197, 200–203,
    211–212, 224–226, 232, 256–258,
    262 (see also Gorhambury: manorial
    court); household management 9,
    107, 127, 171, 177–178, 196, 200, 205,
    208–209, 212–213, 215, 217, 222, 252,
    270, 274–276, 286 (see also Spencer,
    Edward); provisions for sons 107–
    109, 111–113, 126–127, 129–130, 133–
    136, 139, 141, 144, 148–149, 151,
    154, 170–172, 176–177, 193, 204, 207–
    210, 214–216, 218–219, 221–223, 227,
    232–235, 241–247, 249–250, 252,
    256–257, 259–260, 262, 273
motherhood 11–17, 77–78, 80–84, 89–93,
    95, 123, 125, 146–147, 190–191, 194
    (see also Bacon, Lady Anne: counsel:
    maternal counsel)
religious belief 5–6, 17–19, 35, 104, 112,
    138, 151–152, 171, 180–182, 203–204,
    220, 222, 225, 228, 231, 233, 235, 273,
    275–276 (see also Aylmer, John; Bèze,
    Theodore de; A Parte of a Register)
religious patronage 24, 61–68, 77–78, 87–
    89, 96
sisterhood 27–28, 55–58, 150, 207, 209,
    242
stepmotherhood 69–74, 79–80, 288 (see
    also Bacon, Sir Edward; Bacon,
    Sir Nathaniel; Bacon, Sir Nicholas
    II; Peryam, Lady Elizabeth (née
    Bacon); Wyndham, Lady Elizabeth
    (née Bacon))
translations: John Jewel's Apologia Ecclesiae
    Anglicanae 6, 59–61; Ochino's ser-
    mons 5–6, 8, 51–54
widowhood 9, 18–19, 24, 27, 39, 81–86,
    88, 109, 152, 238, 282, 285; and 1
    Timothy 5:9–10 18–19, 38, 108, 142,
    197–198, 202, 218, 220, 265, 282, 288
Bacon, Lady Anne (née Gresham) 11, 36, 69–
    71–74, 80
Bacon, Anthony passim but see especially:
    childhood 71–72, 77–78, 210
    European travels 12–13, 80–86, 89–
        93, 110, 134, 280; prosecution for

sodomy 13, 93 n. 178; return to
    England 3, 12–13, 17, 99–101
finances 29–31, 102, 118, 150, 185, 194,
    200, 214, 228, 239, 242–243, 246–
    247, 285–288 (see also Barley estate:
    sale of manor)
health 34–35, 99, 105–106, 126, 130, 142,
    145, 150, 153, 172, 180, 190–191, 195,
    197–198, 205, 225, 227, 232, 260, 273,
    277–278, 287
local politics 16, 20–21, 42, 114, 119, 176
relationship with aunt Elizabeth Cooke
    Hoby Russell 27–28, 153, 207, 209,
    261
relationship with the earl of Essex 15–16,
    153, 224
relationship with mother, passim but see
    especially: intelligence provision 21–
    22, 122, 140, 143, 161, 163–166,
    169, 238–239, 245, 248, 250–251,
    253, 258–262, 269, 274; reactions to
    maternal counsel 118–119, 134, 140,
    143, 145, 156, 184–187, 189, 241, 243,
    251, 287 (see also Bacon, Lady Anne:
    counsel: maternal counsel); requests
    for provisions from Gorhambury
    22–23, 31, 107, 109, 111, 148–149, 151,
    177, 204, 207–208, 218, 221, 241 (see
    also Bacon, Lady Anne: mistress of
    Gorhambury: provisions for sons)
relationship with uncle Lord Burghley
    (see Cecil, William, Lord Burghley:
    relationship with Bacon nephews)
residences (see London: Bishopsgate
    Street, Chelsea, Essex House, Gray's
    Inn; Redbourn, Hertfordshire)
Bacon, Sir Edward 72, 81–82, 129 n. 357
Bacon, Francis, Viscount St Alban 21, 44–
    45, 72 n. 110, 99–101, 111, 114, 120, 122–
    123, 125, 129, 133, 135, 138–139, 143,
    146–148, 150–152, 154–155, 157, 160–
    161, 165–166, 169–170, 174, 176, 179,
    183–185, 188–189, 192–194, 196, 198,
    202, 205, 209, 210–211, 217, 219, 221,
    227, 233–234, 239, 242, 254, 259, 273–
    274, 286–287
    childhood 11, 71–72, 77–78, 210
    finances 29–31, 121, 124–125, 136, 141, 147,
        150, 157–158, 182, 194, 200, 226, 228,
        247–249, 252, 278, 288
    health 34, 136, 143, 190–191, 205, 229
    letters 101, 157–158, 169–170, 178–179,
        183–184, 192–193

relationship with the earl of Essex 15, 122, 133, 140, 149, 163–165, 224
relationship with mother: reactions to maternal counsel 22, 105, 117, 125, 170 (*see also* Bacon, Lady Anne: counsel: maternal counsel); requests for provisions from Gorhambury 22, 31, 170, 184 (*see also* Bacon, Lady Anne: mistress of Gorhambury: provisions for sons)
relationship with uncle Lord Burghley (*see* Cecil, William, Lord Burghley: relationship with Bacon nephews)
residences (*see* London: Gray's Inn; Twickenham Park, Middlesex)
Bacon, Sir Nathaniel 7 n. 28, 11, 30 n. 149, 42, 44, 69–70, 72–74, 79–80, 102 n. 197, 173 n. 576, 272
Bacon, Sir Nicholas I 27, 57–59, 71, 74 n. 122, 102 n. 197, 102 n. 199, 104 n. 206, 108, 115 n. 273, 118, 176, 188, 195 n. 684, 201–202, 216, 219, 246–247, 252, 256, 270, 278–279, 284–285; death 2–3, 11–12, 14, 29, 80–82, 247; fatherhood 125, 135, 280; health 31, 35, 71, 162, 180, 195, 278; lord keeper 9, 118; marriage 6–9, 39, 61–68; religion 6, 8–9, 77–78 (*see also* Bacon, Lady Anne: marriage)
Bacon, Sir Nicholas II 11–12, 19, 29–30, 35, 44, 71, 72 n. 111, 79–80, 146–147, 149, 181, 193, 272, 288
Bacon, Robert 23–24, 243, 283–287
Bacon, Susan 57–58
Bailey/Bayly, John 210
Baithforde/Bashford(e), servant of Anne Bacon 109, 134, 155
Barley estate, Hertfordshire (Minchenbury, Abbotsbury, and Hores) 33, 115–118, 136–137; sale of manor 29–30, 108, 120, 122, 128, 138, 142–147, 280
Barnet, Hertfordshire/London 272
Bath, Somerset 35, 129–130, 133, 148, 151
Báthory, Sigismund, prince of Transylvania 250
Baylye, Robert 105, 179
Bedfords manor, Essex 58
Berault, Michel 13, 89–93
Bèze, Théodore de 6, 12, 25, 38–39, 80–86, 133–134
Bingham, Sir Richard 271–272
Birch, Thomas, *Memoirs of the Reign of Queen Elizabeth* 2
Blanchard, Honoré 80–81

Boldero, Francis 71, 158, 188
Bonner, Edmund, bishop of London 26, 182
Bradley, Rudolph 26, 112, 189, 207 n. 761, 280–281
Bressey, Edmund 287 n. 1267
Briscoe, Edward 279 n. 1230
Brocket, Sir John 134, 174
Brocket, Thomas 175, 178, 192, 194, 212, 215, 234
Brooke, William, tenth Baron Cobham 255, 274
Bunne, William 225
Burbage, Edward 108
Burbage, James 205 n. 746
Burbage, William 108
Burgh, Thomas, Lord Burgh 260
Burghley (*see* Cecil)
Burston manor, Hertfordshire 30, 104, 211 n. 790
Butler, Sir Henry 119
Butlers manor, Hertfordshire 103 n. 202, 155–156, 196

Caesar, Sir Julius 24, 253, 260 n. 1108
Cambridge University 55–56, 65, 72; St John's College, Cambridge 56 n. 23; Trinity College, Cambridge 72, 74 n. 123, 81 n. 154, 283 n. 1251
Carpenter, Anthony 105, 171
Carpenter, Thomas 105, 171
Cartwright, Thomas 13
Castol, Jean 133–134, 161
Cecil, Mildred, Lady Burghley (*née* Cooke) 3–9, 14, 27, 35 n. 174, 36, 39 n. 188, 44, 55–57, 58 n. 34, 83 n. 158
Cecil, Robert, earl of Salisbury 15, 20, 27–28, 42, 45, 120 n. 306, 163–165, 179, 187–188, 198–200, 209, 248–249, 253, 258, 269–272, 274
Cecil, William, Lord Burghley 6–8, 11, 27, 39, 42 n. 200, 44, 55–56, 79–80, 101, 115–118, 135, 194, 209, 239, 249, 272, 286–287; relationship with sister-in-law Anne Bacon 18–19, 23–24, 87–89, 146–147, 217–218, 269, 284–285; relationship with Bacon nephews 12, 14–15, 28, 93 n. 178, 110, 140, 146–147, 149, 153, 163–166, 176, 179, 193, 199, 261
Cheddar, Somerset 278
Cheke, Sir John 55–56
Christian IV, king of Denmark 239, 258

Cicero, Marcus Tullius 8, 57 n. 28
Clark, Henry 115, 118
Clark, John 119, 278–279
Cleves, Anne of, queen of England 58
Clifford, Sir Conyers 271–272
Clifford, Margaret (née Russell), countess of Cumberland 228
Cocke, Henry 24 n. 110
Cockthorpe manor, Norfolk 74
Coke, Sir Edward 15, 140, 163, 165 n. 545, 184 n. 642
Coke, John 4
Colney Chapel, Hertfordshire 102
Coltman, Mr 225
Coningsby, Sir Ralph 119
Conisby, Humphrey 114
Cooke, Anne (see Bacon, Lady Anne)
Cooke, Lady Anne (née Fitzwilliam) 3–6, 53–54, 59 n. 39, 95
Cooke, Sir Anthony I 3–5, 55–56, 57 n. 29, 86, 95, 192 n. 666
Cooke, Anthony II 3, 5
Cooke, Edward 3
Cooke, Elizabeth (see Russell, Lady Elizabeth)
Cooke, Erasmus 181, 193, 212, 233
Cooke, John 4
Cooke, Katherine (see Killigrew, Lady Katherine)
Cooke, Lady Margaret (née Pennington) 4
Cooke, Margaret (see Rowlett, Lady Margaret)
Cooke, Mildred (see Cecil, Mildred, Lady Burghley)
Cooke, Richard 3
Cooke, Sir Richard 4
Cooke, William 3
Corneillis, Michael 124, 136
court, English royal 105, 200, 217, 233, 236
Cox, Richard, bishop of Ely 4
Crewe, Thomas 32, 115–117, 126–127, 129–130, 133–134, 161, 188, 193, 201, 203, 212, 220–222, 241, 257
Crosby, John 33, 177, 185, 193, 197, 200, 203, 207, 209, 215, 225–226, 228, 232, 246–247, 259, 272, 276, 286
Culford Hall, Suffolk 288

Dawyes/Dawys, servant of Anne Bacon 222, 233
de Vere, Anne (née Cecil), countess of Oxford 58
Dell, William 32, 126–127, 144–145, 160, 171

Dering, Anne (see Locke Dering Prowse, Anne)
Dering, Edward 9
Devereux, Frances (née Walsingham), countess of Essex 21, 206, 231, 254, 264
Devereux, Robert, earl of Essex 2 n. 6, 3, 15–16, 18, 20–21, 26, 36, 37, 39, 40–42, 122, 129, 133, 135, 140, 148–150, 153, 163–165, 194, 199, 206, 208, 217, 224–225, 227, 229–231, 236–240, 245, 248–250, 254, 254 n. 1074, 255–256, 258, 261–268, 272, 277, 282–283, 286
Dike, William 26, 181, 252, 282–283
Dixon, William Hepworth 2
Dorball/Dorbull 159
Downing, William 32, 158, 160, 201, 203, 222, 224, 257, 261
du Plessis-Mornay, Charlotte (née Arbaleste) 13, 92–93 n. 178
du Plessis-Mornay, Philippe 13, 92–93 n. 178
Dudley, Anne (née Russell), countess of Warwick 14, 42 n. 201, 187, 228
Dudley, Robert, earl of Leicester 9, 87 n. 166, 115, 118

Edney, Francis 124
Edward VI, king of England 4, 8, 53
Egerton, Stephen 27, 209 n. 772, 213–214
Egerton, Thomas, Viscount Brackley 15, 140
Elizabeth I, queen of England 9, 12, 14–15, 17, 21, 23, 28, 61, 63, 88, 101–102, 115, 118, 120 n. 307, 122, 132–133, 135, 140, 143, 153, 161, 163–166, 195, 198–199, 219, 228, 233–236, 239, 248, 250, 254–255, 258, 260, 263, 266, 274, 281
Elsdon, Mr 107, 175
Erasmus, Desiderius 7 n. 28, 36, 69
Ewer, William 224

Faunt, Nicholas 12, 14, 24, 99–100, 162 n. 521, 166, 177
Fawcett/Forsett/Furcey, goodman 201–202, 255, 258
Field, John 27
Finch, John 38, 103, 125, 137, 143, 151–152, 154, 156 n. 488, 157 n. 494, 158, 158 n. 503, 160, 232
Finch, Mrs, wife of John 154, 156–158, 160–161
Finch, Richard 158
Finch, William 158–161
Fitzwilliam, Sir William 4
Fletcher, Richard, bishop of London 207, 233

Forsett (*see* Fawcett/Forsett/Furcey)

Fortescue, Sir John 158

France 12–13, 21–22, 89–93, 117, 131–132, 143, 161, 245, 251, 258–259, 261, 280; Newhaven expedition (1562–3) 256; Treaty of Greenwich (1596) 248, 258; Triple Alliance (1596) (*see* Auvergne, Henri de la Tour d')

Franklin 178

Freeston, Sir Richard 58

French Stranger Church (*see* London: French Stranger Church)

Frowick(e), Henry 119, 269

Fuller, Nicholas 116, 280

Fulwood, William, *The Enimie of Idlenesse* 38

Furcey (*see* Fawcett/Forsett/Furcey)

Gifford, Sir George 271–272

Giggs Clement, Margaret 4

Goad, Captain Francis 18 n. 78, 21, 41, 131–132, 239–240

Goodere, Sir Henry 115 n. 273, 116

Goodman, Godfrey, bishop of Gloucester 1, 33

Goodrich, Thomas, bishop of Ely and lord chancellor 14, 67

Gorhambury manor, Hertfordshire, *passim* but see especially: 9, 11 n. 46, 22–23, 25–26, 30–34, 69 n. 97, 127, 129, 135 n. 399, 176, 195, 220, 241–242; manorial court 32, 106, 160 n. 512, 192 n. 666, 200–201, 203, 222, 224, 257; Playdells farm 212 (*see also* Bacon, Lady Anne: Gorhambury)

Gosnold, Henry 21, 45, 166, 169

Gotheram, Thomas 149, 155–156, 171, 177–179, 183, 209, 211–215, 242

Goyon, Jacques de, comte de Matignon 110

Gragg 156

Gray, Mr 111

Gray's Inn (*see* London: Gray's Inn)

Gresham, Anne (*see* Bacon, Lady Anne (*née* Gresham))

Gresham, Lady Anne (*née* Ferneley) 69, 73

Gresham, Sir Thomas 11, 69

Grimell/Grimwell, goodman 111, 137

Groom, servant of Anthony Bacon 202–203, 209, 212, 215, 223, 247

Haddon, Walter 1 n. 1, 4, 7–8, 36, 55–57

Hampton Court Palace, Surrey 195

Harvey, George 29, 121, 124, 147

Hawgood 222

Hayward, Sir Rowland 101

Heath, Nicholas, archbishop of York and lord chancellor 251 n. 1055

Henri IV, king of France 12, 21, 93 n. 178, 131–132, 143, 161, 248

Henshaw, Thomas 179

Heydon, Sir Francis 119

Hickes, Sir Michael 165

Hoby, Sir Edward 21, 120, 122, 274–275

Hoby, Lady Margaret (*née* Dakins) 209 n. 782

Hoby, Sir Thomas 3 n. 8

Hoby Russell, Lady Elizabeth (*see* Russell, Lady Elizabeth)

Holmes, Matthias 218

Holt 244

Horace (Quintus Horatius Flaccus) 7, 65, 188, 231–232

Hores (*see* Barley estate, Hertfordshire)

Houghton, Peter 274

Howard, Charles, first earl of Nottingham 248, 258

Howard, Henry, earl of Northampton 16, 27, 42, 206–207, 209, 217, 223, 235, 277, 286

Howard, Philip, thirteenth earl of Arundel 42, 207

Howard, Thomas, fourth duke of Norfolk 62, 65–66, 207

Huicke, Dr Robert 162

Humphrey, the butcher 126, 211, 226, 228

Ireland 217–218, 271 n. 1173; Nine Years' War 21, 250, 258, 260–262, 269–270

James VI, king of Scotland (later also James I of England) 258

Jeanne d'Albret *see* Albret, Jeanne d', queen of Navarre

Jennings, Gabriel 124

Jewel, John, bishop of Salisbury 6, 60 (*see also* Bacon, Lady Anne: translations: *Apologia*)

Jones, Edward 123

Kellet, John 221

Kemp, Bartholomew 126–127, 129, 138, 158, 166–170, 173–176, 181, 210

Kemp, Nicholas 167

Kempe, David 181

Killigrew, Lady Katherine (*née* Cooke) 3–5, 9, 158 n. 501
Knight, John 213
Knight, Robert 109, 113, 138, 158, 193
Knight, Thomas 109, 126, 144, 171, 232, 235, 252, 285, 287
Knollys, William, first earl of Banbury 258

la Fontaine, Robert Le Maçon de 161, 269
Laceby, Robert 160
Lambeth conference (1584) 87
Large, John 268
Large, Robert 202, 211–212, 232, 242
Lawrence 103, 168, 170, 188, 200, 235, 252
Lawson, Thomas 12–13, 16, 33, 42, 99–100, 110–111, 186, 193, 210–211, 216, 227, 232
le Preux, Jean 133
The Life of Severus Alexander 7, 240
Locke Dering Prowse, Anne (*née* Vaughan) 9
Lockey, Richard 34, 159–160
London: aldermen 21, 30, 101, 143, 145–147, 274; Bishopsgate Street 16, 179–180; Bull Inn, Bishopsgate Street 16, 179–180; Cannon Row 58; Chelsea 16, 207, 217, 219–220, 222; Doctors' Commons 24, 253; Essex House, the Strand 16, 44, 229–230, 239, 273, 275; French Stranger Church, Threadneedle Street 17, 22, 100, 225, 231 (*see also* Castol, Jean; la Fontaine, Robert Le Maçon de); Gray's Inn *passim* but see especially 16, 21, 41, 131, 158, 165, 170, 180, 198, 229; Lambeth 63, 260; Paul's Cross, St Paul's Cathedral 88; Wimbledon 57 n. 29, 58; York House, the Strand 9, 11 n. 46, 170, 210
Lopez, Roderigo 21, 161, 164

manorial courts (*see* Gorhambury, manorial court)
Mantell, Hugh 32, 141, 223
Marks manor, Essex 29, 121, 124–125, 138, 147, 170
Marsh, Thomas 193
Mary I, queen of England 8, 251
Maurice of Nassau 250–251
Maynard, Sir Henry 108, 117
Maynard, Ralph 114
Mehmed III, sultan of the Ottoman empire 245, 250
Meriden/Meryden, Warwickshire 102

Mills, William 124
Minchenbury (*see* Barley estate, Hertfordshire)
Moore, Sir Edward 250
Moorer, Robert 30, 163, 194, 242–243, 246–247
More, Margaret (*see* Roper, Margaret)
More, Sir Thomas, lord chancellor 14, 67
Morgan, Hugh 30–31, 242, 246–247
Morice, James 120
Moschopulus, Manuel, *De ratione examinandae orationis libellus* 3 n. 8, 5
Moseley, John 176

Napsbury manor, Hertfordshire 30, 115–118, 278–279
Neville, Lady Anne (*née* Killigrew) 158 n. 501
Neville, Sir Henry 158
Newton, Thomas 180 n. 619, 181
Nonsuch Palace, Surrey 235, 260
Norris, Sir John 262
North, Roger, Lord North 258
Nunn, George 71

Ochino, Bernardino (*see* Bacon, Lady Anne: translations: Ochino's sermons)
O'Neill, Hugh, second earl of Tyrone 250, 258
Osborne, John 79, 212
Osborne, Mrs, wife of John 212–213

Paget, William, first Baron Paget 251
Parker, Margaret (*née* Harleston) 14, 62
Parker, Matthew, archbishop of Canterbury 6–7, 9, 14, 23, 45, 58–68
Parliament 21, 87, 120, 122
A Parte of a Register 27, 138
Paternoster, Bernard 72
Paulet, Lady Margaret (*née* Harvey) 287–288
Percy, Dorothy (*see* Perrott Percy, Lady Dorothy, countess of Northumberland)
Percy, Henry 123, 125
Pérez, Antonio 16, 42, 123 n. 323, 125 n. 337, 207, 223, 249
Perrott Percy, Lady Dorothy, countess of Northumberland 245
Peryam, Lady Elizabeth (*née* Bacon) 12, 226, 228–229
Peryam, Sir William 12, 226, 228–289
Peter, the cook 110–111
Peter, 'little', servant of Anthony Bacon 24, 41 n. 192, 128, 157, 161, 165, 178, 253–254

Petit, Jacques 113, 175, 196, 221
Philip II, king of Spain 251
Pindar 7, 204
Pinner park and farm, Middlesex 108 n. 231, 280
plague 136, 151, 155, 179, 197, 200, 256
Preston, miller 197, 225
Publilius Syrus 7, 231
Puckering, Sir John 119, 122, 155, 166, 210

Rame, Francis 192, 201, 203
Rawley, William 44
Read, Mrs 73, 210
Reade, Mr 171, 211
Redbourn manor, Hertfordshire *passim* but see especially 25–26, 30, 33–34, 102, 128, 138, 155, 172, 176, 182, 185, 194, 204, 209–210, 213, 219, 242, 270, 280, 287–288
Rich, Lady Penelope (*née* Devereux) 254
Richmond Palace, Surrey 233, 235
Risbrough, bailiff of Barley 136
Rockett, Thomas 256–258
Roewly, Paul, servant 268
Rolff, goodman 104, 167–168, 211
Roper, Margaret (*née* More) 4
Rowland, servant of Anne Bacon 244, 275
Rowlett, Lady Margaret (*née* Cooke) 3–5, 27, 57, 115 n. 273, 275 n. 1194
Rowlett, Sir Ralph 115 n. 273, 116, 275 n. 1194
Russell, Anne (*see* Dudley, Anne, countess of Warwick)
Russell, Lady Elizabeth (*née* Cooke) 1, 3–5, 9, 18 n. 79, 23, 27–28, 38, 42, 57, 120 n. 306, 150, 153, 207, 209, 228 n. 908, 242, 261
Russell, Francis, second earl of Bedford 228
Russell, Margaret (*see* Clifford, Margaret, countess of Cumberland)
Russell, William, first Baron Russell of Thornhaugh 262

Sadler, Thomas 231
St Albans, Hertfordshire 114, 119, 139, 155, 159, 176, 197, 238, 269–271, 278–279; archdeaconry court 25–26, 104, 181–182, 256–257
Sallust 7, 63
Saunders, John 278 n. 1219
Selwin/Selwyn, Edward 141
Seneca, Lucius Annaeus, 'the Younger', 7–8, 195, 267

Scudamore, Sir John 184
Scudamore, Lady Mary (*née* Shelton) 21, 184 n. 640, 195
Shardeloes manor, Amersham 80
Shrimpton, Robert 278 n. 1219
Sidney, Sir Robert 161
Skinner, Thomas 274
Skipwith, Stephen 275 n. 1194
Skipwith, William 275 n. 1194
Smith, 'old', possibly Richard Smith 112, 172, 256, 258
Smith, Dr Richard 150, 162, 227, 235
Smith, Richard 157
Smith, Sir Thomas 55–56
Smyth, Robert 259, 285–287
Smyth, Thomas 64–65
Spain 22, 245; Cadiz expedition (1596) 247, 250, 254, 262–263, 266; Calais, siege and fall (1596) 238, 251, 255–256
Spedding, James 2, 33 n. 167
Spelman, Lady Eleanor (*née* l'Estrange) 173
Spelman, Sir Henry 173 n. 576
Spencer, Edward 26, 33, 122, 127–128, 130, 174, 176, 189, 191, 195–196, 212, 216
Spencer, Alderman John, 30, 122 n. 317, 143, 145–147, 280 n. 1233
Spencer, Robert 250
Stafford, Lady Dorothy (*née* Stafford) 21, 233–235, 264
Stafford, Sir Edward 163
Standen, Anthony 12, 16, 42–43, 135, 137, 140, 150 n. 466, 206, 227, 232
Stanhope, Sir Edward 18, 26, 38, 253–254, 280–282
Stanhope, Thomas 24, 253
Stanley, Elizabeth (*née* de Vere), countess of Derby 262–263
Stanley, William, sixth earl of Derby 263
Stiffkey Hall, Norfolk 74
Stretley, Thomas 183, 189, 194, 279
Sylva, Bartholo 9

Talbot, Elizabeth (*née* Hardwick), countess of Shrewsbury (Bess of Hardwick) 1, 107 n. 222
Talbot, Gilbert, seventh earl of Shrewsbury 248, 259, 262
Talbot, Mary (*née* Cavendish), countess of Shrewsbury 107
Tenison, Thomas, archbishop of Canterbury 44
Terence (Publius Terentius Afer) 7, 76, 174, 179, 276

Thomas, John 279
Tille, Mr 222
Townshend, Lady Jane (*née* Stanhope) 73
Townshend, Sir Roger 73 n. 116
Travers, Walter 87 n. 166, 217–218
Trinity College, Dublin 218
Trott, Nicholas 30 n. 145, 112, 142–143, 145–147, 160, 178, 183, 185, 189–192
Twickenham Park, Middlesex 129, 133–134, 152, 170, 180, 217, 287
Tyrell, Edward 283 n. 1251
Tyrell, Mrs, wife of Edward 283–284

Verstegan, Richard 6

Walker, John 65
Walsall, John 11, 74–79
Walsingham, Frances (*see* Devereux, Frances, countess of Essex)
Walsingham, Sir Francis 12, 99 n. 185, 195 n. 684
Walsingham, Lady Ursula 21, 206, 231
wardships 23–24, 101, 283–287
Waxam, Norfolk 74
Wentworth, Peter 21, 122
Wharton, John 205
White, Anne (*née* Cecil) 217

Whitgift, John, archbishop of Canterbury 24, 87 nn. 165–166, 100, 120 n. 306, 138
Wiburn, Percival (*see* Wyborn, Percival)
widowhood (*see* Bacon, Lady Anne: widowhood)
Wilblood, Humphrey 25–26, 104, 108, 127, 138, 171, 182–183, 204, 233
Wilcox, Thomas 26, 45, 93–98
Wildblood, Humphrey (*see* Wilblood, Humphrey)
Willett, Andrew 9, 127, 136, 183
Windridge manor, Hertfordshire 30, 177 n. 603
Wingfield, Robert 8
Winter/Wynter, goodman 34, 148, 159–160, 172, 226, 228, 234, 271–272
Witherton, Thomas 212
Woodhouse, Lady Anne (*née* Bacon) 74 n. 120
Woodhouse, Sir Henry 74 n. 120
Woodward 202, 208, 234
Wyborn, Percival 25, 104, 127–129, 133 n. 391, 142–144, 178, 227, 273, 275–276
Wyndham, Lady Elizabeth (*née* Bacon) 11, 70, 73
Wyndham, Sir Francis 70

Yates, Edward 168–169, 249, 251–252, 259